D1190577

THE MEDIAEVAL ACADEMY OF AMERICA

PUBLICATION NO. 38

THE NOTATION
OF POLYPHONIC MUSIC
900-1600

THE NOTATION
OF POLYPHONIC MUSIC
900-1600

By

WILLI APEL

Fifth edition

Revised and with Commentary

THE MEDIAEVAL ACADEMY OF AMERICA
CAMBRIDGE, MASSACHUSETTS
1953

The publication of this book was made possible by grants of funds to the Academy from the Carnegie Corporation of New York, the American Council of Learned Societies, the Committee on Musicology of the American Council of Learned Societies, and the Weyman Foundation of the Department of Music of Harvard University.

Printed in U. S. A.

TO

ARCHIBALD T. DAVISON

Quid valet subtilitas
ubi perit utilitas.
Speculum Musicae.

PREFACE

A BOOK on musical notation, especially the first one to appear in the United States of America, can hardly have a more appropriate introduction than the following passage from Waldo S. Pratt's article 'On Behalf of Musicology,' which appeared in the first volume of *The Musical Quarterly*, in 1915:

It is true that only those with exceptional training, peculiar access to materials, and leisure for long and hard labor can hope to discover. and publish that which is new to the scientific world. But a humbler type of 'original research' is possible for all, that which discovers to the student what he knew only from the authorities. Every such effort toughens the muscles of the reasoning faculties, and helps to set us free from the bondage to mere tradition and the idolatry of mere authority, which debilitates the mind like insidious poison.

These words serve as an eloquent expression of the raison d'être of a book whose aim is 'to set us free from the bondage to mere tradition,' which hopes to enable the student to 'discover what he knew only from the authorities,' and which is designed to prepare him for 'original research' in the field of early music.

Twenty years have elapsed since Johannes Wolf published the first and, to the present day, the only complete study on musical notation. The extraordinary merits of this book do not need to be emphasized here, since they are known to every student of musicology. It suffices to say that a score of years has by no means outdated it or rendered it useless. Today it is still an excellent example of what it was meant to be, namely, a 'Handbuch der Notationskunde' or, in other words, a work in which the entire field of musical notation from the earliest periods to the present day is treated. So broad a scope necessarily involves the inclusion of much material of infrequent occurrence and of subordinate importance; and on the other hand, a rather cursory treatment of material which, from the student's point of view, is certainly deserving of more thorough discussion. The unavoidable shortcomings of so comprehensive a plan as is carried out in the *Handbuch*, together with the natural progress in musicological research made during the last twenty years, constitute the point of departure of the present book, and indicate its position in the literature on the subject: it deals exclusively and thoroughly with those forms of musical notation whose problems the student is most frequently called upon to solve in his studies, namely, the notation of polyphonic music prior to 1600.

The book sets forth the familiar systems of notation, such as the white mensural notation, in a new way which, it is hoped, will be found more adequate and informative than former presentations. It also deals with many problems hitherto neglected or insufficiently clarified, for instance, the various notational systems of the thirteenth century. It is hoped, therefore, that it will prove to be of interest not only to the novice, but also to the scholar well versed in the subject.

Great care has been taken to arrange and to expound the material in such a manner as to make the book useful for both the students and teachers in universities and colleges, as well as for self-instruction. Indeed, it follows rather closely courses given by the author at Harvard University from 1937 to 1941. The arrangement and methods employed in these courses have proved so satisfactory that the writer feels justified in applying them here. The fundamental idea has been to renounce the principle of historical development and to treat the matter in nearly reverse order, i.e., by beginning with the latest stage of evolution and, by means of a methodical explanation of the problems encountered there, to prepare the student for the study of the earlier systems. This procedure is justified by the fact that the development of notation from 1100 to 1600 is characterized by a gradual simplification and rationalization, by steps leading from extremely vague notions to the laws and principles prevailing in our days. Thus, an arrangement of the material in the reverse order is in harmony with one of the most elementary principles of pedagogy, i.e., to proceed from the known to the unknown.

Another principle observed in this book is to avoid as much as possible everything of purely theoretical importance. Since the explanations of the theorists of the thirteenth to the sixteenth century have been of great value in solving many problems of early notation, a great deal of attention has been given them in the publications by Bellermann, Riemann, Wolf, and others. But from the present state of our knowledge it seems desirable to eliminate as much of this material as possible, and to make the sources of actual music the basis for investigation and explanation.

The discussions are based entirely on photostatic reproductions of original sources, not on printed versions such as frequently appeared in previous publications on our subject. This seems to be desirable since often the intrinsic problems are artificially changed or partly eliminated by the transliteration of the old style of writing into modern print.

In order to provide practice for the student, transcriptions of the facsimiles have not, as a rule, been given in full, but only as much of them as has been deemed necessary in order to illustrate the principle. For the same reason, these transcriptions are assembled in a separate appendix, to which the student may prefer not to resort until he has tried to find a solution of his own.

There remains the pleasant duty of expressing my sincere gratitude to all those who, in one way or the other, have helped to make possible the publication of this book. First of all, I wish to refer the reader to its first page, on which the name of my revered and dear friend, Professor Archibald T. Davison, appears; and I wish to add that this dedication is not only the expression of personal friendship, but an acknowledgment of active participation. Indeed, it was his kind interest that enabled me to give the courses which form the basis of the present book; it was at his suggestion that the book was begun; and it was his unflagging enthusiasm which has encouraged me time and again to devote my best energies to making it what he wanted it to be.

With the foregoing reference to the inaugurator of this book as a point of departure, I may be allowed to proceed in chronological order. The preparatory studies and the completion of the manuscript have been made possible chiefly through a grant from the Milton Fund of Harvard University. The considerable expense involved in the enlargement of microfilms has been borne largely by the Isham Memorial Library of Harvard University whose remarkable collection of photographic reproductions of early music sources, started by the present writer, includes practically all the material he has been working with. The difficult task of securing photographic reproduction from European libraries has been greatly facilitated by the kind cooperation of Mme Odile de Van, Paris, and of the authorities at the British Museum and at the libraries of Florence, Modena, Turin, and Naples. For the revision of the text and similar matters I am deeply indebted to Dr Everett B. Helm and Dr Lloyd Hibberd, both of Cambridge, who have spent many hours of tedious and patient work upon the manuscript. Dr Hibberd, who has been working with me in this field for several years, has also given many useful hints which have greatly contributed towards the clarification of difficult explanations. For the reading and translation of the mediaeval French, Italian, and Latin texts I have had the very good fortune to have the advice of Professor George B. Weston and Dr John P. Elder, both of Harvard University.

As regards the publication of the book, I am most deeply indebted to the Mediaeval Academy of America, Cambridge, for having considered this book to be worthy of inclusion in their series of scholarly publications, and, in particular, to their secretary, G. W. Cottrell Jr, for his active interest and his most efficient handling of the many problems involved in the preparation of the publication. I also wish to express my gratitude to the Academy's secretaries of publication, Dr Paul L. Ward and his successor, Dr Henry M. Willard, for their great patience and meticulous care in reading the manuscript and the proofs. Last, not least, due acknowledgment must be made to the American Council of Learned Societies, to its Committee on Musicology, to the Weyman Foundation of the Music Department of Harvard University, and to the Mediaeval Academy of America for their financial aid without which all the other efforts would have failed to reach their ultimate goal.

WILLI APEL

Cambridge, Massachusetts
December 1941

PREFACE TO THE FOURTH EDITION

The practical test to which this book has been put within the past eight years has shown its general usefulness and, at the same time, has brought to light its deficiencies. Most of these are in the nature of minor errors, misprints, or linguistic slips. Serious objections, however, have been raised to parts of the chapter on Square Notation.

I am very glad to have the opportunity of correcting these deficiencies, not, as in previous printings, in a make-shift manner, but on the basis of a revised edition. The chapter on Square Notation has been to a large extent rewritten, after careful examination of the suggestions received from other scholars.

In many instances the text, although essentially correct, appeared to be in need of amplification, qualification, or additional information. This material has been gathered in a Commentary (pp. 437–451), to which reference is made by means of asterisks added on the margin of the main text.

Grateful acknowledgment is made of the valuable assistance received from Dom Anselm Hughes, O.S.B., Mr Gustave Reese (New York University) and Mr Oliver Strunk (Princeton University). My particular gratitude goes to Dr Manfred F. Bukofzer (University of California) for his active collaboration on the chapter on Square Notation, and to Dr A. T. Davison (Harvard University) who, on the basis of his teaching experience, has made many valuable suggestions for improvement and correction.

The book has been kindly received by many scholars and by a great number of students. While mentioning this fact it is only fair to state that, in the opinion of one esteemed colleague, 'M. Apel (*The Notation of polyphonic music*, 85) a totalement faussé le problème de la notation mensuraliste,' and that, in the same writer's view, 'La fausse perspective de l'ouvrage de M. Apel est encore mise en évidence par l'ordre antichronologique de ses démonstrations.' The reader is warned.

February 1949

W. A.

PREFACE TO THE FIFTH EDITION

A number of errors have been corrected. Several items have been added to the Commentary.

January 1961

W. A.

CONTENTS

Page

LIST OF FACSIMILES xv

ABBREVIATIONS xviii

INTRODUCTION xix

PART I: THE NOTATION OF SOLOIST MUSIC

   I. KEYBOARD SCORES 3

   II. KEYBOARD PARTITURAS 16

   III. KEYBOARD TABLATURES 21

      A. German Keyboard Tablatures 21
      B. Spanish Keyboard Tablatures 47

   IV. LUTE TABLATURES 54

      A. Italian and Spanish Lute Tablatures 56
      B. French Lute Tablatures 64
      C. German Lute Tablatures 72

PART II: THE NOTATION OF ENSEMBLE MUSIC:
      WHITE MENSURAL NOTATION

   I. NOTATIONAL SIGNS 87

      Notes 87
      Ligatures 87
      Rules for Ligatures 91
      Subsidiary Symbols 94

   II. MENSURATION 96

      A. *Tempus, prolatio,* and *modus* 96
      B. *Tempus imperfectum cum prolatione imperfecta* . . 100
      C. *Tempus perfectum cum prolatione imperfecta* . . . 107
        Imperfection 107
        Alteration 112
        Punctus divisionis 115
      D. *Prolatio perfecta* 120
      E. *Modus* and *maximodus* 124

Page

III. COLORATION 126

    A. Coloration in *tempus imperfectum cum prolatione imperfecta* 127

    B. Coloration in *tempus perfectum cum prolatione imperfecta* 130

    C. Coloration in *prolatio perfecta* 136

    D. Half-Coloration 142

IV. PROPORTIONS 145

    A. History and Terminology 145

    B. *Proportio dupla* and *tripla* in General 148

    C. *Proportio dupla* 151

    D. *Proportio tripla* 155

    E. Other Proportions 157

        Proportio quadrupla 157

        Proportio sesquialtera 158

        Proportio quintupla, sesquitertia 160

        Successive Proportions 161

    F. Augmentation 163

    G. Examples 168

    H. Canons 179

    I. Proportional Time Signatures and Tempo . . . 188

PART III: THE NOTATION OF ENSEMBLE MUSIC: BLACK NOTATION

  I. INTRODUCTION 199

  II. PRIMITIVE NOTATION 204

  III. SQUARE NOTATION 215

    A. General Characterization 215

    B. Modal Notation 220

        The Rhythmic Modes 220

        The Ligatures 223

        Repeated Notes 225

        Plica 226

        Examples 230

        Extensio modi 234

        Fractio modi 235

        Conjuncturae 240

        Consonance and Dissonance 244

Page

Notation of the Tenors 245
Notation of the Upper Parts 252
Examples 254
C. Syllabic Notation 258
D. Duplum Notation 267
E. Motet Notation 271

IV. PRE-FRANCONIAN NOTATION 282

A. The Codex Montpellier, fasc. II–VI 284
Notation of the Tenors 286
Examples 289
Duple Meter 290
Notation of the Upper Voices 294
Ligatures 296
Plica 298
Examples 298
B. The Codex Bamberg 302
Notation of the Tenors 303
Notation of the Upper Voices 304
C. The Codices Torino and Huelgas 306

V. FRANCONIAN NOTATION 310

A. The Franconian System 310
Single Notes 310
Ligatures 312
Examples 315
B. The Innovations of Petrus de Cruce 318
C. The Roman de Fauvel 325
The Tenors; *modus* and *maximodus* 327
Red Notes 328
Notation of the Upper Parts 330
Semibreves signatae 332
Conjunctura and *plica* 333
Examples 334

VI. FRENCH NOTATION 338

A. The Innovations of the *Ars Nova* 338
B. The Notation in the Works of Machaut 343
Imperfection and Alteration 344
Determination of the Mensuration 346

			Page
	Ouvert and *clos*		349
	Examples		352
	C. The Notation of the Later Sources		360
VII.	ITALIAN NOTATION		368
	A. The Origin of Italian Notation		368
	B. The Principles of Italian Notation		369
	Divisiones		370
	Note Forms		371
	C. Examples of Italian Notation		374
	D. The Early Stage of Italian Notation		382
VIII.	MIXED NOTATION		385
	A. General Characterization		385
	B. Examples of Mixed Notation		386
	C. Syncopation		395
IX.	MANNERED NOTATION		403
	A. General Characterization		403
	B. Principal Features		404
	Signs of Mensuration		404
	Special Notes		405
	Coloration		405
	C. Examples		407
	D. Discussion of Examples from Other Publications		426
COMMENTARY			437
INDEX			453
APPENDIX: TRANSCRIPTIONS			

LIST OF FACSIMILES

Page

1. Marcantonio da Bologna, *Recerchari, motetti, canzoni* 5
2. Attaingnant, *Quatorze gaillardes* 7
3. MS London, Br. Mus. *Add. 29996* 11
4. Mulliner Book, MS London, Br. Mus. *Add. 30513* . . . 13
5. MS London, Br. Mus. *Add. 29996* 13
6. Ascanio Mayone, *Primo libro di . . . capricci* 17
7. Buxheimer Orgelbuch, MS Munich, Stb. *Mus. Ms. 3725* . 25
8. Arnolt Schlick, *Tabulaturen etlicher Lobgesang* 27
9. MS Basle, Univ. Bibl. *F IX 22* (Kotter) 29
10. MS St. Gall, Stiftsbibliothek *530* (Sicher) 31
11. Bernhard Schmid, *Tabulatur Buch* 35
12. Vienna, Stb. *Ms. 18491* (Regina Clara Im Hoff) 36
13. Bach, Orgelbüchlein, MS Berlin, Stb. *P 283* 39
14. Ileborgh tablature, Philadelphia, Curtis Institute 41
15. Conrad Paumann, *Fundamentum*, MS Wenigerode *Zb 14* . 45
16. Antonio Valente, *Intavolatura de cimbalo* 51
17. Antonio de Cabezon, *Obras de musica* 53
18. Luys de Milan, *Libro de musica* 57
19. Petrucci, *Intabolatura de lauto* 63
20. Denis Gaultier, *La Rhétorique des dieux*, Berlin, Kupferstich-
    kabinett *Ms. 142* 73
21. Hans Judenkunig, *Ain schone . . . Underweisung* . . . 79
22. Hans Newsidler, *Ein newgeordnet . . . Lautenbuch* . . . 81
23. Dufay, *Quel fronte signorille* (MS Oxford, *Canon. 213*) . . 103
24. Benet, *Sanctus* (Trent Codex *92*) 105
25. *Dangier tu m'as tollu* (Chansonnier Laborde) 109
26. Dufay, *Ave regina* (MS Oxford, *Canon. 213*) 119
27. Pierre de la Rue, *Kyrie* (*Misse Petri de la Rue*) 121
28. Leonel Power, *Anima mea* (MS Florence, *Magl. XIX. 112 bis*) 135
29. *Monsieur* (Munich, Stb. *Cim. 351a*) 137
30. Ockeghem, *Et resurrexit* (MS Rome, *Chigi cod. C. VIII, 234*) 139
31. Lantins, *Ce ieusse fait* (MS Oxford, *Canon. 213*) 141
32. Bartholomeus de Bononia, *Vince con lena; O dolce conpagno*
    (MS Oxford, *Canon. 213*) 143

Page

33. Tinctoris, *Proportionale musices* (MS Brussels) 153
34. Ockeghem, *Kyrie* (MS Rome, *Chigi cod. C. VIII, 234*) . . 165
35. Isaac, *Ideoque* (*Choralis Constantinus*) 169
36. Isaac, *Piae vocis laudes* (*Choralis Constantinus*) 171
37. **Isaac, *Dico ego* (*Choralis Constantinus*)** **174**
38. Isaac, *De radice* (*Choralis Constantinus*) 173
39. Lantins, *Je suy exent* (MS Oxford, *Canon. 213*) . . . 177
40. Obrecht, *Kyrie* (*Missa Si dedero*, tenor) 183
41. Obrecht, *Kyrie* (*Missa Si dedero*, other parts) 185
42. *Tu patris* (*Musica Enchiriadis*) 205
43. *Ut tuo propitiatus* (MS Oxford, Bodl. Libr. *572*) . . . 205
44. *Viderunt hemanuel* (MS Paris, Bibl. Nat. *lat. 3549*) . . 211
45. *Alleluia vocavit Jhesus* (Codex Calixtinus) 213
46. *Go; Flos filius est* (MS Florence, *plut. 29.1*) 229
47. *Descendit de celis* (MS Wolfenbüttel *1206*) 233
48. Instrumental dances (MS Brit. Mus. *Harl. 978*) 239
49. *Benedicamus Domino* (MS Florence, *plut. 29.1*) . . . 247
50. (a) *Scio cui credidi*; (b) *Alleluya* (MS Paris, Bibl. Nat. *lat. 15139*) 249
51. *Varicus clausulae* (MS Florence, *plut. 29.1*) 255
52. (a) *Mulierum*; (b) *Domino* (MS Florence, *plut. 29.1*) . . . 257
53. *Hac in anni janua* (MS Wolfenbüttel *677*) 259
54. *Hui main-Hec dies; L'autre jor-Flos filius* (Chansonnier Roy, Paris, Bibl. Nat. *frç. 844*) 273
55, 56. *Laus Domino—Eius; Homo quo vigeas—Et gaudebit* (MS Wolfenbüttel *1206*) 275, 281
57. *Candida virginitas—Flos filius* (MS Brit. Mus. *Add. 30091*) 285
58. *Ave beatissima—Ave Maria—Johanne; Salve virgo—Ave lux—Neuma* (Codex Montpellier) 291
59. *Diex je—Amors qui ma—Et super* (Codex Montpellier) . . 293
60. *Mout me fu—Robins—Portare* (Codex Bamberg) 305
61. *Hei diex—Mal latus—?* (MS Torino, Bibl. Reale *42*) . . 307
62. *Et in terra pax* (Codex Huelgas) 309
63. *Huic ut—Huic ut—?* (Codex Montpellier) 316
64. *Diex qui—En grant—Aptatur* (Codex Montpellier) . . . 317
65. *Aucun ont—Lonc tans—Annuntiantes* (Codex Montpellier) . 321
66. *Firmissime—Adesto—Alleluia* (Roman de Fauvel) . . . 329
67. *Garrit gallus—In nova fert—?* (Roman de Fauvel) . . . 331
68. Machaut, *Ne pensez pas* (MS Paris, B. N. *frç. 1584*) . . . 353
69. Machaut, *Dous amis* (MS Paris, B. N. *frç. 1584*) 357

Page

70. Machaut, *Biaute qui toutes* (MS Paris, B. N. *frç. 9221*) . . . 359
71. *Kyrie* (MS Cambrai, Bibl. Comm. *Ms. 6*) 363
72. J. Tyes, *Et in terra pax* (Old Hall MS) 365
73. Jacopo da Bologna, *Aquil' altera; Fortune* (MS Paris, B. N. *ital. 568*) 375
74. Bartolinus de Padua, *Perche cançato* (Codex Reina) . . . 377
75. *Benedicamus Domino* (MS Paris, B. N. *ital. 568*) 379
76. *Or qua conpagni* (MS Rome, *Rossi 215*) 383
77. Giov. de Florentia, *Naschoso el viso* Landini, *Chol gli occhi;* (MS Florence, Bibl. Naz. *Panc. 26*) 387
78. Landini, *Se pronto* (Codex Squarcialupi) 391
79. Landini, *Nessun ponga* (Codex Squarcialupi) 393
80. Paolo (tenorista), *Benche partito* (MS Paris, B. N. *ital. 568*) . 399
81. Paolo (tenorista), *Amor tu solo* (MS Paris, B. N. *ital. 568*) . 409
82. *Je la remire;* Machaut, *Se vous n'estes* (Modena, Bibl. Est. L. *568*) 411
83. *Je ne puis* (Codex Chantilly) 413
84. Anthonellus, *Dame gentil* (MS Modena, Bibl. Est. L. *568*) . 415
85. *Tout houme veut* (MS Torino, Bibl. Naz. *J II 9*) 419
86. *Biaute parfaite* (Codex Reina) 421
87. Jacopinus Selesses, *En attendant* (MS Modena, Bibl. Est. L. *568*) 423
88. Baude Cordier, *Belle bonne* (Codex Chantilly) 427

ABBREVIATIONS

I. Books and Periodicals

AfMW *Archiv für Musikwissenschaft*, Leipzig, 1918–1927.

AHdM G. Adler, *Handbuch der Musikwissenschaft*, 2 vols., Berlin, 1929.

AM *Acta Musicologica*, Copenhagen, 1928–.

CS E. Coussemaker, *Scriptorum de musica medii ævi nova series*, 4 vols., Paris, 1864–1876.

DTOe *Denkmäler der Tonkunst in Oesterreich*, Leipzig, 1894–.

GdM J. Wolf, *Geschichte der Mensuralnotation*, 3 vols., Leipzig, 1904.

Gr. Rom. *Graduale Romanae Ecclesiae*, Paris, 1924.

GS M. Gerbert, *Scriptores ecclesiastici de musica*, 3 vols., St Blasien, 1784. Facsimile edition, Milan, 1931.

HdN J. Wolf, *Handbuch der Notationskunde*, 2 vols., Leipzig, 1919.

JfMW *Jahrbücher für musikalische Wissenschaft*, Berlin, 1863, 1867.

Km. Jb. *Kirchenmusikalisches Jahrbuch*, Leipzig, 1885–1911.

MfM *Monatshefte für Musikgeschichte*, Berlin, 1869–1904.

MQ *The Musical Quarterly*, New York, 1915–.

MuT H. Bellermann, *Die Mensuralnoten und Taktzeichen des XV. und XVI. Jahrhunderts*, Berlin, 1858, 1930.

OH H. E. Wooldridge, *The Oxford History of Music*, vol. 1, Oxford, 1901.

RHdM H. Riemann, *Handbuch der Musikgeschichte*, 5 vols., Leipzig, 1904.

SchT J. Wolf, *Musikalische Schrifttafeln*, Bückeburg, 1930.

SIMG *Sammelbände der Internationalen Musikgesellschaft*, Leipzig, 1899–1914.

VfMW *Vierteljahrsschrift für Musikwissenschaft*, Leipzig, 1884–1894.

ZfMW *Zeitschrift für Musikwissenschaft*, Leipzig, 1918–1935.

ZIMG *Zeitschrift der Internationalen Musikgesellschaft*, Leipzig, 1899–1914.

II. Technical Terms

a p.a.	*a parte ante*	*Mx*	*maxima*
a p.p.	*a parte post*	*p.a.*	*punctus additionis*
B	*brevis*	*p.d.*	*punctus divisionis*
c.o.p.	*cum opposita proprietate*	*S*	*semibrevis*
D	*duplex longa*	*Sf*	*semifusa*
F	*fusa*	*Sm*	*semiminima*
L	*longa*	*t*	*tactus*
M	*minima*		

INTRODUCTION

THE DISCIPLINE of musical notation comprises a knowledge of the methods of writing down music. In general, it is concerned with music of all periods, but the term 'notation' is usually employed with special reference to those cases in which the forms of the signs and the principles governing their use are essentially different from those to be found in modern practice. Thus, the field of notation proper covers European music from the beginning to the seventeenth century, and the music of all other nations outside of the European development in so far as it is preserved in writing.

Within this field one meets with a large variety of types of notation. Therefore, it will be our first task to attempt a survey of them. This task is rendered more difficult by the fact that in the previous publications on the subject classifications and terms have been used which upon closer examination do not always prove unambiguous or appropriate. It has been deemed necessary, therefore, to make a new survey of the whole field and, accordingly, to introduce certain changes in the traditional terminology.

Our classification is based upon two considerations, the first of which deals with the number of parts of a given composition, and the second with the number of participants performing the composition. The former point of view leads to a division of music into two chief categories, namely, music consisting of only one part, and music including more than one part or, in other words, monophonic and polyphonic music.[1] To the former field belong the music of the ancient Greeks, the entire tradition of the Gregorian chant, of the Latin sequences and hymns, of the Italian laudi and Spanish cantigas, also the music of the French troubadours and trouvères, of the German Minnesingers and Meistersingers, that of the Byzantine and Russian liturgies, and finally the vast repertory of Oriental music and similar bodies.[2] The second category, that of polyphonic music needs no further description.

[1] The term 'polyphonic' is used throughout the present study to include all music comprising more than a single line of melody (monophonic music) whether the number of parts is strict or free, and whether the texture is contrapuntal or harmonic.

[2] A monograph on Notation of Monophonic Music, planned as a continuation of the present book, is under preparation.

Although there are certain ties of relationship which exist between monophonic and polyphonic music, the two fields are clearly marked off from each other. This is also true of their notation. Without considering details it will suffice to mention a basic feature which clearly distinguishes the notation of monophonic music from that of polyphonic music, namely, the arrangement. Monophonic music has always been written in a purely linear arrangement of the signs, i.e., in a single line following the course of the melody and, obviously, it can only be set down thus. Polyphonic music, however, includes both horizontal and vertical relationships; here, various methods of arrangement are possible. Two principles must be distinguished which may be called, for our convenience, score-arrangement and part-arrangement.

By the term score-arrangement we refer to a scheme in which the voices of a composition are written one underneath the other, arranged in such a way that simultaneous tones appear in a vertical or nearly vertical alignment. In modern practice, this principle is shown in the piano score or in the orchestral score.

The term part-arrangement applies to music which is written without regard to the vertical coincidence of the tones, each part being treated as a notational entity distinct from the others and appearing on a different section of the page or two opposite pages (choir book notation), or in different books (part books, *Stimmbücher*). A modern example of the latter method is the different parts of a string quartet.

Historically, score-arrangement is the earliest method of writing used for polyphonic music. All the earliest documents of part music illustrate the practice of the vertical arrangement of the voices, a principle which was applied to text-syllables (*Musica enchiriadis*, ninth century; see Facsimile 42), to letters (Guido of Arezzo, *Micrologus*, ca. 1000; see Facsimile 43), to neumes (School of St. Martial; see Facsimiles 44, 45), and to notes (School of Notre Dame, ca. 1200; see Facsimiles 46 ff.).

* Score-arrangement gave way to part-arrangement in the second quarter of the thirteenth century (see Facsimiles 57ff). This change is one of the various innovations which accompanied the rise of the motet (see p. 271). In the documents of the period from about 1250 till 1450, the parts of a composition are almost always written on different sections of a page or of two opposite pages, in certain standard allocations (see p. 283). Manuscripts of the late fifteenth century, such as the Glogauer Liederbuch (ca. 1470), furnish the earliest examples of a more recent practice, namely, that of writing in part-books (*Stimmbücher*), one book for the discantus, one for the altus, etc. This method was generally adopted for the printed publications of choral music in the sixteenth

century. With the establishment of regular barring (about 1600) and the rise of orchestral music, score-arrangement reappears, displacing part-arrangement which has survived only in the separate parts used in orchestral and in chamber music.

We now come to the second principle of classification mentioned above, namely that based upon the number of performers. This point of view leads again to a division of music into two categories, namely music performed by a group of participants and music performed by a single musician. In the field of monophonic music this distinction is of relatively little value, at least from the standpoint of notation. However, it has a very real significance if applied to the field of polyphonic music. Here it leads to a distinction between two species of polyphonic music, namely, polyphonic music for a group of performers (one at least to each part), and polyphonic music for a single performer (executed on a keyboard instrument or a lute). For these two types of part music the terms 'polyphonic ensemble music' (or simply ensemble music) and 'polyphonic soloist music' (or simply soloist music) will be used in this book. The term ensemble music almost covers the field which is traditionally designated as vocal or choral music, but also includes instrumental pieces for a group of players. Polyphonic soloist music is, of course, necessarily instrumental music.

By mentioning the terms vocal and instrumental we touch upon a much discussed problem, namely that of the use of these two mediums in music prior to 1600. Whereas, according to the view of nineteenth century historians, nearly all the music written before 1600 was vocal music (*a cappella*), more recent investigations have made it clear beyond any doubt that instruments played an important part in the performance of the so-called vocal music, at least prior to 1550. Owing to this discovery the terms vocal and instrumental music lose much of their significance and can no longer be considered as an appropriate basis for classification, as they have been over and over again. Indeed, such a classification not only is ambiguous but also results in a rather arbitrary separation of what are closely connected styles (for instance, a textless instrumental piece by Obrecht and a vocal motet by the same composer), as well as in an amalgamation of widely different ones (for instance, a so-called organ ricercare by Willaert—actually chamber music for, e.g., three viols—and a genuine organ ricercare by Cavazzoni).

A much more solid and useful basis of classification is furnished by our above distinction between ensemble and soloist music.[1] The former

---

[1] This dichotomy has been emphasized by the present writer in a paper on 'The Importance of Notation in Solving Problems of Early Music' (published in: *Papers Read by Members of the Ameri-*

category naturally includes what is commonly called vocal or choral music, but does not rule out instrumental participation in the performance of such music, and also includes purely instrumental pieces written 'in vocal style,' such as the ricercares of Willaert, and other examples of sixteenth century chamber music. On the other hand, the category of soloist music includes instrumental music of an entirely different character, that is, organ and lute music which comprises such totally contrasting forms as the prelude and the toccata alongside others which, although borrowed from ensemble music, underwent typical changes when adopted into the soloist repertory (coloraturas, cadential passages, 'Freistimmigkeit,' etc.).

These brief hints must suffice here in order to indicate how our classification can be supported by considerations of style and form. More important, from the point of view of this book, is the fact that it is most clearly indicated in the notational systems used for the two classes under consideration. If, for the moment, we restrict ourselves to the period in which the question 'vocal-instrumental' and, consequently, our substituted dichotomy of soloist and ensemble, attain acute importance (*ca.* 1250–1600), a very simple and categorical statement can be made,
∗namely, that music written in part-arrangement is ensemble music, and music written in score-arrangement is soloist music.[1] From the scores of early ensemble music (prior to 1250), the scores for soloist music, usually known as tablatures, are distinguished by special features such as the use of figures and letters, or the writing of several parts on one staff, etc.

The notation for ensemble music includes mensural notation, a term which refers to the use of strictly measurable and unambiguously determined notational characters, which were introduced about 1250 by Franco of Cologne (see p. 310). It is customarily divided into two large categories, that of black (mensural) notation (1250–1450) and that of white (mensural) notation (1450–1600). The former falls again into a number of systems which represent distinctly different phases of a continuous development (see p. 199). The notational systems antecedent to mensural notation are treated in this book under the headings of 'Primitive Notation' (*ca.* 900–1150), and of 'Square Notation' (*ca.*

can Musicological Society, Washington, 1938), and has been elaborated in L. Hibberd, *The Early Keyboard Prelude, a Study in Musical Style* (Harvard dissertation, unpublished, 1941).

[1] For the discussion of certain objections which might be raised with regard to the first part of this statement, see p. 61 of the paper mentioned in the previous footnote. A startling example of the failure to distinguish between ensemble and soloist music is embodied in the recent publication of the *Ricercares* of Annibale Padovano (Edition de l'Oiseau de Lyre, Paris, 1934), in which these compositions are offered as organ music with pedals(!) and all manner of modern registration.

1175–1225), with 'Pre-Franconian Notation' forming the transition to 'Franconian,' i.e., the first true mensural notation.

As has been remarked above, the notational systems for soloist music are usually called tablatures. According to the instrument to which they belong, they are customarily distinguished as organ tablatures, lute tablatures, guitar tablatures, etc. Further distinctions are made according to nations. Thus, one speaks of German and Italian organ tablatures, of Spanish and French lute tablatures, and so forth.

Unfortunately, these customary classifications are not entirely satisfactory. Their chief disadvantage—to mention only one point—lies in the fact that the notation used in the sixteenth century sources of English, Italian, and French organ music is essentially the same as that employed in the piano score of the present. This means, first, that the customary distinction between 'English organ tablatures,' 'Italian organ tablatures,' and 'French organ tablatures' is a national, not a notational, classification. It means, second, that from a methodical point of view, the name 'Italian organ tablature' (or English or French, but not German) could and should be applied to nineteenth century piano compositions. Yet, one would, doubtless, hesitate to refer to a Beethoven pianoforte sonata as an example of Italian organ tablature.

To avoid these and similar ambiguities yet another classification and terminology within the field of soloist music have been adopted in this book. We shall distinguish between sources written exclusively with notes and others in which letters or figures are used. It is only to the second class that the name tablatures will be applied. To this class belong the Spanish organ (or, more accurately, keyboard) tablatures (written in figures), all the lute tablatures (written in figures or letters), the late German keyboard tablatures (written in letters), and the early German keyboard tablatures (written partly in letters and partly in notes).

In the other group, in which music is written exclusively with notes, we may further distinguish between the following species: notation of the whole composition on two staves (or, occasionally, on a single staff of double extension), and notation with an individual staff for each part (mostly four staves). The first type is that of the present piano score. Therefore, we shall refer to this notation as keyboard score.[1] It embraces the Italian, French, and English 'organ tablatures.' The other species (single staff for each voice) is the so-called partitura, which was employed

---

[1] In view of the fact that in the sixteenth century organ, harpsichord, and clavichord employed the same repertory to a large extent, the terms 'keyboard score,' 'keyboard tablature,' etc., are preferable to terms such as 'organ score,' or 'organ tablature.'

especially by the Italian composers of the seventeenth century. When used for writing keyboard music we may call it conveniently keyboard partitura.

The understanding of the above explanations will be facilitated by the accompanying chart which shows the varieties of notation in a methodical and approximately chronological order.

MONOPHONIC MUSIC	NOTATION FOR ENSEMBLE MUSIC		NOTATION FOR SOLOIST MUSIC			
	Score Arrangement	Part Arrangement	Keyboard Scores Two Staves	Keyboard Partituras Four Staves	Tablatures Letters and Figures	
					Keyboard Tablatures	Lute Tablatures
Greek Notation (400 B.C.–200 A.D.)	*Primitive Notation* syllables, letters, neumes, Dasian signs (9th–12th cent.)					
Darian Notation (ca. 900)						
Letter Notation (9th–12th cent.)	*Square Notation* ligatures, notes (ca. 1175–1250) for further classifications, see p. 219.	*Black Mensural Notation* black mensural notes (ca. 1250–1450) for further classifications, see p. 199.				
Neumes (9th–12 cent.)						
Chorale Notation, Roman (12th–20th cent.)		*White Mensural Notation* white mensural notes (ca. 1450–1600)			*Old German Keyboard Tablature* (ca. 1325–1550)	
Chorale Notation, Gothic (13th–15th cent.)			*Italy, France, England* (16th cent.–present)		*Spanish Keyboard Tablature* (16th century)	*Spanish-Italian Lute Tablature* (16th century)
Byzantine Notation (10th–18th cent.)					*New German Keyboard Tablature* (ca. 1550–1700)	*German Lute Tablature* (16th century)
Russian Notation (11th–17th cent.)	*Partition Scores* (1600–present)			*Italy, Spain, Germany* (17th century)		*French Lute Tablature* (16th–18th cent.)
The notational systems of monophonic music are described in HdN I, 11–197.						*Tablatures for the guitar, violin, flute, etc.* (17th century)

POLYPHONIC MUSIC

SURVEY OF NOTATIONAL SYSTEMS

PART I

THE NOTATION OF SOLOIST MUSIC

I. KEYBOARD SCORES

THE METHOD of writing keyboard music in a manner similar to that of the piano score of our day occurs first in an Italian publication of 1523, namely: Marcantonio da Bologna, *Recerchari*, *Motetti*, *Canzoni* (Venice), a page of which is shown on Facsimile 1. Two staves* of six lines each are used, the upper staff for the right hand, and the lower staff for the left. From the standpoint of contemporary mensural notation (see p. 85 ff) two features are particularly interesting since they indicate an advance which was not reached in the writing down of ensemble music until several decades later. These features are the bar-line and the tie. As they are both employed in a very consistent and logical manner, one might well conclude that various prior attempts in this direction had been made (regarding bar-lines see p. 9).

The clef sign at the beginning of each staff indicates middle c (c¹). The mordent-like sign at the end of the staff is the *custos* (guardian, also called 'direct') which refers the player to the first note of the same part in the next staff. The note-values are: *brevis* (B), *semibrevis* (S), *minima* (M), *semiminima* (Sm), *fusa* (F), *semifusa* (Sf).[1] Their forms, together with those of the corresponding rests, are indicated in the following chart which also includes the modern signs derived from them.

	B	S	M	Sm	F	Sf
Old form of notes:[2]	◻	◇	♩	♩	♩	♩
Modern form of notes:	(◻)	○	♩	♩	♪	♪
Old form of rests:						
Modern form of rests:					♪	♪

Each note (or rest) is equal to two, and only two, notes (or rests) of the next smaller value. This is another progressive feature of keyboard and lute notation in contrast to contemporary mensural notation, in which a note was equal to two or to three notes of the lower grade, according to the 'mensuration' (perfect or imperfect, see p. 96). The

[1] The abbreviations: *B* (*brevis*), *S* (*semibrevis*), *M* (*minima*), *Sm* (*semiminima*), *F* (*fusa*), and *Sf* (*semifusa*) will be used throughout the book.

[2] These notes are called 'white notes' ('white notation') although only the larger values are actually white.

3

ledger lines for notes above or below the staff are not drawn separately for each note, but continuously for a group (cf. measures 1–2 and 9–10). In the chord-like formations of the left hand (measures 8–10) the single *M* placed between the two triads belongs to the middle voice and is preceded by another *M* in the same voice (middle tone of the first triad).

The dots which appear rather frequently below or above single notes (upper staff, measure 3, 4, 6, 8; lower staff, measure 3, 5, 6, 7) indicate chromatic alterations, either flatting or sharping. Since at that time the use of chromatic tones was still limited, no confusion arose from this summary method. It was understood that a B, an E, or an A could only be flatted, whereas an F, a C, or a G could only be sharped. Thus, in this notation, a B with a dot is a B-flat, and an F with a dot is an F-sharp.

Although, from the evolutionary point of view, the *S* corresponds to the modern whole note, it appears advisable to reduce the note values in the transcription. i.e., to transcribe the *S* as a half note, and the other values correspondingly. Reductions of this type may be applied to all early music through the end of the sixteenth century. The preservation, customary in scholarly publications, of the original note values brings about an appearance of sluggishness which is highly detrimental to an understanding of early music. It also has led to a great uncertainty concerning the question of tempo in early music. There will be a fuller discussion later of the principles of reduction of note values to be applied to compositions in mensural notation (cf. the chapter on Proportional Time Signatures and Tempo). In the case of keyboard and lute music the practice of the sixteenth century is too varied and involved to allow for the establishment of general principles. As a rule, the transcription of the *S* as a half-note will lead to a satisfactory result, i.e., to the representation of the beat in moderate tempo by a quarter-note. Whatever scale one chooses, should, of course, be indicated at the beginning of the transcription.

The transcription of the first four measures is given in the appendix, No. 1. An interesting feature of the piece is the 'Freistimmigkeit' (cf. four voices in meas. 4, 5; three in meas. 1, 2, 6-7; full chords in the last measures). In a case like this, attempts to bring about correct part-writing (by the introduction of rests) are of no avail.

Seven years after Marcantonio's publication, we encounter the same method of notation in France in seven books of keyboard music published by Attaingnant in 1529–30. Facsimile 2 is taken from one of these books, *Quatorze gaillardes, neuf pavanes, sept branles et deux basses danses, le tout reduit de musique en la tabulature de jeu d'orgues* . . . (Paris, 1530).

FACSIMILE I

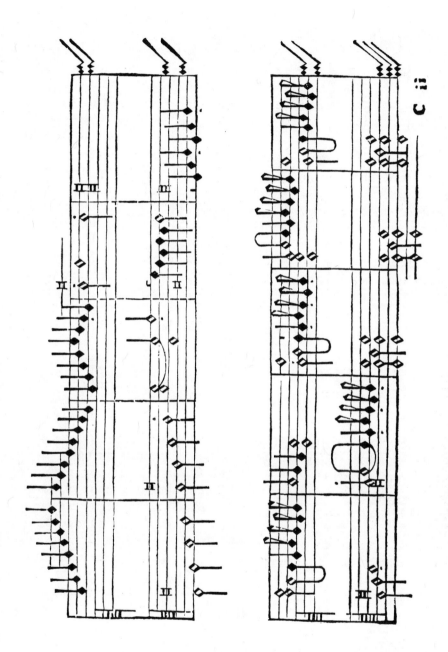

Marcantonio da Bologna, *Recerchari, motetti, canzoni.* Venice, 1523

In Attaingnant's publications we already find the modern staff of five
lines.   However, it was not until about 100 years later that this method
became generally accepted.   The notes of smaller value are slightly
different from those of Marcantonio's book.   The *Sm* does not appear
here as a blackened *M*, but as a white *M* with a flag, ⚐ .   Accordingly,
the *F* appears as a white note with two flags, ⚑ , whereas the *Sf* is a
blackened *F*, ♩ identical with that of the Italian book.   This ambiguity
in the forms of the *Sm* and *F* occurs also in the sources of mensural notation from 1450 to 1550, with preference given to the black shapes (see
* p. 87).

Three signs for chromatic alteration are used in Attaingnant's books:
the flat, the sharp, and the dot.   The former two (the sharp very rarely)
are used preferably for chords, whereas in melodic formations the dot is
employed almost exclusively.   As in the book of Marcantonio da
Bologna, the dot has the function of raising or lowering a note by half-
step, according to which is the more natural direction.   However, in
Attaingnant it has a third meaning, that is, cancellation of a B flat in
the signature, as is illustrated by the following two examples (in example
b, the dot belongs to the higher, not the lower note)[1]:

It may be noted that in Attaingnant's books, as well as in many other
examples of early keyboard music, the arrangement of the notes within
the measure differs somewhat from the modern practice.   If, for example, a long note occurs in the lower staff against a group of smaller
notes in the higher, the long note is not placed at the beginning, but in
the middle of this group (see measure 6).   Furthermore, in order to save
space, the notes in any one part are written as closely together as possible, with the result that notes which are to be played simultaneously
often do not appear in a strictly vertical alignment (see measure 1).

Attaingnant uses smaller note values than does Marcantonio.   They
may, therefore, be transcribed without reduction, that is, with the *M*
represented by a half-note.   The one- and two-flagged white notes, then,
correspond to the quarter- and eighth-notes.

[1] Cf. W. Apel, *Accidentien und Tonalität*, Strassburg, 1937, p. 49 (examples 146, 148).

FACSIMILE 2

Attaingnant, *Quatorze gaillardes* . . . Paris, 1530
From pages 14 , 15

The beginning of the branle commun is transcribed in the appendix, No. 2.   In the third measure, the change from the cadential F-sharp to the truly melodic F is worth noticing—and, of course, preserving.   So is the change from E to E-flat in the first measure of the last brace.

Other interesting examples of sixteenth century keyboard scores occur in England.   The English keyboard literature of this period embraces two schools, that of early Tudor music (*ca.* 1520–1560) and that of the virginalists (*ca.* 1570–1620).   It is especially in the first group that we find many notational features of interest.   The sources of this period are listed here in a tentative chronological order (the dates are estimates):

> London, Brit. Mus. *Roy. App. 58* (circa 1520)
> London, Brit. Mus. *Roy. App. 56* (circa 1520)
> London, Brit. Mus. *Add. 15233* (circa 1530)
> London, Brit. Mus. *Add. 29996* (circa 1550)
> Oxford, Christ Church College, *MS 371* (circa 1550)
> London, Brit. Mus. *Add. 30513, Mulliner Book* (circa 1560)

Among the composers are: Hugh Aston (1480?–1522), John Redford (1491?–1543?), William Blitheman (?–1591), Thomas Allwoode and Master Shepard (probably contemporaries of Blitheman), as well as many others.

The compositions in these sources are written on two staves, of six, seven or eight lines each.   A *Tui sunt celi* (at the end of *Add. 15233*) and a few other compositions are notated on a single staff of twelve or thirteen lines, a manner of writing which occurs also in the sources of the virginalistic period (Fitzwilliam Virginal Book).[1]

These manuscripts display various features indicating that the English, in their notation of keyboard music as well as in many other respects, clung to older traditions to a degree unknown in other countries.   These conservative features make English keyboard notation individual and offer new and interesting problems to the student.

---

[1]The practice of notating all the parts of a piece on one single staff should not be confused with a method widely used in early music (prior to 1250; see Facsimile 53 and Coussemaker, *Histoire de l'harmonie au moyen-age*, Paris, 1852, pl. 24, 25), in which two (or more) different staves are put together as close as possible, probably to save space. A single staff proper would entail the validity of one and the same clef for the entire staff; but in these early examples we find the same clef (C) indicated twice on different lines, so that actually each part has its own clef and, consequently, its own staff.   In fact, in music of this period a single staff for two or more parts is impracticable since all the parts have approximately the same range.

Apart from insignificant instances of a purely demonstrative character, such as occur in certain theoretical writings (e.g., Martin Agricola, *Musica instrumentalis*, 1529, p. 50), the use of a single extended staff for the notation of several parts is exhibited only in keyboard music.   The oldest examples are found in the Ileborgh tablature (see p. 40 ff, Facsimile 14), and in the tablature of Wolfgang Neuhaus (see p. 40).   See also *HdN* II, 259.

Among these features is first the absence, or at least the inconsistent use, of bar-lines. The modern principle of barring is carried out with remarkable regularity in all the Italian and French sources of keyboard music and, as will later be seen, in almost all the tablatures for both keyboard and lute. Indubitably, its introduction marks one of the greatest advancements of the notation of solo music (keyboard and lute) over mensural notation (ensemble music). The English organists, however, did not accept this innovation until the middle of the sixteenth century. Even in the sources after this time (Mulliner Book, Fitzwilliam Virginal Book) bar-lines are used rather sparingly and inconsistently, so that frequently long measures of uneven length result. All the earliest *MSS* would seem to have lacked bar-lines in the original writing; however, such lines have been added frequently by a later hand. In some cases, they are strangely crooked or bent, due to the fact that the scribes of the original paid little attention to the vertical alignment of the notes.

The composition beginning in the second brace of Facsimile 3 (*II. versus*) serves as an example. Here, as in many cases of manuscript music, the chief difficulty lies in the obscurity of the handwriting rather than in the intrinsic problems of notation. The clefs are those of modern practice, namely the G-clef in the upper staff, the F-clef in the lower one. The G-clef is a G with a loop added whereas the F-clef is a sort of C followed by a sign which looks like two minims turned head to head. This shape is explained as a gradual transformation of the letter F. Here follow certain of the main forms of the F-clef, in chronological order[1]:

It should be noted that, in all these shapes, the note f is on the middle line of the staff although with the first three characters the dots or strokes appear a semitone higher than with the other, more recent ones.

The signs above and beneath the clefs are flats (B-flat). For the transcription, a reduction 1:2 (*M* = quarter-note) appears to be appropriate. The system of barring depends upon whether $\frac{2}{4}$- or $\frac{4}{4}$-meter is chosen for the rendition in modern notes. The latter method (two *S* to the measure) makes more familiar reading and is, perhaps, preferable. However, in music of the period under consideration, a musical phrase may well consist of an uneven number of *S*, thus leading to a cadential

---

[1] See the Facsimiles nos. 44 (twelfth century); 49, 50, 64 (thirteenth century); 73, 74 (fourteenth century); 31, 33 (fifteenth century); 27, 35 (sixteenth century). Examples of the C-clef occur on nearly all the facsimiles, while the much rarer G-clef is shown on nos. 44, 33 B and C, 35, 3, 4, 5, 6, 8, 9, 10.

close in the middle of a measure. Hence it will occasionally be found necessary to introduce a single measure of $\frac{2}{4}$ or $\frac{6}{4}$. At any rate, in music of this rather archaic type, modern barring should not be understood to entail regular accent, but only to serve as a guide for the eye.

The beginning of the transcription is given in the appendix, No. 3. The 'original' bar-lines do not always conform with the duple meter chosen for the modern writing. Of stylistic interest is the repeated occurrence of the diminished triad in root position (E G B-flat). In the next-to-last "measure" of the original the tenor part is one *M* short. An *M*-rest seems to be missing between the *S* on a and the *M* on b, or else the missing value is supplied by the *M* on g in the bass.

A second conservative feature of the English keyboard scores is the use of ligatures. Ligatures are a typical device of the notation for ensemble music from 1200 to 1600, but were not used for the writing down of soloist music, except in England. A full explanation of the ligatures will be given later (p. 87 ff). For the present purpose it will suffice to mention one special type, namely the so-called *ligatura cum opposita proprietate*, which is characterized by an upward dash to the left side of the first note. Such a ligature embraces two notes which appear either in form of two adjoining squares or that of a diagonal body (*ligatura obliqua*) the beginning and end of which determines the two notes it represents. The value of these two notes is always an *S* each:

A third peculiarity of English keyboard notation is the use of blackened notes. For certain purposes, which will be explained later, the white *B*, *S* and *M* were replaced by others which show black heads, a change which was referred to as coloration or blackening. Special forms were used for the 'blackened' *Sm*:

	B	S	M	Sm
normal:	♮	◇	♩	♩
blackened:	◼	◆	♩	♩(♩)

It should be noticed that the blackened *M* is identical in shape with the normal *Sm* and that the blackened *Sm* looks like the normal *F* (or in its second form, like the *M*). Which note is represented by one of these ambiguous forms appears from the context, i.e., chiefly from the form of the *S* used in the passage under consideration.

In the English manuscripts, the only sources of keyboard notation employing blackened notes, coloration serves two different purposes which must not be confused. Coloration is frequently used only to

FACSIMILE 3

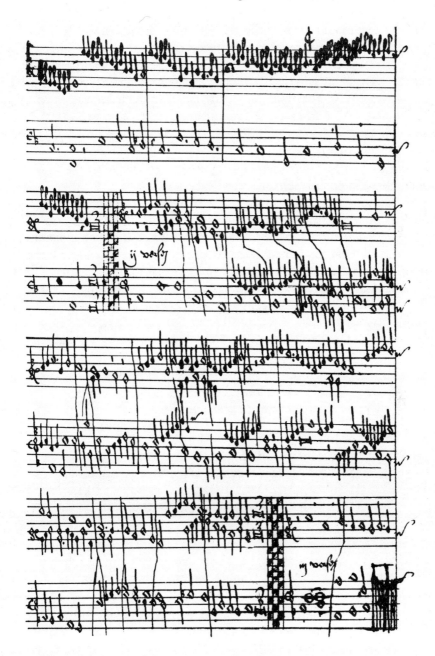

MS London, British Museum *Add. 29996* (*ca.* 1540)
Page 160'

mark off a middle voice from the neighboring ones.   An example of this
practice is to be found in the *Salvator withe a meane* from the Mulliner
Book (Facsimile 4).   Here the middle voice is written in blackened notes
which have the same value as the corresponding white notes.   Moreover, the middle voice is parcelled out between the upper and lower
staves, indicating whether it is to be played with the right or with the
left hand.   Why this blackening of the middle part was used in some
pieces, and not in others, is a difficult question to answer.   In the present
instance, one might suppose that it has some connection with the expression 'meane' of the caption, a term which, in all probability indicates a
middle part of special importance, perhaps a cantus firmus.[1]   Still, such
coincidence is not present in every case.

More interesting, but more difficult also, is the use of coloration for
another purpose, that is, the introduction of ternary rhythm.   In this
function, coloration represents an important feature of mensural notation and will be explained later in detail (see p. 126 ff).   Here it will
suffice to say that a blackened *S* equals two-thirds of a white *S* and that
a blackened *M* is half of a blackened *S*, thus equalling one third of a
white *S*: ♩-⅓○;♦-⅔○ .   Therefore, a blackened *S* and *M* together equal
a white *S*, and so do three blackened *M*:♦♩-○;♩♩♩-○ .   A blackened
ligature (cf. the first measure of the second brace) equals, of course,
two blackened *S*.

As far as the transcription into modern notation is concerned, two
methods are possible which may be indicated as follows:
Beginning of the '2. verse' (Facsimile 5):

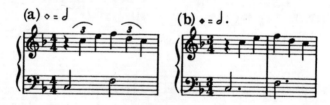

The first method is to be recommended when the ternary rhythm
occurs only occasionally, while the second is to be used when it obtains
throughout a piece.   In the English sources, the latter type is by far the
more frequent—perhaps, indeed, the only one.   If, then, the second
method (b) is adopted, the blackened *M* becomes the ordinary quarter-
note, the blackened *S* the half-note, and the white *S* the dotted half-note
of $\frac{3}{4}$-meter.   However, the latter value is also indicated by a dotted
black *S* (beginning of the 6th staff).   The sign .32. at the beginning

[1] Cf. C. Pfatteicher, *John Redford*, Kassel, 1934, pp. 63-65

FACSIMILE 4

Mulliner Book
MS London, British Museum *Add. 30513* (ca. 1560)
From page 42′

FACSIMILE 5

MS London, British Museum *Add. 29996* (ca. 1540)
From page 9′

means 'three against two' (*proportio sesquialtera*), and merely serves to explain and confirm the meaning of the blackened notes.

The second brace of the piece shows some interesting rhythms in the bass part. The blackened notes *M M S S* at the beginning indicate a rhythm which can be rendered more properly, if two ¾-measures are replaced by one ³⁄₂-measure, a change of rhythm which is frequent in the courantes of Bach (see the explanations on 'courante-coloration,' p. 127). The fourth measure of the bass is an example of syncopation, which, according to early theory, consists of the breaking up of a normal group by the intercalation of longer values. Indeed, a metrical group (one ¾-measure) is formed by the initial black *M* and the final black *S*; however, these two notes are separated by five white *S* in the value of a dotted half-note each. See the transcription in the appendix, No. 4.

Let the foregoing suffice to show the beginnings of that musical notation which today has the most extended usage, and which is now the only one employed for keyboard music. To be sure, its further development and eventual universal acceptance were not achieved immediately. The keyboard score found least objection in England, where it became, in the hands of the virginalists, a convenient means of notating music composed in an idiomatic keyboard style. It was retained in France and Italy, though a rival appeared in the form of the keyboard partitura, which, because of ease of polyphonic reading, was frequently preferred around 1600, especially for works in a contrapuntal style, such as canzonas, ricercares, etc. Germany, on the other hand, was the last country to adopt the keyboard score. Joh. Ulrich Steigleder's *Ricercar Tabulatura*[1] of 1624 appears to be the earliest German example of this notation. In southern Germany, because of the Italian and French influence which prevailed there, this manner of writing quickly became established in general usage. In northern and central Germany, however, even to the end of the seventeenth century, the organ composers remained true to the national method of notation, the German organ tablature (see p. 21 ff). Not until the beginning of the eighteenth century, after the decline of the great north-German tradition in organ music, and the rise of the musical rococo (Mattheson, Telemann) was the keyboard score universally accepted in northern Germany.

The notation on two staves was called in Italy 'intavolatura,' a name which occurs already in the second-oldest source of Italian organ music, that is, the *Intavolatura cioè recercari canzoni himni magnificati* (Venice, 1542) of Hieronimo di Marcantonio da Bologna (i.e., Girolamo Cavazzoni, the son of Marcantonio da Bologna). For this reason the notation

---

[1] The only extant copy of this publication, for which Steigleder himself engraved the copper plates, is in the Landesbibliothek, Stuttgart.

under discussion is frequently referred to in modern writings as the Italian organ tablature, for instance in Joh. Wolf's *Handbuch der Notationskunde* (*HdN*), II, 272 ('Italienische Klavier- und Orgeltabulaturen'). Similar names are used for the keyboard scores of French or English origin ('Französische . . . Tabulaturen, Tabulaturen der Virginalisten').

A practically complete list of French, Italian, and German keyboard scores is given in *HdN* II, 270–279. This list deserves a few comments to enable the student to make best use thereof. The heading 'Französische Orgel- und Klaviertabulaturen' denotes keyboard scores which have five lines in each staff. The title 'Italienische Orgel- und Klaviertabulaturen' includes sources in which other numbers of lines occur, e.g., $\frac{6}{6}\frac{5}{8}\frac{6}{9}$, etc. In this class there is a special group 'Handschriften' (p. 275) which includes a number of English documents, namely, the manuscripts from London, British Museum. It would be more logical to list these with the group: 'Tabulaturen der Virginalisten.' In fact, Add. 29996 appears in both groups. Finally, since a special grouping called 'Deutsche Klaviertabulaturen' is made, it should include German publications (Pachelbel, Froberger) which appear elsewhere in Wolf's list. The name 'Deutsche Klaviertabulaturen' should not be confused with the name 'Deutsche Orgeltabulaturen,' which indicates an entirely different system of notation (*HdN* II, 19). In the terminology of the present book the former term means keyboard scores of German origin; the latter signifies German keyboard tablatures.

II. KEYBOARD PARTITURAS

WE NOW turn to a consideration of those documents of keyboard music in which a separate staff is used for each voice-part of the composition. The earliest books written in this manner are certain Italian publications of the late sixteenth century (see p. 19). Frequently, this kind of notation is indicated in the titles by terms such as *Partitura* (*di canzone*) or (*Canzone*) *spartiti;* while titles like *Intavolatura* (*di cembalo*) or (*Toccate*) *intavolate* point to a notation on two staves (keyboard score).

Facsimile 6 serves as an example of the keyboard partitura, a notation which scarcely offers any problems. The four clefs indicate g, c, c, and F. The forms of the *F* and *Sf* are: ♪♪ . The sharps appear in a diagonal position (see tenor, second measure, second note).

As in Attaingnant's publication (p. 6), the notes within a measure are written here without regard of their vertical coincidence, in order to save space. The bar-lines (which are omitted at the beginning and at the end of the staff) mark off groups of two, three or four *S*. Since a transcription without reduction appears to be musically correct, each bar of the original divides into several measures in the modern writing. In the last bar, the altus seems to be too short, since there are only three *S* as against four in the other voices. However, from the standpoint of early notation the writing is correct, since the missing *S* is supplied by a part of the final *L* which, therefore, sounds ✳ ahead of the *L* of the other voices. See appendix, No. 5.

Of particular interest is the absence of sharps in various passages—such as the third bar of the original—which, from the point of view of nineteenth century tonality, would seem to call for a sharped F. Cases of this sort which, as is well-known, abound in early music, raise the question as to the necessity or justification of the 'editorial accidentals' which appear no less abundantly in many modern editions of early music. A thorough discussion of the problem of accidentals or, as it is frequently called, of *musica ficta*, would far exceed the limitations of this book. Instead, another approach to this important matter has been adopted, that is, short discussions of the special cases arising with the various musical illustrations to be considered. Only this much need be said in general: the generosity with which editorial accidentals have been inserted in most modern editions of early music far exceeds what can be supported and justified by scholarly evidence. Preferences created by

FACSIMILE 6

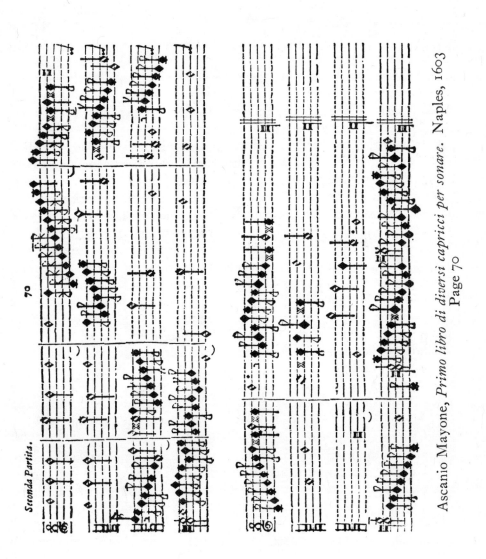

Ascanio Mayone, *Primo libro di diversi capricci per sonare.* Naples, 1603
Page 70

the harmonic idiom of nineteenth century classical music have been allowed to play much too great a rôle in this matter, and a few generalities taken from theoretical writings have been adopted as the answer to a question which actually calls for separate and detailed investigations in every period, perhaps in every single document. It is gratifying to see, however, that, within the last decade, things have taken a turn for the better, and that a number of recent editors have been more judicious and reserved in the question of editorial accidentals.[1] As far as the sources of keyboard and of lute music are concerned, this writer has called attention to the fact that the original accidentals are, as a rule, perfectly reliable and do not need correction or completion, save in some special cases.[2]

As regards the piece under consideration, no editorial sharps are needed. It is a typical example of a sixteenth century phenomenon (especially frequent in keyboard music) which combines a major tonality for harmonic formations (dominant triad with the leading tone) with a strictly diatonic, i.e., modal, scale for melodic progressions, particularly in rapid passages. Very informative in this respect is the passage at the end of the second staff (alto), which starts with a (harmonically conditioned) F-sharp, but continues with a (melodically justified) F of the descending scale. The corresponding passage of the discant shows that in this source sharps have no prolonged validity (as throughout the modern measure), since both the first and the second C are provided with an accidental.

As mentioned above, the partitura, because of its clearer display of polyphony, was frequently preferred around and after 1600 to the notation on two staves. As a matter of fact, it turns out to be especially suitable for the presentation of pieces in strict counterpoint such as ricercares, canzonas, fantasias and capriccios. It is unsuited for pieces in an idiomatic keyboard style such as variations, preludes or toccatas in which full chords with more than four notes may frequently occur. However, in the early seventeenth century, strict counterpoint was so commonly regarded as the foundation of organ style that sometimes even toccatas were set for four parts and notated in partitura. The works of the Neapolitan masters Giov. Maria Trabaci and Ascanio Mayone contain interesting examples of this practice which was, to be sure, of only transitory importance.[3]

[1] See, for instance, D. Plamenac, *Johannes Ockeghem, Sämtliche Werke, Messen I-VIII*, p. xv; L. Ellinwood, *The Works of Francesco Landini*, Cambridge, 1939, p. xlii.

[2] See W. Apel, *Accidentien und Tonalität*, pp. 29, 43.

[3] For a discussion of these works, see W. Apel, 'Neapolitan Links between Cabezon and Frescobaldi' (*MQ*, 1938).

The earliest documents of keyboard partitura[1] are certain Italian publications of the late sixteenth century, for instance:[2]

1577: Cipriano de Rore, *Tutti i madrigali . . . a quattro voci spartiti et*   *
accomodati per sonar d'ogni sorte d'istromento perfetto . . .* (Venice)
1577: *Musica de diversi autori; la bataglia francese et canzon d'uccelli.
Partite in caselle per sonar d'istrumento perfetto* (Venice)
1580: Antonio Valente, *Versi spirituali . . . spartiti per suonar negli
organi . . .* (Naples)

In the early seventeenth century, the partitura spread from Italy to other countries, and appeared at practically the same time in Portuguese and German publications:

1620: Manoel Rodriguez Coelho, *Flores de Musica pera o instrumento de
tecla et harpa* (Lisbon) (. . . for keyboard instruments and the harp)
1627: Hans Steigleder, *Tabulaturbuch darinnen dass Vater Unser . .*
(Strassburg)
1624: Samuel Scheidt, *Tabulatura nova* (Hamburg)

The title of the last publication is of special interest since it refers expressly to a 'new tablature,' i.e., to a new kind of notation not employed theretofore in Germany.   The reader will realize that the word 'tabulatura' for this notation is, to say the least, not in harmony with the terminology observed in this book in which the term tablature is reserved for notations with letters or figures. Even from the point of view of that time, the denomination of a partitura as 'tablature' was not ordinary.   It would seem that it was the word 'nova' rather than 'tabulatura' which was emphasized by the title of Scheidt's book. In the preface, the author refers to his notation in a few sentences which are cited here, as they throw an interesting light on the whole situation of notation as it was in Germany in the early seventeenth century:

Quod . . . singulae voces quinis et non senis lineis Anglico-Belgico more descriptae, in gratiam organistorum Germanorum factum, cum plerisque tabulatura illa Anglico-Belgica omnino ignota . . ., in qua sex lineae dextram, sex itidem sinistram manum concernunt, vocibus ita confuse inter se positis ut saepius etiam mediocriter in Musicis versatus haereat, et quae

[1] A practically complete list of partituras is given in *HdN* II, 276 and 307.
[2] The first two of these books contain arrangements of ensemble music (madrigals, chansons) for a keyboard instrument (*instrumento perfetto* means the 'harmonic' instruments—organ, harpsichord, etc.—in contradistinction to the 'melodic' instruments, viol, flute, etc.).

It is interesting to note that the partitura was used first for soloist music (either arranged from ensemble music—see above—, or original—as in the case of the publications of Valente and others—) before it was used for the writing down of orchestral music (earliest instance the *Ballet comique de la Royne*, 1582; see Grove's *Dictionary of Music and Musicians*, 1938, article 'Score').

notula Cantum, Altum, Tenorem vel Basin repraesentet, addubitet. Ea
de causa quamlibet vocem vides hic seorsim positam . . .

The single voices are written here on five lines and not on six, as is the
Anglo-Flemish usage. This has been done for the convenience of the
German organists, most of whom are completely ignorant of the Anglo-
Flemish tablature. In this tablature we find six lines for the right hand
and six for the left, and the voices are put together in so confusing a manner that even a fairly well-experienced musician will hesitate and wonder
which notes to attribute to the discantus, altus, tenor, or bass. For this
reason, one finds here each voice placed on a separate staff . . .

Scheidt's reference to an 'Anglo-Flemish' tablature is easily understood
from the fact that the English tradition of keyboard music was adopted
by the Netherland composer Sweelinck, of whom Scheidt was a pupil.
This musical lineage explains also why Scheidt was familiar with the
English keyboard score on two staves of six (or more!) lines each, in
contrast to his countrymen who, according to himself, were ignorant of
it. In order not to trouble the German organists with the 'vocibus ita
confuse inter se positis' of the keyboard score, he prefers the principle
of the keyboard partitura, in which one finds 'quamlibet vocem . . .
seorsim positam.'

Apparently, when Scheidt published this book, both notations, the
keyboard score and the keyboard partitura, were unknown in Germany.
From the fact, however, that he rejects the score notation as unsuitable
for the German musicians, it would appear that the notation used in
Germany before this time was related more closely to the principle of
the partitura than to that of the score. We shall find this supposition
confirmed in the following consideration of the national German keyboard notation before Scheidt, the German keyboard tablature.

III. KEYBOARD TABLATURES

A. German Keyboard Tablatures

THE GERMAN keyboard tablature is characterized by the use of letters instead of notes for some or all of the parts.

The method of denoting pitch by the letters a, b, c, etc. of our alphabet originated in the ninth century.[1] In that period, various systems were in use, some of which applied the letters A–P to the tones of two octaves (this system is commonly, but not quite accurately, called Boethian notation; cf. *HdN* 1, 38 and G. Reese, *Music in the Middle Ages* [New York, 1940], pp. 134, 135), whereas others repeated the letters A–G for the various octaves. The treatises of the ninth and tenth centuries also vary with regard to the initial tone of the series, as appears from the following tabulation:

modern:	G	A	B	c	d	e	f	g	a	b	c′	d′	e′	f′	g′	a′	b′	c″
I.		A	B	C	D	E	F	G	H	I	K	L	M	N	O	P		
II.		A	B	C	D	E	F	G	H	I	K	L	M	N	O	P		
III.	(E)	F	G	A	B	C	D	E	F	G	A	B	C	D	E	F	(G)	
IV.		Γ	A	B	C	D	E	F	G	a	b	c	d	e	f	g	α	

or: { a b c
        a b c

I: *Scholia Enchiriadis* (*GS* 1, 209).
II: *Anon. II* (*GS* 1, 342); this system has been used also in various musical sources, for instance, in the 11th-century MS Montpellier *H. 159* where it is used in combination with neumes (see *HdN* 1, 44), and in the famous two-part piece *Ut tuo propitiatus* from MS Oxford, *Bodley 572* (see p. 207; Facsimile 43).
III: Notker Labeo (*GS* 1, 96); Hucbald (*GS* 1, 118); Bernelinus, (*GS* 1, 326).
IV: Oddo of Cluny (*GS* 1, 253, 265), hence the name Oddonic letters; the double letters were also used by Guido of Arezzo.

Since the mediaeval scale included the tone B-flat in addition to the B-natural, separate indication of these degrees was necessary. They were both designated by the letter b, this being written in two shapes, round: ♭ (b molle) for the B-flat, and square: ♮ (b quadratum) for the B-natural. In later usage, the square b assumed the following shape: ♮ , and was, especially in Germany, falsely identified with the

[1] Letters were also used in Greek notation; see *HdN* 1, 16 ff.

21

letter h, the round form being called simply: b. This nomenclature and manner of writing, i.e., h for B-natural and b for B-flat, is found in all German tablatures and persists to the present day in Germany. It may be noticed that another variant of the square b lead to the sign ♮ for the natural, and still another to the sign ♯ for the sharp. Thus, all the material for our notation of accidentals, the flat, the sharp and the natural, developed from one original sign, the letter b.

Although in the Middle Ages the letters remained restricted chiefly to the theoretical and pedagogical fields, they attained practical importance in the German keyboard tablatures of the fifteenth and sixteenth centuries. The origin of this peculiar method of notation can be traced back to an English manuscript of the early fourteenth century (*ca.* 1325). Two leaves from the MS Brit. Mus. *Add. 28550*, the so-called Robertsbridge Codex, contain the earliest preserved example of what is usually called German organ tablature. The justification of the name 'German' lies in the fact that the same notation, slightly more developed, appears one hundred years later in Germany alone of all countries (Ludolf Wilkin tablature, 1432),[1] where it was adopted exclusively for the writing down of keyboard music until Scheidt's *Tabulatura Nova* (keyboard partitura) and Steigleder's *Ricercar Tabulaturen* (keyboard score), both from 1624. Even after this date, many important sources of keyboard music, particularly those from North-Germany, were written in this notation.

It is customary to distinguish between two types of German keyboard tablatures. The first was in use from the early fifteenth century to the middle of the sixteenth century and is usually referred to as 'old German organ tablature.' In this type, letters are employed for all the voices except the highest which is written in notes. The second period opens with the books of the colorists (Ammerbach, 1573), and is known as 'new German organ tablature.' Here, all the parts are written in letters.

1. OLD GERMAN KEYBOARD TABLATURES

We shall start our explanations of this notation by a discussion of an example taken from the so-called Buxheimer Orgelbuch, *ca.* 1460. The reason for our choice lies in the fact that in this source for the first time the principles of this notation appear firmly established, whereas the earlier manuscripts show certain peculiarities which demand special consideration and which, therefore, will be discussed later.

The piece in question, a composition by Boumgartner (Facsimile 7),

---

[1] Cf. L. Schrade, *Die handschriftliche Ueberlieferung der ältesten Instrumentalmusik*, Bonn, 1931; W. Apel, 'Early German Keyboard Music' (*MQ*, 1937).

is in three parts. The upper part is written in notes; the two lower ones
are written underneath in two rows of letters. The notes appear on a
staff of six or seven lines, with a C-clef. The forms are those of the
so-called black notation such as had been used in mensural notation
prior to 1450:

$$S \quad M \quad Sm \quad F$$

The rests are those of the table, p. 3.

A comparison of these notes with those of white notation used in the
former specimens shows that the smaller values have here one more
flag. For instance, the *F* is here a double-flagged note, as against the
one-flagged shape of white notation. In order to escape confusion in
this matter it is imperative to avoid flat identification of any of these
signs with those, similar in appearance, of modern notation (e.g., eighth-
or sixteenth-note). They should always be referred to by their ancient
names and determined in relation to the *semibrevis*, the identity of
which is always clear. The corresponding modern notes will have to
be determined on the basis of the reduction chosen. It will be seen
that, if the reduction is 1:2, the double-flagged *F* becomes the double-
flagged sixteenth-note of the modern system.

The flags of successive *Sm* and *F* in descending line are frequently
drawn as one coherent line, somewhat similar to the cross-strokes
of modern notation. Still, there is a difference which should not be
overlooked, if possible errors are to be avoided. A group of four *Sm*,
for example, is always written thus: , i.e., with the flag of the last
note extending a little to the right side of the last stem. On the other
hand, in a group like this: (cf. the first measure), the last note is
not a *Sm*, but a *M*, the whole group being equal to: *Sm, Sm, M*. Similarly, the group of five connected notes at the end of measure 3 consists
of four *F* and a *Sm* as the last note.

The stems of the *M*, *Sm* and *F* invariably proceed upwards. Downward stems, such as appear occasionally (measures 2, 7 and 8) indicate
chromatic alteration. This alteration may be sharping or flatting, depending on the note in question (cf. the remarks about the chromatic
dot in French and Italian keyboard scores, pp. 4, 6). Thus the double-
stemmed note in measure 2 is an F-sharp *M* while the second to the
last note in the first brace is a B-flat *S*. This manner of indicating
accidentals by a sign directly connected with the note excludes the
presumption of prolonged validity, at least as a principle.

In the third and fourth staves of our example, there are notes with a downward stem to which a little triangular loop is attached: ♪ This sign, which should not be confused with the plain downward stem, indicates an ornament which in later sources (e.g., Joh. Buchner, *Fundamentum sive ratio vera*,[1] *ca.* 1520) is called a mordent. It may be transcribed by our modern sign of the simple shake: ∿, although its execution was probably somewhat different. According to Buchner, the main note was not to be played twice or three times, but held, and only the auxiliary note was quickly repeated, a technique similar to that used for a trill on the violin. If both the mordent and chromatic alteration are desired for one tone, the alteration is indicated by a diagonal dash: ♪

The letters a, b, c, etc. used in the German tablatures have their present-day meaning (with h denoting B-natural, b denoting B-flat). Special attention is needed in order to avoid confusion of the letters c and e. For instance, in the second brace, the third and fifth letters of the upper row are both e, whereas the corresponding letters of the lower row are both c. Two octaves are distinguished in a way similar to that of modern practice, the lower being indicated by plain letters and the higher by a dash above the letter: c̄ (one-line c). Where these octaves begin and end has to be determined separately for each manuscript, since the scribes differ in this regard. In the present case, it appears from the immediate succession of b and c̄ (cf. measures 3, 5) that the new octave starts with c̄.

The capital letters, which usually appear at the beginning of a piece, are merely decorative; in later sources, however, they signify the lowest octave (see p. 30).

The indication of chromatic tones in the letter-notation is a feature of special interest and of considerable importance for the study of accidentals in the period under consideration. Whereas the B-natural and the B-flat are distinguished by different letters (h and b), all the other chromatic tones are indicated by a little loop or scroll attached to the letter, as follows:

c#	d#	f#	g#

[1] Buchner's *Fundamentum*, which includes an extensive treatise on composition' as well as a large collection of organ pieces, exists in two *MSS:* Zurich, Stadtbibliothek, *cod. 284*, and Basle, Universitäts-bibliothek, *F I 8.* A large portion of the *Fundamentum* has been published by C. Paesler in *VfMW* v; see also E. V. Werra, in *Km. Jb.* 1895, and W. Nagel in *MfM* xxiii.

FACSIMILE 7

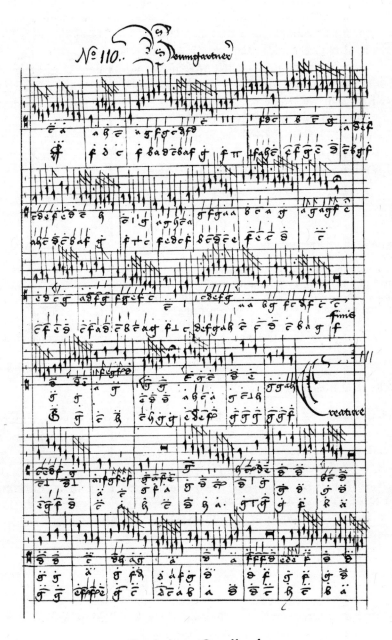

Buxheimer Orgelbuch
MS Munich, Staatsbibliothek *Mus. Ms. 3725 (ca.* 1460)
Page 61

This scroll is an abbreviation of the Latin syllable -*is* which was taken over by German terminology to indicate sharping (*cis* = C-sharp). Indeed, except for the B-flat, all chromatic tones are invariably designated as sharps, for instance, E-flat as D-sharp, A-flat as G-sharp. The observation of this principle brings about what would seem to be, at first glance, a rather strange use of enharmonic equivalents. For instance, in the third measure of the present example, the sixth letter of the lowest row is b, and the corresponding letter of the higher row is d-sharp. The actual meaning is the fifth E-flat to B-flat.

Above each letter there is a sign indicating its time value. These signs are similar in appearance to the note values to which they are equal, and are obviously derived from them:

B (tern.)	*B* (bin.)	*S*	*M*	*Sm*	*F*
⋯	⋅⋅	⋅	│	↾	↾

For the transcription (see appendix, No. 6), a reduction 1:4 of the note values seems appropriate. The piece is an interesting example of fifteenth century Lydian, characterized by the prevalence of B-natural in the melody, and by a change from B-natural to B-flat in the lower parts, the former being preferred for ascending, the latter for descending lines. No editorial accidentals are needed. The tendency to avoid chromatic tones in quick passages and ornamenting figures—already observed in a previous example—here leads to interesting formations (cf. the succession F♯-F in meas. 2, and B-B♭ in meas. 6 of the third brace). Occasionally, the distinction of octaves appears to be inaccurate, in the letter-notation. The frequent crossing of the lower parts is a characteristic of the style of the Burgundian School (Dufay, Binchois, fl. *ca.* 1440) to which all the pieces of the Buxheimer Orgelbuch belong, most of them being * intabulations of Burgundian chansons.

The next source of German keyboard tablature to be considered is Arnolt Schlick's *Tabulaturen etlicher Lobgesang und Lidlein uff die Orgeln und Lauten* (Mainz, 1512). Except for a single musical illustration contained in Sebastian Virdung's *Musica getutscht* of 1511, it is the earliest instance of keyboard music published in print. Facsimile 8 shows the first page of the book.

In contrast to the Buxheimer Orgelbuch Schlick uses white notes, as follows:

S	*M*	*Sm*	*F*	*Sf*
○	♩	♪	♬	♬

Chromatic alterations are indicated by a small loop attached to the note (cf. the sixth note of the example).

In the letter-notation, tones of the great octave (below c) are designated by a horizontal dash beneath the letter. It is probably from

FACSIMILE 8

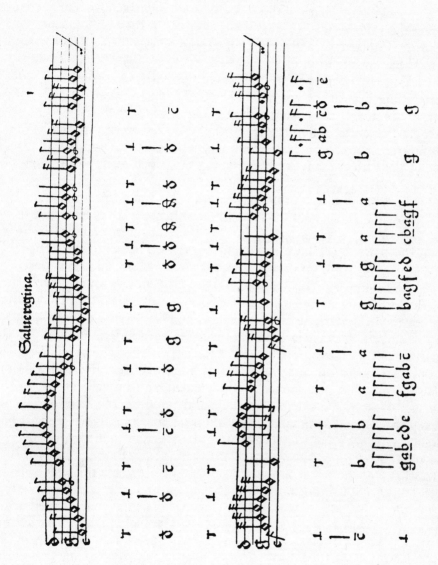

Arnolt Schlick, *Tabulaturen etlicher Lobgesang und Lidlein. Mainz, 1512*
Page 1

this method of indicating the lower tones in a manner 'contrary' to that used for the one-line octave, that the name contra-octave (also contra-bassoon, etc.) originated.[1] The metrical values are indicated by the same signs as in the Buxheimer Orgelbuch, except that the dot indicating an *S* is lacking, a letter without a rhythmic sign being understood as having the value of an *S*. The T-like symbols in the first and third row are *S*-rests affixed to a fragment of a staff line, which alternate with *M*-rests having the form of an inverted T.

There are no bar-lines in this tablature; instead, groups of notes representing a measure are marked off into blocks separated by small spaces. In the present composition, *Salve Regina*, each block contains three *M* (six *Sm*). The fifth group contains one *Sm* too many; but, as a compensation, the seventh group is one short. Apparently, the last note of the fifth and the sixth group has to be tied over, so that syncopation results.

It is interesting to note that the parts of this composition, in contrast to those of the Buxheimer Orgelbuch, **move in separate ranges,** and that the arrangement of the parts in the tablature corresponds to their respective ranges, the lowest voice being written in the lowest row, etc. This arrangement, natural as it is, is not always observed in the German keyboard tablatures. In the sources after Schlick, one usually finds the lowest part written immediately underneath the melody, i.e., as the highest row of letters, so that the following order results: discant, bass, alto, tenor. Some scholars have considered this curious method as an anticipation of the thorough-bass practice, with its characteristic emphasis on the discant and the bass. Another explanation, and a more plausible one, has been given by O. Kinkeldey,[2] who calls attention to the fact that in some books of mensural notation the four parts are arranged in a similar manner, with the bass underneath the discant on the left-hand page, and the other voices on the right-hand page.

Facsimile 9 from Kotter's tablature of 1513 (Basle, Universitäts-bibliothek, *F IX 22*) illustrates this arrangement (cf. the first chord, with f written on top of ī and c̄).[3] Other features of this tablature are:

1. The notes are the black characters of the Buxheimer Orgelbuch; however, instead of the lozenges we have the round heads still in use in modern notation.

2. In a series of *F* or *Sf*, only the first note of the group bears the

---

[1] In modern usage, the term contra-octave signifies the octave below the great octave.
[2] *Orgel und Klavier im 16. Jahrhundert*, Leipzig, 1910, p. 190.
[3] The inscription reads: *Anabole* (Greek, prelude) *in fa*, *Jo*(hannes) *Kot*(ter).

FACSIMILE 9

MS Basle, Universitätsbibliothek *F IX 22 (ca. 1513)*

stem and flag indicating time-value, whereas the following notes are written only as heads. Naturally, these are meant to be notes of the same value: ♪... - ♫♫ .

3. The sign of the mordent is a small loop, similar to that used in Schlick (cf. the first note). Chromatic alteration is indicated by a downward stem carrying a diagonal dash (cf. the first note of the second staff).

4. In the letter-notation, tones of the two-line octave are indicated by a double letter with a horizontal dash: $\overline{cc}$ (cf. second brace, end of the middle row of letters).

5. In the letter-notation, consecutive *F* or *Sf* are indicated, not by single rhythmic signs but in a manner similar to that of the cross-stroke in modern notation: ‖‖ . These fence-like marks form a striking feature of all the later German keyboard tablatures.

A transcription without reduction is recommended (♩-♩). This means that the double-flagged *F* becomes a one-flagged eighth-note, thus leading to what looks like a doubling of the smaller values. There are several instances of incorrect writing in this piece. The rest after the first note of the top voice should be an *F*-rest, instead of an *Sf*-rest. The *fusa*-rest in the second staff should be dotted. In the next measure, the first note of the highest row of letters is indicated as a dotted *M*, that is, equal to *M + Sm*, whereas its actual value is only *M + F*. The whole piece is reproduced in W. Apel, * *Musik aus früher Zeit*, vol. 1 (Mayence, 1932).

The notation just described is typical of all the examples of German keyboard tablature in the first half of the sixteenth century. They offer few difficulties, except those presented by their graphological peculiarities. With many of the handwritten documents a preliminary study is necessary to determine the meaning of the different signs indicating letters. This task is best accomplished by a consideration of letters in vertical arrangement (chords) or in simple melodic formations such as scales and schematic coloraturas. The following table shows the forms of Kleber's manuscript tablature of 1520–24 (Berlin, Staatsbibliothek, *Mus. Ms. Z 26*):

F G A B H c c♯ d d♯ e f f♯ g g♯ a b h

The letters c and e are particularly apt to be confused.

Facsimile reproductions from Kleber's tablature are given in *HdN* II, 26 and in *SchT*, p. 16.

FACSIMILE 10

MS St. Gall, Stiftsbibliothek *530* (*ca.* 1525)
Page 10

A page from Fridolin Sicher's tablature of about 1525 (Library of the Monastery St. Gall, *530*[1]), written in more hasty characters, may serve as a final illustration of the old German keyboard tablature (Facsimile 10). It contains an *In dulci jubilo*, and the beginning of a *Resonet*. A peculiarity of this tablature is the writing of the rhythm ♩♪ in this manner ⅄♪ , which is applied to notes as well as to letters. For the benefit of those whose several hours labouring has not been wholly successful, it may be said that both pieces are transcribed in H. J. Moser's ✳ *Frühmeister der deutschen Orgelkunst* (Leipzig, 1930).

2. New German Keyboard Tablatures

In the second half of the sixteenth century the writers of keyboard tablatures began to use letters not only for the lower parts, but for the melody also. It is this exclusive use of letters for all the voices that distinguishes the so-called new German keyboard tablature from the earlier type. To the modern mind, this change appears bizarre. One would expect to find a gradual decline in the use of letters and an increased use of notes, yet actually the development proceeds in the opposite direction. Nevertheless, the new method is perhaps not so illogical as it seems to be at first sight. As a matter of fact, letters are rather convenient symbols for tones, particularly since they obviate the use of the staff which always has been a source of trouble, especially in printing music. The high cost of publishing music written on a staff may have been a decisive factor in the adoption of the new system. The use of letters also saves space, as can be seen on Facsimile 9, in which the three rows of letters occupy no more space than one row of notes. Even J. S. Bach still resorted to the letter-tablature in some of his autographs when the paper did not offer sufficient space for a staff.[2]

The books of new German organ tablature include the printed publications of the so-called 'colorists,' Nikolaus Ammerbach (1571, 1583), Bernhard Schmid (1576, 1577), Jacob Paix (1583), Bernhard Schmid, the younger (1607), and others. They also include numerous seventeenth century manuscripts, many of which are listed in *HdN* II, 32ff.

These tablatures do not call for general explanations beyond those previously given, except for a consideration of the metrical signs. While the German keyboard tablatures of the first half of the century show

---

[1] Cf. W. R. Nef, 'Der St. Galler Organist Fridolin Sicher und seine Orgeltabulatur' (*Schweizerisches Jahrbuch für Musikwissenschaft*, VII, 1938).

[2] *Orgelbüchlein* (Berlin, Staatsbibliothek, *Mus. Ms. P 283*), pp. 9, 17, 22, 26, 30; see Facsimile 13.

a rather confusing variety of rhythmical signs (see the explanations in *HdN* II, pp. 20, 23, 27), a new and uniform practice, originating in the Italian lute books (see p. 62), appears in the sources now under consideration. The *S* is always represented by a plain vertical stroke which formerly denoted the *M*. Accordingly, the signs for the smaller values show two more flags than the corresponding signs of mensural notation, as appears from the following chart:

	S	M	Sm	F	Sf
mensural notation (*figure de musica*):	○	↓	↓	♪	♬
tablature (*figure de sonatori*):	│	♪	♬	♬	♬

The Italian names are those of Don Bartolomeo Lieto's *Dialogo quarto di musica*, 1559; see *HdN* II, 64.

The correctness of this concordance is attested not only by various theoretical writers, but also by a comparison of pieces preserved in both systems of notation (e.g., the innumerable intabulations of motets, chansons, etc.).

Modern editors have frequently overlooked or dismissed these facts, and have transcribed pieces from German tablatures on the basis of a merely external similarity of metrical signs, i.e., of the number of flags, so that, e.g., the *Sm* of the tablature became a sixteenth-note of modern writing.[1] This actually means a reduction 1:4 of the note values, which is definitely too great for the period under consideration and which considerably obscures matters of tempo and of style. The proper reduction for the sources under consideration is 1:2 which means that the metrical signs of the tablature lose one flag. In external aspect, such a change has, of course, the appearance of the reverse procedure, that is, enlargement 1:2. Once the situation is clearly understood, there would seem to be little danger of referring to it as what it seems to be (enlargement) rather than what it really is (reduction). It is interesting to note that the above-explained principles still hold good in the case of J. S. Bach, who, whenever he uses letter-notation for the closing measures of an organ-chorale, replaces the whole note (i.e., the old *S*) by the plain vertical stroke. Naturally, no actual reduction of time-values is permissible in music so late as Bach's, which means that the metrical signs of his tablature lose two flags.

The printed examples of this notation offer scarcely any problems. Facsimile 11, from the *Tabulatur Buch* of B. Schmid, the younger, of 1607 serves as an example. The simple stroke representing the *S* appears in the form of the letter J. The rhythmical signs for the smaller

[1] For instance, W. Merian in: *Der Tanz in den deutschen Tabulaturbüchern*, Leipzig, 1927.

values are combined in fence-like drawings similar to those of the tablature of Kotter (Facsimile 9). Likewise, the lines indicating higher octaves are drawn as uninterrupted horizontal strokes for an entire group of
notes: a g f e (end of the first line). If, in such a group, some notes
belong to the two-line octave, separate dashes are added on top of the
long dash: c b a g. Note that the letter c has the shape of the modern
letter r (see the explanations on seventeenth century French lute tablatures, pp. 71, 72). Apparently, the one-line octave begins here with
the letter h, not c, as appears from a consideration of the bass line at
the top of the page.

The pieces on this pages are transcriptions into German tablature of the 'toni' (preludes
in the different modes) which originally appeared—in keyboard score—in the *Intonazioni
d'organo di Andrea Gabrieli, et di Gio: suo nepote*, of 1593. The two first columns of the
page are occupied by the conclusion of the *Secundus tonus* which is a fifth lower than the
Secundus tonus transpositus per quintam superiorem (the first C-sharp on the page corresponding to the G-sharp at the beginning of the third column). Of particular interest
is the clash between the harmonically conditioned C-sharp in the initial measure of the
page and the melodic C in the bass-line:

The reader is advised to compare his transcriptions with the very inaccurate reprints
of the *Intonazioni* contained in L. Torchi's *L'Arte musicale in Italia*, vol. III, p. 131 ff.
Torchi and many other writers ascribe these pieces to Giovanni Gabrieli, whereas B.
Schmidt names Andrea Gabrieli as the composer. Stilistic considerations doubtless
support the latter's view (see A. Gabrieli's toccatas in the same volume).

In the numerous manuscript specimens of the new German keyboard
tablature, the chief obscurity lies in their graphological peculiarities.
Facsimile 12, taken from the *Klavierbuch der Jungfrau Regina Clara Im
Hoff* (Vienna, Staatsbibliothek *Ms. 18491*) of 1629, serves as an example:[1]

G A B h c c#   d d# e f f# g g# a b

In both pieces of our facsimile (*Fillis sass in einen Bötgen*, and *Falscher Schäffer ist das
recht*) the number of voices alternates between three and four, in a manner characteristic

[1] Compare these characters with those of Kleber's tablature, p. 30.

Bernhard Schmid, *Tabulatur Buch von allerhand . . . Praeludiis, Toccaten, Motteten, Canzonetten, Madrigalien und Fugen.* Strassburg, 1607
From folio A IV

FACSIMILE 12

Klavierbuch der Jungfrau Regina Clara Im Hoff
Vienna, Staatsbibliothek *Ms. 18491* (1629)

of the keyboard style of the mid-seventeenth century (Froberger). The tiny hooks appearing underneath certain letters (e.g., the first and third at the beginning) are signs of ornamentation the exact meaning of which is doubtful (mordent?). Occasionally, the metrical signs appear within the row of letters, indicating rests. The third brace is transcribed in the appendix, No. 7.

In the seventeenth century, the new German organ tablature spread particularly in North Germany. Not only are all the important collections of organ music in that period thus written down,—for instance, the famous Lüneburger Tabulaturen (containing compositions of Tunder, Reinken, Hanff, Buxtehude and others),—but also contemporary instrumental and even vocal scores. Interesting examples are to be found in the edition by G. Harms of the complete works of Buxtehude (Hamburg, 1925–37; see vols. 5, 6).[1]

Facsimile 13 is a page from J. S. Bach's Orgelbüchlein in which tablature is used whenever the page reserved for an organ chorale did not provide enough space. We leave it to the student to decipher—of course, without the aid of the Peters edition. Let it suffice to point out that the rhythmic signs of the tablature are the traditional ones (with two flags more than those of the ordinary notation), and that the four-flagged sign (corresponding to the sixteenth-note) is replaced by the figure 4.

3. THE EARLIEST SPECIMENS OF GERMAN KEYBOARD TABLATURE

We began our consideration of the German keyboard tablatures with the Buxheimer Orgelbuch, since it is the earliest document showing the principles of this notation fully developed. The few sources preceding it display certain primitive features which make them interesting subjects for individual studies rather than examples for general explanations. In fact, most of them have been dealt with in monographs to which the interested student is referred. Here we must restrict ourselves to a few brief remarks.

The reproduction on p. 38 shows part of a page from the oldest extant document of keyboard tablature, contained in the early fourteenth century MS Brit. Mus. *Add. 28550* (Robertsbridge Codex). The upper voice of the two-voiced composition (an instrumental estampie, not a prelude; of. the erroneous designation in Frotscher, *Geschichte des Orgelspiels* [Berlin, 1935], 1, 62), is written on a staff with notes, while the lower one appears underneath written in letters. In order to clarify the grapho-

[1] See also p. 17 of *SchT* and G. Harms, *Samuel Scheidts Werke*, 1937, vol. 5.

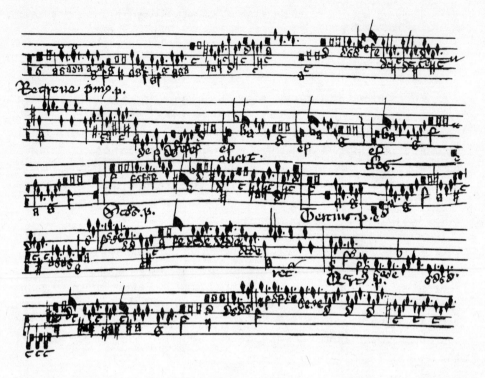

logical obscurities of the original, there follows a transliteration of the first line.

A thorough understanding of the staff-notation requires a knowledge of the Italian mensural notation of the fourteenth century (see p. 384). Suffice it to say that the *brevis* is the unit of time-measurement, equivalent to our beat and, therefore, best transcribed as a quarter-note. Three such *breves* form a measure of $\frac{3}{4}$ (*modus perfectus*). The smaller values are combined in groups equalling a *brevis* and marked off from one another by dots (*punctus divisionis*). Rhythmical differentiations within such a group are obtained by the use of stemmed *semibreves*. The *S* with a downward stem is half of a *B*; the plain *S* is half of a *B* or a quarter of a *B* depending upon whether there are two or four such notes in a group; the *S* with an upward stem (*minima*) is one-eighth of a *B*. The small circles on top of the first two *S* are probably orna-

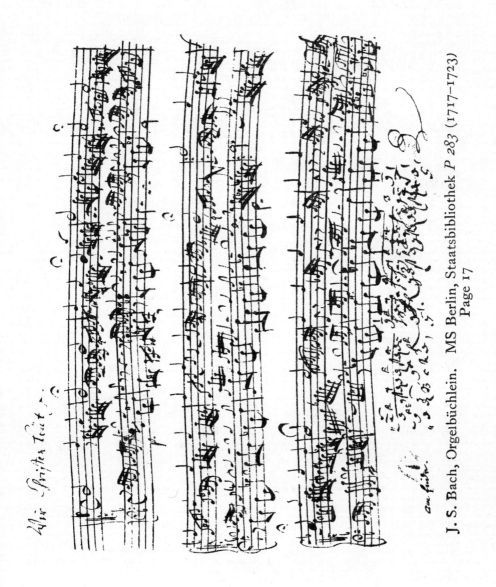

J. S. Bach, Orgelbüchlein.   MS Berlin, Staatsbibliothek *P 283* (1717–1723)
Page 17

ments (mordent?). The white *B* would seem to indicate prolongation of the preceding black *B*.

In the letter-notation, the letter *s* (abbreviation of Lat. *sine*, 'without') indicates a rest. The sharp-like sign stands for the B-natural (see p. 21 f). Following is the transcription of the beginning:[1]

It is not until one hundred years later that we again meet examples of this same notation, all of which are of German origin. They are listed here in an approximate chronological order:[2]

1. Tablature of Ludolf Wilkin, 1432 (Berlin, Staatsbibliothek, *theol. lat. quart. 290*)
2. Tablature of Adam Ileborgh, 1448 (Philadelphia, The Curtis Institute of Music)
3. Tablature of Wolfgang de Novo Domo (Neuhaus), *ca.* 1450 (Hamburg, Stadt-und Universitätsbibliothek, *ND VI No. 3225*)
4. Fragments of a tablature, *ca.* 1450 (Breslau, Dominikanerkloster)
5. *Fundamentum organisandi magistri Conradi Paumanni*, 1452 (Werniger - ode, Library of Fürst Stolbergk, *MS Zb 14*)
6. Tablature, anonymous, *ca.* 1450 (Erlangen, Universitätsbibliothek, *729*)

The most important of these sources, namely, the tablatures of Ileborgh and Paumann, may be briefly considered here.

Facsimile 14 shows the first page of the Ileborgh tablature. It begins with the following lines of Latin text, incorporating many abbreviations (not preserved below), as was customary at the time:

Incipiunt praeludia diversarum notarum secundum modernum modum

---

[1] For further studies of this *MS* see the facsimiles in H. E. Wooldridge, *Early English Harmony*, London, 1897, 1, pl. 42-45, as well as the transcriptions and explanations by J. Wolf (*Kirchen-musikalisches Jahrbuch*, 1899; *AfMW* 1; *GdM* 1, 357; *GdM* 111, no. 78; *HdN* 11, 5) and J. Handschin (*ZfMW* xii, xiii). The *primus punctus* of the above piece is also contained in W. Apel, *Musik aus früher Zeit*, 11. The transcription in *Early English Harmony*, 11, 1913 (H. V. Hughes) contains numerous errors.

[2] Literature (a) general: L. Schrade, *Die ältesten Denkmäler der Orgelmusik*, Münster, 1928; W. Apel, 'Early German Keyboard Music' (*MQ* xxiii). (b) Special: W. Apel, 'Die Tabulatur des Adam Ileborgh' (*ZfMW* xvi); F. Feldmann, 'Ein Tabulaturfragment des Breslauer Dominikaner-klosters' (*ZfMW* xv); F. W. Arnold and L. Bellermann, 'Das Lochamer Liederbuch . .' (*JfMW* 11); K. Ameln, *Locheimer Liederbuch und Fundamentum organisandi*, Berlin, 1925 (facsimile edition).

FACSIMILE 14

Tablature of Adam Ileborgh (1448)
Philadelphia, The Curtis Institute of Music
Page 1

subtiliter et diligenter collecta cum mensuris diversis hic inferius annexis per fratrem Adam Ileborgh Anno Domini 1448 tempore sui rectoriatus in stendall.

Here begin preludes in various keys according to the modern manner (in modern style?), cleverly and diligently collected, with diverse *mensurae* appended hereinbelow, by brother Adam Ileborgh, in the year of our Lord 1448, during the time of his rectorate in Stendall.

Above the first staff one reads:

Sequitur preambulum in C et potest variari in d, f, g, a.

There follows a preamble in C which may be transposed into the keys of d, f, g, a.

This preamble is written on a staff of eight lines, with six letters, namely, C, G, D, F-sharp, C, g underneath.   The rhythmic interpretation of the melody presents difficulties, owing to the absence of bar-lines, and to the employment of a special note not encountered in our previous studies, i.e., ♪ .   This shape of note, with a one-flag stem both upward and downward, occurs in the Italian sources of the late fourteenth century with various meanings.[1]   In all cases, it signifies a small note-value, a meaning which is in harmony with the practice of Paumann's *Fundamentum*, as will be seen subsequently.   In the Ileborgh tablature, however, this interpretation fails to lead to a satisfactory result.   A closer study of the codex shows that the sign in question has here an opposite meaning, namely, that of a long note.[2]

In his monograph on the Ileborgh tablature this writer has called attention to the strikingly free, rhapsodic character of the preambles, suggesting that it was this rambling style to which the words 'secundum modernum modum' referred.   A similar lack of definiteness is to be found in the various notational signs, none of which seems to have an accurate and invariable meaning.   The double-stemmed note, for example, may have the character of a *longa*, a *brevis* or a *semibrevis*, according to the context.   Likewise, the notes of familiar form can hardly be identified with any definite quantity of duration.   Under these circumstances it appears that no accurate transcription into modern notation is possible. The version given below will, at least, afford an insight into the notational problems of this specimen.

The letters written underneath the staff present another peculiar

[1] Cf. *GdM* I, pp. 298, 306, 327, 352, 354; *HdN* I, 313. See p. 405 of the present book.
[2] See W. Apel, 'Die Tabulatur des Adam Ileborgh' (*ZfMW* xvi), p. 193.

difficulty. If one tries to play them together with the corresponding tones of the upper voice, he will easily see that the resulting two-part composition does not make sense. Especially strange is the fact that the last note of the lower voice should be g—which fits very poorly with the C-tonality of the whole piece. The solution of the puzzle lies in the fact that two successive letters always are to be played simultaneously in pairs, as if they were arranged vertically, instead of horizontally.

Thus, the single row of letters actually represents two voices:

This curious manner of writing loses its apparent oddity and becomes logical and plausible if perceived as an expression of a special technique, i.e., of the double pedal. The letters, then, indicate tones to be played on the pedal[1] in such a way that, with each pair, the first one is to be played with the left foot and the second with the right foot. A transcription of this preamble follows:[2]

Our facsimile shows two other preambles, each written in two parts on a single staff, without letters. From the historical point of view, this manner of writing is interesting as the earliest indication of that principle which is utilized in the keyboard-score, that is, the writing of several parts on one staff. The reason for the use of this notation

[1] Cf. the inscription at the bottom of Facsimile 14: *Preambulum bonum pedale sive manuale*. This is the earliest known indication of pedal in musical sources. Regarding the use of pedal in the Buxheimer Orgelbuch see A. Schering, *Studien zur Geschichte der Frührenaissance*, Leipzig, 1914, p. 144 ff.

[2] See the article in *MQ* XXIII, p. 213, from which the above illustration has been reproduced by permission of the publishers.

Similar notational features occur in the Wilkin-tablature (1432), a page of which is reproduced in *SchT*, p. 32/33. The pairs of letters to be found in the measures of the first staff denote simultaneous tones, as in Ileborgh. The double-stemmed note also has the same meaning as in the Ileborgh tablature, that is, of a fermata. The various shapes used for these held tones are worth noticing. At the bottom of p. 32, a two-voice *Kyrie* is notated in letters exclusively. Its primitive style reminds one of the organum of the tenth century.

instead of that employed in the first preamble, is probably to be found
* in the word *manualiter* which excludes pedal performance.

A peculiarity of this MS is the indication, in the letter notation, of
the tone G-sharp, not as an altered (raised) G, but as an altered (lowered)
A, e.g., (p. 7):

D   A   E   A♭   D   A =

It will be remembered that just the reverse practice is found in the
Buxheimer Orgelbuch and in the later sources, in which flat tones (E-
flat) are written as sharps (D-sharp).

The last document of German organ tablature to be considered here
is the *Fundamentum organisandi Magistri Conradi Paumanni Ceci de
Nuerenberga Anno 1452* (Foundations of Composition by the Blind
Master Conrad Paumann from Nuremberg), which is preserved jointly
with the Lochamer Liederbuch.   The student who has read the explanations concerning the slightly later Buxheimer Orgelbuch will be familiar
with the general notational principles of the *Fundamentum*.[1]   The
following remarks deal with the peculiarities of this manuscript.

1.   Chromatic alteration is indicated by a downward stem which
usually carries a small diagonal dash. The following three forms are
used indiscriminately: ♪♪♪ , with the second being the most frequent
one.

2.   The chromatic sign, in any of its three shapes, signifies either
sharping or flatting, depending upon the tone with which it is associated.   See the explanations on the 'chromatic dot' in the early Italian
and French keyboard scores (pp. 4, 6).[2]

3.   The note form ♪ , known to us from the Ileborgh tablature,
occurs frequently in the *Fundamentum*, though with a different meaning.
It nearly always follows a *M*, together with which it expresses a dotted

---

[1] The Buxheimer Orgelbuch also contains a *Fundamentum organisandi C.P.C.* (Conradi Paumanni
Caeci) which is a more complete version of that in the MS from 1452.   The first page of this *Fundamentum* is shown in *SchT*, p. 97.

[2] J. Wolf's remarks about the chromatic alterations in the *Fundamentum* (*HdN* ii, 15) are somewhat obscure, particularly the statement: 'Merkwürdigerweise gewinnt er den Ton b ebenfalls als
Kreuzton von der Stufe h aus.'   The inherent contradiction of this remark results from Wolf's
assumption previously made that all the altered tones of the top voice are sharps ('er sieht in der
Oberstimme alle alterierten Töne als Kreuztöne an').   The incorrectness of this statement becomes
especially evident from a study of the facsimile-page reproduced in Wolf's book (p. 14, *Des Klaffers
neyden*).   The third measure shows the chromatic stem used in connection with the tone a; doubtless, what is here meant is an a-flat, not an a-sharp.   The false relation between this a-flat and the
a-natural of the lower voice is a typical and frequent stylistic feature of this period and of 16th century music.

FACSIMILE 15

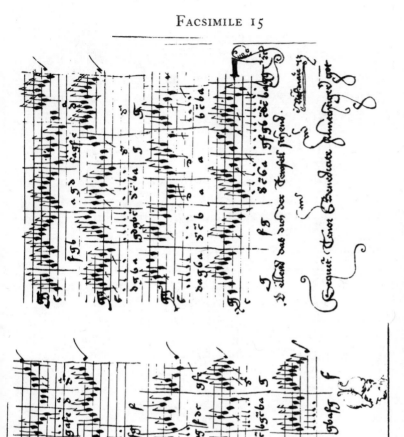

Conrad Paumann, *Fundamentum organisandi.* MS Wernigerode, Library of Count Stolbergk, *Zb 14* (1452)
Pages 76', 77

rhythm: ♩♪-♩.♪-♩.♪ . Occasionally, (for instance, on p. 79, st. 5, meas. 2 of the facsimile edition) it follows upon a *S*: ♦♪♦♩-♩♫♩♩ .

It should be noticed that this interpretation, though commonly accepted,[1] is not entirely satisfactory. The most obvious objection is that the same dotted rhythm is frequently expressed in the ordinary manner, by a dotted *M* followed by a *Sm*. In fact, both manners of writing repeatedly occur in close proximity (cf. Facsimile 15, last two meas. of syst. 3 and second meas. of syst. 4). Moreover, the theory of a note exercising a 'dotting' influence upon the preceding note is somewhat odd and cannot be accepted without question. However, an explanation is offered by an analogous feature of contemporary mensural notation, that is, the so-called *minor color* which consists of a blackened *S* followed by a blackened *M*: ♦♩ . As is explained on p. 128, the dotted rhythm, ♩.♩.♩.♩, which this combination represents, is a modification of what originally was a triplet rhythm: ♦♩-♩♩ . A similar explanation could be applied to the above notational signs of the *Fundamentum*. In fact, it would be possible to assume that these signs here still retain their supposedly original triplet meaning, an interpretation which would obviate the first of our two objections, as they would then express a rhythm different from that indicated by the dotted *M*. We submit this theory as a possible explanation of this notational peculiarity, and illustrate it by the following transcription of the above-mentioned measures:

4. In the last pages of the *Fundamentum* proper (p. 81, 86, 87; the pages 82–85 and 88–92 are insertions of a later hand) the forms ♩ and ♩ occur repeatedly, probably with the meaning of an ornament (mordent).[2]

---

[1] See the explanations and transcriptions in *JfMW* II and in *HdN* II, 13.

[2] The ornamentations in the *Fundamentum* are explained by J. Wolf as follows (*HdN* II, 16): 'Nur als Verzierungen sind die Formen ♩ und ♩ zu deuten. Vielleicht verbirgt sich hinter ihnen der *flos harmonicus* oder der Mordent. Jedenfalls verbietet sich angesichts der folgenden Stellen die Auffassung als alterierter Ton.' As far as the first form is concerned, these remarks are obscure since, on p. 15 of *HdN*, its meaning as a sign of chromatic alteration is clearly set forth. As regards Wolf's example in support (p. 17, first example), a study of the original (p. 75, last measure) shows that the dash is drawn through the stem horizontally, not diagonally. It serves merely to strike out the downward stem, i.e., to cancel an error of writing.

5. As to the letters, the main octave ends with b (i.e., B-flat) and the one-line octave begins with h (i.e., B-natural). The horizontal dash indicating the higher octave appears frequently in the form of a scroll reminiscent of the modern sign for the mordent. The metrical values of the letters are indicated by small red notes wherever deemed advisable for clarity's sake.

Facsimile 15 shows a two-part composition *Ellend du hast* (Misery, thou hast), a section of which, beginning with measure 6 of the third brace, is transcribed in the appendix, No. 8.

The piece contains various clerical errors, particularly in the upper part, some of which are obvious whereas others require conjecture. In measure four of the fourth brace we suggest changing the second note to an *M*, and the last note to an *S*, half of which would go to the following measure. No editorial accidentals are necessary. Particularly interesting is the cadential ornamentation in the last measure of the first brace of p. 77, with its wavering between F-sharp and F-natural.[1]

In conclusion we wish to call attention to an interesting notational hybrid showing mixed features of German and of French origin, namely, the MS Munich, Staatsbibliothek, *Mus. Ms. 2987.*[2]

B. SPANISH KEYBOARD TABLATURES

The scarcity of documents on Spanish keyboard music of the sixteenth century[3] makes it difficult to investigate the early history of notation in that country. It is not unlikely that Spanish composers of organ music prior to 1550 employed a notation similar to that of the Italian keyboard score. At any rate, shortly after 1550 various attempts were made to introduce a national notation based entirely on figures. The Spanish theorist Bermudo, in his *Declaracion de instrumentos musi-cales* (Ossuna, 1555), deals at length with this question.[4] He advocates a new system of keyboard notation, according to which the white and the black keys from C to a″ are numbered by figures from 1 to 42. His lowest octave is a short octave, containing only eight tones instead of twelve, in the following arrangement:

	D	E	Bb		(black keys)
C	F	G	A	B	(white keys)

---

[1] See the explanations on the 'Schwankungsmordent' in *Accidentien und Tonalität*, p. 23.

[2] See W. Apel, 'Du Nouveau sur la musique Française pour orgue au xvie siècle' (*La Revue Musicale* xviii, 97).

[3] For a survey of sixteenth century Spanish organ and lute music see W. Apel, 'Early Spanish Keyboard and Lute Music' (*MQ* xx).

[4] Cf. O. Kinkeldey, *Orgel und Klavier im 16. Jahrhundert*, 1912, p. 20.

His figures then represent these tones:

1	2	3	4	5	6	7	8	9	10
C	D	E	F	G	A	B♭	B	c	c♯

11	12	13	14	15	16	17	18	..	30	..	42
d	e♭	e	f	f♯	g	g♯	a	..	a′	..	a″

In applying this material to actual compositions, Bermudo uses a
staff which, in spite of its apparent similarity, has nothing in common
with the staves either of the piano score or of mensural notation.   Its
lines do not indicate pitch, but represent the separate voices of the composition, and, accordingly, may vary in number from two to four, five
and even six.   The figures written on a given line indicate the tones of
the corresponding voice.   Here follows the beginning of Bermudo's
example:

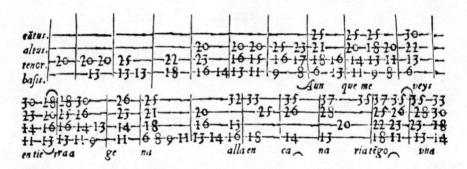

Bermudo also mentions another, more practical method of notation
by figures, i.e., the employment of figures for the white keys only, the
black keys being indicated by sharps and flats.   Here, the number of
figures employed undergoes a substantial reduction, thus making the
system considerably simpler.   Indeed, this notation has been used repeatedly in musical practice.   Joh. Wolf (*HdN* ii, 266) mentions a
manuscript tablature in the possession of O. Chilesotti, written in this
notation.   Another example, of greater importance, is represented by
an Italian publication of 1576, the *Intavolatura de Cimbalo* by Antonio
Valente, who is notable as the earliest known representative of the
Neapolitan school of cembalists, later members of which are Giovanni
Maria Trabaci and Ascanio Mayone.

Facsimile 16 shows a page of this book. The figures 1 to 23 represent the white keys, as follows:

1	2	3	4	5	6	7	8	9	10	11	12
C	F	G	A	B	c	d	e	f	g	a	b

short octave

13	14	15	16	17	18	19	20	21	22	23
c'	d'	e'	f'	g'	a'	b'	c''	d''	e''	f''

A cross (sharp) above the figure denotes the neighbouring black key:

×	×	×	×	×	×	×	×	×	
2	3	4	6	7	9	10	11	13	
D	E	B♭	c♯	e♭	f♯	g♯	b♭	c♯	etc.

short octave

The parts for the right and left hand are separated by a long horizontal line. Above the part for the right hand, metrical signs are given according to a system derived from the Spanish and Italian lute tablatures. The principle of this method is, first, not to indicate different time-values of simultaneous tones, but only the shortest one and, second, to indicate these shortest values only for the first note of a series of equal values, with the understanding that the same metrical sign applies to the following notes until it is cancelled by a different one. This ingenious method, which actually satisfies the requirements of polyphonic music to a remarkable degree, may be illustrated by the following example showing the gradual reduction in the metrical signs:

A. Time value indicated in both voices with each tone:

B. Time values indicated in a single line with each tone:

C. Time values indicated in a single line with each first tone:

The metrical signs used by Valente are those known to us from the tablature of Schmid. The plain vertical stroke is explained, in the preface, as the *battuta over semibreve* (beat or *semibrevis*; see p. 33). In addition to these metrical signs there are, occasionally, special indications given with single notes the duration of which would not be clear without them. These are: ; = $1\frac{1}{2}$ M   : = 2 M   : = 3 M   ? = 4 M (placed behind the figure). The letter t, placed above a figure, indicates a trill or mordent. The first brace is transcribed in the appendix, No. 9.

There is a third species of Spanish keyboard tablature, which, because of a further reduction in the number of figures employed, meets the

needs of practical music still better, and merits attention for its simplicity and clarity.   In this notation, the white keys of one octave, i.e.,
from f to e', are designated by the figures 1 to 7, and the lower and
higher octaves are distinguished by small dashes or dots attached to the
same figures, as is shown in the following chart:

As in the first species of Spanish tablature described by Bermudo,
each voice is represented by a horizontal line on which the figures are
written.   The chromatic alterations are indicated by sharps and flats,
and rhythmical signs are added wherever deemed necessary.   There are
three Spanish publications extant which are notated in this manner,
namely:

> Venegas de Henestrosa, *Libro de cifra nueva para tecla harpa y vihuela* (*Alcalà*,
> 1557).
> (new book of ciphers for keyboard instruments, harp, and lute)
> Antonio de Cabezon, *Obras de musica para tecla harpa y vihuela . . . reco-
> piladas y puestas en cifra por Hernando de Cabezon su hijo* (Madrid, 1578)
> (musical works . . . compiled and notated in ciphers by Hernando
> de Cabezon, his son)
> Francisco Correa de Araujo, *Libro de tientos y discursos de musica pratica*
> (Alcalà, 1626)
> (book of tientos and explanations of practical music).

Of these books, only the second has been available for examination.[1]
From its subtitle *puestas in cifras* . . . one may conclude that the compositions of this book were written first in another notation, but transcribed
by Cabezon's son into 'cifras,' i.e., notation with figures.[2]
To supplement details already given on this notation we might mention that a ♮ (*b durum*, i.e., B-natural) or B (*b molle*, i.e., B-flat) printed
at the beginning of each composition indicates whether the scale to be
used is the Lydian or the F major scale, i.e., whether the tone represented by the figure 4 is a B-natural or a B-flat.   The accidentals ✗
(sharp) and ♭ (flat) are printed, not before the affected notes, but
either below or following them.   The metrical signs are added sparingly
according to the system employed in Valente's book.   There are two

[1] New edition of the works of Cabezon in: F. Pedrell, *Hispaniae schola musica sacra*, Barcelona,
1894-98, vols. III, IV, VII, VIII.
[2] The *Obras* are a posthumous edition; Antonio de Cabezon died in 1566.

FACSIMILE 16

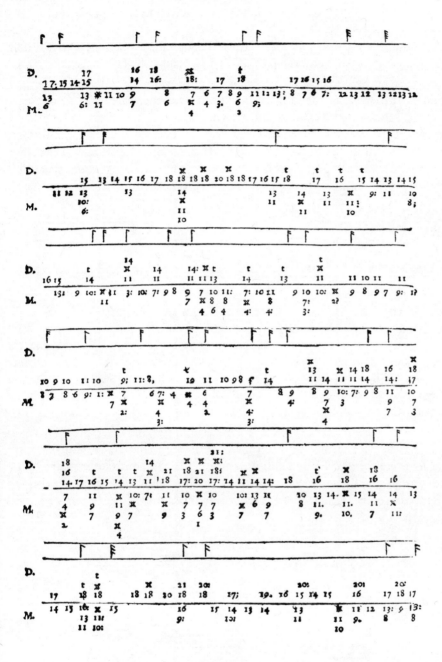

Antonio Valente, *Intavolatura de cimbalo*. Naples, 1576
Page 4

other signs which frequently occur in this tablature, a comma: , and a diagonal dash: /. The former indicates tying of the preceding note, the latter signifies a rest.

Facsimile 17 serves as an illustration. The page contains two short pieces, both in four parts and with a B-flat in the 'signature.' In measures 7 and 8 of the first piece, the figure 3 above the staff indicates triplets; apparently, the eleven notes of the measure fall into three groups of triplets and two plain eighth-notes. The second piece is in ternary rhythm, with three *semibreves* to the measure, as is indicated also by the time-signature ¢3 . In the second measure of the last staff, there is a change to even meter, as is indicated by the semicircle. Following is a transcription of the last five measures of the page:

Actually the sign ¢3 has a more definite meaning than merely to indicate triple meter. It is a proportional sign which signifies threefold diminution (see under Proportions, p. 157). In other words, in the section thus denoted, three notes (three *S*) consume the same amount of time as one note (one *S*) in the section without proportion, marked by the sign ₵ (*tempus imperfectum*, see p. 96). It appears that in the piece under consideration (as well as in many others presenting this problem) a measure of the section in triple meter has the same duration as one of the section in duple meter. In view of this fact a transcription such as given above is misleading, since here the $\frac{3}{1}$-measures seem to be three times as long as they actually are. Below are two renditions which correctly indicate the temporal relationship between the two meters (see also p. 194f).

Antonio de Cabezon, *Obras de musica*. Madrid, 1578
Page 37

IV. LUTE TABLATURES

LUTE TABLATURES play a unique rôle in the field of notation, because they are based on principles fundamentally different from those of all other varieties of notation. If we conceive notation as a link connecting the writer of a composition with its performer, i.e., as an expedient showing the player or singer the tones which the composer wants him to produce, then we must realize that, generally speaking, there is a direct and an indirect way to achieve this goal. In a notation representing the latter method, the player is referred to his instrument through the medium of numerous elements of a distinctly intellectual character, such as pitch, intervals, tonality, accidentals, scales and many other such points. In a notation representing the direct method, however, his fingers are referred immediately to the technical devices of his instrument, the keys, frets, strings, holes, etc. In German terminology, these two species are distinguished as 'Tonschrift' and 'Griffschrift,' terms which may be conveniently translated 'pitch notation' and 'finger notation.'[1]

Although the method of 'pitch notation' is much longer and more complicated, it proves in the end to be by far the more successful one; in fact, nearly all kinds of musical notation belong to this indirect type. There are, however, several notational systems of the opposite type, springing from the very natural desire to avoid burdening the player with intellectual technicalities and to cut short the road leading to practical performance. It is this desire which again and again leads to inventions in the field of piano-teaching, and to popular advertisements such as 'Piano playing learned in ten easy lessons.' Precautions about such short cuts, as far as the piano and other highly developed instruments are concerned, are, we hope, unnecessary. But in dealing with instruments of simpler type and of a more popular character the situation is different. Here, a pure finger notation is occasionally useful and desirable, as for instance with the zither and ukulele.

In the history of notation, the lute is probably the earliest instrument for which a finger notation was invented and developed. Because of

---

[1] In Grove's *Dictionary*, article 'Notation,' the above two types are characterized as 'symbolical' and 'practical,' and as being directed to the 'conceptive' and 'executive' faculty.

the tremendous vogue which lute playing enjoyed in the sixteenth and early seventeenth centuries and the vast literature of lute music created during the period, lute tablature is certainly the most important notation of this kind.[1] We may well assume that the striking popularity of the lute was greatly favoured by the invention of a notation which exempted the player from studying the theoretical foundations of music, and furnished him with the shortest guide to the music itself.

Without considering in detail the history of the instrument (for which the reader is referred to *HdN* II, 35 and various monographs[2]), suffice it to say that the lute was of oriental origin, and that in its earliest preserved description by Al Farabi, the great Arabian writer of the tenth century, it is said to have had four strings tuned in fourths. As early as the twelfth century, the lute had five strings or, more accurately, nine strings in five courses, the highest string being single, while the eight lower strings were arranged in four pairs of equal pitch.[3]

There is no document of music extant for the four or five-stringed lute. The earliest lute tablatures known are designed for a lute with six strings (the five lower ones doubled in unison or octave), an instrument typical of the sixteenth century. Certain features of the German lute tablature (cf. p. 74 ff), however, show clearly that this notation was originally invented for the five-stringed lute, and later on augmented to suit a lute with six strings.

During the sixteenth century, three types of lute tablature were in use, and, according to their native countries, these are called: Italian, French, and German lute tablatures. The Italian type was employed also by the Spanish lutenists. Of all the varieties, only the French survived in the seventeenth and eighteenth centuries.

The basic and common principle of all these tablatures is derived from the fact that there are six strings along the fingerboard of a lute, with a number of frets (nine or more) crossing it, each indicating a chromatic

---

[1] Similar notations were introduced, during the seventeenth century, for other lute-like instruments (guitarre, chitarrone, mandora, angelica, Hamburger Citrinchen, etc.). The notations for these instruments and others, such as viol, violine, flute, have been studied by J. Wolf in *HdN* II, 115-248. Since the literature contained in these tablatures is of a rather subordinate importance—both historically and artistically—it has not been deemed necessary to enter here into a study of this field. The interested reader is referred to the above publication, in which the subject has been treated exhaustively.

[2] O. Koerte, 'Laute und Lautenmusik bis zur Mitte des 16. Jahrhunderts' (Beihefte der *IMG* III, 1901); A. Koczirz, *Oesterreichische Lautenmusik im 16. Jahrhundert* (DTOe XVIII, ii, and XXV, ii); G. Morphy, *Les Luthistes espagnols du XVIe siècle*, Leipzig, 1902; L. de la Laurencie, *Les Luthistes*, Paris, 1928; J. Zuth, *Handbuch der Laute und Guitarre*, Leipzig, 1926-28; M. Brenet, 'Notes sur l'histoire du luth en France' (*Rivista Musicale Italiana*, V, VI).

[3] In the subsequent explanations, we shall not distinguish between string and course, using the former term for either a single string or for two strings tuned in unison or in octave.

step. For example, should an open string give the tone of C, the same
string, if pressed down on the first, second, and third fret, would produce a C-sharp, D, and D-sharp respectively, etc. Thus, there are 54
(or more) intersections available to the player who must know which
ones to touch in a given moment. This information is exactly what he
finds in his tablature. It is only with respect to the manner of signifying these intersections that the tablatures of the various countries differ.

A. Italian and Spanish Lute Tablatures

The earliest extant document of this notation are the lute books
published by Petrucci in the early sixteenth century, namely: *Intabulatura de lauto, libro primo-quarto* (Venice, 1507, 1508). The earliest
preserved book of Spanish lute[1] music is: Luis de Milan, *El Maestro*
(Valencia, 1535). For a special reason it seems advisable to begin our
explanations with an example from the Spanish book and to consider
the notation of the Italian sources later.

In Facsimile 18 six horizontal lines represent the six strings of the
lute. These strings are tuned in fourths and thirds, according to the
scheme: 4, 4, 3, 4, 4. As to the actual pitch of the tuning, there is
some difference of opinion, not only among modern writers, but among
lutenists of the sixteenth century as well, some of them giving the pitch
of the lowest string as A, others as G. In still other sources, the pitch
is left to the will of the player. Hans Neusiedler, for instance, says
(*Ein newgeordnet kuenstlich Lautenbuch*, Nürnberg, 1536): 'zeuch die
oberste Sait so hoch als du magst' i.e., tune the upper string as high as
you like. From a study of those examples in which a voice-part in
staff-notation is added to an accompaniment of the lute in tablature, it
appears that the customary tuning was in G.[2] This statement does not
touch, of course, upon the question of whether the G of the sixteenth
century was the same as the G of the modern concert pitch. Probably
it was considerably lower. But, to take into consideration this circumstance would lead to a transposition not only of the lute music but of
all the music of the sixteenth century—a problem which can not concern

---

[1] The Spanish lute, vihuela, actually is a guitar. However, the tuning as well as the musical
repertory of this instrument connect it much more closely with the sixteenth century lute than with
the seventeenth or eighteenth century guitar. See the article 'vihuela' in Grove's *Dictionary*.

[2] Attaingnant, *Très brève et familière introduction*, 1529 (see p. 66); Diego Pisador, *Libro de musica
de vihuela*, 1552 (cf. *HdN* II, 77 and 108; also *SchT*, 61). In the compositions for voice and lute in
Schlick's *Tabulaturen* (cf. p. 26) the tuning is in A (see the facsimiles in *HdN* II, 42 and in G. Harm's
new edition, p. 14).

FACSIMILE 18

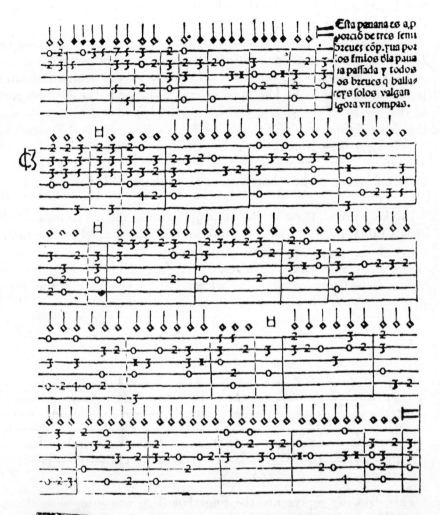

Luys de Milan,
Libro de musica de vihuela de mano, intitulado El Maestro. Valencia, 1535
Folio G VI^v

us here. In the subsequent transcriptions of lute music the G-tuning will be consistently used. In other words, the open strings of the lute give the tones G, c, f, a, d′, and g′.[1]

As mentioned above, each of these strings is represented in our tablature by a horizontal line, with the lowest line standing for the lowest string.[2] On each line, figures from 0 to 9 appear which indicate the frets, with 0 signifying the open string, 1 the first fret etc. According to the tuning of the string, the figure 0 on the lowest line reads G, and the same figure on the fourth line means a. Each subsequent figure stands for a tone which is as many chromatic steps higher as the figure indicates. Thus, figure 3 on the second line means a note which is three half-tones higher than C, that is, D-sharp or E-flat.

In the light of these explanations, to transcribe a composition from such a tablature into modern notation will offer scarcely any problems, although the perpetual counting may prove rather fatiguing. The task of the transcriber may, however, be facilitated by the employment of certain expedients or schemes which show immediately the tone in question. Two schemes of this kind are given here:

A.

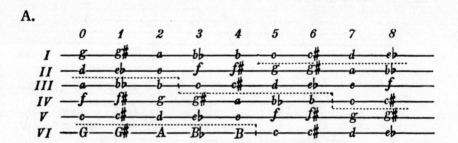

This drawing represents the fingerboard of the lute, with the neck turned to the left side. At each intersection, the corresponding tone is indicated in letters. For greater simplicity, the various octaves have not been identified in the case of each letter, but are merely indicated by three dotted lines marking off the regions of the two- and one-line octaves, the middle octave, and the great octave. The Roman numerals indicate the strings and the Arabic figures signify the frets.

[1] Occasionally, the A-tuning deserves preference, in order to avoid unusual keys; see p. 77.
[2] It is this arrangement of the lines, as will be seen later, which distinguishes Milan's notation from that of other Spanish and Italian lute books (cf. p. 61).

B.

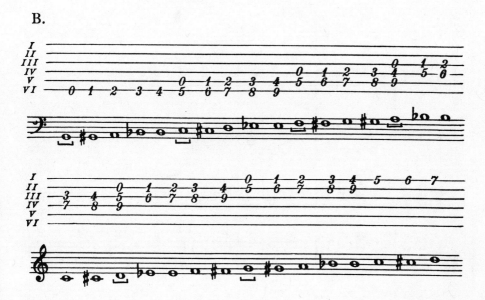

This scheme proves especially convenient, since it refers the transcriber immediately from the signs of the tablature to the notes of modern staff notation.

Diligent practice in transcribing will develop in the student numerous time-saving devices. As a rule it is advisable not to proceed by transcribing complete measures, but to follow each single line of the tablature for the whole piece or a section of it, i.e., transcribing first all the figures on one line, and then proceeding to those of another line. By this method one avoids the confusion caused by continually darting from one line to another. The chart on page 60 illustrates the gradual completion in the transcription of the first staff of Facsimile 18, according to the method outlined.

As with all the lute tablatures, the notation here provides no possibility of indicating different time-values or different rhythms occurring simultaneously in various parts. Only the smallest of simultaneous values is indicated, as in the Spanish keyboard tablatures (Valente, Cabezon; see pp. 49, 50). However, although in these systems the duration of each individual note in the various parts becomes perfectly clear from the polyphonic context, the situation is different in the lute tablatures. Here, the notation as such contains no reference to polyphonic texture, since the lines of the staff do not represent voices—as they do in the Spanish keyboard tablatures—but strings. Moreover, the true lute style is not strictly polyphonic, because of the limitations of lute tech-

nique; rather is it a style which, although frequently including polyphonic elements, treats them freely, and combines them with other manners of writing, such as the homophonic, the figured, and the 'freistimmig.' Therefore, the question arises as to whether a transcription should faithfully retain the time-values of the tablature, or whether it should embody an interpretation of the original as a free polyphonic fabric. Both possible methods may be illustrated by the following example:

Facsimile 18, second staff, measures 5–6.
Strict transcription: Polyphonic interpretation:

J. W. Wasielewski, one of the first to investigate the lute music of the Renaissance, has followed the strict method, in his *Geschichte der Instrumentalmusik im 16. Jahrhundert*, (Bonn, 1878), whereas O. Körte, in his *Laute und Lautenmusik bis zur Mitte des 16. Jahrhunderts* (*Beiheft 3 der Internationalen Musikgesellschaft*, Leipzig, 1901), has strongly advocated the polyphonic interpretation. His method was adopted by practically all the editors of lute music,[1] until L. Schrade, in his reprint of Milan's *El Maestro* (*Publikationen Aelterer Musik* ii, Leipzig, 1927) once more urged strict adherence to the original signs, by declaring the polyphonic interpretation to be tantamount to a falsification of the original.[2]

An objective weighing of the arguments for and against both methods leads to the conclusion that neither can be exclusively preferred. Each has its advantages and its disadvantages. The literal transcription may be recommended especially for the early pieces in free style, such as the preludes (called 'ricercare') of Dalza, Spinaccino, and some of the fantasias by Milan. However, in the case of compositions which are obviously under contrapuntal influence (such as the numerous intabulations of vocal pieces) one could hardly go wrong in allowing such influence to find expression in the transcription. A transcription in a style reminiscent of the free keyboard polyphony of Froberger, Frescobaldi or Bach (in his toccatas, preludes etc.) would seem to be preferable in these cases.

We now turn to a Facsimile (no. 19) from the Italian lute books mentioned above. The principal difference between this tablature and the notation of Milan's book lies in the reversed order of the lines representing the lute strings. The lowest line here stands for the highest string, and the highest line for the lowest string. At first sight, this arrangement appears to be alien and unnatural. As a matter of fact, however, it is more in accord with the practical needs of the player than is the other. The lutenist holds the fingerboard of his instrument in his left hand, and plucks the strings with his right. In doing so, the back of the lute is pressed against the player's body, so that the front, as well as the plane of the fingerboard and the strings, comes to an almost vertical position. This causes the lowest string to lie on top, i.e., in the same position in which it appears in the tablature. The lutenist playing from such a book consequently connects the signs written on the top line directly with the highest string of his instrument which, in sound, is the lowest. Thus, still another intellectual detour is eliminated, and technique and writing are that much more in agree-

[1] E.g., J. Wolf in *Isaac's Weltliche Werke* (*DTOe* xiv, 1); A. Koczirz in *DTOe* xviii, 2.
[2] In a reply to arguments brought forward by O. Gombosi, Schrade has taken a considerably less definite stand. Both articles appeared in *ZfMW*, xiv, p. 185 and p. 357.

ment.   This order is used in all the Italian and Spanish lute tablatures with the single exception of Milan's.

Barring this reversed order of the strings, the explanations previously given hold good.   A deviation of minor importance is that of the metrical signs.   Instead of the complete notes used in Milan's book, we find the same flagged stems as in the new German keyboard tablatures (see p. 33).   In the preface to Petrucci's *Intabulatura de lauto, libro secondo,* they are explained as follows:[1]

Questo sonno li segni: | ⌐ ⌐⌐ ⌐⌐⌐ .   El primo significa la mesura a che devi tegnir: la qual bisogna pigliarla si larga che in qual tempo tu possi dare le botte del numero diminuto: per che lo secondo segno vale per la mita del primo, el terzo per la mita del secondo, . . .

These are the (metrical) signs: | ⌐ ⌐⌐ ⌐⌐⌐ .   The first signifies the measure (beat) to be observed, which has to be taken slowly enough so as to allow for the beats of the smaller values; because the second sign is the half of the first, the third the half of the second, . . .

Additional signs are the 'signs of proportion' (i.e., *proportio tripla,* see p. 148): ⌐⌐ .   The first of these equals one third of an *S,* the second is the half of the first.   Furthermore the signs: ⌐⌐ occur.   The second equals $\frac{1}{3}$ of an *S,* the first $\frac{2}{3}$:[2] | ⌐⌐⌐⌐ ‑| ♩ ♫♫♩ |; ⌐⌐⌐⌐⌐ ‑| ♫ ♫♫♩ |

The figures 10, 11, 12 for the higher frets are replaced by the Roman
 * numerals x, ẋ, ẍ.

It goes without saying that, for transcriptions from this type of lute tablature, the translation scheme (B) of p. 59 must be altered, so that the figures shown there on the lines VI, V, IV, etc. will appear on the lines I, II, III and so forth.

Extensive lists of Italian and Spanish lute tablatures are given in *HdN* II, 66 and 112.   Additional examples for study are available in *SchT,* 18, 70, and 62.[3]

---

[1] Cf. *HdN* II, 53.

[2] See Körte, *Laute und Lautenmusik,* p. 101.

[3] In the lute-books of Fuenllana, Pisador, and others, red figures are used to indicate a vocal part, as against black figures for the lute accompaniment.   See the illustrations in *HdN* II, pp. 109/110 and 113.   Regarding the question whether the red figures were also included in the lute accompaniment, see J. Bal, 'Fuenllana and the Transcription of Spanish Lute Music' (*AM* XI).

FACSIMILE 19

Petrucci, *Intabolatura de lauto. Libro primo.* Venice, 1507
Page 39

B. FRENCH LUTE TABLATURES

The earliest known documents of French lute tablature are two books published by Attaingnant in 1529: *Dixhuit basse dances garnies de Recoupes ei Tordions . . . , le tout reduyt en la tabulature du Lutz* (Paris, 1529), and *Tres breue et familiere introduction pour entendre et apprendre par soy mesme a iouer toutes chansons reduictes en la tabulature du Lutz avec la maniere daccorder le dict Lutz . . .* (Paris, 1529).

From its title and contents, the second book appears to be designed for the self-instruction of the lute student. It is, indeed, of particular interest for us, since it begins with a very detailed explanation of all features of French lute notation. The 'Troys breues rigles pour estre tost et facilement introduict en la tabulature du lutz' which open the book have been reprinted in full by Wolf, *HdN* II, 72. A short abstract will suffice for the present purpose.

1. The fingerboard has eight frets (touches) which are marked by the letters: b, c, d, e, f, g, h, i. Occasionally, a ninth fret is marked k. The letter a is used for the open string.

2. The lute has eleven strings arranged in six courses (ordres), the lowest three of which are doubled in octaves, the fourth and fifth in unison. The highest string, the so-called 'chanterelle,' is a single one.

3. The strings are tuned as usual. As regards pitch, the indications of the book are not definite. We learn that the lowest string may be tuned 'en si bas ton que vouldres.' From the pieces for lute and voice it appears that the lowest string was a G, whatever its actual pitch may have been.

4. The metrical signs are the usual ones, the plain vertical stroke for the 'semibrève,' and those with one to four flags for 'minime, semiminime, crochue, and fredon.' The author says that breves, longae and maximae never occur in lute tablature, since the resonance of a string does not endure beyond a semibreve. Metrical signs, when written on the staff, indicate a rest.

5. The staff (espasse) consists of five lines (rigles). The tones to be produced on the sixth (lowest) string are written underneath the staff.

From the last statement it is obvious that in French tablatures the lines representing the strings are arranged in the same order as in Milan's book, i.e., with the highest string on top. The main difference is the use of letters (the *Introduction* uses capital letters, the later sources use small letters) instead of figures, and of a staff with five instead of six lines.

The reproduction on page 65 shows a *Fortune a bien couru sur moi* from

the *Introduction*. The small dashes which sometimes occur between two letters merely facilitate orientation. The dots appearing under certain notes are fingerings for the right hand, i.e., for the plucking of the strings. The dot refers to the index finger, whereas the neighbouring letters without a dot are to be played with the thumb. If the third or fourth finger is desired, two or three dots are used.

The chief difficulty presented by this piece and, in fact, by a great number of those contained in Attaingnant's two books, is that of meter, or correct barring. As a rule, no bar-lines are given in the original source. Our piece shows grouping in blocks which, however, have no significance since they merely comprise notes of equal metrical value. J. Wolf, in *HdN* II, 76, transcribes the composition in triple meter ($\frac{3}{2}$, reduced, in the following example, to $\frac{3}{4}$):

It cannot be said that this result is altogether satisfactory. Another rhythmic interpretation is suggested by a version of the same piece for lute and voice, which exists in the same book and in which the voice-part is written in alla breve with bar-lines separating measures of four *M* (see the following reproduction; the complete piece in *SchT*, 61):

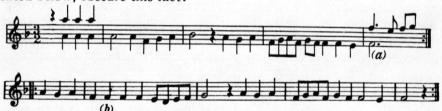

However, the even meter thus suggested proves even less acceptable than Wolf's interpretation, from the point of view of harmony as well as of phrasing. Particularly in the second section, the barring is musically wrong.[1]

An examination of the whole piece from a musical standpoint reveals that the real meter is neither $\frac{3}{4}$ with two up-beats, nor $\frac{4}{4}$ with three upbeats, but $\frac{3}{2}$ with three upbeats. Certain typographical errors, indicated below, obscure this fact:

The notes above the staff indicate certain variants of the lute version. Errors: (a) dot is missing; (b) *S* instead of *M*.

It appears that our piece belongs to the class of 'pavanes' in slow triple meter, of which the piece by Milan (Facsimile 18) is another example. A reduction 1:2 of the above transcription would make the similarity of rhythm still more striking:

Pieces of this type are very frequent in the dance literature of the sixteenth century, but their true rhythm is usually obscured in the original notation. For instance, in the books of the Spanish lute composers Narvaez (1538), Mudarra (1546), and Pisador (1552), all the

---

[1] See also A. de la Laurencie, *Chansons au luth*, Paris, 1934, p. 39.

pieces are barred, but in measures equalling only one *S* each. In modern terms, this means that the bar-lines mark off single beats, not measures. The modern reader, desirous of decreasing the abundance of bar-lines, is naturally inclined to combine two such beats into a measure. It is only after some puzzling over the queer result of his procedure that he discovers that the measure actually includes three beats. The following example, showing (a) the original and (b) the correct modern barring of Luys de Narvaez' *Guardame las vacas* (from the *Libro del Delphin de musica*, Valladolid, 1538) serves as an illustration:[1]

The practice of using even meter (or, at least, bar-lines suggestive thereof) for pieces which, from the musical point of view are indubitably in ternary rhythm, persisted long into the seventeenth century. Numerous examples have been given by Riemann, in his *Handbuch der Musikgeschichte* (cf. II, ii, 195, 196, 296). A particularly striking example is Frescobaldi's *Partite sopra l'aria la Romanesca*, the original barring of which is as follows (see G. Tagliapietra, *Anthologie alter und neuer Musik*, [Milano, 1934], IV, 20):

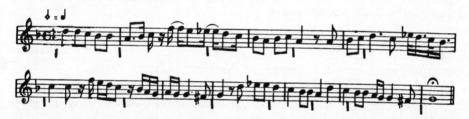

The small strokes underneath the staff indicate the true rhythm, in $\frac{3}{4}$-time without upbeat.

Returning to the lute books of Attaingnant we refer the reader to p. 68 of the *Schrifttafeln*, where he will find a *Basse danse beure frais*, the rhythm of which has been the object of considerable speculation and controversy.[2] We trust that the interpretation in $\frac{3}{4}$-meter, given below,

---

[1] Complete transcription in W. Apel, *Musik aus früher Zeit* II, 14.

[2] In his *Studien zur Vorgeschichte der Orchestersuite im 15. und 16. Jahrhundert* (Berlin, 1925) F. Blume has maintained that there were two types of the *basse danse*, one in duple and one in triple meter. This statement has been strongly criticized by C. Sachs in an article 'Der Rhythmus der Basse Danse' (*AM* III, 107), in which he sums up his opinion as follows: 'Die Basse danse ist zu allen Zeiten und in allen Ländern geradtaktig' (p. 110). In order to support his view, Sachs reproduces

will speak for itself. It should, however, be borne in mind that in dances of this type it is not possible to draw a clear distinction between $\frac{3}{4}$- and $\frac{6}{8}$-meter. The triple rhythm may take the form of three quarter-notes or of three eighth-notes. The rhythm of the last measures of the basse dance is obscured by typographical errors. The last

♪ as well as the following ♪ are printed too far to the right side. The former belongs over the letter c, the latter over $^{a}_{c}$. The next two signs appear a bit too far to the left side; moreover, the second of these, with two flags, must be changed into one with one flag. A correct transcription was given by O. Gombosi in *AM* VII (1934), p. 25.

The notation just explained is maintained in the later French lutebooks of the sixteenth century, for instance:

Adrian Le Roy, *Premier livre de tabulature de luth* (Paris, 1551)
Guillaume Morleye, *Premier, second et troisième livres de tabulature de leut* (Paris, 1552-1558)

the *Basse danse Beure frais* in two rhythmic versions, one by Blume in $\frac{6}{4}$-meter, and one by himself in $\frac{4}{4}$-meter. Unfortunately, the latter is almost as unsatisfactory as the former. The reader is advised to compare these two versions with the transcription given above. It would appear, therefore, that Sachs's categorical statement cannot be accepted.

In this connection, attention may be called to the transcriptions of lute dances contained in H. Bruger's publication, *Pierre Attaingnant* (Wolfenbüttel, 1927). The rhythmic interpretations given here are frequently suspect and some of them indubitably wrong. For instance, the two *tourdion* which, in p. 7 and 14, are rendered in $\frac{4}{4}$-meter with upbeat, actually are in $\frac{3}{4}$-meter (without upbeat), as a dance bearing the name *tourdion* (see the article in Grove's *Dictionary*) may well be expected to be. Both dances show, towards the end of the first section, that change from $\frac{3}{4}$ ($\frac{6}{4}$) to $\frac{3}{2}$ which is a typical feature of the seventeenth century *courante* and which in mensural notation was expressed by coloration (see p. 130 f). On the other hand, the *branle gay* which Bruger (p. 9) transcribes in $\frac{3}{4}$-meter with upbeat, evidently is in $\frac{4}{4}$-meter with upbeat, as appears clearly from the fact that an initial phrase of nine (one plus eight) quarter-notes is repeated. Only in the second section of this dance would Bruger's rendition seem to be correct.

Albert de Rippe de Mantoue, *Premier . . . (sixiesme) livre de tabulature de leut* (Paris, 1554-1558)
Valentin Bacfarc, *Premier livre de tabelature de luth* (Paris, 1564).

A new feature appears in the *Pratum Musicum* of Emanuel Hadrianus (Antwerp, 1584) in which the Italian staff of six lines is used, an innovation which asserted itself throughout the ensuing periods of French tablature. During the seventeenth century, further development of the notational system was necessitated by the increase of the number of strings. In addition to the six strings running over the fingerboard, so-called bass-courses (Bordun-Saiten) were introduced, which ran alongside the others without crossing the fingerboard and the frets. These were, of course, unchangeable in pitch, so that a single sign was sufficient to signify them. The signs for the bass-courses were written underneath the staff representing the six fingerboard-strings. The most common designation was the letter 'a' with an increasing number of dashes: a, ā, á, ȧ. In the following scheme, the tuning of the main strings is indicated as a chord, that of the four bass-courses, as successive notes:

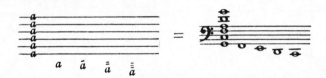

$$a \quad \bar{a} \quad \bar{\bar{a}} \quad \bar{\bar{\bar{a}}}$$

The earliest tablatures utilizing this system of tuning and notation are: Leopold Fuhrmann, *Testudo Gallo-Germanica* (Nürnberg, 1615); Elias Mertel, *Hortus musicalis novus* (Strassburg, 1615); and Jean-Baptiste Besardus, *Novus partus* (Augsburg, 1617).

Numerous lute tablatures of the seventeenth century show long diagonal lines drawn underneath or above a group of letters. The meaning of these signs is explained in *A Briefe and easye instruction to learn the tablature . . . englished by J. Alfred Londenor* (1568);

It is also necessarie to give thee to understande, to what purpose the barres that be drawen bias, under the letters or passages doe serve for, and for thy better understandyng, I have here drawen thee an example at large, and very familier, in the whiche thou shalt not finde one example, trimmed or measured, that thou shalte neede to remove any of thy fingers, from the said measure: the knowledge of the said barre is so necessarie, that hauying founde out, and exercised the same, thou shalte not neede to remove, but those fingers whiche thou shalt be forced, whiche we call close or couert plaie.

Evidently, these bars indicate sustaining of tones or chords, a technique which was called: close or covered play. Approximate transcription:

(Note that in the above example, as in many tablatures, the letters are printed above the line, instead of on the line).

For an explanation of the signs of ornamentation used in seventeenth century lute tablatures, the reader is referred to the detailed studies in *HdN* II, 147-157, in the preface to A. Koczirz, *Österreichische Lautenmusik zwischen 1650 und 1720* (*DTOe* xxv, ii) and, particularly, to Janet Dodge's article: 'Ornamentation as Indicated by Signs in Lute Tablatures' (*SIMG* ix).

In the period between 1620 and 1650, the extraordinarily rapid advance in lute technique made in France led to much experimentation regarding the tuning as well as the indication of the bass-courses. Instead of the signs: a, ā, a̿, a̿ we find the figures 7, 8, 9, 10 (tablature of Friderici, formerly library of Dr. W. Wolffheim), or the signs: a, 8, 9, x (Michelangelo Galilei, *Primo libro d'intavolatura di liuto*, Munich, 1620), which are augmented to: a, 8, 9, x, XI, XII, XIII (7 bass-courses) in the tablature of Dusiacki (Padua, 1620), while still another designation: a, ā, a̿, a̿, 11, 12 is used in the lute book of Virginia Renata von Gehema (Berlin, Staatsbibliothek, *Mus. Ms. 40264*).

Around 1640, a new system, called *nouveau ton* was introduced by the famous lute composer Denis Gaultier (*ca.* 1600–1672). It quickly superseded all the others. Here the main strings are tuned A-d-f-a-d'-f:

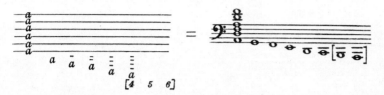

(The symbols in brackets indicate later additions and modifications.)

Facsimile 20 is taken from the famous Hamilton Codex of the Berlin Staatsbibliothek in which the compositions of Gaultier are collected under the title: *La Rhétorique des dieux*.[1] The graphological details of this manuscript are explained below:

Letters	Rhythmic signs
a b c d e f g	♩ ♪ ♪ ♪

The first measures are transcribed in the appendix, No. 10.   *

Gaultier's system remained in use without essential alterations throughout the last period of lute music, that is, till the end of the eighteenth century. More detailed examination of this field is beyond the scope of the present book. Suffice it to say that later lutenists, such as Esaias Reusner (1636-1679), Silvius Leopold Weiss (1686-1750) and others, made frequent use of the *scordatura*, i.e., of alterations of the normal tuning of·the strings for certain pieces or series of pieces (suites). These alterations are indicated at the beginning of the piece in the so-

called *accord*. For instance, the following *accord*:[2]   indicates

that the second bass-course (ā) is the lower octave of the tone indicated by the letter b on the third line, that is, of F♯; and that the fifth bass-course (4) is the lower octave of the tone indicated by e on the first line, that is, of C♯. Hence, the tuning of the bass-courses is: G, F♯, E, D, C♯. Similarly, the *accord*:   leads to the tuning G, F, E♭,

[1] O. Fleischer, 'Denis Gaultier' (*Vierteljahrsschrift für Musikwissenschaft* II, 1886); A. Tessier, *La Rhétorique des dieux*, Paris, 1932.

[2] Cf. H. Neemann, *Lautenmusik des 17./18. Jahrhunderts*, Berlin, 1939, pp. 10, 12, 88.

D, C. The reader is advised to study the *accords* reproduced on the table opposite p. 128 in *HdN* II, in which the complete tunings of various plucked instruments is given. For instance, the following scheme:

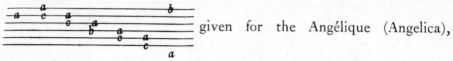 given for the Angélique (Angelica),

an instrument with 16 strings tuned diatonically, shows that, starting with d' as the pitch of the fifth string from below, the pitch of the sixth string (represented by the letter a) is the same as that of the third fret (letter c) of the fifth string, hence, e'. Similarly, the open fourth string is c', because its third fret (letter c) gives the same pitch as the open fifth string (letter a), etc.

Material for further studies in the field of the late French lute tablature[1] is contained in the above-mentioned edition of Neemann, which includes a reproduction of the original together with the transcription into notes. Following are a few brief remarks regarding the examples contained in J. Wolf's *Schrifttafeln*, which may also serve as additional exercise:

Nos. 24, 35, and 73 use the 'old tuning' (*vieil ton*) G-c-f-a-d'-g'. In no. 73, the bass-courses a, ā, ā̄ are tuned F, E, D.

Nos. 27, 36, 51, and 76 are in the 'new tuning' (*nouveau ton*) A-d-f-a-d'-f'. In no. 27, seven bass-courses, tuned diatonically from G to *A*, are indicated by the signs: a, ā, ā̄, ā̄̄, 4, 5, 6. In no. 51, five bass-courses are denoted as follows: a, ā, ā̄, ā̄̄, 11 (11). The strongly curved symbol of this manuscript (and of no. 36) is the letter d, whereas the angular sign is the letter c. The letter c frequently adopts a shape reminiscent of the letter r (cf. no. 76).

The notational system of the French lute tablature was also applied to numerous other stringed instruments, such as the mandora (cf. *SchT*, no. 98), the 'Hamburger Cithrinchen,' a small cittern (cf. *SchT*, no. 26), the viols (cf. *HdN* II, 225 ff.), etc. Whereas Wolf's example for the mandora is in the old tuning (for five strings only: A-d-g-b-e'), the tuning of the Cithrinchen is: c-e-g-b-e'.

C. German Lute Tablatures

During the sixteenth century the German lutenists utilized a notation which, according to Agricola (*Musica instrumentalis deudsch*, Wittenberg, 1529) was invented by Conrad Paumann (1410-1473). Although this

---

[1] See the extensive list of French lute tablatures, printed and manuscript, in *HdN* II, 95 ff.

FACSIMILE 20

LA DEDICASSE.

Denis Gaultier, *La Rhétorique des dieux*
Berlin, Kupferstichkabinett *Ms. 142 (ca.* 1650)
From pages 25′, 26

statement is probably incorrect—an obvious objection being that a blind man is not very likely to have invented a notational system—it illustrates the ancient and somewhat legendary origin of the German lute notation, the principles of which revert to a period antedating considerably the first preserved documents (1512).   Indeed, the relatively ancient origin of this system is revealed by its many primitive and awkward features which form a strong contrast to the rationalized methods of the French and Italian tablatures.   Most striking among these is the fact that the German notation was obviously designed for a lute with only five strings (such as was used in the fourteenth and fifteenth centuries), and was augmented later to suit an instrument with six strings.

In contrast to the French, Italian, and Spanish tablatures, in which the fingers of the player are easily directed by a clear representation of the fingerboard with its strings and frets, the Germans used a notation in which each one of the fifty four or more places on the fingerboard was marked by a special sign—a method reminiscent of Bermudo's forty two figures for the keys of the organ.   Unfortunately, the scheme of the German symbols for the lute is much more confused than Bermudo's plain series of figures.   In order to explain the German tablature we must begin by considering the lute as lacking the sixth (lowest) string (*Grossbrummer*).   The remaining five strings, called *Mittelbrummer*, *Kleinbrummer*, *Mittelsaite*, *Sangsaite*, *Quintsaite* (or *Kleinsaite*) are numbered 1, 2, 3, 4, 5, and are indicated by these figures if used as open strings.   The places on the first fret are marked by the first five letters of the alphabet, a, b, c, d, e, running across the fingerboard.   The second fret bears the five letters f, g, h, i, k, and the same procedure is continued with the following frets.   Since the letters of the German alphabet were then only twenty-three in number, two new signs had to be added for the fifth fret, namely, $\gtrsim$ and 9, called 'et' and 'con.'[1]   For the sixth, seventh, and other frets the alphabet was repeated, either in doubled letters: aa, bb, etc., or in letters with a horizontal dash: ā, ƀ, etc.

Obviously, this method of placing the letters across the fingerboard, following the frets, is less satisfactory than the French method of placing them length-wise, following the single strings.   In the French system, successive letters of the alphabet indicate neighbouring tones of the chromatic scale.   In the German system, they indicate tones which are a fourth or a third apart, while, on the other hand, successive tones of the chromatic scale are denoted by every sixth letter of the alphabet, for

[1] These characters are abbreviations of the Latin syllables *et* and *con*; see A. Cappelli, *Lexicon Abbreviaturarum*, Leipzig, 1928, pp. 78, 408.

instance: a, f, l, etc. The C-major scale c, d, e, f . . . therefore is indicated as follows: 1, f, q, 2(or x) . . .

Although the above scheme of signs for the five upper strings is common to all the German lute tablatures, there is considerable variance regarding the signs used for the sixth string, the *Grossbrummer*, which was added after the notation for the upper strings had already been established. The various notational methods used for this string appear in a picture of the 'Lautenkragen' (fingerboard) contained in Hans Newsidler's *Ein Newgeordnet künstlich Lautenbuch* (Nürnberg, 1536), a reproduction of which is given here:

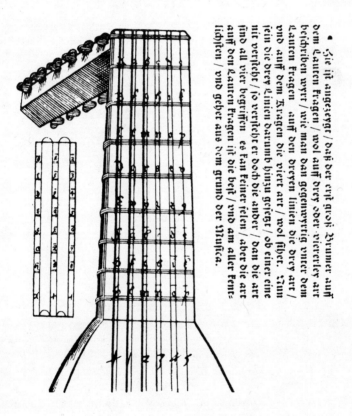

The larger drawing shows the signs for the five upper strings as well as Newsidler's own preference for designating the *Grossbrummer*, namely, the letters A, B, C, D, E, F, G, H for the frets, and the sign ⨎ (at the bottom) for the open string. Other systems are indicated on a small drawing to which the text on the right side pertains. Following is a translation of this text:

Here is shown that the first *Grossbrummer* is designated in three of four different methods. Three of these are shown underneath the *Lautenkragen* on three lines, and the fourth manner is shown on the *Kragen*. The three lines have been added for the benefit of those who may understand one method but not the others. But the method on the *Lautenkragen* is the best and clearest one, and is based on the foundation of music.

The following drawing is a copy of Newsidler's Lautenkragen in modern characters and in horizontal position. To the four methods explained by Newsidler yet another method (III) has been added; this one is used in Arnold Schlick's *Tabulaturen* (Mainz, 1512), the earliest source of German lute music.

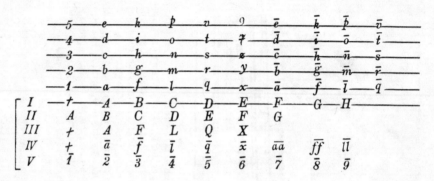

The Roman numerals added at the left side of this chart refer to the following lute books which utilize one or another of the five systems for the *Grossbrummer:*

I. Hans Newsidler, *Ein Newgeordnet künstlich Lautenbuch* (Nürnberg, 1536)
   Sixt Kargel, *Lautenbuch* . . . (Strassburg, 1586)
   Melchior Newsidler, *Teutsch Lautenbuch* (Strassburg, 1574)
II. Hans Judenkunig, *Ain schone kunstliche underweisung* (Vienna, 1523)
   Hans Jacob Wecker, *Lautenbuch* . . . (Basel, 1552)
III. Arnolt Schlick, *Tabulaturen etlicher lobgesang und lidlein* (Mayence, 1512)
IV. Wolff Heckel, *Discant Lauttenbuch*, Strassburg, 1552; *Tenor Lauttenbuch* (Strassburg, 1556)
   Bernhard Jobin, *Das Erste (Das Ander) Buch Newerlessner . . . Lautenstück* (Strassburg, 1572, 1573)
V. Hans Gerle, *Ein Newes sehr Künstlichs Lautenbuch* (Nürnberg, 1552)
   Sebastian Ochsenkuhn, *Tabulaturbuch auff die Lautten* (Heidelberg, 1558)

The transcription of pieces written in the German lute tablature is, of

course, very fatiguing and slow work. The following scheme will facilitate the task:

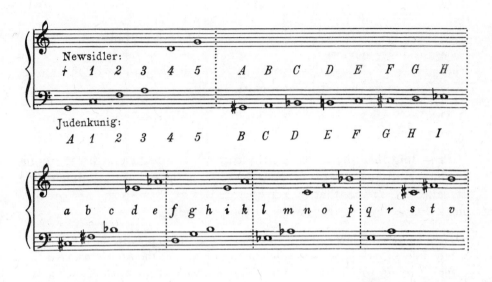

Facsimile 21 from Judenkunig's book of 1523 serves as a first illustration. The transcription presents no difficulties except, possibly, that of
identifying the Gothic letters of the German alphabet, some of which *
are written in a rather quaint fashion. The following transliteration of
the second brace will prove helpful to the reader:

$$
\begin{array}{cccccc}
 & & & & p & o\ 7 \\
s\ s & & s\ \bar{e}\ 9\ p & 7 & z\ \bar{c} & o\ \bar{c} & 7 \\
D\ y\ n\ r & y\ o\ \bar{c}\ s & n\ k\ l & D\ \iota\ l & D\ z\ \iota\ z\bar{c}o & \iota\ \bar{c}\ o\ 7
\end{array}
$$

$$(7 = et;\ 9 = con)$$

The beginning is transcribed in the appendix, No. 11. If instead of the G-tuning the
tuning in A is used, the tonality of the preamble changes from B-flat to C. It goes
without saying that the latter key is intended.

Facsimile 22 shows a piece by Newsidler which is remarkable for various reasons. It is called *Der Judentantz* (The Dance of the Jews) and represents one of the earliest examples, if not the earliest, of satire in music. As in almost all pieces of this genre, the satirical character is expressed by cacophonous dissonances. In fact, our dance is written in a strikingly modern idiom of bitonality such as rarely occurs before the advent of the twentieth century. At the beginning of the music, Newsidler gives the pertinent remark:

The Jew's dance. It must be played very quickly, otherwise it will not sound well.

Preceding this, there is a lengthy explanation dealing with the tuning of the lute. As a matter of fact, our piece is the earliest example of the so-called *scordatura*, that is, a deliberate deviation from the normal tuning. Following is a translation of the passage:

Here follows the Jew's dance, and whoever wants to play it, must tune the lute differently. Now follows the tuning: First, tune the *Mittelbrummer* and the *Kleinsaite* which is next to the *Mittelbrummer*, at the pitch of the figure four (4), and also the *Kleinbrummer*. . . . And the *Obere (Ebrer) Quintsaite* must be tuned equal to the t, then the tuning will be right. Many other dances may also be played with this tuning.[1]

Since the symbols 4 and t denote the tones d and f'♯, the tuning is as follows: G d d a d' f'♯.
Below is a transcription of the first measure of the dance, and of its last measure, immediately before 'Der Hupfauf' (jumping dance, after dance in triple meter):

A complete transcription is contained in W. Apel, *Musik aus früher Zeit*, i, 10. The transcription given by A. Koczirz in *DTOe* xviii is based on a different interpretation of Newsidler's remarks, leading to the following *scordatura*: G d d' d' d' f'♯. However, Koczirz's interpretation is erroneous. The third string (*Kleinbrummer*), which is normally f, cannot be raised to the pitch of d', but can only be lowered to d. His error regarding the fourth string is obviously caused by the words: 'die klein saitten die newen dem mitl Brumer stet' which, indeed, give rise to doubt as to which string is meant by

[1] The sentence: 'Muss gleich lautten. . . . als da 4 gleich lautten' has been omitted in the translation since it merely duplicates the preceding sentence.

FACSIMILE 21

Hans Judenkunig, *Ain schone kunstliche Underweisung.* Vienna, 1523

the term *klein saitte*. Koczirz interprets it as denoting the fourth string (*Mittelsaite*), whereas it actually refers to the fifth string (*Sangsaite*). That the latter interpretation is correct appears particularly from the last measure of the dance (see above) in which, according to the other version, the letter s would indicate an f♯, instead of the c′♯ of our transcription.

Additional examples for the study of the German lute tablature are available in *SchT*, pp. 9, 45, and 59.

Facsimile 22

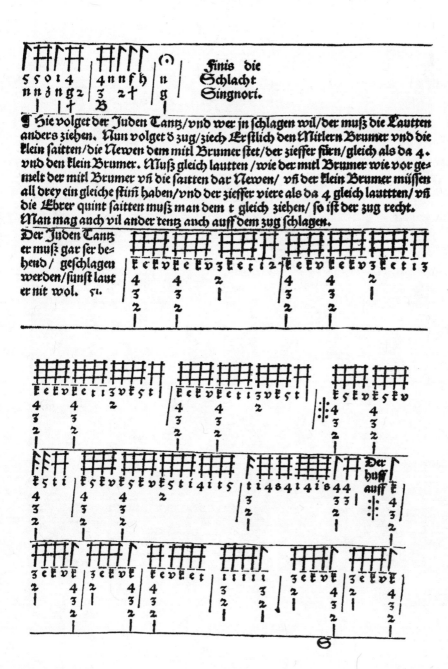

¶ Hie volget der Juden Tantz/vnd wer jn schlagen wil/der muß die Lautten anders ziehen. Nun volget d zug/ziech Erstlich den Mitlern Brumer vnd die klein saitten/die Newen dem mitl Brumer stet/der zieffer süen/gleich als da 4. vnd den klein Brumer. Muß gleich lautten/wie der mitl Brumer wie vor gemelt der mitl Brumer vñ die saitten dar Newen/ vñ der klein Brumer müssen all drey ein gleiche stiñ haben/vnd der zieffer viere als da 4 gleich lauttten/vñ die Ebrer quint saitten muß man dem t gleich ziehen/ so ist der zug recht. Man mag auch vil ander tentz auch auff dem zug schlagen.

Der Juden Tantz er muß gar ser behend/ geschlagen werden/sunst laut er nit wol. 51.

Hans Newsidler, *Ein new künstlich Lautenbuch.* Nürnberg, 1544

PART II

THE NOTATION OF ENSEMBLE MUSIC:
WHITE MENSURAL NOTATION

WHITE MENSURAL NOTATION

HAVING TREATED in the preceding part of our book the notation of music for a soloist instrument (organ, clavier, lute), we
turn now to the notation of polyphonic ensemble music. It is understandable that this field is considerably broader and more difficult than
that which we have hitherto considered. We are presented here with
a seven-hundred-year-long development embracing the period from
about 900 to 1600, during which the principles of notation underwent
such radical changes that a series of different systems arise, each of
which demands a separate study.[1] The student who has made himself
familiar with the notation of the works of Okeghem, Isaac and Josquin
is confronted with entirely different problems when he turns back to the
sources of the French or Italian *Ars Nova*, and again with a new situation in studying the organa of the Notre Dame School or the motets of
the thirteenth century.

During its entire evolution the main, and only real, problem of mensural notation was one of time values and time relationships. Indeed,
the other fundamental problem of notation, i.e., the indication of pitch,
had already been solved satisfactorily before polyphonic music began to
develop. There is only one isolated document of polyphonic music, the
Winchester Troper of the eleventh century, in which the problem of
pitch-determination exists, since it is written in cheironomic or staffless
neumes. In all the later sources, however, the use of the staff, that
ingenious invention of Guido of Arezzo, eliminates this problem; therefore only the other one—that of time values and rhythm—remains.

Considering the history of this problem from its beginnings to the late
sixteenth century, the amount of time, labour and ingenuity spent to
bring about what seems to us but a few paltry results is incredible.
Parturiunt montes et nascitur ridiculus mus, one is tempted to exclaim,
upon discovering that an intellectual struggle of many centuries was
needed in order to find two devices of such utter simplicity, namely, the
bar-line and the tie—devices which were unknown in earlier music but
which, in connection with the principle of binary mensuration, free the
modern musician from the intricacies of mensural notation and provide

---

[1] See the survey of notational systems on p. xxv, and the additional classification on p. 199.

a simple and clear expression of almost every conceivable time value and rhythm.

Such a statement, however, should not lead to a wrong conclusion regarding the value and the importance of early notation. Nothing is more dangerous and misleading in the study of the arts than to regard achievements of the past from the standpoint of technical progress. A superficial observer sees only what has been gained in a fight and not what has been lost. The true historical mind, however, sees that in the history of humanity there is no possibility of perfection, and that there is only a very faint hope of approaching it. Instead, there is something far more important, namely, constant change and ceaseless renewal. It is in this frame of mind that the student should approach the problems of early musical notation. In wrestling with its intricacies he will discover that notation, far from being merely an intellectual puzzle, is in all its various stages the perfect expression of the music it represents. Indeed, apart from the fascination of deciphering obscure systems of writing, his studies will reward him with an insight into the style and structure of early music such as cannot possibly be gained in another way.

As has already been pointed out in the introduction, the development of notation proceeds from extremely vague and ambiguous relationships to ever clearer and more exact indications. At the same time, it progresses gradually from very unfamiliar concepts to those with which we are acquainted in our present-day system. For this reason, as in the section on soloist music, we shall not in the following study pursue the order of the historical development, but begin with that system of notation of ensemble music which is closest to our own, in time as well as in character—the so-called white mensural notation.

I. NOTATIONAL SIGNS

THE WHITE mensural notation[1] embraces the period from the middle of the fifteenth to the late sixteenth century. The name 'white' refers to the use of white notes for the longer values, instead of the black forms of the preceding period. This change is, of course, the result of purely external considerations. Filling in the heads of the notes with black ink involved considerable unnecessary trouble and loss of time. It also may have proved more difficult on thin paper than on the parchment of the earlier manuscripts. Therefore around 1450, the scribes began to leave the notes unfilled. The term 'mensural' comes from *musica mensurata*—a designation used by early theorists to differentiate the regularly measured polyphonic music (motet, etc.) from *musica plana*, i.e., the unmeasured Gregorian plainsong.

Notes. The notes used in white mensural notation are: *maxima (Mx)*, *longa (L)*, *brevis (B)*, *semibrevis (S)*, *minima (M)*, *semiminima (Sm)*, *fusa (F)*, and *semifusa (Sf)*. Their shapes and those of the corresponding rests are as follows:

Of the two forms given for the *Sm* and *F* the black ones are by far the more frequent. Occasionally, both varieties are found in one and the same MS, or even in the same composition with no apparent difference in meaning (see, e.g., Facsimile 30, contra, third staff). The two-flagged *F*-rest is very rare. The *L*- and *Mx*-rests consist of strokes covering two or three spaces depending upon whether the *L* equals two or three *B* (imperfect or perfect modus, see under Mensuration, p. 99).

Ligatures. In addition to the single notes, mensural notation employs certain symbols which represent combinations of two or more tones and

---

[1] The earliest modern explanation of white notation, and one which is still very useful today is A. Bellermann's *Die Mensuralnoten und Taktzeichen des 15. und 16. Jahrhunderts*, published first in 1858 *(MuT)*. J. Wolf deals with this subject in *HdN* I, 381-465.

which are called ligatures.   These forms developed from certain neumes
(i.e., mnemonic signs indicating upward or downward progress of the
melody without showing the exact pitches or the rhythm), such as were
in use during the ninth, tenth, and eleventh centuries for the writing
down of plainsong.   In the earliest stages of polyphonic music the ligatures are used abundantly, as a glance at our facsimiles nos. 44-53
(around 1200) readily shows.   In later times they lose more and more of
their original importance; however, they are still comparatively frequent
in the sources of the fifteenth century.   In the sixteenth century they
gradually disappear and only a few of the simplest forms survive until
the middle of the seventeenth century.

Although we are concerned here with the latest stage in the development of the ligatures, a few words about their history will be helpful in
clarifying certain peculiarities of their form and meaning.

The four simplest neumes were: *punctum, virga, clivis,* and *podatus:*
• ⁄ ⌒ ⌣ .   The first two each indicate a single tone, the *punctum*
normally a shorter one than the *virga*.   Each of the latter two signs
represents a pair of tones which descend in the *clivis* and ascend in the
podatus.   When (around 1150) the neumes changed to the more definite
forms of the so-called Roman chorale notation, these four signs took on

the following shapes: ■ ⁄ ⌒ ⌣ .   These forms are still used today

as neume-like symbols in the liturgical books of the Catholic Church.
However, about 1200 (School of Notre Dame) the same signs were
adopted for the writing down of polyphonic music and, in this function,
acquired definite metrical values.   The two signs for single tones
became *brevis* (*B*) and *longa* (*L*) respectively, whereas, in each of the two
group-signs, or ligatures, the first note became a *B*, the second a *L*.
Thus, the third of the above symbols meant two tones in descending
motion, the first a *B*, the second an *L*, and the fourth signified the same

values in ascending motion, e.g.: ▦▦▦ .

In order to express other combinations of *B* and *L*, these two basic
forms were then subjected to certain modifications, for the indication of
which the terms *proprietas* and *perfectio* were evolved.   These terms
refer to what was then viewed as the 'proper' and 'perfect' rhythmic
sequence, i.e., *brevis* followed by *longa*.   Therefore, a ligature having
this evaluation was said to be *cum proprietate et cum perfectione,* the
former term referring specifically to the first note (*initialis*), the latter

to the last note (*finalis*) of the ligature. The other combinations of *B* and *L*, namely, *L L*, *B B*, and *L B*, were considered as lacking in one or both of the two basic requirements, a condition which was expressed by replacing the word *cum* (with) by the word *sine* (without). Therefore, if a ligature is *sine proprietate* its initial note is not *B*, but *L*; and if a ligature is *sine perfectione* its final note is not *L*, but *B*. There result the four following combinations:

cum proprietate et cum perfectione (*cum-cum*): *B L*
sine proprietate et cum perfectione (*sine-cum*): *L L*
cum proprietate et sine perfectione (*cum-sine*): *B B*
sine proprietate et sine perfectione (*sine-sine*): *L B*

To make these changes in value apparent in the notation the forms of the original ligatures were modified in certain ways, as the following table shows:

Designation	Value	Shape desc.		asc.
cum proprietate et cum perfectione	*B L*	(1)	(2)	(9)
sine proprietate et cum perfectione	*L L*	(3)	(4)	(10)
cum proprietate et sine perfectione	*B B*	(5)	(6)	
sine proprietate et sine perfectione	*L B*	(7)	(8)	

As may be seen from this table the *proprietas*, i.e., the value of the initial note, is determined by the presence or absence of a vertical descending stroke at the left. This principle, simple in itself, is complicated by the fact that in the two original forms *cum-cum*, the descending ligature (1) has a stroke while the ascending one (2) has none. Correspondingly, in the derivative forms *sine proprietate*, the descending ligature is written without a stroke [(3), (7)] and the ascending ligature with a stroke, either on the left or, more frequently, on the right side of the lower note [(4), (8)].

Change in the *perfectio*—that is, the value of the *finalis*—from *L* to *B* is indicated by modifying the shape of the body of the ligature. Two kinds of change are employed, dependent upon whether the ligature ascends or descends. If it ascends, the second note instead of being written vertically above the first as in (2) and (4), is written with the head turned to the right, as in (6) and (8). If the ligature descends, however, the change of *perfectio* is indicated by replacing the square shape of the body by a diagonal one, the so-called *ligatura obliqua*, so that the two forms *sine perfectione*, (5) and (7), result.

Two remarks must be made in regard to the oblique forms. First, such a ligature represents only those tones which are indicated by its beginning and end, not the intermediate tones as the novice might at first think. Therefore: ▨ is c'-g; ▨ is c'-f. Secondly, the oblique form affects only the value of the second note without in any way changing the value of the first note, which is determined solely by the presence or absence of the stroke.

The above-mentioned forms of ligatures constitute the basis of the teaching of Franco (around 1260) and of the mensural notation of the ensuing periods. While, in the succeeding development, the descending forms remained unchanged, the ascending forms underwent further alterations. The most important change resulted from the awkwardness of writing the ascending ligature *cum-cum* [see the form (2) of the table] because of the close proximity of two notes, particularly if the interval was a second. In seeking a more satisfactory form, scribes took their cue from the related form *sine perfectione* [(6), (8)], and employed the same means which, with the first note, were used to indicate the opposite value of the *initialis*, namely, the stroke. There resulted the forms (9), (10), in place of (2) and (4).

To these forms must be added another modification of the two basic signs which is termed *ligatura cum opposita proprietate* (*c.o.p.*). It is indicated by an upward stroke on the left side of the *initialis*. These ligatures are the only ones in which smaller values than a *B* are expressed. In them, each of the two notes has the value of a *S* (see p. 10).

There follows a tabulation of the ligatures as they appear in white notation:[1]

Symbol	Form		Value
	desc.	asc.	
cum-cum	♭	(ᗡ) ♯	B L
sine-cum	♭	(ᗡ) ♯	L L
cum-sine	▷	♯ (♯)	B B
sine-sine	◁	♯ (♯)	L B
c.o.p.	♭ ♭	♭ ♭	S S

[1] The bracketed shapes of the ascending ligatures *cum-sine* and *sine-sine* are exceedingly rare, and their evaluation has been the subject of a heated controversy among fifteenth century theorists. The above interpretation is supported by Tinctoris (*CS* IV, 43) and by Adam von Fulda (*GS* III, 365), but is vigorously denounced by Tinctoris' adversary Gafurius (*Practica Musicae*, 1496, lib. II,

Up to this point we have considered only those ligatures which consist of two notes and which therefore are called *ligatura binaria*. However, the scope of ligatures is considerably enlarged by the numerous forms in which more than two notes can be expressed by a ligature: *ligatura ternaria, quaternaria* etc., as for example: [music notation figures] . In these ligatures all the notes between the first and the last are called *mediae* (middle notes). Each *media* generally has the value of a B, except where it is the second note of a ligature *c.o.p.*, as in the third of the above examples, or where it is marked as a L or Mx, as in the third or fourth example. The reader may try to verify that the four ligatures have the following values: *B B L; B B B B; S S B B B L B; L B Mx B L.*

Rules for Ligatures. Whereas, in the preceding explanations, we have considered the ligatures from the standpoint of historical development, we shall now study them systematically by means of a set of rules from which the value of any ligature can be determined. In theoretical treatises of the fifteenth and sixteenth centuries such rules are given in a rather cumbersome and obscure presentation, or else in the form of Latin or German poems which lack in clarity whatever they gain in shortness.[1] Following is a presentation of these rules in what is intended to be a concise, clear and useful form.

A. Rules about the meaning of the tails.
  1. A note with a downward tail to the right is *L.*
  2. An ascending tail to the left of the initial note makes that note and the following one a *S* each.
  3. An initial with a downward tail to its left side is *B.*

B. Rules for notes not covered under A.
  4. All middle notes are *B.*
  5. An initial note in descending position (i.e., followed by a lower

cap. v; cf. E. Praetorius, *Die Mensuraltheorie des Franchinus Gafurius*, Leipzig, 1905, p. 18), who holds that exactly the opposite values are correct, namely *B-B* for the form without a tail, and *L-B* for that with a tail. Obviously, his interpretation is based upon a comparison of these shapes with their equivalents in square shape, whereas that of the Tinctoris and Adam von Fulda is based upon their similarity with the corresponding oblique forms in descending motion. The two or three examples of the ascending form with a tail which the present writer has encountered in his studies support the latter view, since in each case this form has the value *B-B*. One example (from the Codex Chantilly, *ca.* 1400) occurs on Facsimile 83, fifth staff, last ligature; three others are found on a facsimile from the Old Hall MS (ca. 1450) reproduced in vol. III of A. Ramsbotham, *The Old Hall Manuscript*, Westminster, 1938 (frontispiece, staves 8, 10, and 11). See pp. 364, 412.
  [1] See, e.g., *MuT*, 10.

note) and a final note in descending position (i.e., preceded by
a higher note) are *L*.

6. An initial in ascending position and a final in ascending position
are *B*.

7. A final note in oblique form is *B*.

There follow schematic illustrations of these rules, for the sake of
greater clearness. Diagonal dashes refer to ascending or descending
position; horizontal dashes indicate that the direction has no influence:[1]

A. 1. ꟼ–, –ꟼ–, –ꟼ = *L*

2. ♭–, ♭–, ♭–, ♭– = *S S*

3. ꟼ–, ꟼ = *B*

B. 4. –□– ; –◊–, –◊– = *B; BB*

5. ◊, ◊, ◊ = *L*

6. ◊, ◊ = *B*

7. ◊ = *B*

As experience shows, the rules 1, 2, and 4 are more or less obvious and
are easily remembered. For the others, the present writer has found the
following working rule helpful: ꟼ is *B B* and ♭ is *L L*; a descending tail at the beginning alters the first note, oblique form alters the last.

Since in the determination of a ligature the tails are of prime importance, the student must be warned not to confuse these tails with certain
strokes which merely serve to connect notes of different pitch. Such a
stroke occurs in the example (a) (see below) between the second and the
third note. It has absolutely no influence on the value of the notes; if
the second note were to be a *L*, the stroke would have to extend below
the following note, as that before the last note which actually is a 'tail.'
There might also be some doubt in the student's mind as to whether such
a tail, found in the middle of a ligature, belongs to the preceding or to
the following note, i.e., whether it is a tail attached to the left or to the
right side of a note. However, it may be generally observed that no
note of a ligature may have a tail to the left side except the initial.
Hence, the tail belongs to the preceding note, making it a *L*.

In studying the following examples, the beginner is advised to apply
the rules in their above order.

Example (a) 🎼. The fifth note is *L* (rule 1); the initial is *B* (rule
3); the three following notes are *B* (rule 4); the last note is *L* (rule 5).

Thus the ligature means: *B B B B L L* or, in notes: 🎼 . It

---

[1] A similar method of schematic designation has been used by O. Ursprung in an article on 'Die
Ligaturen, ihr System und ihre methodische und didaktische Darstellung' (*AM* XI).

may be noted that the third and fourth notes could just as well be written in square shapes, instead of in oblique form: . From the viewpoint of logic and simplicity this manner of writing would even be preferable, since the oblique form has real significance only at the end of a ligature in descending position. However, oblique writing is frequently employed elsewhere, probably for its greater ease of writing.

Example (*b*) . The fourth and fifth notes are *L* (rule 1); the first two notes are *S* (rule 2); the third and the sixth notes are *B* (rule 4); the last note is *B* (rule 7): *S S B L L B B:* .

Any note of a ligature may be dotted. If an initial or middle note is to be dotted, the dot is written above that note, e.g.:

In ligatures two successive notes of the same pitch are impossible. If, e.g., this passage: were to be changed so that the third note is d, it must be written thus: .

In acquainting oneself with ligatures, it is useful not only to resolve given forms into single notes but also to follow the opposite procedure i.e., to write a series of single notes in ligature. The following exercise is recommended: Write in ligature each of the three melodic phrases (1), (2), (3), combined with each of the three rhythmic patterns (a), (b), (c):

(1)   (2)   (3)

(a) *B L B B L B*   (b) *S S B B B B*   (c) *L B B L B L*

By combination there result nine melodic-rhythmic formulae each of which is to be written in ligature. The combination (3) (a), for example, is as follows: .

Finally, a few peculiarities of rare occurrence must be mentioned. A rectangular body of double length, with or without a tail, indicates a *Mx:* = *B Mx L;* = *L Mx* (see Facsimile 28). In some earlier sources (MS *Canonici misc. 213* of the Bodleian Library) one finds occasionally forms such as: . Here, the downward dash makes the second note of the ligature a *L*, whereas the upward dash calls for a *B*, thus giving these two forms the values *S L* or *S B* respectively.

As a final example we reproduce the tenor of the *Laudamus te* of an early fifteenth century mass by Arnaldi,[1] contained in MS Bologna, Bibl. Univ. *2216.* The notation is in the black notes of the earlier period which, however have the same significance as the white shapes explained above.

The student may determine the value of each note and, after the study of the following chapter, transcribe it in *tempus imperfectum*.

Subsidiary Symbols. Our study of the graphical signs of white notation will be completed by a brief elucidation of certain subsidiary symbols of reference, repetition, and correction, which are conventionally used in the sources under consideration.

(a) The *signum congruentiae:* ♂.♫.♫ serves to indicate points of coincidence in the various parts. An example of this practice is found in the two texted parts of *Dona i ardenti* of Facsimile 23 (staves 6 and 8). The sign is regularly used in canonic pieces to indicate either the fugal entrance of the imitating part or, in mensuration canons, the places where the various singers have to stop. For an example of the latter practice, see Facsimile 27 and the explanations thereof. Another sign of reference is the *custos* which indicates the pitch of the first note of the next-following staff (see p. 3).

(b) Repetition of sections is indicated in the fourteenth century sources by a simple vertical dash similar in appearance to a *B-* or a *L-* rest (Facsimiles 68 and 70; see the explanations on *ouvert* and *clos*, p. 349). In the fifteenth and sixteenth centuries the sign of repetition occurs in the following shapes: ⁝╫: ╪ ╪ . Another sign of frequent occurrence is the pause, known under names such as *mora generalis, corona, diadema, signum taciturnitatis* or *quietantiae*. The following shapes are used: ⁝ ⟡ ⌒⌒ ⌒ .

(c) If, by mistake, a white note had been written as a full black note, the letter *v* (vacua, empty) was used to correct the error. Some other signs which serve the same purpose and which are probably deteriorations of the letter *v* are shown here: ♫ ♫ ♫˜◦ • .

---

[1] In MS Bologna, Lic. Mus. *37*, p. 3, the same composition is attributed to Z. Micinella.

A dash erroneously attached to a *B* or a *S* was cancelled either by a diagonal stroke through the dash, or by another dash leading in the opposite direction: ♪,♪=◊ .

If notes were written too high or too low, the correction was indicated in the following manner: ♯=♯;♯=♯ . For more details see *HdN* 1, 430.

II. MENSURATION

A. Tempus, Prolatio, and Modus

IN THE PRECEDING explanations we have purposely avoided expressing the characters of mensural notation in modern note values, for the simple reason that such transcription depends upon an additional factor, mensuration. By this term is meant the metrical relation between the value of one note and that of the next smaller degree. In modern notation this relation is always duple—i.e., a given note, unless dotted, is always equal to two of the next smaller species. In mensural notation, however, an undotted note may be either duple or triple—i.e., equal to two or three smaller notes, depending upon the mensuration of the piece and the value of the neighbouring notes. A ternary note is called perfect; a binary, imperfect. These terms go back to the rhythmic concepts of the thirteenth century, when the ternary division was considered perfect because it consists of 'beginning, middle, and end.' The dogma of the Holy Trinity also played some part in this concept and terminology.

In the system of white mensural notation the choice of perfect or imperfect mensuration exists chiefly in the case of two notes, the B and the S. The larger values are usually imperfect, while the smaller notes are always so:

$$Mx = 2\,L;\ L = 2\,B;\ B = 2 \text{ or } 3\,S;\ S = 2 \text{ or } 3\,M;\ M = 2\,Sm;\ Sm = 2\,F;$$
$$F = 2\,Sf.$$

The mensuration of the B is called *tempus*, and exists in the two varieties: *tempus perfectum*, indicated by a whole circle O ; and *tempus imperfectum*, indicated by a semicircle, open to the right C . The mensuration of the S is called *prolatio*. *Prolatio perfecta* is indicated by a dot placed in the middle of these signs, whereas the absence of the dot

* calls for *prolatio imperfecta*. Thus four combinations result:

tempus imperfectum cum prolatione imperfecta:	C ♮=◊◊	◊=♪♪
tempus perfectum cum prolatione imperfecta:	O ♮=◊◊◊	◊=♪♪
tempus imperfectum cum prolatione perfecta:	C ♮=◊◊	◊=♪♪♪
tempus perfectum cum prolatione perfecta:	⊙ ♮=◊◊◊	◊=♪♪♪

To supplement the signs indicating these mensurations, we intend to use occasionally another system of designation which is more easily grasped; namely, to indicate the *tempus* by Arabic figures 2 or 3, and the *prolatio* by the same figures thereafter in italics: *2* or *3*. Thus the four mensurations are also represented by the following symbols: C = [2, *2*]; O = [3, *2*]; ℂ = [2, *3*]; ⊙ = [3, *3*].

An understanding of the meaning of these mensurations is considerably facilitated by an appropriate choice of modern note-values for their transcription. As was the case with the tablatures, a 'literal' rendition of the mensural notes by their modern equivalents in shape, i.e., of an *S* by a whole-note, or an *M* by a half-note (see the table on p. 3) is not to be recommended. This method which was the customary one with editors of the nineteenth century (Bellermann, Proske, Ambros, Commer, and others) has been abandoned in more recent times because of its clumsiness and lack of comprehensiveness, chiefly as a result of Riemann's precedent. Unfortunately the newer publications exhibit no uniformity in the choice of scale of reduction. Many editors transcribe the *semibrevis* as a half-note (1 : 2); others as a quarter-note (1 : 4); others continue to transcribe without reduction. Moreover, in many publications different scales of reduction are chosen for different pieces and, sometimes, for different sections of one and the same composition.

In our discussions of white mensural notation we shall invariably employ a reduction of 1 :4, transcribing the *S* as a quarter-note.[1] In doing

---

[1] The proper choice of modern equivalents for the mensural notes is, of course, closely bound up with the consideration of the tempo for the piece in question. Our basic principle in this matter is, to choose the scale of reduction in such a way that the modern quarter-note becomes the beat in moderately slow tempo, somewhere in the vicinity of M.M. 60. As will be seen later (p. 188 ff), the mensural notes signified not only relative values but had, in a given period, fairly constant absolute durations as well, a fact which makes it possible to choose a uniform scale of reduction for practically all the pieces of any one period, or, at least, of any one type. It must be noticed, however, that, in turning from one period to another, the 'absolute' value of any given note changed considerably, namely from short to much longer durations. This appears particularly in the case of the *B* which, around 1225, designated the shortest value of music (brevis, short), while, in the sixteenth century, it was the longest value in practical use. As a matter of fact, the 'moderate beat' was represented successively by the *L* (1200-1250), the *B* (1250-1300), the *S* (1300-1450), the *M* (1450-1600) and finally the *Sm*, i.e., the quarter-note (1600-present), so that reductions in the ratios of 1:16, 1:8, 1:4, 1:2, and 1:1 appear appropriate for the periods just named.

It will readily be noticed that, as far as the period of white notation (1450-1600) is concerned, the scale of reduction used in our study is not in agreement with the above general explanations which actually would call for a reduction 1:2 (*M* = quarter-note) instead of 1:4 (*S* = quarter-note). Much as the present writer regrets to be inconsistent in a fundamental matter, he has, after much hesitation and deliberation, decided in favor of the reduction 1:4. because this method offers considerable advantage from the notational point of view. It seemed to him that in the present study the clarification of the notation should take preference over other considerations. It may be noticed, however, that even from the point of view of the tempo the transcription *S* = quarter-note is not so, the four above mensurations become the expression of metrical relationships which, in modern notation, are signified by certain simple meters, namely, $\frac{2}{4}$-, $\frac{3}{4}$-, $\frac{6}{8}$-, and $\frac{9}{8}$-meter respectively. As a matter of fact, in [2, 3], e.g., the B, S, and M are in the same numerical relationships as are the (dotted) half-note, the (dotted) quarter-note, and the eighth-note in $\frac{6}{8}$-meter. The following table shows the four mensurations and their modern equivalents:

Mensuration	Meter	Transcription of notes				Example

In theoretical writings, this scheme of four mensurations is broadened considerably by the inclusion of the L and the Mx as additional elements of rhythm. The mensuration of the L was called *modus longarum* (*modus minor*, 'lesser mood') and that of the Mx *modus maximarum* (*modus major*, 'greater mood'). Since each mensuration could be either perfect or imperfect, a system resulted which included 16 combinations of *modus maximarum, modus longarum, tempus* and *prolatio*. A confusing variety of signs for these combinations were invented by the theorists but almost never used in practice. For a survey of them, the reader is referred to the detailed explanations in *HdN* 1, 410-415.[1]

entirely wrong, owing to the fact that the normal tempo of the Flemish music was such as to be capable of being interpreted in two different beats, either M.M. 45, or M.M. 90 (approximately). Thus, one has a choice between two transcriptions, one with S = quarter-note in 'adagio,' or one with M = quarter-note in 'moderato.' The latter is more natural to the modern interpreter; the former is chosen here for the reasons set forth above.

[1] We hope to save the student of this subject unnecessary pains by reminding him that the nomenclature used by the early theorists is far from being consistent and unambiguous. For instance, the terms *major* and *minor* were used not only with reference to *modus*, but also to *prolatio*. However, although in the former connection they designated two different mensurations (*modus maximarum* and *modus longarum*), they signified, in the latter connection, the perfect and imperfect varieties of one and the same mensuration, *prolatio major* and *minor* being identical respectively with *prolatio perfecta* and *imperfecta*. Unfortunately, the latter meaning of the term occurs also occasionally in connection with *modus*. In *HdN* 1, 412, two signs (circles within circles) are reproduced which, accord-

Indeed, from the standpoint of the musical practice the situation is a good deal simpler. The *modus maximarum* (or, as we shall call it, *maximodus*) is of very slight practical importance in the period under consideration (see, however, p. 124). The *modus longarum* (or as we shall call it simply, *modus*) must occasionally be considered in certain types of composition, namely, in the motets and masses which are based upon a *cantus firmus*-like tenor. In these pieces, the upper voices are written chiefly in *B*, *S* and *M* or, in other words, in *tempus* and *prolatio*, whereas the tenor is written chiefly in *L* and *B* or, in other words, in *modus*. Since *tempus* and *prolatio* indicate the rhythmic organization corresponding to the contents of the modern measure, the introduction of *modus* obviously results in the appearance of regular groups of measures, namely, either two (*modus imperfectus*) or three (*modus perfectus*). In a manner analogous to the abbreviations for *tempus* and *prolatio* given above, we shall indicate the *modus* by Roman numerals II or III; thus [III, 3, 2] means: *modus perfectus cum tempore perfecto cum prolatione imperfecta*. Here follows a schematic example of this mensuration:

Discant:

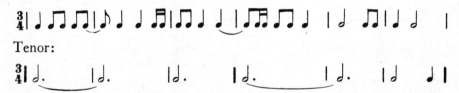

Tenor:

In the musical documents of the period in question the *modus* is not, as a rule, indicated by a special sign, but by the *L*-rests which usually appear either at the beginning or in the course of the tenor. According to whether these rests cover two or three spaces of the staff, the *L* is understood to be imperfect or perfect (see p. 87).

From these explanations it appears that the introduction of *maximodus* would mean the formation of regular phrases each of which includes a regular number of measures. There is only one period in the history of music when such a principle of extremely uniform construction appeared in composition, i.e., the period of Machaut, Dunstable, and Dufay,

---

ing to Adam von Fulda and other theorists have the meaning of: *modus major cum tempore perfecto cum prolatione majori (minori)*. Obviously, in this case *modus major* does not mean *modus maximarum*, but the perfect variety of *modus* in the usual sense, i.e., *modus longarum*. Wolf's explanations on *Taktzeichen* suffer much from his failure to clarify the exact meaning of the various terms, or else, from the inclusion of designations and signs to which no clear meaning can be attached.

who, in some of their 'isorhythmic motets' arrive at the realization of the amalgamation of *maximodus, modus, tempus* and *prolatio* (see p. 356). In those rare cases in which it is necessary to indicate the *maximodus* we shall use italic roman numerals, as for example: [*III*, II, 2, *3*].[1]

As a matter of curiosity, however, it may be mentioned that illustrations of *modus, tempus,* and *prolatio* may also be found in various compositions of the classical period. A particularly interesting example is offered by the variations in Beethoven's pianoforte sonata op. 111, the rhythmic structure of which, in the language of fifteenth century theory, may be described as: *modus maximarum imperfectus cum modo longarum perfecto cum tempore perfecto cum prolatione perfecta* [*II*, III, *3, 3*]:

Here, if one considers the thirty-second-notes as the smallest unit (*minimae*), we find the four subsequent mensurations consistently employed for lengthy sections of the composition:

(a)   three thirty-second-notes to a sixteenth: *prolatio perfecta*
(b)   three sixteenths to an eighth: *tempus perfectum*
(c)   three eighths (beats) to a measure: *modus perfectus*
(d)   two measures to a phrase: *maximodus imperfectus*

We turn now to a detailed consideration of the four combinations of *tempus* and *prolatio*.

B. Tempus Imperfectum cum Prolatione Imperfecta

This mensuration offers no great problems, since the notes are all binary and, therefore, stand in the same metrical relationship to one another as in modern notation. Using our scale of reduction 1:4, the modern equivalent of this mensuration is $\frac{2}{4}$-time. Each measure con-

---

[1] By introducing these abbreviations we hope to achieve greater simplicity and precision than has heretofore been usual. For example, in F. Ludwig's edition of the works of Machaut (*Machaut, Musikalische Werke*, Leipzig, 1929, vol. III, p. 78) the above mensuration is expressed as follows: mo. ma. pf.; mo. mi. imp.; tp. imp.; pr. ma.

tains one *B*, transcribed as a half-note. It is, of course, possible to combine two such measures into one $\frac{4}{4}$-measure, although cases are not infrequent in which this method necessitates the insertion of single $\frac{2}{4}$- (or, $3 \times \frac{2}{4}$, i.e., $\frac{3}{2}$-) measures. For the sake of clarity and consistency, $\frac{2}{4}$-meter is used throughout the book.[1]

To indicate that a note contains three units of the next smaller species, it is dotted as in modern usage. This dot, the so-called *punctus additionis*, also appears in conjunction with ligatures (see p. 93).

Aside from the reduction of note values, the modern notation differs from the old method chiefly by the arrangement of the parts in score, and by the use of bar-lines. Modern scholars have frequently raised objection against the latter device which they felt to be detrimental to an understanding of the polyphonic nature of early music. It also has the disadvantage of entailing a frequent use of tied notes, since values occurring in syncopated position form a characteristic feature of the style of the Flemish polyphony. In various recent publications attempts have been made to eliminate this drawback by replacing the bar-line by the 'Mensurstrich' (mensuration line) which is drawn not through the whole score or through the individual staves, but through the spaces between them. Following is an example illustrating both methods:

(a)

(b)

It is doubtful whether the advantage of the second method—i.e., a greater similarity to the original notation—is considerable enough to compensate for its unfamiliar appearance and greater difficulty of reading. Moreover, it may be noticed that the 'Mensurstrich' cannot be used if different mensurations occur in various voices, as for instance, [3, 2] in the tenor against [2, 2] in the discant, a feature not uncommon in the masses and motets of the earlier Flemish masters. It seems to us that the best device of barring is the bar-line which is drawn through

[1] It goes without saying, but may be stated expressly, that the methods of transcription used in this book have been devised chiefly from the notational point of view, which means that they are designed primarily to clarify the important features of the original writing. For other purposes, scholarly as well as practical, certain changes or adjustments may be advisable.

each stave individually. This method avoids the 'sectional' appearance produced by the long bar-lines of the modern score and yet allows for different barring in each part if necessary. It goes without saying that such bar-lines have only metrical significance, without necessarily implying the added modern meaning of an accentuated first beat. We say 'necessarily,' because a large portion of early music actually is 'bar-line music' in exactly the same sense as music of Mozart and Beethoven—a fact which is usually overlooked in the discussions about the bar-line. To this field belongs the entire repertory of the thirteenth century, practically all Italian music of the fourteenth century, and the various types of sixteenth century chanson (chanson, frottola, villanella, etc.).

We may now turn to a consideration of some examples in [2, 2]. Facsimile 23 shows on the lower half of the page a three-voice chanson, *Dona i ardenti* , by Guillermus Dufay whose name is written in an enigmatical manner, the syllable fa being indicated by the note B-flat which, in the *hexachordum molle* (on f), is fa.

Although the two lower parts carry a flat in the signature, there is none in the discant. This manner of writing is extremely frequent in polyphonic music from the early thirteenth century through at least the beginning of the sixteenth. Its meaning has been the subject of several studies.[1] In an article on 'The Partial Signatures in the Sources up to 1450' (*AM* x; see also *AM* xi, p. 40) the present author has tried to show that the partial absence of a flat in the signature is an expression of a kind of bitonality, namely, of F-major (or D-minor) in the lower parts as against Lydian (or Dorian) in the higher ones. This difference of tonalities bestows upon the music a contrast between 'dark' and 'bright,' between 'heavy' and 'light,' which forms one of the special charms of early polyphonic music and which should not be effaced by editorial accidentals.[2] In fact, the chanson under consideration does not need any emendations, as far as the accidentals are concerned.

The second note of the last ligature of the contra should read f, not g. For the *signum congruentiae* on staff 1 and 3 of the chanson, see p. 94. In transcribing the piece, the student will notice that these signs are not quite correctly placed. The beginning is transcribed in the appendix, No. 12.

Facsimile 24 serves as another example of [2, 2]. These two pages from the Trent Codex no. 92 contain the *Sanctus* of a mass by Benet, which falls into five sections: (1) *Sanctus Sanctus Dominus Deus Sabaoth*; (2) *Pleni sunt celi et terra gloria tua*; (3) *Osanna in excelsis*; (4) *Benedictus qui venit in nomine Domini*; (5) *Osanna in excelsis*. Of these, sections (2) and (4) are in two parts only, as is indicated by the rests in the

---

[1] See the above-mentioned article, p. 4. Also K. Jeppesen, *Der Kopenhagener Chansonnier* (Copenhagen, 1927), p. lxiii f.

[2] This writer was glad to find his view supported by various transcriptions given by H. Besseler in his *Die Musik des Mittelalters und der Renaissance*, Potsdam 1931 (E. Bücken, *Handbuch der Musikwissenschaft*); see the examples 97, 109, 113, and others.

FACSIMILE 23

MS Oxford, Bodleian Library *Canonici misc. 213* (*ca.* 1450)
Page 73

contratenor. Sections (1), (2), and (5) are in [2, 2] and may be tran-
* scribed now.

It will be seen that the two-voice section (2) comprises 16 B (16
$\frac{2}{4}$-measures) plus a final L which is followed by a long vertical dash,
the so-called *finis punctorum*. On the other hand, in the contra there
are rests to the equivalent of only 16 B before the *finis punctorum*. As
a matter of fact, the final L, which usually appears at the end of a piece
or a section thereof, was not considered an exact value, but was supposed
to be held until the leader of the chorus gave the sign for silence. It
is therefore best transcribed as a half-note with a fermata.

This piece is another example of partial signatures. However, the application of the
principles explained in connection with the previous piece, fails to lead to a satisfactory
result here. As a matter of fact, a literal rendering of the parts appears to be impossible
from the melodic as well as from the harmonic point of view, since numerous tritones
(f-b) and clashes such as bb-f'-b' would result. As has been pointed out in the above-
mentioned article (*AM* x), there occurred, around 1450, changes of musical style which,
owing to a greater emphasis of the harmonic point of view (triads in root-position)
obviated the continuation of that bitonality which is frequently encountered in the works
of the preceding period. Generally speaking, the melodic as well as the harmonic context now calls for a much greater use of B-flats in the upper parts than theretofore and,
consequently, for a considerable number of editorials accidentals. The extent to which
such accidentals should be added and the principles, upon which such additions should be
based, represent what may well be called the most controversial and problematic topics
of musicology. Until recently, editors have been inclined to eliminate, by a liberal use
of added accidentals, features which are not compatible with the harmonic system of, say,
the eighteenth century, e.g., the vertical and the horizontal tritone, cross-relations, the
lowered seventh before the octave, etc. Their method was purely empirical or experimental, which means that editorial flats (and sharps) were added after the completion
of the transcription wherever they appeared to be required by the context of the voices.
In place of this rather unsatisfactory procedure another method has been suggested by
the present writer (see the above-mentioned publication), a method which allows one to
determine the flats and naturals *a priori* on a purely horizontal basis, i.e., from a consideration of the part itself. The following rules have been advanced:

The B is natural when occurring in conjunct motion (seconds) from both sides, but
is flat when it is connected by a leap with either the preceding or the following note.
The B occurring as a top-tone is flat.

According to these rules, the B is natural in the combination a-b-c' or c'-b-a, flat in
combinations such as g-b-c', d'-b-a, a-b-a, etc. The justification of these principles lies
in the fact that a progression by leap, either of a third or a fourth, introduces a harmonic
element into the melodic line, while a progression by steps alone remains within the
boundaries of the (modal) scale. That there existed a differentiation between a 'melodic
tonality' with an emphasis of the B-natural and a 'harmonic tonality' with a greater use
of the B-flat appears particularly from the study of sixteenth century keyboard music
(see pp. 8, 26, 34). The 'moderate bitonality' which results from the above method
forms the transition between the earlier, more distinct, type, and the 'monotonality' of
the seventeenth and later centuries.

It goes without saying that the rules given above do not constitute an infallible principle. They are useful, however, as a point of departure—if only, as a point of departure
away from the biased misconceptions which prevailed in practically all the editions
published until recently. If the principles here presented need revision or replacement—

FACSIMILE 24

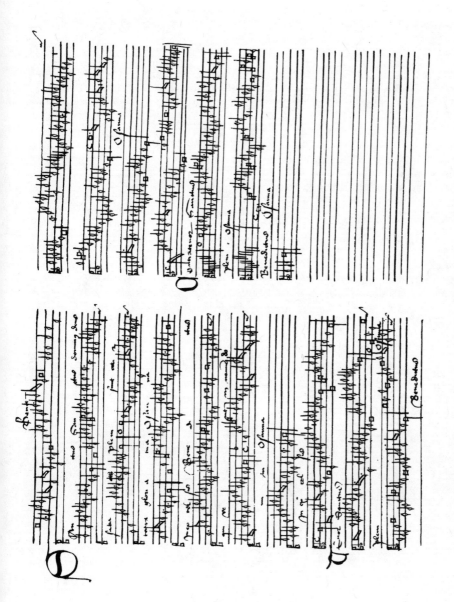

Trent Codex 92. Vienna, Staatsbibliothek *Mss Trient 87–92 (ca. 1475)*
Pages 82', 83

a possibility which this writer readily admits—this can only lead still farther away from the classical system of harmony, toward a still stricter adherence to the original. An indication of such a trend is found in the edition by D. Plamenac of the masses (I–VIII) of Ockeghem, a publication in which progressions such as:  are left intact, while, strangely enough, other combinations of a much less 'offensive' nature are corrected (see the Kyrie of the first mass).

A few remarks may be added with regard to the second problem of *musica ficta*, i.e., the sharped leading-tones in cadences. The closing measure of section (1) in Facsimile 24 illustrates the problem presented by the three-voiced cadence typical of the Burgundian and the early Flemish schools: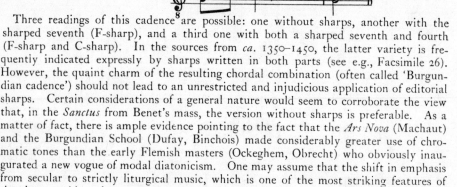

Three readings of this cadence are possible: one without sharps, another with the sharped seventh (F-sharp), and a third one with both a sharped seventh and fourth (F-sharp and C-sharp). In the sources from *ca.* 1350–1450, the latter variety is frequently indicated expressly by sharps written in both parts (see e.g., Facsimile 26). However, the quaint charm of the resulting chordal combination (often called 'Burgundian cadence') should not lead to an unrestricted and injudicious application of editorial sharps. Certain considerations of a general nature would seem to corroborate the view that, in the *Sanctus* from Benet's mass, the version without sharps is preferable. As a matter of fact, there is ample evidence pointing to the fact that the *Ars Nova* (Machaut) and the Burgundian School (Dufay, Binchois) made considerably greater use of chromatic tones than the early Flemish masters (Ockeghem, Obrecht) who obviously inaugurated a new vogue of modal diatonicism. One may assume that the shift in emphasis from secular to strictly liturgical music, which is one of the most striking features of the change taking place around 1450, played a decisive role in the adoption of a tonal system which was much more conservative and 'Gregorian,' so to speak, than that of the previous periods. On the basis of this general view it would be proper to give preference to the sharped varieties of the above cadence in music (particularly secular music) of the *Ars Nova* and of the Burgundian School, as against the diatonic variety in sacred music of the ensuing period, at least through the end of the fifteenth century. It is interesting to note that this tonal change is in inner agreement with the shift from light to dark timbre, from high to low range, from a thin to a fuller texture, which accompany the transition from the Burgundian to the Flemish style. It may also be noticed that in the cadence which closes the first phrase of the *Sanctus* the use of sharped tones is actually prohibited by the B-flat in the contra:

In applying our rules regarding the B to the piece under consideration it will be seen that they lead to satisfactory results, particularly in the section (4), *Benedictus*, which will be considered later (p. 118). In the section (2), *Pleni*, one will probably restrict their application to the obvious case of the tritone (f-b), without changing the B in the fifth measure (second staff of the original, shortly before the syllable 'sunt'), on account of its close proximity to a cadence on C.

As a last example of imperfect mensuration the chanson *Dangier tu m'as tollu* reproduced on Facsimile 25 may be studied. The third and fourth notes on the last staff of the discant are an example of the so-called minor coloration which will be explained later (see p. 128 ff). For the present purpose, it will suffice to say that the third note, a 'blackened *S*,' has the same value as a dotted *M*.

The clef on the last staff of the discant is a G-clef. The beginning of the discant is transcribed in the appendix, No. 13.

C. Tempus Perfectum cum Prolatione Imperfecta

In this mensuration, which in early practice is indicated by a whole circle or, in this book, by the sign [3, 2], the B equals three S: ♮=♦♦♦; all the other values are binary. The transcription into modern notes leads to $\frac{3}{4}$-measures: ○♮◊♦♦♮ =$\frac{3}{4}$|♩.|♩ ♫ ♩| ♩.|

Imperfection. Whereas in *tempus imperfectum* (and, of course, in modern notation) the ternary value of a note is derived from the binary by adding one half, a reverse process takes place in *tempus perfectum.* This process, which leads from the ternary B to the binary and therefore amounts to subtracting one third, is called *imperfection.* Generally it is not indicated by any external sign, but certain circumstances determine when the B remains perfect, and when it becomes imperfect or, as we take the liberty of saying, 'is imperfected.'[1] The following examples illustrate the two principal methods of imperfection, namely, *imperfectio a parte post* (*a p. p.*), i.e., imperfection by a following note, and *imperfectio a parte ante* (*a p. a.*), i.e., imperfection by a preceding note:

a p. p.   ♮◊=|♩♩| *a p. a.*   ◊♮=|♩ ♩|

The following rules must be observed:

[1] The use of 'imperfect' as a verb throughout this book seems justifiable both by the analogy with the verb 'to perfect' and by the exigencies of this subject.

Rules of imperfection (for [3, 2]):

1. A *B* is perfect if followed by another *B* or by a *B*-rest.
2. A *B* is perfect if followed by two or three *S*.[1]
3. A *B* is imperfect if followed or preceded by one or by more than three *S*.
4. If both *imperfectio a p. p.* and *a p. a.* are admissible, the former takes preference.
5. A *B*-rest can never be imperfected; however, a *S*-rest may cause imperfection of a note.

These rules may first be illustrated by the following examples:

NB: In the examples to rule 2 the case of two *S* has not been illustrated because it calls for further explanation (see alteration, p. 112).

It is unnecessary to mention that these rules are not strict laws, but guiding principles. They should be used, not from the standpoint of the mathematician, but from that of the singing or playing musician. In other words, the value of a given note should not be determined by a process of calculation, but by the comprehension of the musical context.

Following are a few supplementary remarks regarding the above rules.

To rule 1: This rule is considered one of the most fundamental of the entire theory. It is frequently given in the form: *similis ante similem perfecta,* i.e., a note is perfect before another one of the same kind.[2]

---

[1] For a possible modification of this rule and the next, see p. 114.

[2] Although this writer has never encountered an exception to this rule, there is an interesting remark in Glarean's *Dodekachordon* of 1552 which shows that such exceptions may have been quite

FACSIMILE 25

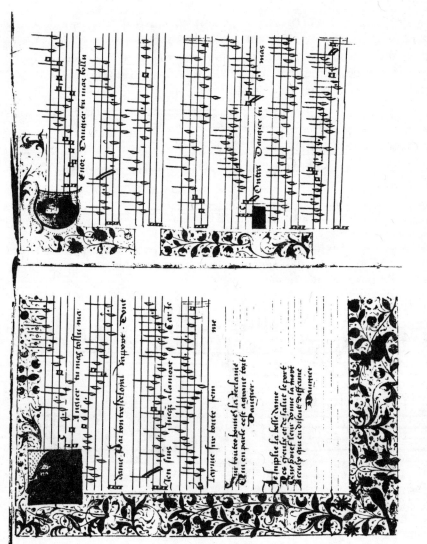

Chansonnier Laborde. Washington, Library of Congress *M2. 1. L 252 (ca. 1500)*
Pages 47', 48

To rule 2: The following example:

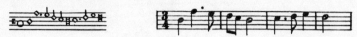

shows that a *B* followed by three *S* may occasionally be imperfect, namely, by *imperfectio a. p. a.*

To rule 3: Although the above examples illustrating this rule show the normal grouping of 1, 4, and 5 *S* placed between two *B*, yet the grouping may differ occasionally, according to the context, namely, if the first *B* is imperfected *a. p. a.* In the following example, for instance, the group of four *S* must be divided into 3 + 1, instead of 1 + 3:

In the following example the imperfection *a. p. a.* of the first *B* necessarily leads to the application of the same imperfection to the second and third *B:*

The flexible character of the principles of imperfection may be illustrated by the following passage from the Trent Codex 89 (p. 246′; see the facsimile in *DTOe* VII):

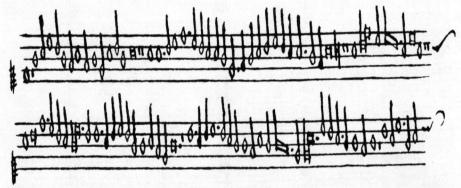

The sharp-like sign after the second *B* (near end of the first staff) means four *B*-rests (two and two). After this follow five perfections (groups to the value of three *S* each; a *punctus additionis* is missing

---

frequent. Here is a translation of this passage (lib. III, cap. XII; p. 214 of the German edition of the *Dodekachordon* by P. Bohn, Leipzig, 1899): 'What shall I say about imperfection? Franchinus [Gafurius] states and maintains emphatically that under no circumstances can a note be imperfected which stands before another of the same species. And yet how frequently does one see this rule broken, not only by mediocre musicians but also by Josquin des Près, the king of singers.'

after the ascending ligature), until we arrive at the first *B* of the second staff. Since this *B* is followed by a long series of *S* (or their equivalents in smaller values) one would expect imperfection *a. p. p.* to take place (see below, version a). This, however, is wrong as appears from the fact that one *S* is lacking at the end of the phrase. Actually, the first *B* of the second staff is perfect, as is also shown by the context of the other voices (version b):

(a)

(b)

Properly, the perfect quality of the initial *B* should be indicated by a *punctus divisionis* (see p. 115).

To rule 5: If a *B* is followed by two *S*-rests, the scribe usually makes a slight but important distinction. When the two rests are on different lines of the staff the first is meant to imperfect the preceding *B*, whereas the second belongs to the next perfection. If, on the other hand, both rests appear on the same line, both belong to the same perfection, and the *B* remains perfect:

The above rules and remarks explain the simplest and most important type of imperfection—the so-called *imperfectio ad totum*, i.e., 'imperfection of the whole' (of the note). In addition, there is an *imperfectio ad partem*, 'imperfection of a part' (of the note), which is discussed at great length by theoretical writers of the period, and which is used occasionally in musical practice. Generically, this term refers to all those cases in which a note is imperfected by a note two (or more) degrees removed from it in value. In the present mensuration this situation occurs chiefly when an *L* is followed or preceded by a *S*. Here, the *L* is considered as being composed of two *B*, one or both of which may be imperfected. Thus, reduction of the *L* from six to five or four *S* results:

More specifically, these examples illustrate the so-called *imperfectio ad partem propinquam (partes propinquas)*, in a contrast to the much rarer *imperfectio ad partem remotam (partes remotas)*, i.e., the imperfection of a note by one (or several) of the third-following degree, for instance, * of an *L* by an *M* in [3, 2]: 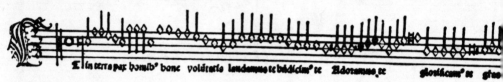 .

The following example, the beginning of the discant of the *Et in terra pax* from Pierre de la Rue's *Missa L'homme armé (Misse Petri de la Rue*, Petrucci, Venice, 1503), illustrates the problems one may encounter in this matter:

The rhythmic as well as the melodic design of the opening phrase would seem to suggest *imperfectio ad partem remotam*, i.e., imperfection of the *L* by the *M*:

However, this is wrong, as one will notice as soon as he comes to the two *B*, near the end of the staff where he will find that there is one *M* too many.   Actually, the *L* is imperfected by two *M*, as follows:

In cases like this where there is a long series of small values between two long values (*B* or *L*), the quickest way of determining the proper rhythm is to work backwards from the final *B*, which—at least, normally—will come at the beginning of a measure. This method, unmusical though it is, is frequently extremely useful.

Alteration. In the above explanations the case of two *S* placed between two *B* (see rule 2) has not yet been considered. In fact, another fundamental concept of perfect mensuration enters here, namely, alteration, which means, the doubling of the value of a note. The principle rule is as follows:

   6. If two *S* are placed between two *B*, the second *S* is doubled.

Examples:

(a)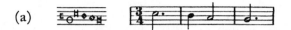

(b)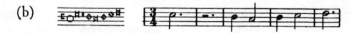

One might wonder why in example (b) the two identical rhythms of measures 3 and 4 are not both expressed by means of imperfection as follows: ♮I◇♮◇♮♮ . This manner of writing, however, is not permissible since it would contradict rule 1, according to which a *B* followed by another *B* must always be perfect. It appears, therefore, that the principle of alteration is the logical corollary of this rule. It is the only way of expressing the iambic rhythm immediately before a *B*.

If, on the other hand, this rhythmical combination is followed by another value, larger or smaller than the *B*, its rendering by means of imperfection *a p. a.* is possible and, indeed, was considered imperative. In other words, the rhythm ♩♩ was to be expressed by alteration ◇◇ only if its rendering by imperfection *a p. a.* ◇♮ was prevented by rule 1. Statements to this effect are to be found in practically all the theoretical treatises, and a strict observation of this principle is encountered in the practical sources. Frequently the following rule is given:

7. A note may be altered only if the succeeding note is of the next higher value. Therefore, the following renditions are correct:

◇◇♮ = |♩♩|♩.|; ◇♮◇ = |♩♩|♩| ; ◇♮♮ = |♩♩|♩.|♩.|

The following two examples from the *Odhecaton* (*Tandernaken*, tenor)[1] are instructive:

The dot of these examples is the *punctus divisionis*, see p. 115.

It must be noticed that occasionally the combination *B S S B* calls for an interpretation which does not conform with the above principles, namely, for imperfection: |♩ ♩|♩ ♩| . According to strict theory, such a meaning ought to be indicated by a *punctus divisionis*, as follows: ♮◇·◇♮ . However, examples calling for imperfection but lacking this dot are not unusual in musical documents. The ambiguity in this matter is explained as the result of an evolutionary shift. In the notation of the thirteenth, fourteenth, and early fifteenth centuries the com-

---

[1] See the facsimile edition, published by *Bolletino Bibliografico Musicale*, Milan, 1932, p. 75.

bination *B S S B* invariably calls for alteration. If in such a group
imperfection was intended, this had to be indicated by a *punctus divisionis*. In the late fifteenth century, however, the iambic rhythm resulting from alteration became obsolete and the principle of alteration
gradually fell into disuse. At this time, therefore, two *S* placed between
two *B* were understood normally to imply imperfection, even without
the *punctus divisionis*. However, the new interpretation did not completely supersede the old one; hence, one encounters a certain ambiguity
in respect to this combination in the sources of the Ockeghem—Josquin
period. The theorists definitely adhered to the old principle (Tinctoris,
see *CS* iv, p. 69; Pietro Aron, see E. Praetorius, *Die Mensuraltheorie
des Gafurius*, p. 47). In the practical sources, however, the opposite
interpretation seems to prevail. Two examples of the combination in
question appear in the beginnings of the nos. 667 and 1418 of the complete list of contents of the Trent Codices, given in *DTOe* vii, p. 52
and 76. A comparison with the transcriptions given in *DTOe* vii, p.
266 and *DTOe* xxvii, p. 16 shows that they both call for imperfection.
However, examples calling for alteration are also frequent. The
question certainly deserves fuller investigation. It appears that, depending on the result of such an investigation, the fundamental rules
(2) and (3) of imperfection (see p. 108) may have to be changed to run
as follows:

2a.   A *B* is perfect if followed by three *S*.
3a.   A *B* is imperfect if followed or preceded by less or more than
      three *S*.

Only in one case was the old principle of alteration never modified.
that is, if the two *S* were written in ligature *c. o. p.*:

8.   Two *S* in ligature *c. o. p.*, placed between two *B*, invariably call
     for alteration.

It may be noticed that imperfection is automatically ruled out in the
combination *B S S B B*, on account of rule 1, and that alteration is
naturally impossible if the second of the two *S* is replaced by its *valor*,
i.e., by smaller notes of the same value, as, for instance, *B S MM B*.

The following example from Obrecht's *Missa sub tuum praesidium*
illustrates both interpretations of the sequence *B S S B*. The first two
S, written in ligature *c. o. p.*, call, of course, for alteration. The third
and fourth *S*, however, must (according to the context of the other

voices) be interpreted as imperfection although the dot is missing:[1]

The following rule corresponds to rule 5:

9. A rest cannot be altered but may cause alteration of a note. Example: O♮⌐◦♮◦⌐♮ = $\frac{3}{4}$|♩.|♩♩|♩♩|♩.| .
The impossibility of altering a rest brings about an unequivocal indication of imperfection in the following combination: *B S(S) B.*[2]

Finally, it may be noticed that the principle of alteration comes into play also in the case of six *S* between two *B*. At first thought, such a combination would suggest two groups of three *S* each, so that the initial *B* remains perfect: ♮◦◦◦◦◦◦♮ = $\frac{3}{4}$ |♩. |♩♩♩|♩♩♩|♩.| . However, if rule 3 is applied, the first *S* would imperfect the preceding *B*, and the last *S* would be altered: $\frac{3}{4}$|♩♩|♩♩♩|♩♩|♩.| . The latter version would seem to deserve preference, but not to the entire exclusion of the former. As in the case of two *S*, alteration is impossible if the last *S* of the group is replaced by smaller values. Hence, in the following combination: *B S S S S S M M B* the first *B* of necessity remains perfect, because otherwise one *S* would be missing at the end of the phrase, before the final *B*.

Punctus divisionis. The above concepts of imperfection and alteration, ingenious though they are, do not prove sufficient for the clear rendering of every rhythmic combination. For instance, the following simple rhythm cannot be expressed in mensural notes by employing only the rules previously given: $\frac{3}{4}$| ♩ ♩|♩♩|♩.| . Indeed, one might suggest either: O♮◦◦◦♮ or: O♮◦◦♮♮ . But the former version means |♩.|♩♩♩|♩.| (rule 2) and the latter |♩.|♩♩|♩.|♩.| (rule 6).

In this case as well as in many others of a similar nature the *punctus divisionis (p.d.)* is used. As the name suggests, this *punctus* is a sign of division and, indeed, serves somewhat in the same capacity as the modern bar-line. For instance, a pair of *S*, placed between two *p.d.*, or between one *p.d.* and a *B*, is understood to constitute a perfection, demanding alteration of the second *S*. Thus, the above problem is easily solved by placing a *p.d.* after the first *S:* ♮◦·◦◦♮ (a; see below).

---

[1] In this example, as also in subsequent ones, groups of imperfection are indicated by a slur, groups of alteration by a square bracket.

[2] Here and in subsequent examples, brackets around *B, S,* etc. indicate rests to the value of these notes.

The *p.d.* is also needed in order to guarantee correct reading of the ambiguous combination *B S S B*. Indeed, ♮◊·◊♮ (b) clearly demands imperfection whereas in ♮·◊◊♮ (c) the dot emphasizes alteration.

Early theorists, delighting in intellectual subtleties, made further distinctions in this matter, introducing various names such as *punctus alterationis, punctus perfectionis, punctus imperfectionis*, etc. Actually, they all amount to the same thing, i.e., a sign of division in perfect mensuration, and they vary only with regard to certain secondary effects. For instance, in the first of the above three examples (a) the *p.d.*, in addition to its main function, causes alteration of the second *S*; hence it was regarded as a *punctus alterationis*. In the third example (c), its effect is to make perfect the first *B* which would otherwise be imperfect. For this reason it was called *punctus perfectionis*. In the second example (b) it was called *punctus imperfectionis* because the two *B* become imperfect. Since these distinctions are nothing but unnecessary complications in terminology, we shall disregard them completely, and shall refer to the sign in question as *punctus divisionis* exclusively.

The *punctus divisionis*, however, differs materially from the *punctus additionis* (or *augmentationis*), which, as explained above (p. 101) is identical with the dot in modern notation. This *punctus* does not mark off perfections, but adds to a given note one half of its value. The essential difference between these *puncti* lies in the fact that the *p.d.* may be employed only in perfect mensuration, whereas the *p.a.* occurs exclusively in connection with imperfect notes. This may be illustrated by the following two examples:

(a) O♮·◊♮ -$\frac{3}{4}$| ♩·|♩ ♩| (b) C♮ ◊♮ -$\frac{3}{4}$|♩|♩ ♩|♩|♩|

Although these two examples are identical not only in appearance but also in the metrical value of the individual notes, the dots serve two completely different functions. In the example (a) the first *B* is normally ternary, and the dot merely prevents it from becoming binary. In the second example, however, the first *B* is normally binary and its value is augmented by the dot.[1]

---

[1] The writers of the fifteenth and sixteenth centuries attempted to simplify the system of the numerous *puncti*, as it occurs in the treatises of the fourteenth century (see, e.g., *GdM* 1, 103 ff; *HdN* 1, 339). Generally, three kinds of *punctus* are mentioned in the writings from 1480 to 1550, namely, the *punctus divisionis, perfectionis*, and *additionis*. Gafurius goes even one step further and reduces their number to two; however, he does not identify the *punctus perfectionis* with the *punctus divisionis*, but rather with the *punctus additionis*. Accordingly, this *punctus* may occur both in perfect and in imperfect mensuration, although it actually serves an entirely different purpose in one and in the other. Unfortunately, this twofold meaning of the 'point of perfection' has been perpetuated by Th. Morley, in his well-known *Introduction to Practical Musicke* (London, 1597) whence it has been

Of course, in the mensuration which we are considering, namely, [3, 2] both types of *punctus* may occur, the *punctus divisionis* referring to the *tempus* which is perfect, and the *punctus additionis* referring to the *prolatio* which is imperfect: ♩♩♩ .

There even occur cases in which both *puncti* coincide, as in the following example where the dot functions as a *p.d.* with respect to the *tempus* by marking off a group of perfection, and as a *p.a.* with respect to the *prolatio* by adding half to the value of the *S*: ♩♩♩ . For an example, see the beginning of the discant of Facsimile 27.

Whether a given dot is a *p.d.* or a *p.a.* is generally apparent from the musical context. If a dot is a *p.a.*, a note of the next smaller species must always follow which provides the other half of the increase. Sometimes, the situation is obscured by the fact that this note does not directly follow the *p.a.*, but is separated from it by notes of greater value as here: ♩♩♩ . At first sight, one might believe this to be a *p.d.*; in such a case, however, there would be no place for the single *M* before the *B*. The interpretation as a *p.a.*, with syncopation following, is evidently correct.

In some documents of white notation the scribes distinguish between the *p.d.* and the *p.a.* by writing the former in a higher position or by giving it the shape of a check-mark: ♩♩♩ ; ♩♩♩ . This practice is observed, though not consistently, in Facsimile 30, in which the *S* is perfect (*prolatio perfecta*) and the *M* is, as always, imperfect.

Facsimile 26, containing a three-voiced *Ave regina* by Dufay, may be studied as a first example of *tempus perfectum*.

In the third measure of the piece we find an example of the 'Burgundian cadence' (see p. 106), with the sharped fourth and seventh. For the final cadence of the piece, a sharp is indicated only for the seventh (discant), not for the fourth (contra), while all the other cadences are without accidentals. Whether or not they should be modified according to the initial cadence, is a question which cannot be definitely answered. The champions of 'editorial accidentals' will, no doubt, argue that the sharps given for the first cadence are meant to indicate the intention of the composer with regard to all the cadences of this composition. The other school of thought will arrive at exactly the opposite conclusion,

adopted into an article by S. T. Warner, published in *Proceedings of the Musical Association*, London, 1918/19 (see also the article 'Notation' in Grove's *Dictionary*, 1938, vl. III, p. 654).

In contrast to all these interpretations, it is interesting to note that as early as the first years of the fourteenth century an eminent theorist has defined the *puncti* exactly as we have done. In Joh. de Muris *Ars discantus* we read (*CS* III, 92): 'How many *puncti* exist in music? Two. Which are these? The *punctus divisionis* and the *punctus augmentationis*. . . . The *punctus augmentationis* cannot be used except in binary numbers of prolations, as for instance in the major or minor prolation, in reference to a note equal to two notes [of the next smaller species].' About the meaning of *prolatio* in the early fourteenth century, see p. 340.

maintaining that the use of accidentals for three tones clearly shows that the other tones were meant to be diatonic. As a principle, this author inclines toward the latter view, because of its stricter adherence to the original. In the measure to the syllable 'sal-(ve)' there is a clear indication of a diminished triad b-d'-f'. As a matter of fact, diminished triads are extremely frequent in music from the thirteenth through the fifteenth century.

This composition also serves to illustrate the problem of text-underlaying in early music. Two facts can easily be seen: first, that the original frequently leaves considerable room for doubt and speculation as to the 'correct' placing of the words, as for instance in the initial phrase of our hymn; second, that in those cases in which the placement of the syllables is unambiguous, the result is frequently contradictory to the modern principles of 'good accentuation,' as, for instance, with the words *radix, angelorum, regina.* In general, it can be said that modern editors and interpreters are frequently misled and biased in this matter by ideas which actually did not prevail until the middle of the sixteenth century (*musica reservata*, Josquin and his pupils).

A transcription of the beginning is given in the appendix, No. 14.

As additional exercise, the transcription of Facsimile 24 may now be completed, by adding the first *Osanna* and the *Benedictus* [sections (3) and (4)]. In the latter section, which is in two parts only, a rest to the value of two *B* occurs simultaneously in both parts. That this is not a slip of writing is shown by the fact that the total of 24 *B* ($\frac{3}{4}$-measures) for this section (exclusive of the final *L*) is also indicated by the number of rests in the contra. This author is at loss to explain this strange interruption from the musical point of view; it may, however, have a
* liturgical significance.

Finally, an example may be studied which illustrates with particular clearness the difference between *tempus imperfectum* and *tempus perfectum.* The first *Kyrie* from Pierre de la Rue's mass *L'homme armé* (Facsimile 27) has *tempus perfectum* for the discant, *tempus imperfectum* for the alto, whereas the bass carries both signatures. This last manner of writing is indicative of canonic procedure. Actually two parts are derived from the bass line, the tenor in [3, 2] and the bass in [2, 2]. As is customary with the 'mensuration-canons' of this period, both parts start simultaneously, the tenor an octave higher, as is also suggested by the position of the question-mark-like *signum congruentiae.* The second of these signs indicates the end of the canonic voice (tenor) which, owing to the larger value of the *B* in [3, 2], does not consume the entire melody given for the bass. In the original edition (*Misse Petri de la Rue*, Petrucci, Venice, 1503) which is in four part books, the tenor (not reproduced here) carries the inscription: *resolutio ex basso.*

As has been pointed out previously (p. 117), the dot after the second note of the discant serves both as a *p.d.* and a *p.a.* In transcribing the piece it will be noticed that the final notes (L) of the various parts occur at different places. They must, of course, be held until the end of the piece. This practice, an example of which occurred already in our

FACSIMILE 26

MS Oxford, Bodleian Library *Canonici misc. 213* (*ca.* 1450)
Page 62

Facsimile 6 (see p. 16), obviates the use of a method which is frequently useful in the deciphering of difficult passages, that is, working backward from the end. See the transcription in appendix, No. 15.

This composition illustrates that problem of *musica ficta* which is most prominent in the sources of the sixteenth century, namely, that of the sharped leading tone. Several times combinations such as d-c-d occur which raise the question as to whether the c should be sharped (*subsemitonium*, lower semitone) or not (*subtonium*, lower whole-tone). Even among the more 'reserved' scholars and editors the inclination toward the *subsemitonium* is so common that it may seem to be almost dangerous to raise a voice of doubt. It is true that the evidence which can be obtained from a study of the sixteenth century keyboard and lute tablatures (particularly the numerous intabulations of motets and chansons) is, on the whole, in favor of the *subsemitonium*, at least for the cadential endings of passages or sections (much less so for leading-tones in the middle of a phrase; see W. Apel, *Accidentien und Tonalität*, p. 62 ff). On the other hand, there is the testimony of so distinguished a writer as Glarean (he cannot be considered a 'theorist' in the ordinary sense of the word) who in his most judicious and detailed analyses of the compositions of Josquin, Isaac, Mouton, and others never mentions the *subsemitonium*, but frequently refers to the 'whole-tone to be added below the fifth g-d', and similar formations (see the above-mentioned publication, p. 63, footnote). Summing up all the evidence available, a very cautious use of sharped sevenths would seem to be most proper for music prior to 1550. For compositions from the second half of the century, the use of the *subsemitonium* will probably have to be increased, particularly, of course, in the secular literature (chanson, madrigal, etc.).

D. Prolatio Perfecta

Prolatio perfecta may occur in combination with *tempus imperfectum* or *tempus perfectum*. In the former combination, indicated by ℂ or, in the present book, by [2, 3] the S equals three M ( ) with all the other values being imperfect. All the rules given for [3, 2] are valid, with the understanding that L, B and S are replaced by B, S and M. Only rule 8 is to be omitted since minims do not exist in ligatures.

It may be noticed that *imperfectio ad partem* (and *partes*) which is quite rare in [3, 2] is not infrequent in the present mensuration:

The combination S M M S, corresponding in *prolatio perfecta* to the ambiguous combination B S S B of *tempus perfectum*, is more likely to call for imperfection than for alteration since the former interpretation leads to a group of two perfect S: a rhythm that better conforms to the imperfect *tempus* than the group of three perfect S, which would result if alteration were applied: . However, the latter possibility cannot be ruled out, particularly in earlier sources.

The tenor of Facsimile 30 (p. 139) may serve as a simple example of this mensuration. Its melody is the famous *L'homme armé*. As will be

FACSIMILE 27

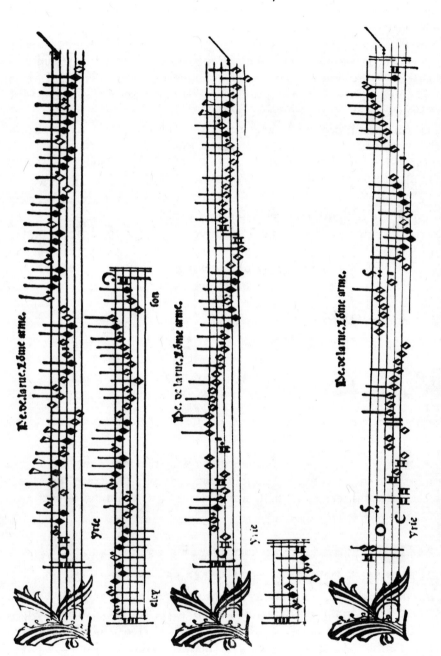

Pierre de la Rue, *Misse Petri de la Rue.* Venice, 1503

seen later (p. 138), its actual pitch is a fifth below the written notes (wrong
clef?).   See also p. 164 for remarks concerning the meter and tempo of
this piece.

In *tempus perfectum cum prolatione perfecta*, a mensuration which is
indicated by the sign ☉ or, in our explanations, by the symbol [*3, 3*],
the *B* equals three *S*(♮-◊◊◊) and the *S* equals three *M*(◊-♦♦♦), while
all the other values are imperfect.

The rules of imperfection and alteration apply without modification,
both in *tempus* and in *prolatio*.   However, the combination of two ternary
groupings brings about certain complications which demand attention.
Particularly the *imperfectio ad partem* (and *partes*), i.e., the imperfection
of the *B* by the *M* occurs more frequently and offers a greater variety
of combinations than in the previous mensurations.

Normally, the *B* equals nine *M*; but it may be reduced by imperfection of various kinds to any number of *M* down to four.   No further
reduction is possible since a value equaling three *M* can be expressed
by a *S*.   The following examples are illustrative:

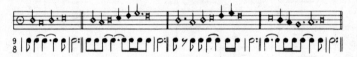

The perfect *B* is transcribed here by the sign ♩: which provides a simple and convenient expression, lacking in modern notation, of a note equalling nine eighth-notes.   It
may be noticed that these two dots are used in the same meaning in an *Ave regina coe-
lorum* from MS *Selden B 26*, f. 12' (reproduced in J. Stainer, *Early Bodleian Music*, I, no.
lvi).

Another peculiarity of this mensuration is the fact that an altered
note may be imperfected.   The following examples illustrate this point,
the theoretical interest of which is greater than its practical importance:

In the first example, for instance, the second *S* is altered from *3 M* to
6 M in order to make up the equivalent of a perfect *B* between the first
and the last *B*; simultaneously, however, this altered *S* is reduced from
6 M to *5 M* by the following *M*.   In the last example, alteration is applied to pairs of *M* as well as to pairs of *S*.   All the dots in these

examples are *puncti divisionis*. As a matter of fact, *puncti additionis* are not possible in this mensuration, except for the smallest values (*M*, *Sm*).

Examples of this kind are more prominent in the theoretical treatises (particularly of the late fourteenth century; see *GdM* 1, 126 ff.) than in the musical sources. On the whole, it must be noticed that pieces in [*3, 3*] are very rare in the manuscripts of white mensural notation. Only the earliest among them contain a few compositions in this mensuration. Two examples from MS *Canonici 213* of the Bodleian Library (Facsimiles 31 and 32, pp. 141 and 143) will be studied later, *in extenso*. However, certain passages may be briefly considered here, in order to illustrate the above explanations.

(H)ughe de Lantins' chanson *Ce ieusse fait* (Facsimile 31) shows no time signature. However, *tempus perfectum* is clearly indicated in the initial phrase of the discant, while the single *M*'s later in the course of this part, as well as the groups of three *M* and the combinations *S M* towards the end indicate *prolatio perfecta*. Here follows the transcription of the beginning:

The rhythm of the measures 7 and 8 is exactly the same as that of our first example illustrating the imperfection of altered notes. In fact, all these examples can be notated in a simpler way, by replacing the altered *S* by a *B*, and by applying to this *B* the methods of imperfection illustrated by our first examples of *tempus perfectum cum prolatione perfecta*.

As a further example, the tenor of the three-voiced *Vince con lena* of Facsimile 32 may be studied. Whereas the rhythm of the group *B S M*, beginning with the eighth note, is clear, the following group *B M S* leaves room for doubt as to whether the *M* imperfects the preceding *B* or the following *S*, in other words, whether the transcription: |♩.♩♪♩.| or: |♩. ♪♩| is correct. The former rhythm would seem to be more natural and indeed is the proper one, as appears from the context of the other parts.

The music for this chanson consists of two sections, the second of which begins with the words *Gia 'namorato* of the discant, and is indicated in the two other parts by the inscription: *S[ecund]a p[ar]s*. Whereas the first section contains various notational devices which will be explained later, the second section is free from such and may therefore be transcribed in full at this point in our study. The first measures are given in the appendix, No. 16. For the complete piece, see p. 151.

E. Modus and Maximodus

As has been pointed out previously (p. 99), *modus* and *maximodus* are mensurations which occur only in the 'Pfundnoten'-tenors of masses and motets. The metrical scheme to be observed with such a tenor is indicated by the length and arrangement of the rests which usually appear at the beginning of the tenor, or else are found somewhere during its course. According to whether these rests cover two or three spaces of the staff, the *modus* is imperfect or perfect, while their grouping together in pairs or in groups of three indicates imperfect or perfect *maximodus*:

[*II*, II]   [*II*, III]   [*III*, II]   [*III*, III]

The imperfect mensurations, as indicated by these signs, usually exist in theory only. Thus, the first sign shows that the L and the Mx are both binary, but does not necessarily imply a regular division into groups of two and twice two measures. Under the second sign we are likely to find (perfect) *modus*, that is, groups of three measures, but rarely any clear evidence of *maximodus* (groups of twice three measures). Examples of perfect *maximodus* (signs 3 and 4) are very rare. They occur only in the isorhythmic motets of Machaut and of some of his followers, such as Dunstable. The tenor of a *Veni sancte spiritus* by Dunstable from the Old Hall MS serves as an example:[1]

According to the mensuration [*III*, III] indicated by the rests, each L equals three B, and three L form a group equivalent to a Mx. Obviously, a first group of three L ends with the *p.d.* which also implies imperfection of the last L by the subsequent B. Another group of the same length is formed by the Mx and the L-rest (it may be noticed that the Mx itself was not admitted to be ternary; in other words, its maxi-
* mum value was six, not nine, B). Between these two groups we find a ligature B B L which, although the second B will have to be altered, would yield only two L. In order to reach the necessary number of three, the L must also be altered. The construction of the second half of the tenor is identical with that of the first. Here follows a schematic tran-

---

[1] The notation of the Old Hall MS is in black notes (see p. 364 ff).

scription of the first half in which the value of each note is given in figures indicating the equivalent number of *B* (rests in parentheses): (9) | 3 3 2 1 | 1 2 6 | 6 (3) | 3 3 3 |. Each *B* equals a ($\frac{3}{4}$-)measure of the upper parts. The sign at the end of the melody indicates that the melody has to be sung three times.

III. COLORATION

THE TERM coloration (*color*) first occurs in the fourteenth century to designate the use of red notes for certain variations from the normal values which, at that time, were written as black notes. In the later period of black notation, white forms were frequently used instead of the red ones. When, in the middle of the fifteenth century, the forms for the normal values changed from black to white ones, the special values expressed previously by white (or red) notes now came to be indicated by black notes so that the practice of 'coloration' became a process of 'blackening.' In current terminology, both terms are used synonymously. Much in the same way as the term 'white notes' comprises some black forms (*Sm, F, Sf*), there is one white form among the 'blackened notes,' namely, the *Sm* which, however, is of rare occurrence (no corresponding forms exist for the *F* and *Sf*):

	L	*B*	*S*	*M*	*Sm*
White notes:	⊨	⊨	◇	♦	♦
Blackened notes:	◢	◼	◆	♦	♦

Although the 'white' *M* and *Sm* are identical in shape with the 'blackened' *Sm* and *M* respectively, the context always discloses which note is meant by ♦ and ♦ . In the following combination, ◇♦♦♦ , all the notes are 'white,' namely, *S, M, Sm, Sm;* whereas in the following example, ◆♦♦♦ , they are all 'blackened,' namely, *S M Sm Sm*, as appears from the form of the *S*.

Coloration is employed to indicate certain changes in note-values and rhythm. The following two rules constitute the basis of this important concept:

1. A blackened note loses one-third of its value.
2. Blackened notes are always imperfect.

According to rule 1, we have: ◼=⅔⊨; ◆=⅔◇ . In other words, three blackened notes equal two white ones: ◼◼◼=⊨⊨ ; ◆◆◆=◇◇ . According to rule 2, we have: ◼=◆◆; ◆=♦♦ . Due to the imperfect quality of blackened notes, none of the principles of imperfection or alteration may be applied to them.

The explanations on coloration given by both early and recent writers are not altogether clear and satisfactory. A real insight into this matter can only be obtained if a strict distinction is made between the coloration applied to imperfect notes and that applied to perfect notes. This difference can easily be demonstrated in modern notation. If, e.g., two ordinary half notes are equalled by three notes, triplets result: $|\,\natural\,\natural\,|=|\,\natural\,\natural\,\natural\,|$; if, however, two dotted half notes are equalled by three notes, the result is not so much a change of note-values as a change of accent, inasmuch as the next-smaller values, namely, the quarter notes, remain unchanged: $|\,\natural\cdot\,\natural\cdot\,|=|\,\natural\,\natural\,\natural\,|$. Since this change of accent, which is equivalent to a change of meter from $\frac{6}{4}$ to $\frac{3}{2}$, is very common in the courantes of the suites by Bach and others, we may be permitted to refer to this type of coloration as 'courante-coloration,' as against 'triplet-coloration' for the former type. We shall now discuss the use of coloration in the various mensurations.

A. Coloration in Tempus Imperfectum Cum Prolatione Imperfecta

In this mensuration *B*, *S* and *M* (even *Sm*) may appear in groups of three blackened in the place of two white notes:

(a) is called *color temporis*, (b) *color prolationis*, whereas a special case of (c), consisting of a blackened *S* and a blackened *M*, is known as *minor color* (see below, p. 128). The following quotation from Cypriano de Rore's *Tutti i madrigali* of 1577 (the earliest instance of the partitura, see p. 19) provides a particularly clear illustration, owing to the score arrangement of the parts:

In this passage the blackened notes appear in groups of three *S*, whereas the following example from the *Odhecaton* (p. 95, *Gentil prince,* contra) shows the use of three blackened *M*:

The figure 3 is added here for the sake of clarity because of the identity in shape between the blackened *M* and the four normal *Sm* preceding them.

Particularly frequent is the simultaneous use of coloration in all the parts, as in the following final passage of Jo. Sthokem's (Stokeghem) *Porquoy je ne puis dire* (*Odhecaton,* p. 18'/19):

Transcription of the discant:

If such sections are of any considerable length, change of meter in transcribing is more convenient than the writing of triplets. If this method is used it is imperative to indicate clearly and accurately the time-relationship between the two meters, as in the following rendering of the above passage:

A specially important case of coloration in *tempus imperfectum* is the so-called *minor color*, consisting of a blackened *S* followed by a blackened *M*—a combination which may also be considered as the half of a *color prolationis* (half of three blackened *S*). No doubt this sequence originally indicated triplet rhythm, in conformity with the general meaning of coloration. In the later fifteenth century, however, its meaning changed into a dotted rhythm, identical with that expressed by a dotted *M* followed by an *Sm*: ♦ ♩ = [♩ ♪] = ♪♩ = ♩. ♪ .

Throughout the sixteenth century both manners of indicating dotted rhythm are used interchangeably, without any difference of meaning. It is not uncommon to find them side by side, not only in the same source, but in one and the same piece. J. Wolf (*HdN* I, 394) cites the following example from Obrecht's mass *Si dedero:*

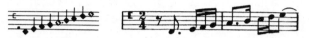

Other instances of the same practice occur in the contra of Facsimile 34 and in the chanson *Dangier tu m'a tollu* (Facsimile 25, p. 109, discant).

Although the second note of the *minor color* agrees in shape as well as in value with the second note of its equivalent in normal notation, these two notes should not be considered wholly identical. In the coloration-group, this note is a blackened *M* whereas, in the dotted manner of writing it is a 'white' or, more properly, a normal *Sm.* In studying a passage like that from Obrecht's mass the reader should not fail to notice this difference, for instance, between the second and the third note.

Minor color appears frequently in connection with half-blackened ligatures *c.o.p.*, as follows: 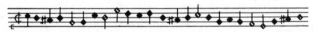 . See the explanations on half-coloration, p. 142.

Finally, as a curiosity we reproduce a passage from a late sixteenth century publication (Didier le Blanc, *Airs de plusieurs musiciens,* Paris, 1579; repr. H. Expert, *Monuments de la musique française de la Renaissance,* Paris, 1924, vol. III, 78) in which the 'inverted' form of the *minor color,* i.e., with the *M* preceding the *S,* is used:

Expert merely transliterates this passage into a rather obscure modern version: ¢ ♩•|♩♩♩♩|♩♩•|♩♩| . A proper transcription would be as follows:

A-près que tu m'eus of-fen - sé, J'in - vo -que d'A-mour

la puis-san-ce, af - fin - que mon cœur fut bles-sé

It is not without interest to notice in this song, not only the influence of the French humanism, with its novel but sterile ideas of 'correctness' in poetry and music, but also an early instance of the iambic rhythm which, under the names 'alla zoppa,' 'lombardic rhythm,' or 'Scotch snap,' is known as a characteristic feature of seventeenth century Italian and English music (Caccini, Monteverdi, Frescobaldi, Blow, Purcell, and others).   Much rarer than the *minor color prolationis*, as the combination *S M* might be called, is the *minor color temporis*, consisting of a blackened *B* and a blackened *S*, an example of which is shown at the beginning of the following chanson from the Chansonnier Laborde (p. 21):

Here, one might be doubtful as to whether to apply the change of rhythm from triplet to dotted notes.   However, the fact that even meter prevails strongly throughout the piece would seem to constitute an argument in favor of such a change:[1]

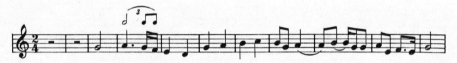

B.   Coloration in Tempus Perfectum cum Prolatione Imperfecta

In this mensuration coloration cannot be applied to the *S*, since this note already appears normally in groups of three.   However, it may be applied either to the *B* or to the *M*.   In the latter case it refers to an imperfect note and, hence, is triplet coloration: ♩.

---

[1] In the seventeenth century, the rhythmic clash caused by triplet-coloration, if used against normal values in other voice-parts, was no longer felt as an interesting subtlety but rather as an unnecessary disturbance.   As a result, explanations occur in this period which interpret such a group in duple rhythm as follows: (see, e.g., *MuT*, 16, referring to a treatise of Melchior Vulpius from 1641!).

It is not impossible to assume that this modification of rhythm made its appearance already in the late sixteenth century.   However, it can certainly not be applied to compositions of Josquin or Isaac, as has been advocated by E. Praetorius who, in his *Mensuraltheorie des Franchinus Gafurius*, on the basis of the above interpretation, arrives at a 'neue Uebertragung' of such compositions (p. 52, 107), rejecting the traditional method as a 'rhythmisches Labyrinth' (p. 106) or 'rhythmisches Zerrbild' (p. 52).   Such statements, resembling in character the familiar outcries over 'crude parallel fifths' and 'unbearable dissonances' hardly need to be refuted.   Suffice it to state once more that throughout the fifteenth and sixteenth centuries coloration in *tempus imperfectum* calls for triplets, with the exception of the *minor color*.

More important is the coloration of the *B*, according to the equation:
◫◫-▪▪▪ . The blackened *B* may, of course, be replaced by smaller
values, or two of them by a blackened *L*. The modern equivalent of
▪▪▪▪▪ is: $\frac{3}{4}|\natural.|\natural.|\frac{3}{2}\natural\natural\natural|$. If two of the $\frac{3}{4}$-measures are combined in one
$\frac{6}{4}$-measure, the courante-character of this rhythm becomes still more
evident: $\frac{6}{4}|\natural.\ \natural.|\frac{3}{2}\natural\natural\natural|$. This type of coloration (*color temporis*) is also
known as *hemiolia temporis* or *hemiolia major*.[1]

If in the above equation the *B* are replaced by *S* we find that there
are six on each side or, in other words, that the white *S* is equal in value
to the blackened *S*, both being represented by a quarter note of our
transcription. It should be noticed that this fact is not in keeping with
the first of our rules of coloration, according to which blackening always
entails a loss of one-third of the value. As a matter of fact, this rule,
in its unlimited application, holds good only in imperfect mensuration.
In perfect mensuration, however, it applies only to the largest value
(i.e., the *B* in *tempus perfectum*, the *S* in *prolatio perfecta*), not to the
smaller ones replacing it. This point will be clarified by the following
chart in which the *L* is considered the common point of departure, and
is, for the sake of comparison, represented by the figure 24:

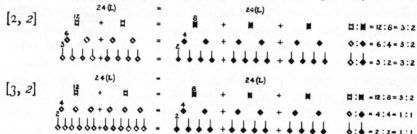

The result of coloration in [*3, 2*] is usually described as a change from
tempus perfectum (*B = 3S*) to *tempus imperfectum* (*B = 2S*). However,
it should be noted that not only does the *tempus* change but also that
the *modus* simultaneously changes, namely from imperfect (*L = 2B*) to
perfect (*L = 3B*). Therefore the result is correctly described as a transition from [II, 3] ([II, 3, *2*]) to [III, 2] ([III, 2, *2*]).

Instead of the method of transcription given above, in which, for the
passage in blackened *B*, two $\frac{3}{4}$-measures are combined into one $\frac{3}{2}$-measure,
modern publications generally retain the original meter as follows:
$\frac{3}{4}|\natural\ \natural|\natural\ \natural|$. Although this rendition is, of course, mathematically correct, it implies a syncopated effect which in our opinion is foreign to

---

[1] *Hemiolia* is Greek for one-and-half.

coloration. The meaning of coloration is not a jazz-like suppression of the strong beat, as in (a), but a change of accent, as in (b):

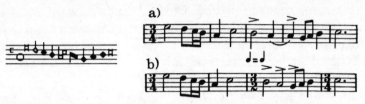

This point may be further clarified by the following consideration. There frequently occur passages in coloration the rhythm of which could easily be expressed in normal notes, and in which, moreover, the writing in white notes actually duplicates the notation in blackened notes. For instance, in the following example the values of the black notes are the same as those of the white notes, namely, 2, 1, 1, and 2 *S*: However, one should not jump to the conclusion that both progressions are plainly identical. There remains, indeed, the above explained difference in phrasing or accent:

This difference is obscured if $\frac{3}{4}$-measures are used for the blackened notes. But it was undoubtedly this change in accent which the old masters wanted to stress by the employment of coloration. H. Bellermann (*MuT*, p. 27) rightly points out that this rhythmical finesse still persists in the works of Bach and Handel, but was lost in the period of the Viennese classics.[1] As an example, he cites the following passage from Handel's *Messiah* in which coloration, although it is not notated, is clearly suggested by the original English text, but is obscured in Mozart's German version:

glo - ry, the glory of the Lord shall be re-vea - led
Eh - re, die Eh - re des Herrn —— wird of - fen-bar

What is true of Handel and Bach is certainly even more true of the masters of the fifteenth and sixteenth centuries, who still possessed a notational method of indicating this rhythmical effect. Unfortunately, in their case Bellermann fails to observe the principle which he expounds so clearly in his remarks concerning Bach and Handel (see, e.g., the passage from Dufay's mass *Se la face ay pale, MuT*, p. 33).

Before transcribing a passage in coloration the student is advised to

---

[1] As is well known, it has been revived by Brahms.

count the number of *B* involved. If there are three *B* (or their equivalent in smaller or larger values), as is normally the case, the passage will occupy exactly two $\frac{3}{4}$-measures or one $\frac{3}{2}$-measure, as in all the above examples. There are cases, however, in which the blackened notes are not sufficient in number to constitute a complete measure, for instance in the following passage from the same mass (see *MuT*, p. 34):

Here, the group in coloration which comprises notes in the equivalent of only two blackened *B*, is completed by a group of white notes (*S M M*) in the value of a third *B*. The use of the white instead of the blackened forms is admissible because they have identical values (see p. 131).

More interesting is a passage from **Hughe de Lantins'** *A madame playsante*, in which the coloration-group is split into two sections by an intermediate section in white notes (see the facsimile no. 4 in J. Stainer, *Dufay and His Contemporaries*, London, 1898):

If one transcribes this passage in $\frac{3}{4}$-meter throughout, one arrives at a result (a) which, although mathematically correct, is musically dull. However, the melody becomes alive and corresponds much more closely to the text (cf. the words 'ung chapelet') if the meter of the transcription is changed according to the notation of the original, as in (b):

These two transcriptions illustrate two different concepts of syncopation, the first of which is based upon the idea of 'omitted strong beats in

unchanged meter,' whereas the second involves an irregular succession of strong beats due to change of meter. While the former meaning is the familiar one (particularly in modern jazz), the latter prevails in early music (particularly in the fourteenth century, see pp. 395 ff, 414) as well as in the works of contemporary composers, such as Hindemith and Stra-
* vinsky, who frequently mix measures of $\frac{2}{4}$, $\frac{5}{4}$, $\frac{7}{4}$, etc.

A similar passage occurs at the beginning of the second staff of Facsimile 23. The student is advised to transcribe the whole piece, Dufay's chanson, *Quel fronte signorille*, which according to the inscription 'Romae ccmposuit' was the fruit of his trip to Italy. We suggest the following manner of transcription (beginning with the last two notes of staff 1):

Slightly more difficult than Dufay's chanson is a motet, *Anima mea*, by Leonel [Power][1] which is reproduced on Facsimile 28. The tenor as well as the contra show several complete groups of coloration (*L B, B B B, B B S S*), each of which is the equivalent of a $\frac{3}{2}$-measure. The single black *B* at the end of the first staff of the tenor has no particular significance; its value of 2 *S* could also be expressed by a white *B*, imperfected by the preceding S. The last black *B* of the contra, however, is part of a split group of coloration, the other parts of which (S S B) are found shortly before. The rhythm of this passage is exactly the same as that from *Quel fronte signorille*.

Particularly interesting is a group of black notes: *B M M S M* which occur in the middle of the second staff of the discant. These notes, which together have the value of a perfect white *B*, must be read in [3, 3] and therefore, must be transcribed as a $\frac{9}{8}$-measure or as triplets within a $\frac{3}{4}$-measure (the *B* is reduced by imperfection to the value of 4 *M*). A similar combination of notes occurs at the end of the third staff, but with two white M instead of the black *S* and *M* of the other group.

---

[1] The composer's name is given in the MS Modena, Bibl. Estense, *L. 471*.

FACSIMILE 28

MS Florence, Biblioteca Nazionale *Magl. XIX. 112 bis* (late 15th century)
Pages 32', 33

The blackened *B M M* of the second group can be interpreted in two ways, either in the triplet rhythm that is clearly indicated in the former group, or else as an example of *minor color temporis*, that is, in dotted rhythm. The relatively early date of the composition (*ca.* 1450) weighs in favor of triplet rhythm which is the original meaning of all coloration groups.[1]

The initial note of the tenor is a *Mx*, as is also the second note of the ligature near the middle of the next staff. A *p.d.* is missing at the end of the first staff of the discant. The Modena MS shows several sharps (evidently all added by a later hand) which would make the following tones B-naturals instead of B-flats: third note of the tenor; sixth note of the second staff of the tenor; fourth-to-the-last note of the second staff of the contra. The beginning of the tenor is transcribed in the appendix, No. 17.

As a last example, Facsimile 29, containing a three-voice chanson ✶ *Monsieur*, may be studied.

This piece illustrates the special difficulties which, in some sources, arise from the careless writing and from clerical errors. Following is a list of the most important ones:
Discant: (1) The clef is missing; the melody begins on c″. (2) The ninth note is probably a plain *S* on c″, not a dotted *M* on d″. (3) The vertical dash near the middle of the second staff is not a B-rest, but a mere sign of demarcation, indicating the beginning of the second section; the same sign occurs in the tenor; however, both voices begin simultaneously with the contra in which there is no such sign. Tenor: (1) The first note of the second ligature is meant to be *L*. (2) The sixth note on the first staff of p. 23 should be white. Contra: (1) The third note after the fermata is stricken out; (2) The next-to-last *S* should be c.
Of special interest is the passage which begins with the eleventh note (e) of the third line (discant), and which recurs on the first line of the right-hand page (beginning with the 16th-note). The original writing shows the combination *S M . Sm Sm Sm*, which yields five *M*. From the context, however, it appears that this passage must fill in a whole measure, or six *M*. In other words, the meaning is not ♩♩♪ ♫ but ♩ ♩ ♪♫ . Apparently, this is not a clerical error but an emergency manner of writing necessitated by the fact that the latter rhythm cannot correctly be expressed in mensural notes.

The use of coloration in *tempus perfectum* persisted throughout the seventeenth century. In many courantes of this period the change from $\frac{6}{4}$ to $\frac{3}{2}$ is indicated by blackened notes. Blackened notes are also frequently used in later sources (after 1550) for the expression of the iambic rhythm which was formerly indicated by alteration, e.g.: ○◆◆◇◾◇◆◾◾ instead of: ○◆◆◇◾◇·◇◆◾ .

C. Coloration in Prolatio Perfecta

Here only one type of coloration is practically possible, namely, that of the *S:* ℭ◆◆◆◆◆ = ⅜|♩·♩·|♩♩♩♩| (*color prolationis, hemiolia minor, hemiolia*

---

[1] In the MS Modena both groups show the same notation, i.e., that of the second group in our MS.

FACSIMILE 29

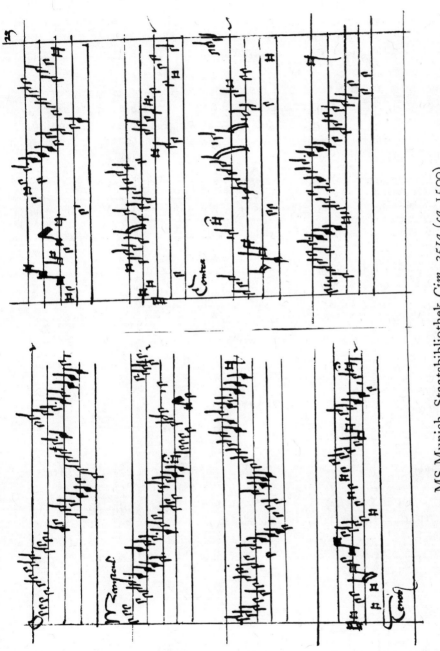

MS Munich, Staatsbibliothek *Cim. 351a* (*ca.* 1500)
Pages 22', 23

prolationis). Aside from the shift to smaller values, the explanations given for *tempus perfectum* apply without modification. Again, coloration affects not only the *prolatio*, which changes from perfect to imperfect, but also the *tempus*, which changes from imperfect to perfect. In other words, the result is a transition from [2, *3*] to [*3*, *2*], or, in modern terms, from $\frac{6}{8}$ to $\frac{3}{4}$.

Facsimile 30, the tenor of which has already been studied, serves as an example. The coloration-group *M M S S* on the second staff of the discant (between 'cum gloria' and 'iudicare vi[vos]') begins in the middle of a $\frac{6}{8}$-measure, so that the following succession of measures: $\frac{3}{8}$, $\frac{3}{4}$, $\frac{3}{8}$ results in the transcription.

In this piece not only the white form of the *Sm* (see p. 87) but also the white form of the *F*, with two flags, is used (e.g., discant, near end of the third staff). The distinction between the *p.a.* and the *p.d.*—the latter being placed higher or lower than the note—is rather consistently carried out. The tenor is erroneously notated a fifth too high, as has already been pointed out. The beginning of the discant and tenor are transcribed in the appendix, No. 18.

In [*3*, *3*], triplet-coloration is of course impossible, due to the absence of binary values. Courante-coloration can be applied in different ways. In *color temporis* three blackened *B* will be equal to two white ones. Since a white *B* equals 9 *M*, the blackened *B* is worth 6 *M*; hence, if a blackened *B* is broken up into two *S*, each of these is worth three *M* and, therefore, equal to the white *S*. Example:

The latter transcription is preferable (three $\frac{6}{8}$-measures are written instead of one $\frac{18}{8}$-measure).

In *color prolationis*, three blackened *S* will be equal to two white ones, thus occupying two-thirds of a full measure. Since the white *S* equals three *M*, the blackened *S* will be equal to two *M*. If, in such a combination, two blackened *S* are replaced by one blackened *B*, this *B* equals in value 4 *M*. Example:

FACSIMILE 30

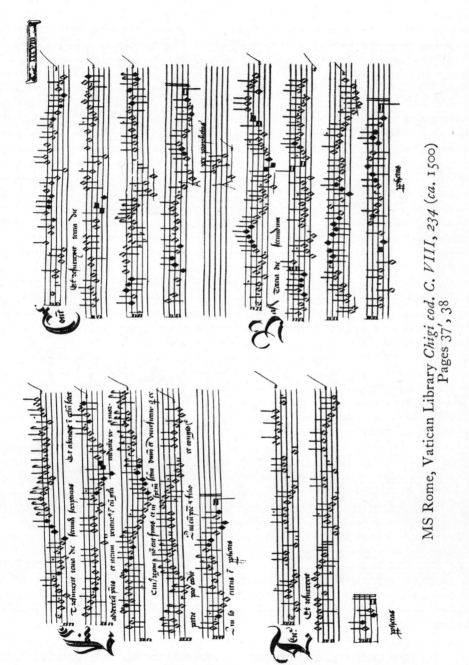

MS Rome, Vatican Library *Chigi cod. C. VIII, 234 (ca. 1500)*
Pages 37', 38

It appears that the value of the blackened notes essentially depends upon whether they form a part of *color temporis* or *color prolationis*. Shorter groups, consisting chiefly of *S*, are likely to be *color prolationis*, longer ones, particularly a group of three *B*, are likely to be *color temporis*. In cases of doubt the proper evaluation must be derived from the context.

Several instances of *color temporis* are found in Hughe de Lantins' chanson *Ce ieusse fait* (Facsimile 31) which already has been considered in part (p. 123). In addition to various examples of the imperfection of the *B* from nine to five *M* (usually in the combination: *S B M*) there is, at the beginning of staff 6, an example of a *L* being imperfected by a preceding as well as by a following *S* which reduce its value from six to four *S*.

The application of our 'rules of the B and B-flat' (see p. 104) is recommended for the discant of this piece which is another example of the partial signatures. Its beginning furnishes a remarkably early instance of the imitation in the fifth. See the transcription in the appendix, No. 19.

The poetical-musical structure of this chanson is that of the mediaeval rondeau, as it originated with the trouvères of the thirteenth century. The music falls into two sections, a and b (b begins with the words *Je seroye plus*, end of the first staff), which are repeated according to the scheme A B a A a b A B (capital letters indicate the refrain, i.e., repeated text). The underlaying of the full text is as follows:

A 1. *Ce ieusse fait ce que ie pence—Et se je fusse en mon pays*
B 2. *Je seroye plus que assouvis—D'avoir une telle chevance*
 a 3. Car iay desyr de l'aliance—De la tres belle au doulx cler vis
A 4. *Ce ieusse fait ce que ie pense—Et se je fusse en mon pays*
 a 5. Donc ne l'ames en oubliance—Si fort y ay mon cuer assis
 b 6. Et si luy plest que ses amis—Soie de tout iay souffisance
A 7. *Ce ieusse fait ce que je pence—Et se je fusse en mon pays*
B 8. *Je seroye plus que assouvis—D'avoir une telle chevance.*

In the modern transcription, the distribution of the text can conveniently be indicated as follows (refrain in italics):

a		b	
1.4.7.	*Ce ieusse*.........	2.8.	*Je seroye*...........
3.	Car iay..........	6.	Et si...............
5.	Donc ne.........		

Examples of *color prolationis* occur in the *Vince con lena* of Dom. Bartholomeus de Bononia (Facsimile 32). The coloration passage near the end of the third staff includes a full group of *color prolationis*, since it consists of notes to the value of three blackened *S*:

FACSIMILE 31

MS Oxford, Bodleian Library *Canonici misc. 213 (ca.* 1450)
Page 46

The two blackened *S* at the beginning of the discant are an incomplete group of coloration and, hence, bring about syncopated rhythm:

For the full discussion of the piece, see p. 151.[1]

D. Half-coloration

Half-coloration is applied to two-note ligatures, particularly *c.o.p.*, and to single long notes. The former procedure, which has already been referred to on p. 129, simply means that of the two notes of the ligature one is normal, the other blackened. The contra (abbreviated *ont[ra]*; the initial C is missing) of a *Quia respexit* from Brussels, Bibliotheque Royale *MS 6428*, serves as an illustration:

The vertical dash through the circle indicates *tempus perfectum diminutum* (see p. 148) which, however, in the present case has no different meaning from the ordinary *tempus perfectum* (see p. 191 f).

The first and second passage in coloration are *color temporis* whereas, in the second line, there is an example of *minor color*. It is interesting to note that the dotted rhythm expressed by the latter is exactly the half of that expressed by the same notes (*S* and *M*) at the beginning of the second passage:

Half-blackening is also applied occasionally to single notes of larger value: . Such a note may be considered as being equal to two notes of the next smaller value, the second of which is blackened. Thus,

---

[1] Blackened notes were also used in those passages, not infrequent in the compositions of Dufay and his successors, in which a single part is notated 'divisi,' i.e., with two simultaneous notes instead of a single one. For an example see the reproduction of the contra of *Exultavit*, p. 192. It is probably this usage which accounts for the sixteenth century English practice of writing a middle part of a keyboard composition in blackened notes (see p. 12).

FACSIMILE 32

Oxford, Bodleian Library *Canonici misc. 213* (*ca.* 1450)
Page 135

in *tempus perfectum* the *L*, instead of equalling in value two white *B* of three *S* each, would be equal to one white *B* and one blackened *B*, with a total of five *S*. Similarly in *prolatio perfecta*, the half-blackened *B* would be equal to 5 *M*, instead of 6. Such notes occur in the *Sanctus* of Isaac's *Missa Paschalis*, which is reproduced on p. 43 of J. Wolf's *Schrifttafeln* and—together with a transcription—in his *HdN* 1, p. 420. Theorists also discuss the value of half-blackened notes in imperfect mensuration. Here, half-blackening would entail a loss of one-eighth of the original value, e.g., the half-blackened *L* would equal 4 + 3 *M*, instead of 4 + 4. Whether these speculations have practical significance this writer is not in the position to say (see *HdN* 1, 403).

IV. PROPORTIONS

A. History and Terminology

THE USE of proportions, that is, of the diminution and augmentation of metrical values in certain arithmetic ratios, is a characteristic feature of the Flemish music of the fifteenth and early sixteenth centuries.[1] Its history, however, goes back to considerably earlier periods. The first traces of this method are encountered in some of the *clausulae* of the period of Perotinus (*ca.* 1200), in which the liturgical melody serving as a tenor appears twice, the second time in half or double the values of the first appearance (see p. 245). The same procedure is normally found in the tenors of the motets by G. de Machaut (see p. 358). Here again, the second section of the tenor repeats the melody of the first in notes of half the value, each *L* being replaced by a *B*, etc. In the later fourteenth century principles evolved which allowed one to indicate the reduction of value, not by actually using smaller notes, but by certain signs of diminution. It is this idea which is the basis of the proportions proper.

The earliest mention of proportions is in the *Libellus cantus mensurabilis secundum Joh. de Muris* (*CS* III, 58), a treatise of the mid-fourteenth century, in which *diminutio* (i.e., *dupla*) is discussed. Proportions are explained more fully by Prosdocimus de Beldemandis, in his *Tractatus practice de musica mensurabili* of 1408. He mentions *proportio dupla, tertia, sesquialtera, sesquitertia* and *dupla sesquiquarta*, and indicates the signs designating them (*CS* III, 218). Guilelmus Monachus, in his *De preceptis artis musice libellus*, (*ca.* 1460) expounds the entire system in a very learned manner, and illustrates it by numerous examples (*CS* III, 277-288). The subject is treated most exhaustively by Tinctoris in his *Proportionale musices*, written around 1480 (*CS* IV, 153-177), and by Gafurius in his *Practica musicae*, Milan, 1497. In this period the system of proportions developed far beyond the bounds of practical application into the realm of pure speculation. Gafurius, for instance, does not hesitate to explain proportions calling for a diminution in the ratio of 9:23. Needless to say, even the theoretical value of such extravagances

---

[1] Nonetheless, the term 'proportional notation,' which is frequently used as a name for mensural notation, is a misnomer.

is doubtful, to say nothing of their bearing on actual music. It will suffice to indicate only briefly these theoretical proportions in a general survey; then we shall proceed to an explanation of those which are of practical application.

The mathematical foundation of the entire system of proportions as given in the above treatises goes back to Boethius.[1] Following his teaching the theorists of the late fifteenth century distinguished between five species of proportions, i.e.: *genus multiplex, genus superparticulare, genus superpartiens, genus multiplex superparticulare* and *genus multiplex superpartiens*. In terms of modern arithmetic, the first genus comprises all fractions the denominator of which is 1, e.g., *proportio dupla* $= \frac{2}{1}$; *tripla* $= \frac{3}{1}$; *quadrupla* $= \frac{4}{1}$, etc. The second genus comprises all fractions the numerator of which is one more than the denominator. In Latin terminology, these fractions were indicated by the prefix *sesqui-* (*semique-*), which actually means addition of the half: $1 + \frac{1}{2} = \frac{3}{2}$. In conjunction with the terms *-altera, -tertia, -quarta* etc., it designates the fractions $\frac{3}{2}, \frac{4}{3}, \frac{5}{4}$, etc. The third species includes fractions in which the numerator is two, three, etc., more than the denominator. For instance, *proportio superbipartiente tertias* means a fraction in which the denominator is 3 (*tertias*), and the numerator is two (*bi-*) more than the denominator, i.e., $\frac{5}{3}$. Likewise, *proportio supertripartiente quintas* is the fraction $\frac{8}{5}$. In the fractions of the fourth species, which in a way is a combination of the first and the second, the denominator must be multiplied by a given number, before one is added. For instance, *proportio tripla sesquitertias* means a fraction in which the denominator 3 (*tertias*) has to be multiplied by 3 (*tripla*) and then augmented by one (*sesqui-*), i.e., $\frac{10}{3}$. Similarly, *proportio quadrupla sesquiquinta* is $\frac{21}{5}$. Finally, in the last species (combination of the first and third) a similar process of multiplication is applied to the proportions of the third genus. For instance, *proportio dupla supertripartiente quartas* means that the denominator is 4 (*quartas*), and that the numerator is $4 \times 2 + 3 = 11$; therefore, the fraction is $\frac{11}{4}$. The inverted fractions are indicated by the prefix *sub-*; for instance, *proportio subdupla supertripartiente quartas* means $\frac{4}{11}$.

These arithmetical proportions are used in mensural notation to diminish or increase the value of a note in certain ratios. As will be explained later (p. 191 ff), the whole system of mensural notation rests upon the

---

[1] Boethius, the authoritative philosopher of the early sixth century, deals with the proportions from the standpoint of arithmetic. Musical theorists of the Middle Ages frequently used the terms to denote ratios of vibrating strings, i.e., intervals. For instance, *sesquialtera* is the fifth because strings sounding c and g are in the ratio of 3 to 2.

principle of a fixed, i.e., unchangeable unit of time, the *tactus*, a beat in moderately slow speed (M.M. 50-60) which pervades the music of this period like a uniform pulse. The *tactus* (*t*) is normally represented by the *S: S = t*, with the other notes being multiples or fractions thereof, e.g., in [3, 2]: *B = 3t, M = ½t*, etc. These normal values of the various notes are called *integer valor*. If a note appears in proportion, its value is that part or multiple of its *integer valor* which is indicated by the proportion. Oddly enough, the proportions are used in mensural notation in exactly the reverse meaning they would seem to indicate. For instance, *proportio dupla* ($\frac{2}{1}$) and *tripla* ($\frac{3}{1}$) do not indicate multiplication, but division of the values by two or three. In other words, all the proportions which are indicated by fractions larger than one (and only these are of practical significance) are diminutions. For instance, the value of a *S* in *proportio dupla* ($\frac{2}{1}$) is $\frac{1}{2} t$, while the value of a perfect *B* in *proportio sesquialtera* ($\frac{3}{2}$) is $\frac{2}{3}$ of *3t = 2t*.

It goes without saying that these calculations are given here merely for purposes of demonstration. For the study of musical examples, appropriate groups of notes rather than single notes should be considered. The general principle may be formulated as follows: In a proportion indicated by the sign $\frac{m}{n}$, m *S* equal n *S* of the *integer valor*. For instance, in the following example: ○ ◆◆◆ $\frac{4}{3}$ ○◆◆◆ the four notes which follow the sign $\frac{4}{3}$ occupy the same space of time as three *S* of the *integer valor*, that is, the same time that is consumed by the three notes preceding the proportion. Similarly, in *proportio dupla* or *tripla*, two or three *S* of the proportion will be equal to one of the *integer valor*. All these facts are easily retained if one understands that in a sign of proportion such as $\frac{5}{3}$ or $\frac{3}{1}$ the denominator refers to the notes preceding the sign (*integer valor*), and the numerator to those following it (proportion).

In addition to the fraction-like signs of the system just explained, certain special symbols were used for the simplest proportions. *Proportio dupla*, also called *diminutio* or *diminutio simplex*, is usually indicated thus: ⊃ ; ₵ ; C2 ; ⦰ ; O2 ; *proportio tripla* thus: C3 ; O3 . In certain early sources, around 1400, the following modifications are used for *proportio dupla:* ₵ ; ⊖ .[1]

Duple and triple proportion are not only the most frequent, but also, in a way, the most difficult ones. Since they have many features in common, it seems advisable to explain their general principles in conjunction.

[1] See Facsimiles no. 39, 71, and 88.

B.   Proportio Dupla and Tripla in General

The following equations may be considered as the basis for the application of these proportions to either *tempus imperfectum* or *tempus perfectum:*

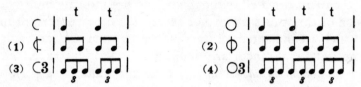

These equations lead to the following scheme of transcription for a series of *S:*

Whereas in the two *integer valor-* mensurations the *tactus* falls on the *S*, it falls, in the proportions, on a group of two or three *S* or, in other words, on an (imperfect or perfect) *B*. It is for this reason that the *integer valor* was called by Italian sixteenth century theorists *alla semibreve,* and the proportion (particularly the *dupla*) *alla breve.* This name, together with the sign ₵ exists still today, the last vestige of the proportional system.

It will be noticed that, in the case of (2) and (3), there exists a certain contradiction regarding the grouping of the *S*, insofar as different groupings are indicated by the plain mensural sign and by its proportional variety. Indeed, whereas the semicircle suggests groups of two *S*, the sign C3 actually calls for groups of three; similarly, whereas the full circle would seem to indicate groups of three *S*, groups of two are actually demanded by Φ . Briefly, both signs of duple proportion, (1) and (2), must be read in *tempus imperfectum* ($B = 2 S$), and both signs of triple proportion, (3) and (4), must be read in *tempus perfectum* ($B = 3 S$).

The schematic example on page 148, bottom, showing four proportional readings of the same melody, serves as a further illustration of this important point.

It appears that with each of our four species the rhythm expressed by a proportional sign can also be expressed in *integer valor*, if the next smaller note values are used, as follows:

(1) ¢ ♮ ◊ ♦ ♦ = C ◊ ♦ ♦ ♦ (2) Φ ♮ ◊ ◊ ♮ = ◊ ◊ ♦ ♦ ◊

(3) C3 ♮ ◊ ♦ ♦ ◊◊ = C ◊ ♦ ♦ ♦ ♦ ♦ (4) O 3 ♮ ◊· ♦ ♦ ◊♮ = ⊙ ◊ ♦· ♦ ♦ ♦ ♦ ◊

Simultaneously with the shift of note values indicated by these equations there occurs a displacement of the mensurations. That which is written proportionally as *tempus* actually is the *prolatio* of the *integer valor*, etc. In order clearly to indicate this important fact, it may be useful to introduce terms such as 'notated *tempus*' and 'actual *tempus*.' In both proportions, then, the following displacements occur:

notated *modus* = actual *tempus*
notated *tempus* = actual *prolatio*.

The observation of these facts is particularly useful in the two quasi-contradictory proportions (2) and (3). When it has been said above that the following sign, Φ, calls for *tempus imperfectum* (in spite of the whole circle), we must now add that this *tempus imperfectum* is only illusory—that is, it appears merely in the writing; in reality, however, it is *prolatio imperfecta*. This same *prolatio imperfecta* is already present in the *integer valor* O, so that actually no change in mensuration occurs.

On the other hand, the triple meter in the *tempus* of the *integer valor* is continued as *modus* in the proportion. As a matter of fact, in practically all cases one will find that the passage in proportion contains groups of three *B* so that it may naturally be interpreted in the sense of *modus perfectus*. This perfect *modus*, then, actually preserves that perfect mensuration which, in the *integer valor*, is represented by the *tempus*. Therefore, it is generally possible to maintain in the proportion the ¾-meter used for the transcription of the integer valor. One might simply say—as the old theorists frequently do—that the whole circle refers, not to the (notated, imperfect) *tempus*, but to the (notated, perfect) *modus*, which, owing to the diminution, becomes the (actual, perfect) *tempus*. In this connection it is interesting to note that various theorists of the sixteenth century, by disregarding the reduction of the note values, adopt the sign Φ as an indication for *modus perfectus*, although without consistency (see the table of Ornithoparchus, *HdN* 1, 413).

The result of the above explanations may be summarized as follows:

The four elementary proportions ¢;Φ;C3;O3 are nothing but the four elementary mensurations C;O;C;⊙ , but written in the next-higher note values and performed with the *tactus* falling on the *B* instead of on the *S*. Their notational and actual significance appears from the following tabulation:

Notated				Actual			

¢ [II, 2]   C [2, 2]
Φ [III, 2]   O [3, 2]
C3 [II, 3]   C [2, 3]
O3 [III, 3]   ⊙ [3, 3]

As an illustration, we reproduce a well-known melody in what may be regarded as the modern equivalent of *integer valor* (O) and proportion (Φ):

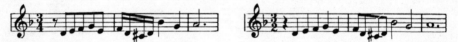

The following example shows the application of the four proportions to one and the same melody. The proportions start with the sign ? , the first three notes being in *intĕger valor*:

After these general explanations, we now turn to the detailed study of the various proportions as they occur in the musical sources.

C. Proportio Dupla

An examination of the sources of the fifteenth and sixteenth centuries reveals interesting and significant changes in the practical application of this proportion. In the earliest manuscripts of white notation (as well as in the latest sources of black notation, see p. 404 f) the *diminutio* is used chiefly in order to introduce into perfect prolation short groups of duplets, which can be rendered in modern writing as under (a) or as under (b):

(a) [musical notation example]

(b) [musical notation example]

Examples are found in Facsimile 32 which already served as an illustration of coloration in [*3, 3*]. Several times, groups of six *S* occur under the sign ⊃. Such a group equals three *S* or, in other words, a perfect *B*, of the *integer valor*, thus filling in one complete $\frac{9}{8}$-measure of the transcription. It is interesting to consider the reason why the desired change of rhythm from triplets to duplets is indicated by a proportional sign, instead of simply changing from *prolatio perfecta* to *prolatio imperfecta*, as follows: [musical notation].

Apparently, the reason is that this manner of writing may be misinterpreted, by considering the *M* as the unchanged temporal unit, instead of the *S*. Thus, the result would be as under (a), instead of as under (b):

(a) [musical notation example] (b) [musical notation example]

The mensuration of the piece is [*3, 3*], $\frac{9}{8}$-meter, with some passages in [*2, 3*], $\frac{6}{8}$-meter. However, neither of these meters is always strictly observed. The section in [*3, 3*], middle of the second staff, includes 12 *M*, instead of 9, and the section in [*2, 3*] beginning near the end of the first line of the contra includes one half-measure ($\frac{3}{8}$) in addition to five full $\frac{6}{8}$-measures.

As has previously been remarked (p. 123), the piece consists of two sections, a and b. Its musical form is that of the *ballata* (the French *virelai*): A b b a A

A:	*Vince con lena* . . . . *al periglioso scoglio*	(ripresa)
b:	Gia n'amorato . . . . a gli amorosi segni	(piedi)
b:	Anci divene . . . . costumi degni	
a:	Unde mie force . . . . tuo che voglio	(volta)
A:	*Vince con lena* . . . . *al periglioso scoglio*	(ripresa)

For the repetition of the *secunda pars* (piedi) a *seconda volta*- ending is provided in the short passage marked *clus* (*cluso*, *chiuso*, French *clos*, 'closed'). The modern rendering of the discant would be as follows:

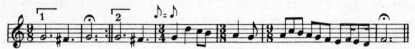

For the distribution of the text the following scheme is convenient:

a		b	
1.5.	*Vince*............	2.	Gia............
4.	Unde............	3.	Anci..........

The reader is advised to transcribe the entire piece, which is also reproduced in Stainer, * *Dufay and His Contemporaries*, p. 60. A transcription of the end of the first section is given in the appendix, No. 20.

The use of *diminutio simplex* described above explains an otherwise obscure remark of Gafurius according to which the sign ꜱ was used to indicate *proportio sesquitertia*, that is, diminution in the ratio of 3:4 (*Practica Musicae*, lib. IV, cap. v; see *HdN* I, 419). Indeed, the equation: ꜱ♦♦♦♦=ᴄ♦♦♦ shows that four *M* of the proportional sign are equal to three *M* of the *integer valor*.

With the rise of a new, 'classical' style under Dufay and Ockeghem, the rhythmic complexities of the earlier period fell into disuse. *Proportio dupla* occurs now chiefly for passages which could just as well be written in *integer valor* (with the next-smaller note values), but which are notated in *diminutio* in order to bestow upon the composition an aura of learning. An example is the first piece (A) of Facsimile 33, which has *diminutio dupla* in one part (*contrapunctus*) against *integer valor* in another (*tenor*). Two *S* of the former are worth one of the latter. If, in the *integer valor*, the *S* is transcribed as a quarter note, the *S* of the proportion becomes an eighth note:

The twelfth note of the fourth staff is an *Sm*, not an *M*.

More justified is the use of *proportio dupla* (as well as the other proportions) in the mensuration-canons, i.e., canons in which several voices are derived from a single written part, by the application of different mensurations. An example showing the simultaneous use of [3, 2] and [2, 2] has already been studied (p. 118). Below is an example by Josquin

FACSIMILE 33

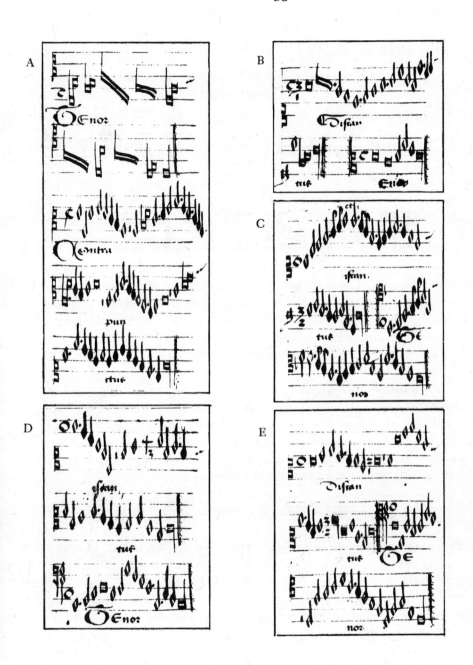

J. Tinctoris, *Proportionale musices*, MS Brussels, Bibl. Royale (*ca.* 1480)
A: page 100; B: page 102; C: page 104; D: p. 106; E: page 102

in which [2, 2] is used in *integer valor* and in *proportio dupla* (from Sebaldus Heyden, *De arte canendi*, Nürnberg, 1540). Both voices begin simultaneously and at the same pitch. Under the upper sign, only the first half of the melody is sung, up to the first *L*.

**Exemplum Tertij Modi, per C cum Ɔ
Duo in unum Iofquini.**

Much more frequent than any of the above applications is the use of ¢ simultaneously in all the parts of a composition or a section thereof, that is, as a general time-signature. From the notational point of view, this method of writing presents no difficulties at all. However, it involves problems of tempo which will be dealt with later in a special chapter (p. 188 ff).

As regards the *proportio dupla* of *tempus perfectum*, our explanations concerning its rhythm may be illustrated by the following passage, from Facsimile 38 (second staff of the tenor): 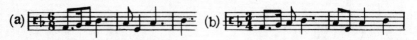 .
If here the *B* were considered perfect, a rendering in $\frac{3}{8}$ (or $\frac{6}{8}$)meter as under (a) would result, whereas, with the *B* being imperfect, a transcription in $\frac{3}{4}$-meter as under (b) would be obtained:

(a) [music example] (b) [music example]

The context shows that (b) is correct (see the discussion of this piece, p. 172).

It must be noted, however, that there are numerous cases in which the interpretation as under (a) is clearly indicated. The passage on page 155 (beginning of the cantus of *Rompeltier*, from *Odhecaton*, p. 27') is a case in point.

Obviously, the *B* is here perfect, the *L* understood to be imperfect, so that the *diminutio* does not entail any change of the rhythmic structure

Om peltier

of the ordinary *tempus perfectum*, but would only seem to double its speed. In other words, the (notated) mensuration is [II, 3], not [III, 2], and its equivalent in the next-smaller values is, therefore, [2, 3], not [3, 2]. Hence the sign ⊕ has the same meaning as C3 , namely, that of a substitute for ⊂ (see p. 195). Another example of *tempus perfectum diminutum* showing ternary grouping of the *S*, is the passage reproduced on p. 142 from the *Quia respexit*.

Actually, examples showing the 'ternary' interpretation are much more frequent in the sources than those for the 'binary,' because the former invariably applies if the sign in question is used as a time-signature, that is, in all the parts simultaneously for the entire piece or a section thereof, whereas the latter usually applies if the sign is used as a true proportional symbol. See the chapter on Proportional Time-Signatures and Tempo (p. 188 ff).

The meaning of *diminutio simplex* in connection with the signs of *prolatio perfecta* ₵;⊕;Ɔ —rather rare combinations—will be explained later (p. 167).

D. Proportio Tripla

In *proportio tripla* of *tempus imperfectum*, C3 , the *B* must, as has been explained above, be read as a perfect note, or, in other words, the *S* must be read in groups of three. To avoid errors one must remember that *proportio tripla*, like all the proportions, is—at least normally—based on the *S* and not on the *B*. This means that the fundamental equation is 3 *S* (*prop.*) = 1 *S* (*int. val.*), not 3 *B* (*prop.*) = 1 *B* (*int. val.*). As a matter of fact, these two interpretations are not necessarily identical. If, in the example ⊂◇◇$^3_1$♮◇◇◇♮ , one considers the *B* as the unit of the proportion, then three *B* under $^3_1$ are equal to one *B* of the *integer valor*, i.e., to two *S* of *tempus imperfectum*. However, if the *S* is taken as the unit, we find that the three *B* under $^3_1$ represent nine *S* which therefore equal three *S* of the *integer valor*. Thus two different interpretations arise:

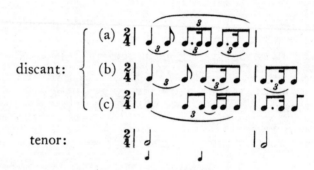

Only (b) is correct. An instructive example of this point is found in the piece from Tinctoris reproduced under (B) on Facsimile 33. Since here the tenor begins with *B*'s, one may be tempted to contrast each of these notes by three *B* (or their equivalent) in the discant. However, the result, indicated below under (a), is evidently wrong. The correct interpretation is obtained if in the tenor each *B* is replaced by two *S*, to each of which correspond three *S* of the discant, as is shown under (b):

The version (c) of this illustration indicates another possible solution which would be obtained on the basis of the relationship $3 B = 1B$, if the *B* of the proportion were interpreted as being imperfect. Although, in the present case, this interpretation cannot be ruled out altogether, it is not likely to be the one intended (see the third measure of the piece). At any rate, it would be in contradiction with the general principles of *proportio tripla*. However, since in music of our period no strict observation of these principles—or of almost any others—can be expected, it has been deemed advisable to call attention to the possibility of such an alternative interpretation, in which the *proportio tripla* refers to the (imperfect) *B*.

More definite statements can be made with regard to the possibility of *proportio tripla* referring to the *M*. As a matter of fact, instances such as the following one are not rare in the sources of the sixteenth century: . According to the general principles of *proportio tripla*, the following transcription would be correct: [musical notation] . However, this is not the intended rhythm, as one may gather already from the fact that unduly quick notes would result. Actually, in a case like this the sign 3 is likely to indicate, not *proportio tripla*, but *proportio sesquialtera*, with the result: [musical notation] . For an example, see p. 159.

The triple proportion of *tempus imperfectum* is frequently indicated by the sign: ₵3 . Properly this would denote a combination of *dupla* and *tripla*, i.e., *proportio sextupla*, particularly in analogy to the sign ₵2 which always signifies *proportio quadrupla* (see below). However, it is not used in this meaning. In other words, the figure 3 does not combine with the *dupla*-stroke, but only modifies its meaning to indicate *tripla* rather than *dupla*.[1]

The *proportio tripla* of *tempus perfectum*, O3 , is the equivalent of ⊙ , as has been previously explained. Theoretically, the difference between C3 and O3 is that, under the former sign, a passage consists of notes to the equivalent of a multiple of two perfect *B* (*modus imperfectus*), under the latter, of three (*modus perfectus*). However, the practical examples of O3 usually show little evidence of notated *modus perfectus* (actual *tempus perfectum*), but rather of notated *modus imperfectus* (actual *tempus imperfectum*), or else of no *modus* at all. A case in point is the discant of a piece from Sebald Heyden's *Ars canendi*, reproduced in *MuT*, p. 71, a passage of which, marked O3 , includes 13 *B*, so that neither full ternary nor full binary measures can be obtained. In the bass of the same piece (see *MuT*, 72) there is another passage in O3 , which opens with two rests in the value of an imperfect *L* each. Obviously the signature C3 would be more appropriate for this passage.[2]

E. OTHER PROPORTIONS

Proportio quadrupla indicates a diminution in the ratio of 1:4. The signs of this proportion are: ⁴:4;C⁴;C4; O⁴; O4 , or combinations of two signs of *proportio dupla*: ₵2; Φ²; Ɔ2; Ɔ²; ƆȻ; Ɒ   Since here the *tactus* falls on the *L*, this proportion is sometimes called *alla longa*. *Proportio*

---

[1] For an example, see Josquin's canon *Agnus dei* and Pierre de la Rue's *Fuga quatuor vocum ex unica*, p. 181.

[2] In the sixteenth century, *proportio tripla* came to be regarded as the proportion *par excellence* and was frequently referred to simply as 'proportio,' 'proportionatus,' etc., while *proportio dupla* was called 'diminutio.' This special meaning also exists in the 'Proportio' or 'Proportz' of sixteenth century German dances in which it indicates variations in triple meter of the main dance (passamezzo, etc.); see, e.g., W. Merian, *Der Tanz in den deutschen Tabulaturbüchern*, p. 77f.

quadrupla always calls for imperfect mensuration of the *B* (*tempus imperfectum*), even if applied to *tempus perfectum* (Φ2). Indeed, under this proportion groups of notated *S* really are groups of *Sm* (of the *integer valor*) which, of course, are always imperfect:

Proportio sesquialtera signifies diminution in the ratio of 3 to 2. Like *tripla* it always calls for perfect mensuration of the *B*, i.e., for groups of three *S*. Each such group, then, is equal in value to a group of two *S* of the *integer valor*. For the transcription into modern notes the same method as that used in *proportio tripla* may be applied:

Since this proportion is the first example of the *genus superparticulare* we shall recall our previous remarks concerning groups of notes in the sections before and under such a proportion (p. 147). Apparently, the fundamental equation of *sesquialtera*, namely, 2 *S* (*int. val.*) = 3 *S* (*prop.*) calls not only for ternary groups (*tempus perfectum*) in the proportion, but also for binary groups (*tempus imperfectum*) in the *integer valor*. Therefore, *sesquialtera* occurs usually in combination with *tempus imperfectum*, and an example such as this: is of purely hypothetical significance. This does not mean to exclude the use of O$\frac{3}{2}$ altogether. It is limited, however, to cases in which the proportion is applied to *M*'s, which are binary in [3, 2]. Example (C) of Facsimile 33 serves as an illustration. Three *M* of the proportion are equal to two of the *integer valor*. The sign at the beginning of the second staff is a g-clef.

It appears that, in [2, 2], *sesquialtera* amounts to the same thing as coloration (*hemiolia*): .

As will easily be seen, *sesquialtera* cannot be used in [3, 3].

It has already been mentioned (p. 157) that *sesquialtera* is frequently indicated, not by the sign $\frac{3}{2}$, but by the sign 3 which normally would call for *proportio tripla*. The following passage from Brumel's *Missa de beata virgine* (only altus and bassus; for the other parts see H. Expert, *Les Maîtres musiciens de la renaissance française*, vol. VIII, p. 19) illustrates this usage:

Apparently, the figure 3 produces here the same effect that it has in the modern writing of triplets: three notes of the triplet-group equal two ordinary notes of the same kind.   Familiar as this may be to the modern musician, it is difficult to explain within the proportional system, and must probably be understood as a mere matter of routine.   The situation is somewhat simpler if the entire piece is written in *tempus diminutum* (*alla breve*, see p. 148). as in the following example (Janequin, *La Guerre*; see H. Expert, *Les Maîtres musiciens de la renaissance française*, vol. VII, frontispiece; cf. the transcription in the same volume p. 36 ff, particularly p. 39) and many similar ones:

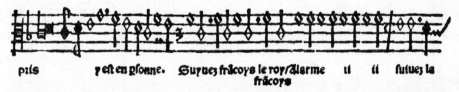

Here one could argue that, under the sign ₵ , two *M* equal one *M* of the *integer valor*, and that, under the sign ₃, three *M* equal one of the *integer valor*; hence the equation ₵♩♩ =C3♩♩♩ , resulting in *sesquialtera*.

Proportio sesquialtera is frequently used in combination with *diminutio simplex*, as follows: ₵³⁄₂ .   Here, the 3:2-relationship of the former proportion is once more halved by the latter, so that the ratio of $\frac{3}{2} \times \frac{2}{1} = \frac{3}{1}$, i.e., *proportio tripla*, results.   This proportion was known as *sesquialtera diminuta*.   The discant and bass of an example from Seb. Heyden, reproduced on the next page, will serve as an illustration (for the other parts see *MuT*, 67):

Proportio quintupla, sesquitertia. Proportions other than those already considered are not likely to be encountered in the musical documents of white notation. However, two examples will be examined here in order to complete the presentation of the subject. Following is an example of *proportio quintupla* from Gafurius' *Practica Musicae:*

The sign $\frac{5}{1}$ indicates diminution in the ratio 5:1, so that 5 *S* of the proportion are equal to one *S* of the *integer valor*, or of the tenor. This proportion is cancelled by the sign for *tempus inperfectum*. Once more, *proportio quintupla* is introduced by $\frac{10}{2}$ which is, of course, identical with $\frac{5}{1}$. For the transcription, one only has to mark off groups of five *S*, each of which has the value of one normal *S*.

Facsimile 33D illustrates *proportio sesquitertia* or, as it is sometimes called, *epitrita* (Greek). The section in proportion, marked $\frac{4}{3}$, contains two groups of four *S* each; each of these groups is equal in value to three *S* or to a perfect *B* of the tenor. For the transcription, the above method of indicating triplets, quadruplets, etc. may be used.

Successive Proportions. If several proportions appear successively in the same part, their effect is cumulative, each of them referring to the preceding ones, not to the *integer valor*. The cumulative result of two proportions is, of course, arrived at by multiplication; e.g., $\frac{2}{1} \times \frac{3}{2} = \frac{3}{1}$, which means that *proportio sesquialtera* in *proportio dupla* is *proportio tripla*. Facsimile 33E serves as an example. Here, the final passage signed $\frac{3}{2}$ really is in *proportio tripla* of the *integer valor*, owing to the preceding *diminutio simplex*. The blackened *L* and *B* at the beginning of this passage obviously equal $4 + 2 = 6$ white *S*, which gives 9 *S* for the entire group; these, according to the proportion, are equal to three *S* of the *integer valor*, or, in other words, of the tenor (see the transcription in appendix, No. 21). A more complicated example illustrating this method is found in *CS* iv, 131-32.

Occasionally, there occur, in the course of a piece, not only various proportional signs (figures, fractions), but also new signs of regular mensuration. The cumulative principle does not, as a rule, apply to these. For instance, in the following succession of signs, O--$\frac{4}{3}$--$\frac{3}{2}$--₵3--2--$\frac{3}{2}$, the first two fractions would accumulate, leading to *proportio dupla* ($\frac{4}{3} \times \frac{3}{2} = \frac{2}{1}$); however, the following *proportio tripla*, being attached to a sign of mensuration(₵), does not multiply with the preceding *proportio dupla*—thus resulting in *proportio sextupla*—but establishes, as it

were, a new beginning, cancelling automatically all the previous proportions.

  An example from Gafurius' *Practica Musicae* serves as an illustration:

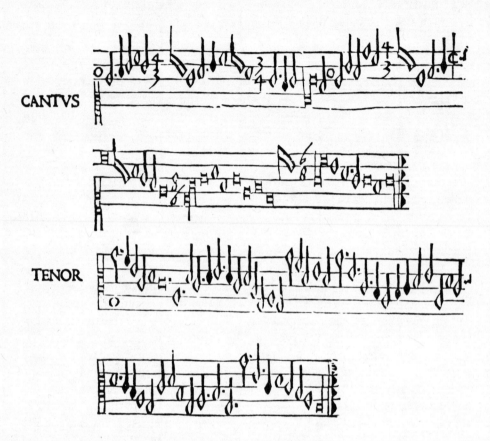

CANTVS

TENOR

The cumulative meaning of the signs is as follows:

$$\text{Signs:}\quad \bigcirc\quad \tfrac{4}{3}\quad \tfrac{3}{4}\quad \tfrac{4}{3}\quad \mathfrak{C}\quad \tfrac{8}{6}\quad \tfrac{6}{8}$$

$$\text{Meaning:}\quad \bigcirc\quad \tfrac{4}{3}\quad \bigcirc\quad \tfrac{4}{3}\quad \mathfrak{C}\quad \tfrac{8}{3}\quad \mathfrak{C}$$

  A special difficulty of this example lies in the irregular length of some
of the sections, which are not always adaptable to the *tempus perfectum*
($\frac{3}{4}$-meter) of the tenor. For instance, the section under $\frac{3}{4}$ which really
is again *tempus perfectum*, contains four *S*, that is, one more than is
required for one full measure. Thus the following section in *sesquitertia*

begins (and ends) on the second beat of a measure. The transcription of the upper part given in the appendix No. 22 may be compared with ∗ that in *HdN* 1, 418.[1]

F. Augmentation

The proportions considered so far are all diminutions. Augmentations are very much rarer, proportional signs such as ½ and ⅔ being used only for cancellation of previous diminutions.[2] There is, in fact, only one special type of augmentation which merits our attention because of its rather frequent occurrence, i.e., that indicated by the familiar sign of *prolatio perfecta*. The following principle must be observed: In *prolatio perfecta* the *tactus* is represented by the *M*, not by the *S*.

This means that under the signs ℂ and ⊙ the *M* takes the temporal value which is normally indicated by the *S*. This principle is particularly important in the case of compositions written in *prolatio imperfecta*, except for one part, usually the tenor, which is notated in *prolatio perfecta*. The singer of such a part determines the relative value of the notes according to the rules of *prolatio perfecta*, but gives the *M* the same real duration which the other singers give to the *S*. Obviously, the result is double augmentation. The *prolatio perfecta* actually becomes *tempus perfectum*, while the *tempus* (*imperfectum* or *perfectum*) indicated by the (semi- or full) circle in reality is *modus* (*imperfectus* or *perfectus*).

Facsimile 34 illustrates this practice. Here, the tenor, containing the melody *L'homme armé*, is notated in ℂ , as against ⊙ in the other parts. The transcription, therefore, is not as under (a), but as under (b):

(a) (b)

In the *Christe*-section all the parts are notated in *prolatio perfecta;*

[1] In this transcription the relationship 3 *S* (*int. val.*) = 4 *S* (*prop.*) is expressed, not by quadruplets, but by dotted notes, because of the fact that three half-notes are equal to four dotted quarter-notes. Wolf's rendering, though correct, makes rather awkward reading, and obscures certain peculiarities of rhythm, such as the varying measures of our transcription. After having read our explanations on the insertion-character' of late fourteenth century syncopation (p. 416) the student will realize that Gafurius, in this example, presents himself as the pupil—one of the last, no doubt—of the musicians of the period of 'mannered notation.'

[2] This usage still occurs in sources of the early eighteenth century, e.g., in F. X. Murschhauser's *Prototypon longo-breve organicum* II, 1707, in which the time-signature $\frac{12}{8}$ is cancelled by the signature $\frac{12}{8}$ (see *DTB* XVIII, p. 154). It goes without saying that in this period the sign $\frac{12}{8}$ has no proportional meaning, but simply indicates measures comprising twelve eighth-notes each. ∗

the entire section must be transcribed in the augmented values, i.e., in $\frac{6}{4}$ (or $\frac{3}{4}$), not in $\frac{6}{8}$. The same procedure applies to the *Et resurrexit* of this mass which has been studied previously (p. 138, Facsimile 30). The student may have already noticed that, with this piece, the normal scale of reduction did not lead to a satisfactory result. Evidently, the notes are much too small to be sung in the speed suggested by our transcription. The reason for this failure becomes apparent now. In this composition, the *M* represents the beat and must, therefore, be transcribed as a quarter-note, not as an eighth-note.

Under these circumstances, one may raise the question as to whether the same principle applies to the pieces on Facsimiles 31 and 32, both of which are in *prolatio perfecta*. However, as will readily be seen, the same considerations of tempo which, with the *Et resurrexit*, constituted a good argument in favor of the application of augmentation, speak strongly against this method in the present cases. This is particularly clear with the piece no. 31, which the principle of augmentation would cause to begin with a series of notes each equalling an entire $\frac{3}{4}$-measure. Indeed, these compositions are not subject to the rule of *prolatio perfecta*, for the simple reason that they belong to an earlier period in which this principle had not yet become established. The following remarks represent an attempt to clarify the 'history of *prolatio perfecta*' during the fifteenth century.

Although Ramis de Pareia, in his *Musica Practica* of 1482, is the earliest theorist to mention *prolatio perfecta* as a *signum augentiae*, an example of this practice occurs already in the Codex Chantilly, a collection of music written around 1400 (see Facsimile 88). However, this would seem * to be a rather isolated case. The musical sources of the earlier part of the fifteenth century (prior to 1475?) as well as the theoretical writings of this period show clearly that the interpretation in question was by no means common or universally accepted. Otherwise Tinctoris, the great authority, would not have failed to mention such a fact in his *Proportionale* (*ca.* 1475). That there existed, however, a great uncertainty and confusion regarding the meaning of the sign ℭ , appears clearly from Tinctoris' explanations. According to him, three different rhythmic interpretations of this mensuration were in use among his contemporaries, none of which, however, agrees with that of Ramis. Without entering into a detailed consideration of his rather roundabout explanations, it will suffice to illustrate the intricate problem by the following table showing four different interpretations of one and the same example:

FACSIMILE 34

Rome, Vatican Library *Chigi cod. C. VIII, 234 (ca. 1500)*
Pages 33', 34

Discant: C◊♩♩◊◊◦╫·◦╫╫   Tenor: ℂ◊♩♩♩♩◊◊

Transcriptions:

A comparison of the number of measures in the various realizations of the tenor shows that (c) is the double of (a), that (d) is the double of·(b), and that (d) is the triple of (a).

(d) is the interpretation called for by the above rule (threefold augmentation); (a), (b), and (c) are those mentioned by Tinctoris (*CS* iv, 171). Of these, he disapproves of (a) (*proportio sesquialtera*, as he calls it with reference to the relationship of the *M* in discant and tenor) as well as of (c) (*proportio subsesquitertia*, again with regard to the *M*), considering (b) the only correct solution. In a way, this interpretation is, indeed, the simplest and most plausible of all. It is based upon the consideration of the *M*, instead of the *S*, as the common unit of time in C(O) and in ℂ(O) . It appears that here two *S* under ℂ are equal to three *S* under C(O) ; hence, Tinctoris calls it *proportio subsesquialtera*. As an example, he cites the following passage from Dufay's mass *De Sancto Anthonio:*

Here, the *M* has the same value under both O and ℂ . The result is simply a change from $\frac{3}{4}$ to $\frac{6}{8}$, the reverse of the change expressed by coloration.

Another example of the same practice is offered by Dufay's chanson *Belle que vous*, which is notated with a different mensuration in each voice-part (see page 167; cf. *DTOe* vii, p. 34, no. 119).

In briefly summarizing the above explanations, we find that in the earlier period of the fifteenth century (Dufay) *prolatio perfecta*, if placed against *prolatio imperfecta*, indicates equal value of the *M*; in later peri-

ods (Ockeghem, Josquin) it calls for threefold augmentation ($M = S$). *
However, in this later period, the augmenting significance of the *prolatio perfecta* could be cancelled by combining its sign with a sign of diminution, in the following way: ¢ : Ɔ : ⦶ . Under these signs, the former interpretation, version (b) of the above tabulation, based upon the equality of the *M*, takes place. It was called *prolatio perfecta diminuta*.

However, even in late documents a lack of correctness in this matter must be reckoned with. Particularly striking is the fact that Seb. Heyden (1540!), although he clearly demonstrates the difference between ℭ and ¢, fails to use the signs correctly in at least one of his examples, an *Et in terra* by Ockeghem. Below is the beginning of this piece (for the complete piece see *MuT*, 79) which calls for equal duration of the *M* in all the parts:

Exemplum Quinti Toni Iohannis Ockegem.

Et in terra. Altus sequit̄ Discantū in Subdiateſſaron.

Baſſus in Subdiateſſaron incipientē Tenorem ‚pſequit̄.

The first part gives two voices in canon, a discant in [2, 2], starting on f, and an altus in [3, 2], starting simultaneously a fourth below (*subdiatessaron* is the lower fourth). The second part also gives two voices in canon; again, the bass starts a fourth below the tenor. The rests written at the beginning of this part are valid, not for the tenor, which actually starts together with the discant and altus, but only for the bass which follows at the distance of four *S*, as is also indicated by the *signum con-*

gruentiae.   Since the bass is in [3, 3], the initial *B*-rest equals in value, of course, *9* M and, therefore, occupies one full ⁹⁄₈-measure of the transcription.   In the continuation of this part, however, there is no evidence of *tempus perfectum* (already the first *B* is made imperfect by the preceding *S*-rest), so that ⁶⁄₈-meter proves more convenient than ⁹⁄₈-meter.   The beginning of the transcription follows:

For the use of ₵ as a general time-signature, see p. 195.

G. Examples

We now turn to the study of a few pieces which show to what a degree of complexity the proportional notation was used—or, occasionally, misused—in the fifteenth and sixteenth centuries.   We begin with some examples taken from Isaac's *Choralis Constantinus*, in Formschneyder's publication (Nürnberg, 1550).[1]

(1)   *Ideoque quod nascetur* (Facsimile 35).   The piece opens in [2, 2] in all the parts, the discant being silent throughout the first section (*Ideoque . . . vocabitur*), which comprises twenty measures.   Towards the end of this section, the three lower parts have a passage in coloration.   The remaining section (*filius . . . dei*) is written in four different signatures: Ø; Ɔ; ₵; ○ .   Naturally, the *proportio quadrupla* of the alto renders the *L*, *B*, and *S* of this part equal to the *S*, *M*, and *Sm* of the tenor (*integer valor*).   In a similar way, the *S* and *M* of the discant (*proportio dupla*) are equal to the *M* and *Sm* of the bass (*integer valor*).   According to the proper interpretation of Ø , the notated mensuration * of the cantus is [III, 2], its actual mensuration [3, 2].   In other words, the modern meter of this part is the same (³⁄₄) as that of the bass, only written in the next greater values.   Of course, the absence of larger notes (*B*, *L*) makes it impossible to arrive at an unambiguous decision in this

---

[1] The original publication is in four part-books.

FACSIMILE 35

Heinrich Isaac, *Choralis Constantinus*. Formschneyder, Nürnberg, 1550

question. In fact, the application of the 'secondary' interpretation of
Φ (notated [II, 3], actual [2, 3]) leads to the same note values, only
arranged in ⁶⁄₈-meter, instead of ³⁄₄-meter. In the transcription of the
closing section, appendix, No. 23, both interpretations are indicated.

(2) *Piae vocis* (Facsimile 36). This example opens in [2, 2] in the
three upper parts, whereas the bass begins with two *B*-rests in [2, 3].
According to the augmenting character of *prolatio perfecta*, each *B* of this
mensuration is the equivalent, not of a ⁶⁄₈-measure, but of a ⁶⁄₄-measure, or,
more conveniently, of two ³⁄₄-measures. Further on, this meter is introduced simultaneously in all the parts, but changes back to duple meter
under c . Toward the end of the piece, the figure 3 introduces *proportio tripla* simultaneously in all the parts. The 'correct' interpretation of
this passage, that is, according to the equation 3 *S* (*prop.*) = 1 *S* (*int.
val.*), leads to an unduly quick rhythm, as is shown below under (a). No
doubt, the actual meaning of the figure 3 is *proportio sesquialtera*, applied
to the *M* (3*M* = 2*M*), as in the instance from Brumel's mass, given previously (p. 159). Therefore, the rendering as under (b) indicates the
proper time-relationship between the *integer valor* and the proportion:

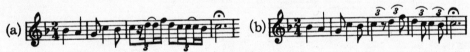

(3) *Dico ego* (Facsimile 37, p. 174) shows *prolatio perfecta diminuta* in the
discant, against *tempus perfectum diminutum* in the other parts. According to our explanations, the former sign simply means [2, 3] without augmentation, that is, ⁶⁄₈-meter (*S* = dotted quarter note). With the *tempus
perfectum diminutum*, again the question arises whether it is the equivalent (written, of course, in larger values) of [3, 2] or of [2, 3], in other
* words of modern ³⁄₄- or ⁶⁄₈-meter. In this example, an unequivocal decision in favor of the latter interpretation is found in the blackened notes
at the end of the alto (and bass). This coloration-group of three blackened *B* is the equivalent of two white *B* and, therefore, suggests (notated)
modus imperfectus and, consequently, actual *tempus imperfectum* for the
white notes. The following two renditions of the end of the alto (beginning with the last *M*-rest) illustrate this point; the 'triplet-coloration', as
under (a), is one quarter-note too short, whereas the 'courante-coloration' as under (b) leads to a correct result:

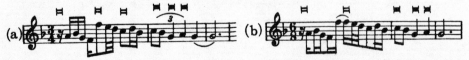

FACSIMILE 36

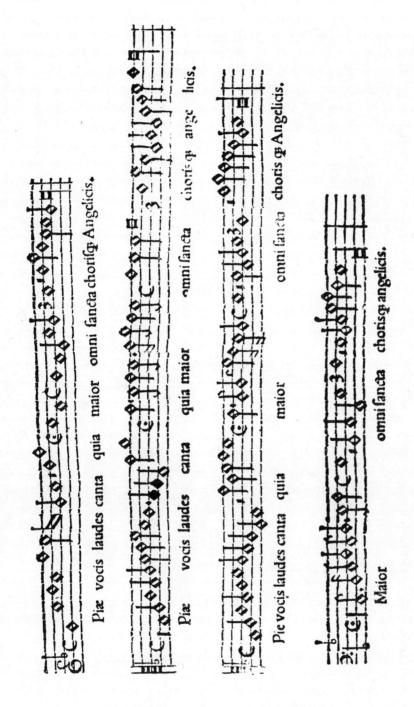

Heinrich Isaac, *Choralis Constantinus*. Formschneyder, Nürnberg, 1550

(4) *De radice Jesse* (Facsimile 38). This piece, which has repeatedly been cited as the *non plus ultra* of proportional complexities, presents quite a few problems, although not nearly so intriguing difficulties as numerous pieces of the late fourteenth and early fifteenth centuries.[1] The following table showing the modern equivalents of the various mensurations will facilitate transcription:

Sign	Notes		Modern equivalent
C	◊ ◊	=	$\frac{2}{4}$ | ♩ ♩ |
O	◊ ◊ ◊	=	$\frac{3}{4}$ | ♩ ♩ ♩ |
¢	◊ ◊	=	$\frac{6}{4}(\frac{3}{4})$| ♩. ♩. |
⊙	◊ ◊ ◊	=	$\frac{9}{4}(\frac{3}{4})$| ♩. ♩. ♩. |
¢(C 2)	⊟ ⊟	=	$\frac{2}{4}$ | ♩ ♩ |
O2	⊟ ⊟ ⊟	=	$\frac{3}{4}$ | ♩ ♩ ♩ |
¢2(¢ ꜿ)	⊟ ⊟	=	$\frac{2}{4}$ | ♫ |
3	◊ ◊ ◊	=	| ♫♪ (3)

A few peculiarities may be noticed. The figure 3 signifies *proportio tripla* (as indicated in the above table), although it always occurs following upon *proportio dupla*. Properly, therefore, its value should be half of those shown in the table. Two explanations for this irregularity are open: either, that the cumulative process does not apply, or that the actual meaning of the figure 3 is, again, *sesquialtera*, which, by combination with the *dupla*, would lead to *tripla*.[2] A similar irregularity attaches to the figure 4 (near the end of the alto and of the bass). In both cases, it is preceded by a sign of *proportio quadrupla* (¢2; ¢ꜿ). However, it does not denote a reduction in the ratio of 1:16 (L = sixteenth-note), but only in the ratio of 1:8 (L-eighth-note). The blackened notes *B S S B* in the discant near the beginning of the second staff have exactly the same values as if they were written in white. They must be considered *a typographical error or else a peculiarity without meaning. The piece is transcribed in the appendix, No. 24.

[1] In *MuT*, 82, this piece is reproduced in mensural notation (after Glarean's *Dodekachordon* and with a different text) as well as in transcription. The latter, however, obscures practically all the notational features of the original. H. Riemann, in his *Handbuch*, II, i, 170, reproduces it from the same source, together with a much more adequate transcription. See also the transcription in *DTOe* XVI, p. 194.

[2] In Glarean's version of the piece (see *MuT*, 82) most of these sections are, more correctly, labelled $\frac{3}{2}$.

FACSIMILE 38

Heinrich Isaac, *Choralis Constantinus*. Formschneyder, Nürnberg, 1550

FACSIMILE 37

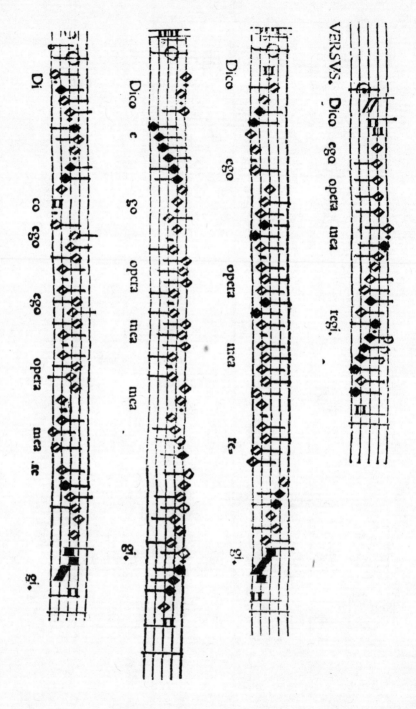

Heinrich Isaac, *Choralis Constantinus.* Formschneyder, Nürnberg, 1550

Finally, two pieces from the Canonici MS may be considered, which illustrate the use of proportions in the early part of the fifteenth century. The notational practice of this period differs in various respects from that of the later sources. In fact, the peculiarities of these examples can only be understood as the inheritance of that stage of black notation which, owing to its unique features of complexity, has been termed 'mannered notation' in this book. Actually, their proper place would be in the chapter thus entitled (see p. 403), rather than here. However, since they are written (possibly, re-written) in white notes, they may stand here as a fitting climax to the student's efforts to cope with the intricacies of the proportional system.

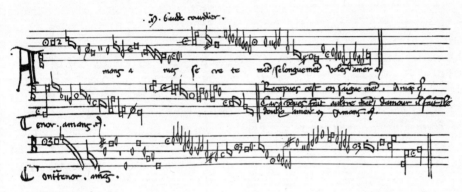

(5) In Baude Cordier's *Amans ames secretement* we find nearly all the signs of mensuration, plain as well as in *proportio dupla* or *tripla*. The exact meaning of these signs (which, needless to say, must frequently be determined by experimentation) will appear from the following table in which all the values are expressed by a temporal unit designated e, which equals the M of the *integer valor* or the eighth-note of the transcription:

	$\mathbb{C}$	$\mathcal{C}$	$\bigcirc$	$\varnothing$	$\bigcirc 3$	C	$\mathcal{C}$	$\odot$	$\odot 2$	$\odot 3$
M =	e		e			e		e		
S =	3e	$^3\!/_2$e	2e	e		2e	e	3e	$^3\!/_2$e	e
B =	6e	3e	6e	3e	2e	4e	2e	9e	$^9\!/_2$e	3e

As appears from this tabulation, the relationship between the four plain mensurations is based upon the equality of the M, not of the S. In particular, the signs of *prolatio perfecta* do not call for augmentation. A transcription of the piece is given in the appendix, No. 25.[1]

[1] A wrong transcription of the beginning of this piece (MS Oxford, Bodl. Libr. *Canonici 213*, p. 123) has been given in E. Dannemann, *Die spätgotische Musiktradition in Frankreich und Burgund vor dem Auftreten Dufays* (Leipzig, 1936), p. 106.

(6) Our last piece, Hughe de Lantins' *Je suy exent* (Facsimile 39), is quite difficult to transcribe, but even more difficult is the proper explanation for some of its notational peculiarities. The piece begins in *tempus* * *perfectum diminutum* in all the parts. In contrast to its 'classical' meaning, this mensuration retains the perfect value of the *B*, as is clearly indicated by the *punctus divisionis* after the first *S* of the tenor, as well as by the coloration-groups at the beginning of the contra. In the later course of the piece, plain *tempus perfectum* appears simultaneously in all the parts (discant, near beginning of the third staff; tenor, beginning of the second staff; contratenor, before middle of the second staff). Notationally, this marks the beginning of a second section which may be considered first because it shows the various mensurations in their normal meaning, and in relatively simple configurations. The tenor continues in [3, 2] throughout ($\frac{3}{4}$-meter). In the contra, the passage marked 2 contains 12 *M*, the value of which is reduced by proportion to 6 *M* or to one full measure of the *tempus perfectum*. The passage in ⊃ , towards the end, introduces a new rhythm: two *B* are equal to one (perfect!) *B* of the *tempus perfectum*. It will be noticed that this meaning of *tempus imperfectum diminutum* is entirely different from that indicated by the sign ¢ in the pievious piece. Whereas there the *B* of the proportion equalled two *M* of the *integer valor*, it equals, in the present case, three *M*. Following is the transcription of the close of the contra:

A similar meaning attaches to the passage in *proportio quadrupla*, Э , of the discant (to the text [*sou*]*lus*). The *L* of the porportion has the same value as the *B* of the simple diminution, that is, half of the *B* of the *tempus perfectum*. Towards the end of the third staff, the sign ¢ introduces change from [3, 2] to [2, 3], that is, from $\frac{3}{4}$-meter to $\frac{6}{8}$-meter. Towards the end of the discant, the sign 2 and the coloration-group of three *M* present a minor problem which, however, the student who has managed to steer safely this far through the notational labyrinth of the composition will have little difficulty in solving.

We now may turn to the study of the first section. Using the mensurations considered so far as a point of departure, one will naturally interpret the *tempus perfectum diminutum* of the opening as half of the *tempus perfectum* of the second section. Thus, three *S* would fill in a $\frac{3}{8}$-measure, instead of a $\frac{3}{4}$-measure. Two such measures may be combined into one $\frac{6}{8}$-measure. The figure 3 found shortly after the begin-

FACSIMILE 39

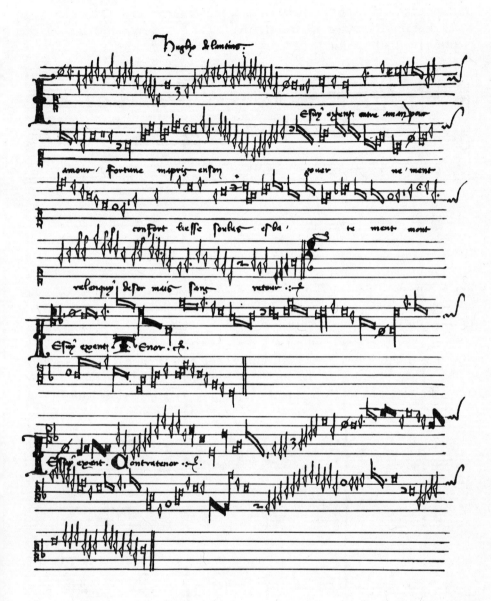

MS Oxford, Bodleian Library *Canonici misc. 213* (*ca.* 1450)
Page 47

ning of the discant (and also in the later course of the contra) refers to the *integer valor*. In other words, with reference to the preceding diminution it indicates, not *proportio tripla*, but *proportio sesquialtera*, so that three *M* take the place of two *M*, or of one *S*. Here follows the transcription of the beginning:

The real problem presented by this piece lies in the fact that a satisfactory rendition of the first section is obtained only if the mensural signs ○ and ⊖ , which occur in the discant and in the tenor of this section, are interpreted as just half of what they represent in the second section. For instance, the *B* of ○ , which in the second section becomes a quarter-note (see the above transcription of the closing measures of the contra), must now be transcribed as an eighth-note. Following is a rendition of the second line of the discant (beginning with the first *B*) and the corresponding portion of the tenor in two versions: (a) according to the exact meaning of the mensural signs; (b) in the halved values which are required by the context of the parts (see the added contra).

Two ways are open for the explanation of this discrepancy.   Either the
signs ↄ and ꞓ are, in the first section, understood to be subject to the
diminution indicated at the beginning of this section, whereas later they
are understood to be in *integer valor*, being placed after the sign of plain
tempus perfectum; or the sign ∅ of the first section has no proportional
meaning, and indicates just simple *tempus perfectum*.   In the latter case,
the entire first section would have to be transcribed in the double values
of those used above.   No doubt, this choice is even less satisfactory than
the first.   From the musical point of view, the extremely long duration
of the various *L* occurring with the text *Je suy exent* ('I am exhausted')
would seem to represent a strong argument against the second version—
unless it is assumed that the composer wanted them to depict the state
of mind of the despairing lover and perhaps—prophetically—that of the
equally despairing reader of the above explanations.   *

H. CANONS

In the music of the fourteenth through the sixteenth centuries, the
term canon (i.e., rule) has a much wider significance than it has in the

ensuing periods and today. It means any kind of prescription that contains a clue to the correct interpretation of music which would otherwise be obscure. Tinctoris, in his *Diffinitorium* (*ca.* 1500, see *CS* IV, 179) defines it thus: 'Canon est regula voluntatem compositoris sub obscuritate quadam ostendens' (A canon is a rule which shows the intention of the composer in an obscure way).

Musicians of the fifteenth and sixteenth centuries certainly succeeded in making this definition come true. The Flemish masters spent no small amount of their ingenuity in devising enigmatical manners of singing a part and in indicating them by inscriptions which, 'though ostensibly vouchsafed for the purpose of giving the student some little insight into the secret of their construction, tend rather, as a general rule, to increase their perplexity' (Grove's *Dictionary*, 1938, vol. II, p. 713). Their delight in these intellectual subtleties has brought them into grave disrepute among the musicians and musical historians of a posterity that had completely lost living contact with the mentality of the Renaissance, and who, being brought up in the tradition of musical romanticism, could not conceive of a composer combining artistic inspiration with clarity of intellect. A more sober and unbiased observer will not be misled into mistaking for a criterion of artistic quality what was merely the playful whim of a culture which followed the motto: *Nihil humanum a me alienum puto*.

A relatively simple manifestation, but one which is of particular interest from the point of view of notation, is the mensuration-canon, i.e., a melody which is performed by various singers simultaneously under different mensurations. Examples of this method occurred already in the tenor and bass of the *Kyrie* of la Rue's mass, *L'homme armé* (Facsimile 27), in Ockeghem's *Et in terra* (p. 167), and in a two-voice canon by Josquin (p. 154). On page 181 we reproduce a three-voice canon from the same composer's *Missa l'homme armé* (from *Dodekachordon*, p. 442). The middle voice is in *integer valor*, (*S* = quarter-note); the lower in *proportio dupla* (*S* = eighth-note). In the upper voice, which is in *diminutio tripla*, three *S* equal one of the *integer valor*. The *signa congruentiae* indicate the stopping points of the two lower parts; since their tempo is slower than that of the upper part they both sing only a portion of the melody, which is sung in its entirety only by the discant. The entrances of the voices are here in the relation of tonic and dominant; they begin simultaneously on d, a and d' (see appendix, No. 26).

The spirit of competition which is so characteristic a trait of the Netherland schools induced Pierre de la Rue to compose a *fuga quatuor*

Ex una uoce tres, ex eiuſdē Io

dociMiſſa Lhome armeſuperuoces muſicales.

A Gnus Dei qui tol-
lis pecca ta mun di mi miſere re
no ſtri.

vocum ex unica, which is easily the most interesting specimen of mensuration-canons. The piece is reproduced here from *Dodekachordon,* p. 445: *

The four voices start simultaneously on G, d, g, d′. The beginning is
transcribed in the appendix, No. 27.

Another type of canon is the use of proportional signs for the repetition of a tenor melody. In fact, this is the earliest known use of proportions. Both Johannes de Muris (*ca.* 1325) and Prosdocimus de Beldemandis (*ca.* 1400) assert that diminution and augmentation serve only to produce an extensive tenor from a shorter melody.

The tenor of Obrecht's mass *Si dedero* (Facsimile 40) shows how this principle was utilized by the early Flemish masters. A single page suffices for the printing of the complete tenor (except the third *Agnus Dei*) of a mass, the discant of which covers nine pages. With each portion of the tenor two, three or four mensurations are given which, together with the sign of repetition at the end, indicate that the musical phrase has to be sung twice, three or four times in succession, each time under a different mensuration. Two of these tenors may be studied here, that of the *Crucifixus* and that of the *Sanctus*.

Four mensurations are indicated at the beginning of the *Crucifixus*. It is to be recommended that one begin transcribing the second and the third presentation of the melody, both of which are in *integer valor*. Contrary to the rules of imperfection the initial *B* is perfect under O . A *punctus divisionis*, which ordinarily would indicate this, cannot be used here since it would be interpreted as a *punctus additionis* under C . The length of the rests preceding the notes also varies according to the mensuration. Under O they equal five perfect *B* or fifteen *S* (five $\frac{3}{4}$-measures); under C , five imperfect *B* or ten *S* (five $\frac{2}{4}$-measures). Under the sign ₵ every note and every rest equals a half of its duration under C . Under the sign of *prolatio perfecta* each *M* equals a *S* of the sections in *integer valor*. The initial rests are worth $5 \times 6 = 30$ *M*, which, owing to the augmentation, take the place of 30 *S*; therefore, in the transcription, the tenor begins with a rest of ten $\frac{3}{4}$-measures. It may be noticed that, under this mensuration, the two pairs of *M* call for alteration, not imperfection (see appendix, No. 28).

The construction of the tenor of the *Sanctus* is still more involved. This tenor consists of two sections of equal design which may conveniently be designated as A and B. Each of these has three signs of mensuration. There result three different versions of A (A_1, A_2, A_3) and three of B (B_1, B_2, B_3), which have to be read in the following order: A_1 B_1 A_2 B_2 A_3 B_3 . A_2 and B_3, both of which are in [2, 2], are composed of six imperfect *B*, inclusive of the two *B*-rests at the end. In A_3 and B_2 these values are halved. In B_1 the second *B* is imperfect, so that, as a result, the passage consists of only three (perfect) *B*, or of five with the inclusion of the rests. Finally, in A_1 the second *B* remains perfect, since a complete perfection, consisting of three perfect *S*, follows. There result

FACSIMILE 40

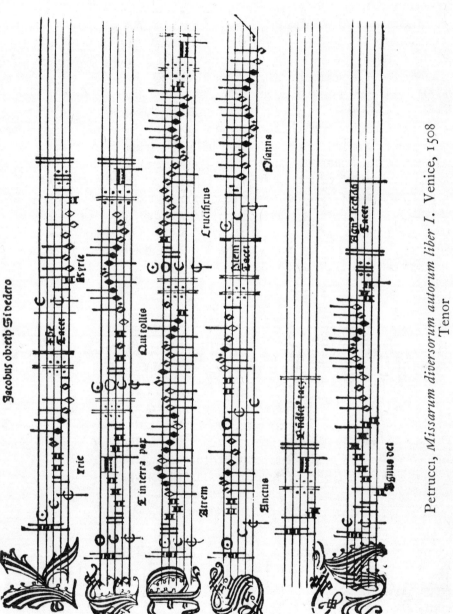

Petrucci, *Missarum diversorum autorum liber I.* Venice, 1508
Tenor

—with the rests included—five perfect *B*, the actual value of which is tripled by the *prolatio perfecta* as a *signum augentiae* (15 measures of $\frac{3}{2}$-meter).   See the transcription in appendix No. 29, which may be compared with that in *HdN* 1, 422.

* On Facsimile 41 we reproduce the other parts of the *Sanctus*, in order to enable the student to make a complete transcription of this piece.

The considerations and calculations involved in the reading of such tenors were not without their difficulties even for sixteenth century singers, not all of whom were so well trained in the intricacies of the proportional system as, for instance, the singers of the papal choir or of other great churches.   This situation became particularly urgent in the case of printed books which, intended to reach a wide clientele, had to be designed in such a way as to accomodate a reader of merely average training and ability.   It was for this reason that Petrucci, who was the first to publish printed editions of masses, frequently added to the proportional tenor a *resolutio*, that is, a transcription in plain mensural values.   Following is the tenor of the *Kyrie* from Obrecht's mass *Je ne demande*, both in its canonic and transcribed version (from *Misse Obrecht*, Venice 1502):

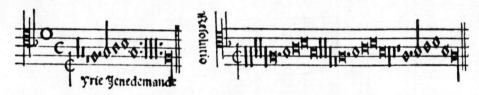

In accordance with the meter of the other parts, *alla breve* is used here for the *resolutio;* each *S* of the original becomes a *B* in the transcription. The reader may first transcribe the tenor in the familiar manner, and then compare it with the 'sixteenth century transcription.'

Another method of writing proportional tenors is illustrated by the following example, taken from Josquin's *Missa Di dadi supra naxagie* (*dadi* = dice; *naxagie* = *N'aray-je*, a chanson by Morton):

The black squares at the beginning signify augmentation in the ratio

FACSIMILE 41

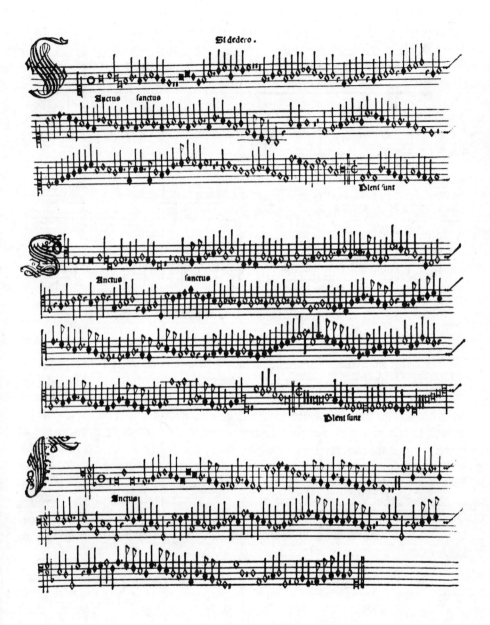

Petrucci, *Missarum diversorum autorum liber I.* Venice, 1508
Superius, Altus, Bassus

indicated by the number of dots (doubling). Again, the student may compare his transcription with the *resolutio:*

For the *Crucifixus* of the mass, the same melody is used in sixfold augmentation:

An example of considerably greater complication, found in the Old Hall MS (*ca.* 1450), is discussed on p. 366 f.

Only brief mention can be made here of the numerous canonic inscriptions which show the intention of the composer 'sub obscuritate quadam.'

Among the simplest are those which direct the singer to read his part backwards. This indication was disguised under expressions such as: 'A est O' (A [Alpha, the first letter of the Greek alphabet] becomes O [Omega, the last letter of this alphabet]), or: 'canit more Hebraeorum' (to be sung in the manner of the Hebrews, with reference to the fact that Hebrew writing is read from the right side to the left), or: 'Vade retro, Satanas' (get thee behind me, Satan), or by the more familiar 'cancriza' (walk like a crab), or by the word tenor spelt backward: 'Ronet,' or thus: 'ɿouǝʇ,' if retrograde motion was to be combined with inversion.[1]

---

[1] The inscription 'Ronet' appears on a four-voice *Et in terra pax* of the MS *52* of the Library Krasinski, Warsaw, reproduced in *SchT*, 5. However, the present writer has been able to arrive at a satisfactory transcription of this abnormally difficult specimen only by disregarding the above inscription and by allowing various other emendations in the notation of the two lower parts, namely: (1) both parts begin after a rest of 16 *B* (with the section 'Laudamus'); (2) both parts are repeated, beginning with 'Qui tollis'; (3) the last four *L* (two rests and two notes) of the tenor must be omitted; (4) the 6th and the 24th note of the tenor (not including the rests) is a *L* each. This author readily admits that these far-reaching conjectures are rather unsatisfactory; he would be glad to be informed
* about a solution which is more in keeping with the notation of the original.

An example is found in the chanson *O dolce conpagno* by Dominicus de Feraria which appears on the lower part of Facsimile 32. The contra. bears the inscription: 'Et d[icitu]r eundo et redeundo,' that is: to be sung going forward and going backward. As a matter of fact, it will be seen that its length is the exact half of that of the discant, and that in playing it twice, the second time in retrograde motion, it combines satisfactorily with this part. However the resulting texture in two parts is not the complete composition, since a third part is indicated 'sub obscuritate quadam' in the text of the discant which reads as follows: 'O dolce compagno se tu voy cantare dyapason piglia senca demorare'—that is: 'My sweet companion, if you wish to sing, please sing the octave without hesitation.' This would seem to indicate that the singer of the third part should follow the discant in the (lower) octave, thus producing a succession of consecutive octaves for the entire composition (see the transcription in J. Stainer, *Dufay and His Contemporaries*, p. 160). Fortunately, this is not the meaning of the inscription. As H. Riemann has shown (*ZIMG* VI, 466), the 'companion' has to sing his part backward, beginning with the last note of the discant which actually is the lower octave of its first tone.

As an example of the complicated tenor technique of the fifteenth century, the tenor of Dunstable's *Veni sancte spiritus* is reproduced below (from *DTOe* VII, 201; cf. also p. xxix of this volume):

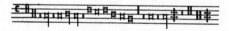

Canon: *Et dicitur prius directe, secundo subverte lineam, tertio revertere removendo tertiam partem et capies diapente, si vis habere tenorem Sancti Spiritus.*

According to this inscription, the given melody must be sung first as written, that is, in [3, 2], which is the mensuration of the other parts. For the first repetition, the direction 'subverte lineam' (turn the staff, i.e., upside down) indicates inversion, while for the third statement retrograde motion is indicated ('revertere') together with transposition to the (lower!) fifth ('capies diapente') and a reduction of the ternary values to binary values ('removendo tertiam partem') or, in other words, transition from [3, 2] to [2, 2]. Not only the 'inverted' but also the 'retrograde' section is preceded by a rest of nine measures, as is suggested by the rests placed at the end of the melody, between the first and the second signs of repetition. A transcription is given in the appendix, No. 30.

It goes without saying that with a canonic inscription like the above—

and there are many which are much more 'obscure'—the exact meaning of the directions has to be worked out by experimentation, that is, on the basis of the transcription of the other parts which usually present no difficulty. H. B. Collins, in his edition of the *Missa O Quam Suavis* (Burnham, 1927) has used this method with remarkable ingenuity, an ingenuity which is certainly equal to that of the man who devised the really diabolical tricks encountered in this composition. The following tenor very nicely illustrates the mentality of the unknown composer whose work, by the way, proves him a great artist as well as a keen intellect:[1]

dia arte contractos.

The use of the smallest note-values for a tenor shows at once that the written values are fictitious. By induction, Collins has shown that their real values are nearly the reverse of those indicated in the writing, the *B*, *S*, *M*, and dotted *S* equalling one, two, four, and six *S* respectively. Thus, the beginning of the tenor reads as follows:

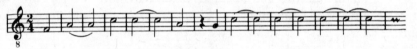

In this interpretation the tenor yields the exact number of 102 *S* which is required by the upper parts, as against $31\frac{1}{2}$ *S* in the writing. The notation, therefore, actually is 'contracted' by an 'art' which, as Mr. Collins aptly remarks, the reader is free to interpret as 'divina' or 'diabolica.'

I. Proportional Time Signatures and Tempo[2]

Our study of the proportions would be incomplete if we pass over what actually is by far their most frequent use, that is, simultaneously in all the parts of a composition or a section thereof. Practically all music of the sixteenth century is written with the alla breve sign ¢ in all the

---

[1] The notation of the MS is in black notes. See p. xxi of the above-mentioned publication.

[2] Although, to the best knowledge of this writer, the above study is the first attempt to attack the problem of the tempo of Flemish music from a musical point of view, there exist several publications in which quotations from theoretical treatises are given, information which, of course, will have to be considered in a more exhaustive and definitive treatment than has been intended here. The most important of these publications are: A. Chybinski, *Beiträge zur Geschichte des Taktschlagens* (Krakau, 1908); E. Praetorius, *Die Mensuraltheorie des Franchinus Gafurius* (*Publicationen der Internationalen Musikgesellschaft* II, ii, Leipzig 1905); G. Schünemann, 'Zur Frage des Taktschlagens und der Textbehandlung in der Mensuralmusik' (*SIMG* 1908).

parts, and the use of signs such as ⏀ , etc. for shorter or longer
sections of motets and masses is very common. From the strictly notational point of view this usage is the least interesting, since, whatever
the meaning of these signs be, it applies equally to all the parts. Therefore the transcriber may simply disregard them or, in order to appease
his scholarly scruples, simply indicate them as they are given in the original, leaving it to the reader to find out what they mean. This method,
together with the practice of using unreduced note values (S = whole-
note, etc.) has been adopted in the great majority of scholarly publications of early music (see the editions of the Trent Codices, of Ockeghem,
of Lassus, of Palestrina, etc.). However, a serious objection must be
raised against this method, namely, that it disregards (and, from the
point of view of the modern reader, obscures) a fundamental feature of
the mensural and the proportional signs: their temporal significance.

There can be no doubt that throughout the history of music prior to
1600 the notational signs indicated not only relative values, as do the
modern notes, but also signified absolute temporal durations. This fact
constitutes a basic contrast to the modern system in which the duration
of a given note, e.g., a half-note, may vary from several seconds (in
largo) to fractions of a second (in prestissimo). That the modern principle of unlimited variability of tempo is of a fairly recent date appears
from a glance at the practice of the seventeenth and early eighteenth
centuries in which the limits of the variability are considerably narrower,
and in which the scarce use of tempo marks points strongly to the existence of 'normal tempi' from which only moderate deviations were admissible. Such a line of development suggests the assumption that, in a
still earlier period, the variability of tempo may have been practically
unknown. This is exactly the situation that existed in music prior to
the end of the sixteenth century.

Before we turn to more detailed explanations it may not be superfluous to corroborate the principle of tempo-stability by some considerations of a general nature. In looking over, for instance, the works of
Orlando di Lasso or Palestrina the uniformity of the notation is striking.
There is nothing comparable to what we find in the works of Bach or,
even more, those of Beethoven, in which one piece may be written chiefly
in large values (whole to quarter-notes), the other in small notes (eighth
to thirty-second-notes), a situation which becomes still more strange—
not to say, 'artificial'—from the fact that the larger values are used for
quick pieces, the smaller ones for slow compositions. The old masters
followed a more 'natural' procedure, by writing all their pieces in the
same note-values, chiefly *brevis*, *semibrevis*, *minima*, and *semiminima*, the

fusa being used only in groups of two for a quick cadential ornamentation in the character of a mordent.

Additional evidence in support of the principle of tempo-stability is found in the fifteenth and sixteenth century theory of proportions, which is essentially based upon the idea of a fundamental and unchangeable unit of time, the *tactus*. In fact, the considerable complexities of this system would certainly present an insurmountable obstacle even for a well trained singer, if they were understood to refer to variable note-values such as prevail in modern music. Actually, the situation was not quite as complicated as the modern reader is inclined to believe. To the singer of this period *proportia tripla* or *proportio sesquitertia* meant a definite and fixed tempo, derived from the *integer valor*, and familiar to him through his long training in a normal tempo which represented for him the natural pulse of music.

The complete absence of tempo marks in the early sources is perhaps not a very strong argument, considering the general 'negligence' of the old masters in so many questions which are of vital interest to us. However, it is interesting and significant that the first tempo marks occur in sources of music for a soloist. To the best knowledge of this writer the earliest remarks of this type occur in the lute pieces of Luis de Milan (*El Maestro*, 1536), according to whom certain sections of his lute fantasias must be played 'a priesa' (quick), others 'a espacio' (slow). That a single player was much more naturally disposed to free himself from the fetters of fixed tempo than the performer of ensemble music is obvious.

More eloquent than the musical sources are the theoretical treatises of the sixteenth century. Practically every theorists gives longer or shorter explanations on the *tactus* as the unit of musical time, and although the positive information to be gained from these explanations is much less clear than we would wish, the important fact is that nowhere is a remark to be found which would give the slightest justification for the assumption that the duration of a note could be varied according to the text, the character or feeling of the piece, or whatever other romantic ideas a modern conductor may have in his mind if he chooses the 'right' tempo for a motet by Palestrina or by Byrd. In the sixteenth century there existed only one way of changing the temporal duration of a given note, that is, by proportions. Thus the proportional signs, if used simultaneously in all the parts, represent the tempo marks, nay, the metronomic marks, of the fifteenth and sixteenth centuries.

After this blunt statement, the situation may seem to be much simpler than it is. Actually, the establishment of tempo-stability as a principle of early music is only the basis for numerous questions of detail most of which are bound up with evolutionary changes. It goes without saying that this principle does not imply stability of tempo throughout the entire early history of music, but only during certain periods, or in certain schools, or for certain 'standard' types of music. Even in this more limited sense the term should not be interpreted too rigidly, and should be considered as the indication of a guiding idea rather than as a strict law.

The following explanations in no way attempt to present an even approximately exhaustive study of the problem of tempo, a study which would certainly fall outside the scope of the present book. Only a few typical examples will be studied which serve to clarify the temporal meaning of the proportional signs.

As has already been pointed out (p. 147), the fundamental conception of tempo in sixteenth century music was the *tactus*, a unit of time-measurement comparable to a slow to moderate beat which was represented (in *integer valor*) by the *S*. Although the indications concerning the duration of the *tactus*, such as are found in various treatises, are much less clear than we would like them to be, yet they are sufficient to show that the *tactus* was a temporal unit equal to M.M. 48, more or less.[1] Such a tempo, that is, *S* = M.M. 48, is indeed quite adequate for the major portion of the sacred music of the Flemish era, which is practically always written in *B*, *S*, *M*, *Sm*, and *F*, the latter value being used only in groups of two as a quick 'cadential mordent.' The *Kyrie's* by Ockeghem and de la Rue, as well as the *Sanctus* by Benet (Facsimiles 34, 27, 24) serve as examples.

Another example, shown on p. 192 (from MS Florence, *Magl. xix, 112 bis*), shows a section in ⊂ followed by one in ¢ . This change is accompanied by a striking shift from the shorter to the longer values, the section ¢ being written mostly in *B*, *S*, and *M*. Evidently, the *tactus* which, in the first section, falls on the *S*, falls here on the *B*. Similar examples are frequent in the works of the late fifteenth and early sixteenth centuries, and may be studied in publications such as A. W. Ambros, *Geschichte der Musik*, (Leipzig, 1889), vol. v (e.g., pp. 4-5), or D. Plamenac, *Johannes Ockeghem, Sämtliche Werke, Messen I-VIII* (Leipzig, 1927). If, in these examples, the sign ¢ is interpreted in its strict proportional meaning, the result is a change of the note values without any real change of tempo, the same durations (M.M. 48, 96) now being represented not by *S* and *M*, but by *B* and *S*. This interpretation is not wholly satisfactory, since it marks the sectional use of ¢

[1] The number 48 has been chosen here as an average value because it is divisible by two as well as by three.

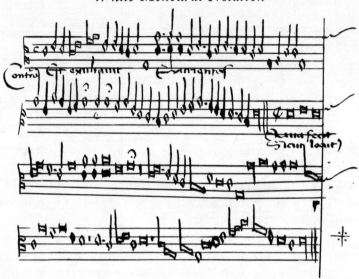

as a mere externality of writing without any real significance. We prefer to think that it really meant a different tempo, the reduction of the values being somewhat different from the exact halving. A possible explanation will be offered below.

During and after the Josquin period the sign ₵ was universally adopted as a time-signature, to the almost complete exclusion of the signs of *integer valor*, C and ○ . We now find under this sign exactly the same note values, *B* to *F*, which formerly were used under the sign C , as a quick perusal of the editions of Lassus and Palestrina will readily show. Obviously, a real *diminutio dupla* of the temporal values, i.e., $S =$ M.M. 96, leads to a tempo which is much too quick. The fact that the same note values appear here and in the Facsimiles 34, 27, and 24 suggests the theory that there really was no change in tempo, the *S* having approximately the same value now under ₵ as it had formerly under C .

No attempt is made here to explain why the sign ₵ was so universally adopted throughout the sixteenth century, without any apparent significance and meaning. Possibly its adoption is bound up with the introduction of the *tactus major* and the *tactus minor*, terms which indicate, not different tempi, but different conductor's beats for the same tempo, the latter having two movements of the hand in place of one of the former.

A similar situation is encountered in the case of the *tempus perfectum diminutum* Φ . As has already been pointed out, this sign, if used as a common time signature, always calls for ternary mensuration of the *B*, in

contrast to its correct meaning as a proportional sign. As regards the
tempo of this meter, the same ambiguity exists as was previously encountered. The following reproductions (from the *Odhecaton*) illustrate this point. Obviously, a much quicker tempo is demanded for the
'Rompeltier' than for the 'Est possible.' Whereas the latter is approximately in the tempo of the *integer valor* ($S = 48$), the former is in double
that speed, $S = 96$, or $B = 32$.

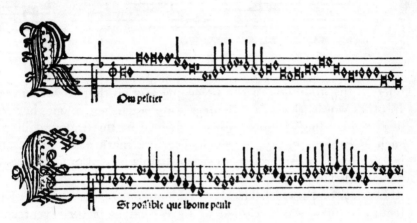

In the latter interpretation which, no doubt, is the earlier and the
original one (see our remarks regarding Facsimile 88, p. 425), we arrive
at a new value, $B = $ M.M. 32, for the *brevis perfecta diminuta*. Considering the general importance of *tempus perfectum* in the period of Dufay
and Ockeghem, it is not impossible to assume that this value of the *brevis
perfecta diminuta* was also used in *tempus imperfectum diminutum*. This
would lead to the value $S = 64$ for ₵ , that is, to a really different tempo
for the sections in diminution we have been considering previously.[1]

In turning to a consideration of *proportio tripla* we find a somewhat
simpler situation. The meaning of the signs C3 , or $\frac{3}{1}$, or simply 3, conforms with their strictly proportional significance: three S (or a perfect
B) consume the time which is normally allotted to the single S, thus leading to the tempo: B (*pf.*) $= $ M.M. 48. On page 194 is an example (from
MS Modena, Bibl. Estense, *L. 471*).

In the sources of the sixteenth century, the sign 3 occurs most frequently for shorter or longer sections in compositions marked ₵ (for
examples, see Ambros v, 106, 151, and numerous pieces in Lassus,
Palestrina, etc.). Here it must be noted that as a rule the *tripla* does not

---

[1] For an example, see Facsimile 71, p. 363.

refer to the *diminutio* of the preceding section, but to the *integer valor*. In other words, three *S* of the *tripla* are equal, not to one, but to two *S* of the preceding section.   Clear evidence of this is found in passages such as Ambros v, 112, in which measures marked ¢   and 3 alternate in both parts, or Ambros v, 76, where tripla is used in four parts against a cantus firmus in unchanged values.

The use of ¢ , which largely predominated in the sources of the sixteenth century, was discarded to a great extent in the seventeenth century.   In this period, pieces written in c frequently include sections marked 3 or ³₁, a designation which, of course, indicates exact triplication of the speed of the preceding section in *integer valor*.   The following example (from G. Muffat, *Apparatus musico-organisticus II*, 1690; reproduced from A. G. Ritter, *Zur Geschichte des Orgelspiels*, II, 156) serves as an illustration:

Passages of this kind are frequently a cause of fundamental errors on the part of performers and conductors who, mislead by the long notes occurring under these signs, usually take them much too slow, interpreting the sign $\frac{3}{1}$ as a mere metrical indication similar to the familiar $\frac{3}{4}$, and overlooking its proportional significance. Below is a rendering which clarifies the temporal relationship between the two sections. It is interesting to note that in a document as late as this the notational principles of *tempus perfectum* are still strictly observed (see the use of undotted *B* for ternary, and of blackened *B* for binary values):

Turning back to the Flemish era, it may be noted that there existed a variety of proportional time signatures for quick triple rhythm, such as $\Phi : C_3 ; C_2^3 ; \mathbb{C}_2^3 ; \mathbb{C}$. These were all used to indicate that meter and tempo which normally should have been denoted by $\mathbb{C}$. Actually, however, this sign is practically never used after 1450 (1500?) as a time signature, on account of its then firmly established character as a *signum augentiae*.

Considering the fact that some of the above proportional signs denote *proportio dupla*, others *proportio tripla*, it is tempting to speculate whether they might have signified different degrees of speed, possibly as follows:

	O	$\Phi : \mathbb{C}$	$C_3 : \mathbb{C}_2^3$	C_2^3
B:	16	32	48	24
S:	48	96	144	72

Some support of such a theory can be gained from a comparison of two related pieces by Ockeghem, reproduced in Ambros V, 12 and 18, to which the interested reader is referred. However, in this question, as well as in the whole subject of the temporal significance of the mensural and proportional signs, extensive special studies will be necessary before definitive statements can be made.

PART III

THE NOTATION OF ENSEMBLE MUSIC: BLACK NOTATION

I. INTRODUCTION

IN TURNING to a study of black notation one is confronted with a situation entirely different from that presented by white notation. Of course, the use of black notes instead of white ones is merely an external difference.   More notable is the fact that the signs and rules prevailing in the former system differ in many respects from those to be found in the latter.   The chief contrast, however, is one of intrinsic structure, that is, the contrast between a phenomenon of a stable and one of an evolutionary character.   For, whereas white notation is a consolidated system which, during its period of existence, underwent only slight modification, black notation must be comprehended as an historical process.   Throughout the twelfth, thirteenth, and fourteenth centuries the mechanics of notation were in a state of continuous flux and rapid change, produced and paralleled by an evolution in musical style the progress of which lies mainly in the field of rhythm.   The development leading from the entirely free and unmeasured rhythm of the twelfth century organa, through the rigid uniformity of the thirteenth century modal meter, to the singular rhythmic complexities of the late fourteenth century, brought about a continuous succession of notational problems: as soon as one of them was settled, others arose and inaugurated a new phase.   Naturally, under such conditions, it is difficult to draw exact lines of demarcation.   It is, therefore, with due reservation that the following classification is presented:

I.   Primitive notation (ninth through the twelfth century)
II.   Square notation (late twelfth and early thirteenth centuries)
III.   Pre-Franconian notation (middle of the thirteenth century)
IV.   Franconian notation (second half of the thirteenth century)
V.   French notation (*ca.* 1300-1450)
VI.   Italian notation (middle of the fourteenth century)
VII.   Mixed notation (late fourteenth century)
VIII.   Mannered notation (late fourteenth and early fifteenth centuries).

Square notation is also called 'modal notation' (see p. 218). The systems IV to VIII are usually termed 'black mensural notation.' The term 'French notation' for the system V is not meant to suggest a contrast to the previous systems which, of course, are all of French origin, but to the contemporary Italian notation (VI). It should be noted that the system of French notation, by the adoption of white notes, led, around 1450, to the white mensural notation.

The treatment of this large field obviously demands an entirely different method from that used in the preceding chapters. In place of methodical and systematic explanations, given frequently in the form of rules, we must treat the subject in a more flexible manner, and must approach it chiefly from the evolutionary point of view. More consideration must be given here to the theoretical writings, which in these early periods prove to be important and generally reliable sources of information and which, in spite of their aura of scholasticism, are closer to the musical practice of their period than the treatises of the late fifteenth and sixteenth centuries are to theirs.

The following table provides a general view of the most important sources, both practical and theoretical, of black notation, together with references to modern publications. The chronological arrangement has been made on the basis of the notational characteristics rather than the date of completion of the manuscripts. The difference between these two dates may in some instances be quite considerable, especially in the case of manuscripts which are preserved only in copies from non-existent originals.[1] As a rule, the 'notational' date of a source will correspond with the position it occupies in the historical development, since the original system of notation was generally preserved even by later copyists.

[1] A case in point is offered by the Codex Wolfenbüttel 677 (*W*₁) of the School of Notre Dame, which has been frequently accepted as having been written around or even after 1300 (see, e.g., the Introduction to F. H. Baxter, *An Old St. Andrews Music Book*, p. xiii, and G. Reese, *Music in the Middle Ages, p. 297*). However, the present writer has always been skeptical about this late dating, and was gratified to find his view supported by no less an authority than Prof. E. K. Rand of Harvard University, who pointed out to him that the minuscule, rather than the majuscule, form of the final *s*, as well as the more regular *a* of minuscule Carolingian script, suggest a mid-thirteenth century date for the codices *W*₁ and *Fl*, that is to say, only a few decades later than the period represented by their contents.

SOURCES OF BLACK NOTATION

Musical Sources	*Theoretical Sources*

I. PRIMITIVE NOTATION (9th-12th centuries)

a. *Syllables, Letters*

Musica enchiriadis, Scholia enchiriadis ca. 900 (*GS* I, 152, 173).
Guido d'Arezzo, *Micrologus*, ca. 1000 (*GS* II, 2).
Ad organum faciendum, 11th cent. (Coussemaker, *Hist. de l'harmonie*, 229).

'Ut tuo propitiatus,' 11th cent. (see p. 207).

b. *Cheironomic Neumes*

Winchester Troper, ca. 1050 (W. H. Frere, *The Winchester Troper*, 1894).

c. *Diastematic Neumes*

MSS of St. Martial, ca. 1150: Paris, B. N. *lat. 1139, 3719, 3549;* London, Br. M. *Add. MS. 36881.*
Codex Calixtinus of Santiago de Compostela, ca. 1150 (P. Wagner, *Die Gesänge der Jakobusliturgie*, 1931).

II. SQUARE NOTATION (1175-1225)

Four sources of Notre Dame, ca. 1250·
1. Wolfenbüttel *677* (*W*₁); facs. in J. H. Baxter, *An Old St. Andrews Music Book*, London, 1931.
2. Florence, Bibl. Laur. *pluteus 29 codex 1* (*Fl*); also known as *Antiphonarium Mediceum*.
3. Madrid, Bibl. Nac. *Hh 167* (*Ma*).
4. Wolfenbüttel *1206* (*W*₂).
London, Br. M. *Egerton 2615* (*LoA*).
London, Br. M. *Egerton 274* (*LoB*).
Paris, B. N. *15139* (formerly *St. Victor 813*).
Paris, B. N. *frc. 844*, 'Chansonnier Roy' (*R*); facs. in J. B. Beck, *Le Manuscrit du Roi*, Philadelphia, 1938.
Paris, B. N. *frc. 12615*, *Chansonnier Noailles*' (*N*).

III. PRE-FRANCONIAN NOTATION (1225-1275)

Paris, B. N. *lat. 11266.*
London, Br. M. *Add. 30091.*

Discantus positio vulgaris, ca. 1225 (*CS* I, 94).

Codex Montpellier, Montpellier, Fac. des
Méd. *H 196 (Mo)* fasc. II-VI; facs. and
transc. in Y. Rokseth, *Polyphonies du
xiiie siècle*, 4 vols., Paris, 1936-39.
Codex Bamberg, Bamberg, Kgl. Bibl. *Ed.
IV. 6 (Ba)*; facs. and transcr. in P.
Aubry, *Cent Motets du xiiie siècle*, 3 vols.,
Paris, 1908.
Codex Torino, Torino, Bibl. Reale, *man.
var. N. 42.*
Codex Huelgas or *Burgos*, *(Hu)*; facs. and
transcr. in H. Anglès, *El Codex musical
de Las Huelgas*, 3 vols., Barcelona, 1938.

Anon. VII, *ca.* 1250 (*CS* I, 378).
Joh. de Garlandia, the elder, *ca.* 1250
(*CS* I, 96).
Pseudo-Aristoteles or Magister Lambert,
ca. 1250 (*CS* I, 269).
Amerus, *ca.* 1275 (J. Kromolicki, *Die Prac-
tica Musicae des Amerus*, Berlin, 1909).
Dietricus, *ca.* 1275 (H. Müller, *Eine
Abhandlung über Mensuralmusik*, 1886).
Anonymous Sowa (H. Sowa, *Ein glossierter
Mensuraltractat 1279*, Kassel, 1930).

IV. FRANCONIAN NOTATION

Codex Montpellier, fasc. VII-VIII (see
above).
Paris, B. N. *frc. 146 (Roman de Fauvel)*,
ca. 1315; facs. in P. Aubry, *Le Roman de
Fauvel*, Paris, 1907.

Franco of Cologne, *Ars cantus mensur-
abilis, ca.* 1260 (*CS* I, 117).
Walter Odington, *ca.* 1280 (*CS* I, 235).
Anon. IV, *ca.* 1280 (*CS* I, 327).
Robertus de Handlo, *Regulae* (*CS* I, 383).
Anon. III (*CS* I, 319).

V. FRENCH NOTATION

Codex Ivrea (Ivrea, Libr. of the Chapter).
Machaut-MSS (G. de Machaut, 1300-
1377): Paris, B. N. *22545/46, 1584, 1585,
1586,9221; MS de Vogüe*, Paris. See F.
Ludwig, *G. de Machaut, Musikalische
Werke*, Leipzig, 1928, II.
Numerous French and English fragments;
see *AfMW* VII, p. 195 ff. and 219 ff; also
GdM I, 176.
Compositions contained in the MSS listed
under 'Italian Notation.'
Prague, Univ. Bibl. *XI E 9;* see F. Kam-
merer, *Die Musikstücke des Prager Kodex
XI E 9*, Prag, 1931.
Codex Apt (Apt, Library of the Chapter),
ca. 1400; transcr. in A. Gastoué, *Le Manu-
scrit . . . d'Apt*, 1936.
Cambrai, *MS 6 (Cambrai A)*, *ca.* 1425.
Rome, Bibl. Vat. Urb. *lat. 1411;* see *GdM*
I, 192.
Bologna, Lic. Mus. *cod 37;* see *GdM* I, 197.
Bologna, Bibl. Univ. *2216;* see *GdM* I,
199 ff.

Joh. de Garlandia, the younger, *ca.* 1300　*
(*CS* i, 389, 424).
Ph. de Vitry, *Ars nova, ca.* 1325 (*CS* III,
13).
Joh. de Muris, *Musica practica*, 1321
(*GS* III, 292). See also *CS* III, 46, 59, 68.
Speculum musicae (by Jacobus of Liège?),
ca. 1325 (*CS* II, 322).
Theod. de Campo, *ca.* 1350 (*CS* III, 177).
Verulus de Anagnia, *ca.* 1350 (*CS* III, 129).
Simon Tunstede, *ca.* 1350 (*CS* IV, 254).
Anon. V (*CS* III, 379).
Prosdocimus de Beldemandis, *Tractatus
. . .* , 1408 (*CS* III, 200).
Joh. Ciconia, *Liber de proportionibus*,
1411 (see *HdN* I, 333).
Guilelmus Monachus, *De preceptis. . . . li-
bellus, ca.* 1450 (*CS* III, 273).

Old Hall MS (College of St. Edmunds,
England); new ed. by A. Ramsbotham,
3 vols., Burnham, 1933-1938.
(The last four sources date from the first
half of the fifteenth century).

VI, VII. ITALIAN NOTATION; MIXED NOTATION

Rome, Bibl. Vat., *MS Rossi 215*, see J.
Wolf in *Jahrbuch Peters*, 1938.
Florence, Bibl. Nac. *Panc. 26*; see *GdM* 1,
244.
London, Br. Mus. *Add. 29987*; see *GdM* 1,
268.
Paris, B. N. *ital. 568*; see *GdM* 1, 250.
Florence, Bibl. Laur. *Pal. 87*, (*Squarcial-
upi Codex*); see *GdM* 1, 228.
Paris, B. N. *f. fr. nouv. acq. 6771*, (*Codex
Reina*); see *GdM* 1, 260.

Marchettus de Padua, *Pomerium, ca.* 1320
(*GS* III, 121). See also *CS* III, 1
Anon. VII (*CS* III, 404).
Ph. de Caserta (*CS* III, 118).
Anon. X (*CS* III, 413).
Antonius de Leno (*CS* iii, 307).
Prosd. de Beldemandis, *Tractatus . . . ad
modum Ytalicorum*, 1412 (*CS* III, 228);
see C. Sartori, *La Notazione Italiana del
Trecento*, 1938.

VIII. MANNERED NOTATION

Modena, Bibl. Estense *L. 568*
Chantilly, Musée Condé *1047*.
Torino, Bibl. Naz. *J II 9*.
Compositions contained in Paris, B. N. *ital.
568* and *f. fr. 6771* (see under VI, VII).

Bibliography:

I: *OH*, 45-101; M. Schneider, *Geschichte der Mehrstimmigkeit*, Berlin, 1935,
vol. II.
II: *OH*, 102-371; F. Ludwig, *Repertorium organorum recentioris et motetorum
vetustissimi stili*, Halle, 1910, particularly p. 42-57; *HdN* 1, 198-237; G. Jacobsthal, *Die Mensuralnotenschrift des 12. und 13. Jahrhunderts*, Berlin, 1871;
W. Niemann, *Die abweichende Bedeutung der Ligaturen in der Mensuraltheorie
der Zeit vor Johannes de Garlandia*, Leipzig, 1902; H. Sowa, *Ein anonymer glos-
sierter Mensuraltraktat 1279*, Kassel, 1930.
III: *HdN* 1, 237-250;
IV: *HdN* 1, 250-286; *GdM* 1, 37-62; II, III, nos. 1-12.
V: *HdN* 1, 330-362; *GdM* 1, 63-214; II, III, nos. 13-37; F. Ludwig, in *SIMG* VI,
607; H. Besseler, in *AfMW*, VII, VIII.
VI, VII: *HdN* 1, 287-329; *GdM* 1, 28-36 and 215-288; II, III, nos. 38-63.
VIII: *GdM* 1, 289 ff, 328 ff; II, III, nos. 64-70.

For additional literature see: G. Reese, *Music in the Middle Ages*, p. 451 ff.

II. PRIMITIVE NOTATION

THE EARLIEST preserved documents of part music are the instruc-tive examples of parallel organum, contained in the *Musica En-chiriadis* (*GS* I, 152) and in the *Scholia Enchiriadis* (*GS* I, 173), two MSS of the ninth century.[1] Here a staff of a varying number of lines (four to eighteen) is used, the interspaces of which represent the successive de-grees of the scale. Instead of using notes or similar signs, the syllables of the text are placed in the proper interspaces, as is shown in Facsimile 42a (text: 'Tu patris sempiternus es filius'). The pitch is further clari-fied by means of the signs of the so-called Dasia notation, written at the left of the staff. This system, which is a mediaeval imitation of the an-cient Greek notation,[2] utilizes four basic signs for the tones of the tet-rachord d e f g, and others (derived largely from these by changing their position from upright to horizontal, or their direction from right to left, as in Greek notation) for one lower and two-and-half higher tetrachords which repeat the basic tetrachord in exact transpositions of the fifth. There results a curious scale which avoids diminished fifths but, as a consequence, includes augmented octaves, as follows:

G   A   B♭ c | d   e   f   g | a   b   c′ d′ | e′ f′♯ g′ a′ | b′ c″♯

The letters *t* (or *t*°) and *s*, indicating *tonus* and *semitonus* (whole-tone and semitone) are added in some of the examples as a further clarification of pitch. It must be noticed, however, that their indications frequently contradict (or correct?) those of the Dasia scale proper. For instance, the example of Facsimile 42a contains, according to the fundamental scale, a B-flat in the lower part, while the letter *t* placed between the lowest signs would call for a whole tone above A:

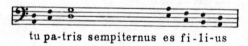

tu pa-tris sempiternus es fi-li-us

[1] The notation of the *Musica* and *Scholia Enchiriadis* was first correctly interpreted by Ph. Spitta, in *VfMW*, v. See also *HdN* I, 31, and G. Reese, *Music in the Middle Ages*, pp. 126, 254, and Bibli-ography. For various details of the above explanations I am indebted to Mr. Lincoln B. Spiess who is preparing a study on 'Consonance and Dissonance from the Ninth to the Fourteenth Centuries.'

[2] See, for instance, *HdN* I, II ff and various monographs on Greek music mentioned in the bibli-ography of G. Reese's book.

FACSIMILES 42a, 42b

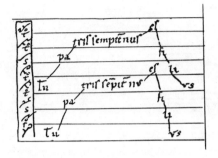
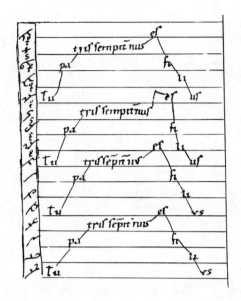

Musica Enchiriadis (9th century)

FACSIMILE 43

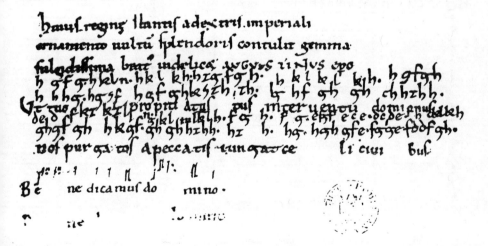

MS Oxford, Bodleian Library *572* (11th century)

In Facsimile 42b, which shows a four-voice organum, the intervals are indicated only for the higher octave of the scale, probably in order to permit the singers of the two lower parts to introduce the necessary chromatic alterations:

* This is not the place to enter into a discussion as to what is the intended reading of these examples. It may be noted, however, that our two facsimiles (the only ones which were available for this book[1]) are not entirely characteristic. More typical is the manner of writing illustrated by the reproductions given below,[2] in which only a small number of the Dasian signs are used and repeated in transpositions which are indicated by additional signs.

P No/ qui vivimus benedicimus

Pr. XI. No/ qui vivimus

Or. VIII. No/ qui vivimus

H No/ qui vivimus benedicimus

Pr. IIII. No/ qui vivimus

A No/ qui vivimus benedicimus

---

[1] See H. B. Briggs, *The Musical Notation of the Middle Ages*, London, 1890, pl. 17.
[2] For the complete reproductions, see *GS* I, pp. 185, 186.

For instance, in the first reproduction the signs for the segment d — b appear three times, while the letters A, H, and P, written in front of the sign for a, indicate that the three singers start with A, a, and a' respectively (for the meaning of the signs A, H, P see the explanations on p. 21). In the second reproduction the same segment appears twice, and the three singers start, according to the roman numerals, on the fourth, eighth, and eleventh degrees of the scale (beginning with e), that is, on a, e', and a' (the letters *Pr.* and *Or.* designate the *vox principalis* and the *vox organalis*). The second tone of the *organalis* is F-sharp.

A more advanced type of organum is represented by the curious illustrations of another 'Hucbaldian' treatise (reproduced in *CS* II, 74 ff) which—at least in Coussemaker's reproduction—look like an engineer's design for the construction of a bridge rather than like musical notation. *
Small circles indicate the positions of the tones in the Dasian scale, and vertical or diagonal lines somewhat vaguely connect simultaneous sounds. Following are a few examples taken from Coussemaker (*CS* II, 77) and their transcription:

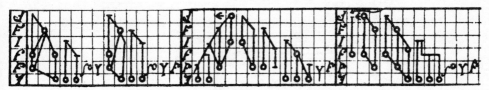

In the tenth century various systems of letter-notation were evolved (see p. 21). Such letters are used in the eleventh-century treatise, *Ad organum faciendum*[1], for the writing down of organa in contrary motion ('new organum,' see *OH* I, 74), for instance:

c a b G F e c d c a b G
C D F D F E F G F E F G
Alle   lu   ia

Al-le - lu - - ia

A particularly interesting specimen of part music written in letter-notation (the only one preserved outside of treatises) is the famous *Ut tuo propitiatus* from the codex *572* of the Bodleian Library, Oxford

[1] E. Coussemaker, *Histoire de l'harmonie au moyen-âge*, Paris, 1852, p. 229. See *OH* I, 77 ff.

(Facsimile 43). This composition, although of a later date (eleventh century) than the one just considered, employs a more ancient system of signs, in which the letters a — p designate the tones of two octaves from A to a' (so-called Boethian notation; see the system II of the table p. 21). Following is a transliteration of the beginning of the piece:

h g f g . h k l n . h k   l k h . h i g f g h.   .

h h h g . h g ? f . h g   f g h . k ? i h i h.

Ut tuo   pro-pi-ti- a-   tus (interventu Dominus nos pur-
                                                       gatos a peccatis iungat coeli
                                                       civibus)

The question mark in the lower row stands for a sign, vaguely reminiscent of a 5, the meaning of which has been variously interpreted (see *RHdM* I, ii, 141 and *OH* I, 92). We suggest interpreting it as indicating pro-
✱longed duration of the preceding tone:

Despite the great authority which H. Riemann deservedly enjoys as a musical scholar, the reader must be expressly warned against his rhythmical version of the above piece—as well as against those of numerous other melodies reproduced in his *Handbuch*. These versions are the result of his principle of 'Vierhebigkeit' (Hebung, i.e., accent), a theory according to which, throughout the history of music, all musical phrases comprise four accents, i.e., two or four measures or multiples thereof. Accordingly, Riemann forces the above melody into two $\frac{4}{4}$-measures, coordinating it to the four accents of the text: 'út tuó propítiátus.' Actually, 'Vierhebigkeit' is a principle which plays a basic and universal rôle only in the music of the eighteenth and nineteenth centuries. If applied to mediaeval compositions it usually leads to procrustean deformities of which Riemann's rendition of the piece in question furnishes one of the most monstrous examples.

A great number (over 150) of two-part organa are preserved in the eleventh century Winchester Troper. Unfortunately, they are written in cheironomic[1] neumes the deciphering of which is extremely dubious,

---

[1] Neumes are called cheironomic (staffless, *in campo aperto*) if their writing gives no clear indication of pitch; otherwise they are called diastematic or heighted.

to say the least. A discussion of their notational problems is beyond the scope of the present book, since it would presuppose a study of the neumes. Suffice it to say that the organal parts are not written together with the liturgical melodies, but appear in separate sections bearing inscriptions such as 'Incipiunt melliflua organorum modulamina super dulcissima caelestia praeconia.'[1]

In turning to the sources of the twelfth century we enter upon more solid ground. A large repertory of two-part organa written in diastematic neumes is contained in the manuscripts from St. Martial at Limoges and in related sources.[2] A reproduction from the MS Paris B. N. *lat.* *3549* (p. 151'/152) may serve as an example (Facsimile 44).

With each line of the text, two rows of neumes of the Aquitanian (i.e., southern French) type are given, separated by a horizontal line. The neumatic signs are written on staff lines, which are scratched in the parchment and, therefore, barely visible in a photographic reproduction. They have been redrawn in our facsimile.

The composition is a trope (i.e., inserted text and music) to the Christmas gradual *Viderunt omnes fines terræ* (see *Grad. Rom.*, p. 33). Following is the complete text:

Viderunt Hemanuel patris unigenitum
In ruinam Israel et salutem positum
hominem in tempore, verbum in principio
urbis, quam fundaverat, natum in palacio
omnes fines terræ salutare Dei nostri . . . .

The second line of the poem is to be sung to the music provided for its first line; the continuation of the original text (*omnes fines* . . .) is sung in plainsong.

The pitch of the various tones is clearly indicated (clef-letters c, g, f). The writing of group signs in a strictly vertical position is a characteristic feature of the Aquitanian neumes; these signs must always be read from top to bottom. The contrapuntal coincidence of the two parts is somewhat vaguely indicated by the alignment of the neumatic signs; in cases of doubt the observation of consonances provides a helpful clue. The main problem offered by this notation is that of time values and rhythm. F. Ludwig, in *AHdM* I, 179, gives a transcription of *Viderunt Hemanuel*, in which triple meter—apparently suggested by the modal rhythm of the thirteenth century—is introduced for the beginning of the piece, while for the long melisma on '(unige)ni-' irregular groups of eighth-notes are used in such a manner that frequently a group of three, four or five notes in one part is placed against a group of two, three, or four notes respec-

[1] See W. H. Frere, *The Winchester Troper* (publications of the Henry Bradshaw Society, vol. VIII), plate 7. A number of transcriptions, necessarily of a tentative character, are given in M. Schneider, *Geschichte der Mehrstimmigkeit*, Berlin, 1935, vl. II.

[2] See the list of sources, p. 201.

tively in the other part. This rendition is open to several objections. The introduction of triple meter for the beginning of the piece is without foundation and is bound to lead to a misconception of the rhythmical context, even if this meter is treated freely, as is demanded by Ludwig's inscription: 'In rhythmisch freiem Vortrag.' On the other hand, the use of, e.g., four notes in one part against a group of five notes in the other is rather too vague an indication of how the two parts should be combined. Finally, the grouping of the notes and the vertical alignment of simultaneous notes is frequently not in agreement with the writing of the original.

The fact that a transcription presented by so outstanding and scrupulous a scholar as Ludwig is open to severe question only goes to illustrate the difficulty of the situation. The present writer is far from pretending to be able to offer a 'correct solution' of the problems presented by the piece under consideration. Properly speaking, no transcription into modern notes is possible for music of this kind, and even a rendering by means of the modern signs of Gregorian chant (Roman chorale notation) is not without its difficulties. One must content himself with a sort of clarified copy in which signs as similar as possible to those of the original are used. We suggest a method of transcription the details of which will become sufficiently clear from the following table:

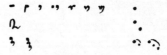

The first three single signs are called *punctum*, *virga*, and *apostropha*. Their difference in meaning is rather problematic and need not concern us here. Even more obscure is the exact meaning of the ornamentations indicated by other symbols for a single note such as reproduced above. The group sign of the second line is the *clivis*, while the signs on the last line are a combination of the *punctum* and the *apostropha*, or else the liquescent form of the *clivis*, also known as *cephalicus* (see the explanation of the neumes in *Liber usualis missae et officii*, Rome, 1937, p. vii).

The proper combination of the notes of the upper voice with those of the lower voice presents great difficulty. In the rendition given in the appendix, No. 31, the observation of consonances has been the main guide, together with the vertical alignment of the characters as they appear in the original. This method has almost everywhere led to a satisfactory result, except for one or two places where a second (d-e) could not be avoided. However, it may be noticed that the use of this interval (in a weak position) is clearly indicated in the 'syllabic section' to the syllable '(tem)po(re).' For more information on the mediaeval theory of consonance and dissonance, see p. 244 f.

FACSIMILE 44

MS Paris, Bibliothèque Nationale *làt. 3549* (12th century)
From pages 151′, 152

From the standpoint of the technique of composition the use of chains of notes in the upper voice (duplum) against single notes in the lower voice (tenor) deserves our attention, particularly if considered in contrast with the strictly syllabic treatment of the section 'hominem . . . pala(cio).' Here we find an early intimation of a differentiation in musical styles which was bound to have far-reaching consequences, and which will play a fundamental rôle in the ensuing discussions of square notation—that is, the distinction between melismatic and syllabic style.

Closely contemporary with the sources of St. Martial is the Codex Calixtinus of the cathedral of Compostela (northern Spain), a page of which is reproduced on Facsimile 45.[1] It contains, beginning in the middle of the first brace, a two-voiced *Alleluia vocavit Jhesus*, at the beginning of which the name Magister Goslenus, episcopus Suessionis, possibly indicates the composer. Each part is written in diastematic neumes of a type similar to those of St. Martial. Their reading, which may offer some difficulties to the novice, will be facilitated by the following transliteration of the beginning, reproduced from P. Wagner's publication, into modern plainsong notes:

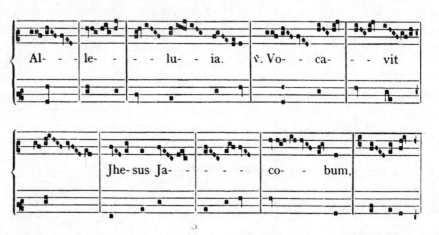

Certainly, these twentieth century 'neumes' are a very convenient—in fact, the most satisfactory—means of 'transcribing' pieces of this early period, the free melismatic rhythm of which would necessarily be destroyed by the signs of measured notation.[2] There is only one point which does not become sufficiently clear from the above transliteration, that is, the coincidence of the upper part with the lower part, if the latter

---

[1] From P. Wagner, *Die Gesänge der Jakobusliturgie zu Santiago de Compostela*, 1931.

[2] Cf. Handschin's measured transcription of a three-voice *Congaudeant Catholici* from the same MS in *ZfMW* VIII, 336.

FACSIMILE 45

Codex Calixtinus. Cathedral of Santiago de Compostela (12th century)
Pages 189′, 190

is written in group-characters. For instance, already with the opening 'measure' of the *Alleluia* the question arises how to align the two notes of the tenor with the ten notes of the duplum. There is, apparently, no hard and fast rule for this. However, the guiding principle will be quickly understood if the composition is viewed from the point of view of two singers performing it. Obviously, the singer of the duplum will take the lead, and the singer of the tenor will follow suit, beginning simultaneously with the first note, and changing to the second note somewhere in the middle of the melisma (always with the first note of a group sign, of course), where a suitable consonance[1] occurs. As an illustration, there follows the 'transcription' of some measures in characters which will make easier reading to the student not familiar with the signs of modern plain-song notation:

Naturally, there is quite a considerable latitude in the question of the vertical alignment. The student will notice that the above arrangement brings about rather bold 'appoggiaturas' which could be avoided if the notes of the tenor were postponed to coincide with the end of a melisma, rather than with its initial note, for instance:

This method has been used by H. Anglès in his transcription of a *Benedicamus* from the Codex Calixtinus (see his *El Codex de las Huelgas*, III, 47). Although it gives satisfactory results, as far as the consonances are concerned, it leads to a very uneven distribution of the notes of the tenor, or else, to fermatas at the end of the phrase which interrupt the flow of the musical line. It is for this reason that the other method, as a rule, would seem to deserve preference.

[1] See the explanation of consonances, p. 244.

III. SQUARE NOTATION

A. General Characterization

THE LATE twelfth century is a highly important period in the history of polyphony. The then newly constructed cathedral of Notre Dame at Paris became the center of a musical activity of greater intensity and of more important consequences than that of any previous period. In striking contrast to the extremely slow progress of polyphonic music during the preceding centuries, there now begins an era of precipitate change. A significant feature illustrating the importance of this period is the fact that here, for the first time, musical activity steps out of the obscurity of anonymous and collective creation, and enters the stage of individual achievement and personal contribution. Magister Leoninus, 'optimus organista,' (greatest composer of organa) and Magister Perotinus Magnus, 'optimus discantor et melior quam Leoninus,' (greatest composer of discant, and greater than Leoninus)—as they are called by the English Anonymous[1]—are the leading figures of the School of Notre Dame. Leoninus was the creator of the Magnus Liber Organi which represents a complete cycle of two-part organa (*organa dupla*) for the ecclesiastical year. His successor Perotinus (*ca.* 1160-1235) rewrote this repertoire in a more 'crystallized' style which is characterized by a greater rhythmic preciseness (modal meter) and by the increase of the number of parts from two to three and, occasionally, four (organa tripla, quadrupla). He also added a large number of short compositions, mostly in two parts, the so-called clausulae ('Ersatzklauseln') which were designed to be used as substitutes for certain sections of the complete organa. For instance, to the organum *Audi filia* (et vide et inclina aurem tuam quia concupivit rex) which is preserved in W_1, p. 19',[2] there exist clausulae for the sections 'fili-,' 'filia,' 'et inclina,' and 'concupivit rex' (in *Fl*, p. 168; reproduced in *SchT*, p. 14). Naturally, the complete organum as well as the clausulae use for their tenors the liturgical plainsong melody of *Audi filia*, which is the verse (℣) of the gradual *Propter veritatem* for Assumption (see *Gr. Rom.*, p. 561).

In strong contrast to the liturgical organa and clausulae there is a

[1] *CS* I, 342.
[2] Page references are always to the modern pagination of W_1.

third type of composition, namely, conductus. A conductus has no relationship to plainsong, either textually or musically, but is simply a
musical setting of a Latin poem. In the period under consideration,
these poems are usually religious lyrics, addressed to the Virgin, a Saint,
or dealing with other religious matters. Later examples frequently refer to social conditions or to political events. A great portion of the exceedingly large repertory of conductus is purely monophonic (conductus
simplex). Here, we are interested only in the conductus in two, three or
four parts (duplex, triplex, quadruplex).

As regards the musical style, as well as the notational methods applied
to these forms, there exists a fundamental distinction resulting from the
fact that the text can be treated in two different ways: either syllabically,
i.e., with one note to each syllable; or melismatically, i.e., with extended groups of notes to each syllable. This distinction exists, of
course, already in Gregorian chant, in which the psalm tones are in a
simple syllabic style, while the graduals, alleluias, etc. are for the most
part in a highly ornate melismatic style. The same distinction occurs
in early polyphony, as appears from Facs. 44 (p. 211), where the section
'hominem . . . pala-' is syllabic in both parts, while the closing passage,
on 'ci-o,' is melismatic.

In the School of Notre Dame the distinction between these two methods
gains considerably in clearness and importance. Melismatic and syllabic
style, which formerly were used side by side, now become rather completely
segregated, the former being used mainly for organa and clausulae, the
latter for conductus. The organa of this period are based on (untroped)
graduals and alleluias, as well as on the *Benedicamus Domino,* a salutation
used at Vespers. The plainsong melodies of these chants consist of
passages in 'group style' (one to four notes to a syllable) in alternation
with others in 'melismatic style' (ten to forty notes to a syllable). This
distinction entails an important difference in polyphonic composition.
The passages in group style were transformed into tenor sections consisting of single prolonged notes each of which serves as a sort of 'pedal
point' for an extended complex of notes in the upper part or parts (*duplum,
triplum, quadruplum*). The melismatic passages, on the other hand, were
transformed into tenor sections of continuous motion, by organizing the
plainsong melisma in a strictly metrical pattern, according to one of the
rhythmic modes. The upper parts added to these sections contain only
slightly more notes than are found in the tenor, for instance, three against
one. A good illustration of these methods is found in the *Benedicamus Domino* of Facs. 49 (p. 247). The plainsong melody consists of a passage in group
style, 'Benedicamus,' which is followed by a highly melismatic passage,

'Domino. Consequently the organum consists of a first section with widely spaced tenor notes, and of a second section showing continuous motion in the tenor. Sections of the latter type are called *clausulae*, while the term 'organal style' is used for sections based on sustained notes.

Although syllabic treatment almost completely disappears in the strictly liturgical music, it becomes clearly established, in compensation, as the main style of the polyphonic conductus. The reason for this difference of treatment is clear enough. In genuinely liturgical music—plainsong as well as polyphonic music—the text has a mystic significance which elevates it beyond criteria such as 'clear pronunciation' or similar requirements of modern singing. Its existence, like that of God, is eternal and independent of actual apperception on the part of men. With the conductus—as well as with other extraliturgical texts (tropes)—the situation is entirely different. Here the words express new thoughts of individual minds and are meant to convey a new message to the audience. Here audibility and clear pronunciation are matters of prime importance. Hence, syllabic treatment is most suitable.

The development of forms and styles that has just been outlined is paralleled by one of notational signs and methods. A comparison of the sources of the School of Notre Dame (chiefly the four more or less complete copies of the Magnus Liber Organi: W_1, *Fl*, W_2, and *Ma*,—see the table p. 201; Facsimiles 46-50, etc.) with those of the preceding period (Facsimiles 44, 45) shows in the first place a striking difference of the notational characters. Towards the end of the twelfth century, the Aquitanian neumes assumed more definite shapes, characterized by the use of square forms. Thus they changed into what were later to be called notes and ligatures, e.g.:

It is the use of these new shapes which led to the adoption of the name square notation (German: Quadratnotation[1]) for the notation under consideration.

In conformity with the above dichotomy of styles—syllabic and melismatic—there evolved two fundamentally different systems of notation, one in which the tones are represented primarily by single signs, and another in which the tones are written in group-characters, i.e., ligatures. They may fittingly be called syllabic and melismatic notation. Theorists of the thirteenth century frequently refer to these two

[1] The term has been introduced by F. Ludwig.

types of notation by the terms 'notatio cum litera' and 'notatio sine litera.' A particularly clear description is found in Anon. IV (*CS* I, *343*):

> Notandum est quod differentia est dicendo cum litera et sine litera quoniam sine litera fiat ligatio punctorum . . . quantum plus poterit. . . . Cum litera vero quandoque fit ligatio quandoque non; sed in majore parte plus distrahuntur quam ligantur.
>
> A difference is to be noted between singing with and without text. When there is no text, the notes are bound in ligatures as much as possible. But when a text is present, the notes will be partly bound in ligature and partly not. But they will more frequently be written separately than in ligature.

A glance at the Facsimiles 46 and 53 will readily show the difference between *notatio cum litera* and *notatio sine litera*. The remark of Anon. IV regarding the use of ligatures in syllabic notation refers to the occasional use of groups of two or three notes in place of a single note.

Further distinctions must be made within the field of melismatic style (and notation). One of the most influential innovations of the late twelfth century is the introduction of modal rhythm. The long chains of notes in the duplum which, in the period of St. Martial, were sung in free plainsong-like rhythm (see our transcription of Facsimiles 44, 45) are now subjected to an extremely rigid rhythm characterized by the regular alternation of long and short notes. Whereas previously the vertical alignment of the parts (duplum and tenor) was regulated by a sort of sympathetic understanding between the singers, it now is based upon strict meter or, in other words, upon those principles which, in thirteenth century theory, are referred to as *discantus* (J. de Garlandia; see *CS* I, 106):

> Discantus est aliquorum diversorum cantuum consonantia secundum modum et secundum equipollentis equipollentiam.
>
> *Discantus* is the consonant alignment of different parts according to a (rhythmic) mode and to the equivalence of equivalent values.

This *discantus* style is most clearly expressed in those works which must be ascribed to Perotinus, the 'optimus discantor,' and his contemporaries, that is, in the organa tripla and quadrupla, and in the numerous clausulae. However, the transition from the freely flowing rhythm of St. Martial to the rigid modal meter of the Perotinus-era was by no means sudden and without intermediate steps. In fact, the earliest sources of square notation (W_1 and, to a certain extent, Fl) contain a large number of organa and certain shorter pieces (chiefly polyphonic settings of the *Benedicamus Domino*) for which the applicability of modal rhythm must be considered extremely doubtful, to say the least. These pieces are, of course, all in two parts, with a quick duplum over sustained notes of the tenor. In fact, the addition of a third part (triplum), similar in rhythmic design to the duplum, was possible only on the basis of strict meter, that is, of modal rhythm or *discantus*.

There exist, therefore, two different types of melismatic polyphony: an earlier one, presumably connected with Leoninus, which is always in two parts and which clearly shows traces of the free style of St. Martial; and a later one, introduced by Perotinus, which admits of two, three or four parts and in which all the parts are regulated by modal meter. * This stylistic distinction leads to a similar dichotomy of notation, for which the terms duplum notation and modal notation will be used in the present book.

In the last period of the School of Notre Dame, probably around 1225, occurs the rise of one of the most important musical forms, the motet. As is well known, the earliest motets are exact imitations of clausulae, the only difference being that the upper part, originally a melisma *sine litera* (vocalisation), is provided with a full text. This important innovation was accompanied by a notational change, that is, transition from modal notation to syllabic notation for the upper part or parts. Thus, at the end of the development we see the two styles, which formerly had become clearly differentiated from each other, combined in a new form.

Our discussion of square notation, therefore, falls into four sections: * syllabic notation (simple conductus); duplum notation (organa dupia of the earlier, Leoninus period); modal notation (organa and clausulae of the Perotinus period); and motet notation (earliest motets). In order to clarify ideas, there follow four short examples illustrating these four types of polyphonic style:

These are taken from the following sources: (a) Reproduction p. 264;
(b) Facs. 49, p. 247; (c) Facs. 46, p. 229; (d) Facs. 55, p. 275.

B. MODAL NOTATION[1]

We first turn to a study of modal notation which holds a central
position within the entire field of square notation.

The Rhythmic Modes.   Modal notation is based on two values, a long and a
short, called *longa* and *brevis*.   These occur in certain stereotyped rhythmic patterns which are called *modi*.   The complete system of the rhythmic modes, as explained in the theoretical writings of the thirteenth century (*Discantus positio vulgaris*, Joh. de Garlandia, Franco, Odington,
etc.) comprises six modes, namely:

First mode: pattern *L B*	Fourth mode: pattern *B B L*
Second mode: pattern *B L*	Fifth mode: pattern *L L*
Third mode: pattern *L B B*	Sixth mode: pattern *B B B*

A voice written in a given mode repeats the pattern of that mode several times.   Thus, a melody in the first mode would have the following
rhythm: *L B L B L B . . . ,*

The first mode was, no doubt, the earliest, as it is also by far the most
frequent one.   Its pattern, *L B L B . . .* or, in modern notes ♩♪♩♪... ,
established that ternary meter which became the basis of the entire system.   The second mode shows the reverse order of values.   It should,
however, not be understood as a first mode with an upbeat; the accent
falls here, not on the *L* but on the *B:* ♪♩♪♩ ... .   The third mode would,
on the basis of the same values for the *L* and the *B*, lead to duple meter:
♩♪♪♩♪♪... .   However, in order to be combined with the two other
modes, its rhythm had to be adapted to ternary meter.   This was done
by making the *L* a ternary value, and by doubling the value of the second
B, as follows: ♩.♪♪♩.♪♪... .[2]   It is here that we find the root of three

---

[1] The subsequent explanations on modal notation represent the first attempt to give a detailed
description of the subject.   The earliest studies in this field, such as G. Jacobsthal's *Mensuralnotenschrift des 12. und 13. Jahrhunderts* (Leipzig, 1871), and W. Niemann's *Ueber die abweichende Bedeutung der Ligaturen in der Mensuraltheorie der Zeit vor Johannes de Garlandia* (Leipzig, 1902), are
concerned exclusively with the theoretical writings of the thirteenth century.   The explanations in
HdN I, pp. 202-237, deal only with the fundamentals of modal notation, chiefly with the notation
of the six modes.   Much more informative is the concise study contained in the chapter 'Exkurs II:
Ueber Quadratnotation und modale Rhythmik' of F. Ludwig's *Repertorium organorum recentioris
et motetorum vetustissimi stili* (Halle, 1910), from which various fundamental considerations have
been borrowed for the present study.

[2] Much speculation and controversy has been caused by the fact that several thirteenth century
theorists refer to an early tradition in which the *L* was equal, not to three, but to two *B*, as for

important concepts of mensural notation, namely, perfection, alteration, and imperfection. In the complete system of the modes, the ternary *L* of the third mode was considered the normal value and termed perfect (see p. 96), whereas the binary *L* of the first two modes was called imperfect. The term alteration (from Latin *altera*, second) refers to the fact that it is the second of the two *B* which is doubled. It goes without saying that the rhythmic formula for the third mode must be read in $\frac{6}{8}$-meter, not—as has occasionally been surmised—in $\frac{3}{4}$-meter. Obviously, the latter interpretation would bring about a rhythm which is not compatible with the $\frac{3}{8}$- (or $\frac{6}{8}$-) meter of the first and second modes.

The three remaining modes present no new features. The fourth mode merely inverts the pattern of the third. The fifth consists of a succession of ternary *L*; and the sixth comprises only *B*, in groups of three. Here follows a table of the six modes in modern notation:

One might well ask why, in this table, $\frac{6}{8}$-meter has been used for all the modes instead of only for the third and fourth mode for which it is natural. The reason is that, in modal notation, the other modes normally repeat their $\frac{3}{8}$- pattern an even number of times, so that the musical phrases naturally fall within the scheme of $\frac{6}{8}$- measures. The use of this meter usually facilitates the task of transcription. There are, however, a number of cases in which this meter cannot be applied (see pp. 245, 251f).

Another question suggested by the above scheme is that of the modern note values chosen for the transcription. That a reduction of the ancient values is necessary, is apparent. Even the most 'conservative' editors have never gone as far as transcribing a composition in the first mode in *L* and *B*: ⊓¤⊓¤ . In older books (Coussemaker, Wooldridge)

instance Walter Odington in the following remark (*CS* 1, 235): 'Longa autem apud priores organistas duo tantum habuit tempora' ('the *L* equalled only two beats with the early composers of organa'). H. Riemann, with his well-known propensity for the even numbers in rhythm and in phrasing, was quick to seize upon these remarks and to surmise a pre-modal era in which duple time was prevalent, possibly as the result of some folk-like influence. Leaving aside the latter argument, which has too frequently been misused as a compliant *deus ex machina*, it can easily be seen that Riemann's theory is based upon a wrong conclusion, namely that a binary *L* necessarily entails binary meter. Such a conclusion is correct only with the third and fourth modes, but not with the first and second, in which the alternation of a binary *L* with a *B* results in triple time. Odington's remark, therefore, gives only additional evidence of the chronological order, outlined above, of the appearance of the modes.

a reduction 1:4 (whole and half-notes) is chosen for the rendering whereas more recent writers prefer a reduction 1:8 or even 1:16. The last is used here because it corresponds with our general principles of tempo-transcription, according to which that note which represents the beat of the music—in the present case the *L*—, is rendered by the modern quarter-note.

Brief mention must be made of a nomenclature derived from the identification of the six modes with certain metric feet of Greek poetry, namely (in the above order of the modes): trochaic – ᴗ, iambic ᴗ –, dactylic –ᴗᴗ, anapaestic ᴗᴗ –, molossic – – –, and tribrachic: ᴗᴗᴗ. Although this terminology is widely used in modern writings, it has little historical significance and justification. The only mediaeval theorist to mention these terms is Walter Odington who also goes in for such scholarly terms as *proceleumaticus* and *pyrrichius* (*CS* 1, 240f). It is perfectly clear that his references to Greek poetry are the result of personal antiquarian studies, and that, in contrast to a wide-spread opinion to be found in Wolf's *HdN* (vol. 1, p. 202) as well as in many books on music history, they do not offer the slightest evidence of the rhythmic modes having developed from the poetic meters of the ancient Greek.

The application of the modes to melodies of various length leads to a further concept of modal theory, i.e., *ordo* (pl. *órdines*). The ordo refers to the length of a musical phrase, indicating the number of times the modal pattern is repeated before a rest:

Primus ordo	Secundus ordo	Tertius ordo
1.		
2.		
3.		
4.		
5.		
6.		

* Every ordo is followed by a rest, the duration of which is determined by the mode; it equals one *B* (eighth rest) in the first mode, two *B* in the second, etc. As may be inferred from our previous remarks regarding the use of $\frac{6}{8}$-measures for all the modes, the second (fourth, sixth) ordo of the first, second and sixth mode are relatively rare.

Certain thirteenth century theorists considerably broaden the above system of modes and ordines by the introduction of the so-called *modi imperfecti* in addition to the above *modi perfecti*. The various ordines of the imperfect modes are derived from those of the perfect modes by the omission of the final note, e.g., *tertius ordo primi modi imperfecti:* |♩♪♩♪|♩♪♪.|. These imperfect modes, which are treated in great detail by Anon. IV (*CS* 1, 329 ff) and others, have no practical significance and may be completely disregarded by the student.

In turning to a study of the manner in which these modes were used in actual music and expressed in writing it must first be said that the theoretical system does not in every respect conform with the actual data. If considered from the standpoint of the musical sources of this period, it proves to be too complicated in certain respects and too much simplified in others. The latter point will become apparent in our discussions of *extensio modi* and *fractio modi*, while the former point is illustrated by the fact that only four of the six modes, namely, the first, second, third and fifth are commonly used, the fourth and the sixth being extremely scarce.[1] Of the four modes commonly employed, the first mode is not only by far the most frequent, but also almost the only one to appear with all those rhythmic modifications and variants which constitute the real problem of modal notation.[2]

The Ligatures. In the previous explanations of the modi we have purposely indicated the metrical values by modern notes and have avoided using early forms for the *L* and *B*, such as ¶▪ . The reason is that modal notation, although essentially based upon these two values, does not employ notational signs for them, but for combinations thereof, such as occur in the modal patterns; and these are the ligatures in their earliest stage of development. This fact may seem surprising at first; but it will easily be understood when it is realized that modal notation is a melismatic notation which developed from the melismatic passages of the organa of St. Martial.

The ligatures used in modal notation form the starting point of a development the final phase of which is well known to us. The various stages of this development can conveniently be described by the use of

[1] With regard to the fourth mode, Dietricus remarks: 'but it is not in use' ('sed non est in usu').
[2] Two examples written in a free modification of the second mode are discussed at the conclusion of the study of modal notation.

the terms *proprietas* and *perfectio*.   In modal notation all the ligatures
are *cum proprietate* and *cum perfectione;* in pre-Franconian notation ligatures *sine proprietate* and *cum opposita proprietate* are added, occasionally ligatures *sine perfectione;* and finally, in Franconian notation all the
forms are used with equal frequency, and their rhythmical value is determined clearly and unambiguously by definite rules which persisted
until the end of the sixteenth century.

The following table shows the more common ligatures of modal notation, all the *binariae* and *ternariae*, as well as some *quaternariae*.   It also
includes some of the varieties known as *conjuncturae* (marked c) which
are frequently preferred for notes of the descending scale, particularly
for combinations of four to six and more notes:

Binariae	Ternariae	Quaternariae	Quinariae

In addition to the ligatures single notes are used, but very sparingly
and only for special purposes.   As in conductus notation, they occur
usually with a short stem which in some cases is missing.   Occasionally,
a single note with a head of about double length is found.   This is the
so-called *duplex longa* (D) which later becomes the *maxima.*

In order to provide a simple and short designation of these signs Fried-
rich Ludwig in 'Exkurs II' of his *Repertorium organorum recentioris et
motetorum vetustissimi stili* has introduced a system of abbreviations as
follows: 2 li for a *ligatura binaria* (two note ligature); 3 li for a *ligatura
ternaria* (three note ligature) etc.; 1 si for a single note; 2 si for a group
of two single notes, etc.   For the present purpose we propose a somewhat
simplified system, i.e.: *1* for each single note; *2* for a *ligatura binaria; 3*
for a *ligatura ternaria,* etc.   Thus, *1 3 3 3* means a single note followed by
three *ligaturae ternariae.*

For the writing down of the modes these ligatures are used in certain
standard combinations each of which is characteristic of one of the
modes (see p. 225).

From this illustration it appears that the value of the notes of a given
ligature is by no means invariable, but depends entirely upon the mode.
The *ternaria,* e.g., has the value ♩♩♩ in the first mode; ♩♪♪ in the
second mode; ♪♩♩. in the third mode; and ♩.♩.♩. in the fifth mode.   The
binaria is always *B L* (either ♩♩ or ♪♩) in the examples given there.
However, it will be seen that it is likewise capable of various other meanings, under special circumstances.

Combination	Example	Transcription
1. *3 2 2 2 2*		
2. *2 2 2 2 3*		
3. *1 3 3 3*		
4. *3 3 3 1*		
5. *3 3 3*		
6. *4 3 3*		

The small vertical stroke which appears at the end of each *ordo* is the so-called *divisio modi*, which indicates a rest.

Repeated Notes. For obvious reasons of writing, two successive tones of the same pitch (unison) can never occur in ligature. Therefore, whenever the melody would call for repeated notes within a ligature, this ligature must be broken up into single tones or smaller ligatures (see p. 93 f).

The following examples show some of the deviations caused in the first mode by repeated notes:

There are, of course, no set rules for the writing of these anomalous combinations. In the sources the same melodic and rhythmic phrase may be found expressed in several different ways, as, for instance:

It may be noticed that as a result of these anomalies the *ligatura binaria* appears in a new metrical meaning, namely as *L B*.

The Plica. The *plica* ('fold') is an important auxiliary symbol of square notation. It is indicated by downward or upward dashes attached to a note. These dashes occur in connection with single notes as well as with the final note of ligatures. The original form of the *nota plicata* is explained as the square-shaped modification of the liquescent neumes, *epiphonus* and *cephalicus*, from which the *plicas* developed:

$\smile$ *(epiphonus)* = ⬚ *(plica ascendens)*

$\cap$ *(cephalicus)* = ⬚ *(plica descendens)*

While these single *plicas* are frequently used in syllabic notation (see p. 260), in modal notation the *plica* occurs chiefly as *ligatura plicata*. Here it is indicated by an upward or downward dash added to the right side of the *finalis*. If the *finalis* is in ascending position and, consequently, written above the preceding note, the *plica*-dash is difficult, if not impossible to attach. This problem was solved in two different ways. Either a single *nota plicata* was written immediately after the ligature; or the head of the finalis was turned to the right side, so that the dash could be added. Following are all the forms of the *binaria plicata*, and some examples of *ternaria* and *quaternaria plicata:*

(a)

(b)

The *plica* sign indicates an ornamenting tone, somewhat in the character of a grace note, to be inserted between the note to which it is attached and the next written note. According to the direction of the dash this ornamenting tone is above or below the written note.

The explanations of the *plica* by the theorists are not entirely satisfactory. The following passage from the treatise of Magister Lambert (Pseudo-Aristotle, *CS* I, 273 a) is typical:

Unde notandum est quod plica nihil aliud est quam signum dividens sonum in sono diverso per diversas vocum distantias, tam ascendendo quam descendendo, videlicet per semitonium et tonum, per semiditonum et ditonum, et per diatessaron et diapente. . . . Fit autem plica in voce per compositionem epiglotti cum repercussione gutturis subtiliter inclusa.

. . . the *plica* is nothing but a sign indicating that a tone is divided into a different tone, in various intervals both ascending and descending, such as half tone and whole tone, minor and major third, fourth and fifth. . . .

The *plica* is performed in singing by the partial closing of the epiglottis combined with a subtle repercussion of the throat.

As regards the performance of the *plica*, a problem somewhat irrelevant to the purpose of this book, one must be content with the information given in the above and in similar statements. Evidently the *plica*, which is derived from the liquescent neumes (*cephalicus*), belongs to the same species of ornaments as, e.g., the French 'aspiration' or the German 'Nachschlag.' More relevant to our study is the problem of determining the pitch and value of the extra tone indicated by the *plica*. For the sake of clarity we shall carefully distinguish between *plica*-note and *plica*-tone. The former term refers to the written note to which the *plica*-dash is attached; the latter to the extra tone called for by the dash.

The pitch of the *plica*-tone depends upon the pitches of the *plica*-note and the next-following note. If these two notes are the same, then the *plica*-tone is the upper or lower second, depending on the direction of the stem. If the interval between the two notes is a third, the second in between is meant to be filled in. If it is a second, one may have to choose the upper or lower third. In many cases, however, the second will prove more satisfactory, causing anticipation of the subsequent note. In regard to the larger intervals, the instructions of the theorists are even less clear than in the previous cases. Apparently, the interpretation was governed chiefly by the musical context which, indeed, rarely leaves room for doubt.

Concerning the second question, that of the metrical interpretation, the general principle is that *plica*-note and *plica*-tone together consume the same time as that to be assigned to the note if it were written without *plica*. Since, in actual application, this note always turns out to be a L (last note of a ligature), there are only two possibilities: either this L is imperfect, in which case the *plica*-tone gets the half of the full value; or it is perfect, in which case the *plica*-tone is allotted one-third of the full value. On this point Magister Lambert speaks with perfect clarity (*CS* I, 273):

[Plica perfecta] habet autem omnem potestatem, regulam et naturam quam habet perfecta longa, nisi quod in corpore duo tempora tenet et unum in membris . . . [Plica imperfecta] . . . continet unum tempus in corpore et reliquum in membris.

The perfect *plica* has the same function, value, and nature as the perfect *longa*, except that it contains two *tempora* in the note (*corpus*), and one in the tone (*membrum*). The imperfect *plica* contains one *tempus* in the note and the rest in the tone.[1]

---

[1] *Tempus* denotes in the thirteenth century the duration of the *B*. See p. 283.

It appears that the *plica*-tone was not a sort of a short grace-note, but had a definite metrical value, comparable to that of the normal notes. It was only the special manner of singing (see p. 235) that distinguished it from them.   Therefore, transcriptions in which the *plica*-tone is rendered by the modern symbol ♪ (see *HdN* I, 225) are misleading, as are others in which they are transcribed as ordinary notes without any distinction.   We suggest the use of small notes, as illustrated in the following examples:

That the *plica*-tone has the full value of a *B* is confirmed by the fact that, according to various theorists, *plica*-ligatures could be used to express the sixth mode.   Joh. de Garlandia gives the following example (*CS* I, 101):

This manner of notating the sixth mode has been misinterpreted by both Niemann and Wolf.[1]   In *HdN* I, 232, Wolf cites the following as illustrations of the sixth mode:

or

The two examples in modal notation, however, do not mean the same thing, as Wolf assumes.   The transcription which accompanies them is correct only for the first example, whereas the second would result in the following much longer melody (using Wolf's scale of reduction):

At the beginning of a composition or a section thereof one frequently finds a single note followed by a *plica*-note of the same pitch: ▪♩ .   This

---

[1] See A. Michalitschke, *Theorie des Modus*, Regensburg, 1923, p. 62.

FACSIMILE 46

MS Florence, Biblioteca Medicea-Laurenziana *plut. 29.1*
(13th century)
From pages 11, 11′

combination usually indicates a *plica duplex longa*. There is an obvious
similarity of appearance between this sign and forms given in the second
row (b) of the illustration of *ligaturae plicatae* (p. 226). However, in
these forms the use of a separate plica note is a mere expedient of pen-
manship and does not, as a rule, indicate *duplex longas*.[1]

Examples. The principles of modal notation just explained may be illustrated by a few relatively simple examples.

   (1)   Facsimile 46 (p. 229) contains a three-voice clausula *Go*, the tenor of
which is taken from the verse (V) *Vir-go Dei* of the gradual *Benedicta es
et venerabilis* (see *Gr. Rom.*, p. [99]).[2] The liturgical melody appears
twice, beginning for the second time with the eleventh ligature (the initial ligature is the *ternaria* written slightly to the left of the letter G).
The two upper parts are in the first mode, and show various examples of
unison-writing and of *plica* ligatures. The tenor is evidently in the fifth
mode. Every two ordines of the tenor correspond in length to one ordo
of the upper parts:

[1] I am greatly indebted to Mr M. F. Bukofzer for pointing out the correct meaning of these forms
of *ligaturae plicatae*. The (b)-forms (as we may call them with reference to the illustration) are
probably the earlier ones, since they are the only ones used in W_1. In F and W_2 both forms occur,
the (b)-form being preferred when the *finalis* is a *L*, the (a)-form when it is a *B*. See, e.g., Facs. 47
(p. 233), second column, second staff, next-to-the-last ordo; and Facs. 46 (p. 229), seventh staff,
end of fourth ordo, and eighth staff, middle of sixth ordo.

[2] We seize this opportunity to emphasize the importance of tracing the liturgical tenors of the
organa, clausulae and motets back to their original sources, that is, to the melodies of the Gregorian
chant. This task is greatly facilitated by F. Ludwig's standard publication, *Repertorium organorum
recentioris and motetorum vetustissimi stili* (Halle, 1910), which is an invaluable aid in all research
connected with the School of Notre Dame. The strictly scientific character of this book, which is
written in the form of a detailed catalogue of all the sources of this period, makes it difficult to read;
however, a study of its somewhat cryptic language and its complicated system of abbreviations
amply repays the effort. As a guide to such a study, it may be remarked that the above clausula
Go is listed on p. 61, and that the sign M 32 given there refers the reader to the complete index of
the *Magnus liber organi de Gradali et de Antiphonario* contained on pp. 65-75. The organa *de
Antiphonario* are marked O1 — O 32 (O = Office), those *de Gradali* M 1 — M 59 (M = Mass).
Under M 32 (p. 72) the reader finds listed the gradual (*Gr*) *Benedicta* with its verse (V) *Vir-go dei*

The fourth, seventh, and ninth ordo of the upper parts contain irregular combinations of ligatures which indicate *extensio* or *fractio modi* (see p. 234ff; particularly p. 237).

(2) The conductus *Hac in anni janua* (Facs. 53, p. 259) closes with a three-voice vocalization on (acti)-'o' (beginning after the first *divisio modi* of the last brace), which is written in a mixture of the third mode, *1 3 3 3*, and the second mode, *2 2 2.* Here follows the transcription:

(3) Facsimile 47 (p. 233) contains an organum triplum *Descendit de celis* from W_2. In order to facilitate orientation, the various sections of the composition have been marked by letters. Several of these sections show the normal combinations of ligatures explained previously. Thus, the sections (a), (f), and (h) are in the first mode (*3 2 2 . . .*), (b) and (e) in the third (*1 3 3 . . .*), (d) in the second (*2 2 2 . . .*).

The vertical strokes usually are signs of *divisio modi,* indicating rests the length of which depends on the mode, according to the previous explanations (see p. 225). Some of them, however, have a different meaning, that is, to call the singer's attention to a change of syllables in the text. To this category belong the sixth stroke of brace 1 (change from 'Des' to 'cen') and the second stroke of brace 2 (change from 'cen' to 'dit'). F. Ludwig, who was the first to call attention to these syllable dashes (*Silbenstriche;* see *Repertorium,* p. 49), rightly pointed out that they give proof of the vocal (vocalizing) nature of the organa in all their parts. It will be noticed that in most of these cases the interpretation of the dash as a rest is prohibited by the appearance of *plica* notes which naturally call for immediate joining with the following note. The practical result of these considerations is that the *quaternaria* at the end of section (a) is not preceded by a rest, but follows immediately after the *binaria plicata,* filling

which is the source for the tenor of the above clausula. The full texts and the liturgical melodies of the graduals, alleluias, etc. are found, of course, in the ritual books of the Catholic Church, either in the *Antiphonarium Romanum* (complete service for the office) and the *Graduale Romanum* (complete service for the mass), or, more conveniently, in the *Liber Usualis* which contains the most important chants from both books.

a measure in the rhythm *B B B L* (*fractio modi*). A similar case occurs on
the right-hand column, first brace, where the next-to-the-last stroke is
not a *divisio modi*, but a syllable dash indicating change to 'ce.' These
signs may be reproduced in the transcription as breathing marks.

The section (d) shows the familiar groups of the second mode, particularly in the middle part (duplum) which has the final *ternaria* required in
this mode. Since the triplum closes with a *binaria*, the first note of this
ligature would have to be extended from a *B* into a *L* (*extensio modi*).
Section (i) finally, notated in *ternariae*, would seem to indicate the fourth
mode. The fact, however, that the triplum begins with *1 2* suggests another interpretation, that is, to start in the first mode and to continue
thereafter in the sixth mode. The musical design of this section, with its
extensive use of short sequential patterns, would seem to lend itself more
naturally to the continuous motion of the sixth mode than to the halting
rhythm of the fourth which, moreover, is very rarely used (see p. 223).

For the major part the transcription of the organum presents no difficulties, once the correct start is made. In order to facilitate transcription
some of the crucial measures are shown below.

FACSIMILE 47

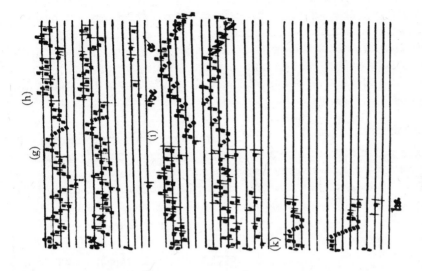

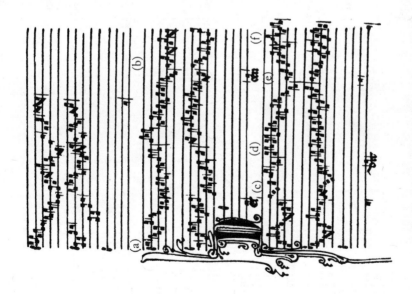

MS Wolfenbüttel, Herzogliche Bibliothek *1206*, formerly *Helmstedt 1099* (13th century)
Pages 7', 8

In *Fl*, which is another source for *Descendit de celis* (see the facsimile in *OH*, p. 208), the second tenor note, c, for the syllable 'cen' appears right after the first note, d, at the beginning of section (b), not at its end, as in *W₂*. We have adopted the version from *Fl* because it eliminates some strongly dissonant combinations such as d-f-c′ and d-e-a which occur in *W₂*. This may be the place to remark that the exact placement of the tenor notes in the organal sections is often uncertain. For instance, the note to the syllable 'cen' could just as well be placed on the second beat of the measure, coincident with the final notes of the upper parts.

The preceding explanations cover all the sections of *Descendit* except (c), (g), and (k). It will be seen at a glance that these differ from the others by their shortness and by the irregular groups of the ligatures and *conjuncturae* found in them. Furthermore, they all occur immediately before a change of syllable, that is, at the end of the main divisions of the organum. These are the so-called *copulae*, which are described by various theorists of the thirteenth century as a separate species of polyphonic music, side by side with discantus and organum (Joh. de. Garlandia, *CS* i, 175a). Garlandia (*CS* i, 114a) also tells us that 'discantus cannot be considered as perfect without having connecting *copulas* (*nisi mediante copula*),' and that 'copula forms the connection (*est inter*) between discant and organum.' In spite of their shortness these passages offer many problems (see p. 241).

If the normal pattern of the rhythmic modes were always strictly observed in the compositions of our period, their interpretation and transcription would present little difficulty. Actually, examples of this pure type are relatively rare and uncharacteristic. Usually the elementary pattern of the mode is modified by either omission or addition of tones, modifications which are expressed in notation by irregular combinations of ligatures. It is these anomalies which present the chief problems of modal notation.

Extensio modi. This term is used here to denote the occasional omission of a *B* (eighth-note of the transcription). Such a modification of the modal pattern is very frequently used at the end of an ordo. Below are a few typical examples:

(a) and (b) are first mode; (c) and (d) are second mode.

Most of the ordines of Facsimile 46 show this type of *extensio*. The following examples illustrate the omission of a *B* in the middle of an ordo:

(1) *Fl*, p. 7', *Mors* (beginning of the upper part):

(2) *W₁*, p. 50, clausula *Ta* (from the *Alleluia, Ascendens Christus* [in altum captivam duxit captivi-ta-tem . . .]):

Fractio modi.[1] This term signifies the opposite procedure of *extensio modi*, that is, the breaking up of the normal pattern of the modal rhythm into smaller values, preferably of the *L* into two *B*. It may be illustrated by the following example (*W₁*, p. 22, third brace):

An already familiar means of introducing *fractio modi* is the *plica*. In fact, many examples exist showing that the *plica* and the above notational method were used interchangeably for the introduction of passing-notes. For instance, a comparison of our Facsimile 47 with the reproduction of the same piece from *Fl* given in *OH* 1, 209, reveals the following variants of notation (fourth ordo from the beginning):

---

[1] See Anon. IV, *CS* 1, 336-339.

The following passage from W_1 p. 162 (middle of the fifth brace) shows the simultaneous use of both methods:

Occasionally, the breaking up of the normal pattern may be carried to even smaller values, equivalent to sixteenth notes in the transcription, for instance (W_1 p. 21, *Notum fecit*):

A comparison of the above examples of *fractio modi* with those of *extensio modi* shows that there is no clear notational distinction between these two opposite modifications. It is chiefly this lack in clarity which makes modal notation difficult. As a matter of fact, the same combination of ligatures may denote two, and sometimes even more, different rhythms, resulting in different lengths of the phrase, for instance:

No definite rules can be given concerning the application of one or the other interpretation in a given case. The main consideration in this matter is the coordination of the parts according to the thirteenth-century principles of consonance and dissonance (see p. 244). Naturally, the tenor should always be transcribed first. In compositions with two (or three) upper parts a clue to the correct coordination is often found in what may be called the "rule of corresponding ligatures." In fact, a ligature in the duplum usually corresponds in position to one in the triplum, except for such deviations as are caused by repeated tones, *extensio modi*, etc. Although it cannot be applied strictly, this rule often proves helpful.

The student is now prepared to complete the transcription of the clausula *Go* (Facs. 46, p. 229). The fourth ordo has *fractio modi* in the triplum, while *extensio modi* would seem to be indicated for the close of the duplum [see Figure, (a)]. However, the version given under (b) is probably preferable, if only from the point of view of corresponding ligatures.

(a)   (b)

At the end of the seventh ordo we find three single notes each of which equals an *L* (dotted quarter-note). It is interesting to notice in this ordo (duplum) a clear tendency to distinguish between a *brevis*-like and a *longa*-like shape for the single note. The former occurs at the beginning of the ordo for unison-writing, the latter for *extensio modi*:

The end of the clausula presents some difficulties, owing to the great number of notes in the upper parts. The following transcription (beginning in the tenor with the eighth ordo of staff 6) would seem to be correct, in spite of the dissonance in meas. 5. The upper parts close with a *copula* (coda) showing the ligatures of the second mode. Although the mode never changes within the main part of a clausula, examples suggesting a change of mode in the coda are quite frequent (see the close of 'domino' in Facs. 49, p. 247, and of *Sanctus* and *Sancte spiritus* in Facs. 51, p. 255).

Our facsimile also includes a three-voice clausula *Flos filius est*, which will be considered later (p. 251).

Facsimile 48 contains a number of textless pieces, evidently instrumental dances in two parts, from the slightly later MS, Brit. Mus. *Harl. 978*. The two parts are marked 'cantus superior' and 'cantus inferior.' The first three lines of the page are occupied by the lower part of a piece, the higher part of which is given on the preceding page (see the complete reproduction and transcription in *HdN* 1, 224). The cantus inferior, which is evidently in the first mode, shows a few simple cases of *fractio modi*, for instance in the last ordo of the first staff:

There follows on the page a piece with a remarkably regular rhythm and structure. Each part consists of eight ordines, each of which comprises eight perfections (seventh ordo) and, therefore, yields four $\frac{6}{8}$-measures in the transcription. The piece (as well as the others of the facsimile) belongs to the class of *ductia*, a mediaeval type of dance music consisting usually of four short sections each of which is repeated: aa bb cc dd. The present example shows an even simpler structure, since the third and fourth phrases reiterate the first and second, but transposed a fifth above and transferred from the cantus inferior to the cantus superior. The basic scheme of our *ductia* is therefore:

> Cantus superior: (counterpoint) a   a   b   b
> Cantus inferior: a   a   b   b   (counterpoint)

In every ordo some deviation or other from the normal scheme of ligatures, *3 2 2 2 2 2*, occurs. Some of these deviations, e.g., the writing *1 2* (instead of *3*) at the beginning of the first and second ordo of the cantus inferior, are obviously caused by repeated notes and, therefore, do not entail a modification of the basic rhythm of the first mode. Others, e.g., the sequence *3 2 3 2 2* (superior, first ordo) indicate extensio modi: | *L B L' B | L' L B | L' B L' B | L' —* |, while the sequence *3 2 2 2 3 2* (superior, third ordo) indicates fractio modi: | *L B L' B | L' B L' B | B'B B L' B | L' —* |. More problematic is the rhythm of the sequence *3 2 3 3 1* (inferior, third ordo). Here it is only by comparison with the rhythm of the upper part that the solution is found, namely: | *L B L' B | L' L B | B' B B L' | L' — /*. The first three ordines of the upper part are given in transcrip-

FACSIMILE 48

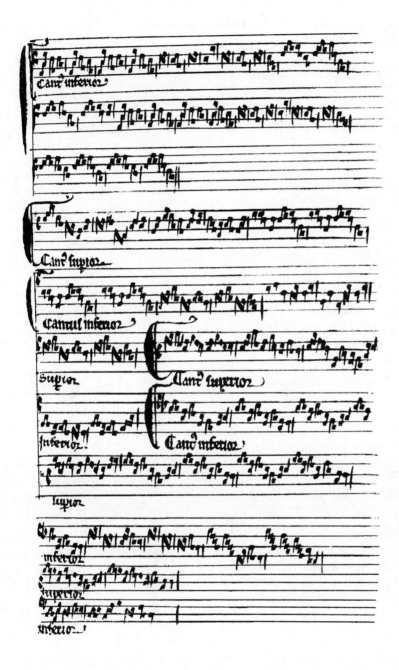

MS London, British Museum *Harleian 978* (13th century)

tion in the appendix, No. 32. For a discussion of the second piece, see p. 242.

Conjuncturae. Particularly vague and equivocal symbols are those many-note ligatures which appear in the form of *conjuncturae* or *currentes,* that is, of a single note or a *binaria* (*ternaria*) followed by a series of three to seven or more isolated notes of the descending scale, written in a form like that of the later *semibrevis:* ⟨notation symbols⟩ .

Already the name *currentes* (from *currere,* to run) indicates that quick notes are involved here. However, the question as to their exact rhythmical meaning has caused considerable confusion as early as the late thirteenth century, because the diamond-shaped notes were mistaken for real *semibreves* which, in that period, had already become established as independent values. Originally, these shapes have nothing to do with *semibreves,* but are transformations of the dots characteristic of the neume *climacus:* ⟨symbol⟩ .

We have already pointed out that the simplest *conjunctura,* that is, the *conjunctura ternaria,* is identical in meaning with the ordinary *ligatura ternaria.* Very informative in this respect is the section (i) of Facsimile 47. As additional evidence, the following passage from the Ms Madrid *Hh 167* (*Ma*) may be quoted:

As far as the *conjuncturae* with four, five, etc. notes are concerned, their value is much more variable. The following rule, which is supported by evidence from theoretical as well as musical sources, may serve as a point of departure:

> In every ligature the last note is an *L,* the next-to-last note is a *B,* and all the preceding notes are equal to one *L* (see Anon. IV, *CS* I, 341, *Omnis figura ligata . . .*).

Examples illustrating this rule are given below under (a). However, the context often requires certain adjustments, such as are indicated under (b), (c), and (d):

For the interpretation of symbols composed of both ligatures and *currentes* the following examples may serve as a guide:

Modern scholars have frequently been misled by the *semibrevis*-like characters of the *conjuncturae*. The following passage from *Ma*, together with its transcription by Aubry (*Iter Hispanicum*, Paris, 1908, p. 11) and the (approximately) correct transcription, may serve as an example:

The cadential sections (e), (g) and (k) of the organum *Descendit* (Facsimile 47) illustrate the highly equivocal character of the *conjuncturae* of many notes. Several variants of transcription are deliberately given in the appendix (No. 33), some of them based on the notational variants found in other sources. They are meant to warn the reader not to expect a 'correct solution' of problems of this type. He will derive the greatest benefit by trying to tackle these passages, and by comparing his results with our transcriptions, as well as with those given in *OH* 1, 209 ff, where the whole organum is transcribed.   A comparison of our facsimile with the reproduction of the same piece from *Fl*, given in the same book, as well as with that from *W₁*, to be found on p. 76′ of J. H. Baxter's publication (*An Old St. Andrews Music Book*) will reveal to him the importance of consulting different sources whenever these are available.   A fourth source for this organum is the MS Brit. Mus. *Egerton 2615 (LoA)*, p. 82.′ Following is a reproduction of the final passage (k) from this manuscript:

A rhythmic variant suggested by this manner of writing is given in the appendix, No. 33.

A special type of *conjunctura* which occurs in some later documents of modal notation is the following, characterized by a diagonal stem attached to the left side of the initial note: ⟋•• .   This symbol indicates shorter notes than the normal *conjunctura ternaria;* in fact, it has the same meaning as the later ligature *cum opposita proprietate: S S B.*   It occurs repeatedly in the last dance piece of Facsimile 48, the beginning of which is transcribed here:

The transcription of this piece presents few difficulties, owing to the fact that it falls into regular phrases of eight perfections each, or, of four ⁶⁄₈-measures of modern notation.   The *binaria plicata* at the end of staff 6 means *B + L plicata*, while the similar form occurring simultaneously in the *cantus inferior* (third-to-the-last sign of staff 7) means *B + D plicata*.

Another notational peculiarity of interest is the use of single notes in the diamond-shaped form of the *semibrevis* (see the closing ordines on the last two staves). Actually, these notes are not *S*, but represent a peculiar manner of writing the *B* which is found in various sources of English origin. The first to point out this peculiarity was H. E. Wooldridge, in his detailed discussion of *Sumer is icumen in* to which the reader is referred.[1] The same shape occurs in the last fascicle of W_1 (see p. 191' and others of the facsimile edition), the English origin of which has been pointed out by J. Handschin.[2] Following is a transcription of the close

of our dance piece (upper part):

Our lengthy explanation of modal notation may seem very unsatisfactory to the reader, who naturally expects to obtain concise information and a reliable clue to the problems of this notational system. It certainly will appear even more annoying when, upon trying to make transcriptions of his own, he finds himself confronted with many questions for which our explanations contain no answer. Unfortunately, this situation cannot be remedied since vagueness and ambiguity is an inherent characteristic of modal notation. As early as the late thirteenth century musicians were fully aware of this fact. About 1275 Anon. IV very adequately summarizes the situation in following sentences (*CS* 1, 344):

> . . . in antiquis libris habebant puncta equivoca nimis, quia simplicia materialia fuerunt equalia, sed solo intellectu operabantur dicendo: intelligo istam longam, intelligo illam brevem, et nimio tempore longo laborabant, antequam scirent bene aliquid quod nunc ex levi ab omnibus laborantibus circa talia percipitur mediantibus predictorum, ita quod quilibet proficerit in una hora quam in septem ante quoad longum ire.
>
> Maxima pars cognitionis antiquorum fuit in predictis sine materiali significatione . . . prout habebant respectum superioris ad cantum inferiorem, et docebant alios dicendo: audiatis vos et retineatis hoc canendo. Sed materialem significationem parvam habebant, et dicebant: punctus ille superior concordat cum puncto inferiori, et sufficiebat eis.

In the old books the signs were all too equivocal because the fundamental signs [*B* and *L*?] were alike. The singers proceeded only by their intellect, saying: I see that this one is a long, that one a breve. Thus they labored a long time before they learned something which today anybody can easily learn by means of the above explanations if he wants to do so, so that

[1] *OH* i, 326ff. See also M. F. Bukofzer, *Sumer is icumen in* (1944), p. 83ff.

[2] *ZfMW* 1932. See also pl. 10 (p. 55) in A. Hughes, *Worcester Mediaeval Harmony* (Worcester, 1928).

today every student will achieve more in one hour than formerly in seven.

The knowledge of the ancients was chiefly oral tradition without written fixation. They paid attention to the relationship between the upper and the lower part and taught by saying: listen carefully and remember it by singing. But they had little notational fixation and merely said: this note of the upper part coincides with this note of the lower part; and that satisfied their needs.

Weighing these pertinent remarks, the student will realize that only by long experience and patient practice may he expect to acquire some facility in this field of study. As a further aid to this goal, there follow a few remarks of a more empirical nature, as well as a number of additional examples.

Consonance and Dissonance. As is intimated by the words of Anon. IV, a knowledge of the early thirteenth century principles of consonance and dissonance is of foremost importance. These principles call for consonances on the strong beat although, between these, dissonant combinations are admissible. The consonances of this period are, according to the theory of the time, the unison, octave, fifth, and fourth. In musical practice, the third as well as the augmented fourth (diminished fifth, tritone, e.g., f-b) also are admitted as consonant intervals, although they appear much less frequently than the others. The sixth is regarded as a dissonance in theory as well as in practice. It must be borne in mind, however, that a strong dissonance, such as a second, is admissible even on the main beat if it is immediately resolved into a consonance, e.g.:

Various examples of this practice occur in our Facsimile 47 (*Go*, transcription, meas. 18, 19 etc.). An interesting and adequate explanation of these appogiaturas of the thirteenth century is given in the following remark by Johannes de Garlandia (*CS* 1, 107a):

Sed duo puncti sumentur hic pro uno, et aliquando unus eorum ponitur in discordantiam, propter colorem musice. Et hic primus sive secundus; et hoc bene permittitur ab auctoribus primis et licenciatur. Hoc autem invenitur in organo in pluribus locis et precipue in motetis.

However, two notes may be put in the place of one, and sometimes one of them is treated as a dissonance, in order to add color to the music. This tone may be either the first or the second. This method is fully approved and permitted by the best authorities and it is to be found repeatedly in organa, and especially in motets.

The observation of consonances is practically the only reliable clue in transcribing pieces in modal notation whenever, as is frequently the case, writing of the ligature fails to indicate clearly the rhythm. The student is strongly advised never to consider a transcription satisfactory unless it conforms with the principles of consonance and dissonance. The observation of consonances is helpful also in determining the pitch of tones in ligatures written carelessly.

Notation of the Tenors. It is advisable always to start with transcribing the tenor which, owing to the greater simplicity and regularity of its rhythm and notation, gives a desirable basis for the interpretation of the duplum and triplum. The chief types of tenor-notation are as follows:
1. All single notes, for instance: ❘ꞁꞁ ꞁꞁ❘ꞁꞁꞁꞁ ꞁꞁ ꞁ❘ꞁꞁ❘ꞁꞁ❘ . This notation evidently indicates the fifth mode. Usually the ordines contain a varying number of notes. Examples showing regular groups of, e.g., 4 *L* are rare, except for the very frequent pattern of 3 *L* which, however, is usually notated in ligatures (see p. 248, under Ic). Tenors consisting of irregular groups of single notes (Ludwig, in *Repertorium*, p. 43, calls them *Simplices-Gruppen* and uses the abbreviation σγ) occur chiefly in compositions of the Leoninus period and, therefore, represent the oldest type of modal rhythm used for the tenors. Examples are found in Facs. 46 (p. 229), *Do;* Facs. 49 (p. 247), 'domino;' Facs. 50a (p. 249), *Scio;* and Facs. 51 (p. 255), *Et occurrens.* Owing to the varying numbers of *L* found in these groups the $\frac{6}{8}$-meter cannot be insisted upon in the transcription. Usually the *divisio modi* indicates a rest to the value of a *B* (eighth-note), so that, in the case of 3 (or 5) *L* an extra $\frac{3}{8}$-measure (or a $\frac{9}{8}$-measure) results.
2. The notation of the tenor in single notes sometimes indicates values of double length, namely, the *duplex longa* (*D*). There is hardly any clear notational distinction between the *L* and the *D*; however, the presence of the latter will generally be suggested by the greater distance of one sign from the other which is caused by the greater number of corresponding notes in the upper parts. An interesting example is the final section of an organum *Benedicamus domino*, which is reproduced on Facsimile 49. Here, the plainsong for the syllable 'do-' occurs twice: first (end of the fourth brace) in the following grouping: d f d c / d f g d / e c / . . . , then (beginning with the next-to-last ordo of the fifth brace) in different ordines: d f d c d / f g d / e c d / . . . . Whereas, for the second presentation, the single notes of the tenor represent ordinary *L*, to be transcribed as dotted quarter-notes (see below, b), those of the first

section must be given the double value (see below, a), in order to account for the considerably greater number of notes in the discant:[1]

Sometimes the decision on this point is not easy, due to the equivocal nature of the upper part as well as of the tenor. On Facsimile 50a, a two-voice *Scio cui credidi* from the slightly later MS Paris, B. N. *lat. 15139* (also known as *St. Victor, 813*) is reproduced, the upper part of which shows the familiar ligatures of the third mode. In order to make the tenor conform with the discant, its single notes must be interpreted as *D*:

However, in the present example it is also possible to read the discant in the sixth mode and the tenor as a succession of *L*. In fact, this probably is the correct version since in this Ms the *D* is often indicated by slightly enlarged heads (see the end of *Alleluya* on Facs. 50, p. 249).[1]

---

[1] In this connection it may be pointed out that the anonymous treatise from 1279, which has been edited by Sowa, contains interesting information about the possibility of reshaping a piece in a different mode, a procedure which was called 'transmutatio.' See Sowa's edition, p. xix ff, and his article in *ZfMW* xv.

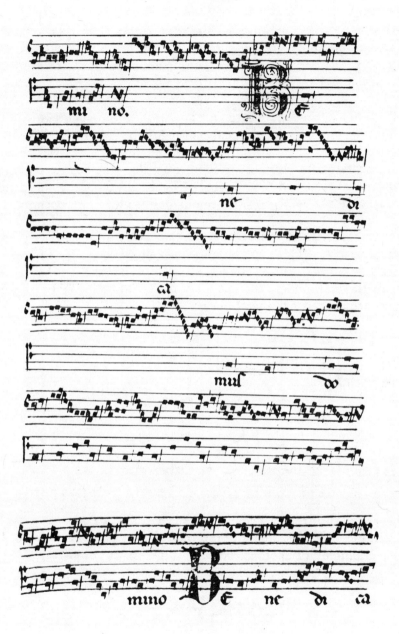

MS Florence, Biblioteca Medicea-Laurenziana *plut. 29.1*
(13th century)
From pages 87′, 88

An interesting detail are the numerous deviations from the normal pattern of ligatures, *1 3 3 3*, for instance at the end of the first and the second ordo, as well as within the third ordo, where *3* is replaced by *2 1*. These deviations are conditioned by the change of syllables, as indicated in the tenor. The ordo 'depositum' contains more notes than can easily be accommodated by the four *L* of the tenor. A possible solution is given in the appendix, No. 34a.

On Facsimile 50b we reproduce an *Alleluya* from the same source. The tenor is one of the few examples showing regular groups of *L*. The upper part goes even further than that of *Scio* in the direction of quick motion, and represents an interesting attempt to utilize the restricted means of modal notation for the rendering of lively rhythms. Some details, particularly in the final *copula*, remain doubtful. See appendix, No. 34b.

3. Frequently, the tenor is written in *ternariae*, either exclusively or in connection with *L*. These combinations usually indicate the fifth mode, as under (c); occasionally, however, they must be read in the quicker rhythm of the first mode, (a) or possibly the second (b). The following groupings are the most frequent ones:

I.

|3 |3 |3

Ia | ♩ ♪♩ 𝄾 | ♩ ♪♩ 𝄾 | ♩ ♪♩ 𝄾 |

Ib | ♪♩ ♪𝄾𝄾 | ♪♩ ♪𝄾𝄾 | ♪♩ ♪𝄾𝄾 |

Ic | ♩. ♩. | ♩. 𝄾. | ♩. ♩. | ♩. 𝄾. | ♩ ♩. ♩. | ♩. 𝄾. |

II.

11 |3 |11 |3 |

IIa | ♩. ♩𝄾 | ♩ ♪♩𝄾 | ♩. ♩𝄾 | ♩ ♪♩𝄾 |

IIb | ♩. ♪𝄾𝄾 | ♪♩ ♪𝄾𝄾 | ♩. ♪𝄾𝄾 | ♪♩ ♪𝄾𝄾 |

IIc | ♩. | ♩. 𝄾. | ♩. ♩. | ♩. 𝄾. | ♩. | ♩. 𝄾. ♩. ♩. | ♩. 𝄾. |

In IIc the first of the two single notes is actually a *D*.

An example of Ic is the tenor of the clausula *Go*, Facs. 46, p. 229. The following beginning of another clausula *Go* (*Fl*, p. 165) illustrates Ib:

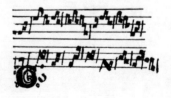

FACSIMILES 50a, 50b

MS Paris, Bibliotheque Nationale *lat. 15139* (13th century)
From pages 285', 283'

The ligatures of the upper part clearly indicate second mode which, therefore, must also be assumed for the tenor. The following transcription reveals a rhythmic peculiarity which is more frequent in the compositions of our period than one might expect it to be, that is, an overlapping of the phrases of the two parts, caused by the fact that an ordo of the discant begins in the middle of a ⁶⁄₈-measure:

The same cross-rhythm occurs even more consistently in the following clausula, *(Fl,* p. 165′) the tenor of which is an example of Ia:

In determining the rhythm of the upper part (the first ordo belongs to the preceding piece) one will have to rely chiefly upon the principle of consonances (octaves, unisons, fifths, fourths), since another clue, frequently useful, completely fails us here, namely, the principle of the vertical alignment of simultaneous sounds (particularly on the second brace). Towards the end of the piece the transcription is not without difficulties, and remains to a certain extent dubious (see the appendix, No. 35).[1]

The following *Regnat (Fl,* p. 167) shows the combination II in the tenor. Since the duplum has about the same number of notes as the tenor, only the rhythm of the first or second mode, i.e., IIa or IIb, comes into question. The ligature-writing of the duplum once more suggests

---

[1] A derivative motet exists in *Mo,* No. 194 (facsimile and transcription in Y. Rokseth, *Polyphonies du XIIIe siècle,* i and iii).

second mode. In the second statement of the tenor two ordines, corresponding to the last two ordines of the first line, are missing.

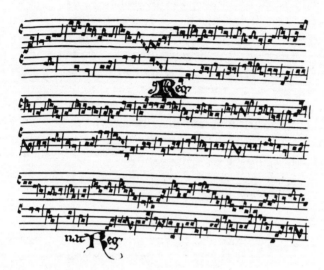

Transcription of the beginning:

In the following *Regnat* (*Fl*, p. 167) the tenor is in the fifth mode (IIc) as appears from the considerably greater number of notes contained in the duplum:

Finally, the three-voice clausula *Flos filius* from Facsimile 46 (p. 229) may be considered. This example is interesting because it clearly shows that the normal scheme of $\frac{6}{8}$-measures cannot always be insisted upon. The tenor, after an initial ordo of two *L*, has the combination *3 2*, i.e., the secundus ordo of the first mode. From the context of the parts it appears that this combination comprises only three perfections (three groups of the value of $\frac{3}{8}$ each), without a fourth perfection being supplied by a $\frac{3}{8}$-rest. The modern equivalent of each such ordo is a $\frac{9}{8}$-measure, so that the rhythm of the beginning is as follows: $|\frac{6}{8}\, \downarrow \!\!\downarrow \gamma |\frac{9}{8}\, \downarrow\!\downarrow\,\downarrow\!\uparrow\!\downarrow\,\downarrow\!\uparrow\!\downarrow\gamma|\downarrow\!\downarrow\,\downarrow\!\uparrow\!\downarrow\,\downarrow\!\uparrow\!\downarrow\gamma|\ldots$.

The transcription of the upper parts is not without difficulties. The student is advised to transcribe first the duplum, then the triplum, always paying attention to the consonances. A particular problem is presented by the concluding measures, in which it is difficult to reconcile the rhythms suggested by the notation of the different parts. Evidently a free performance, involving some sort of ritardando, is intended here. The beginning of the triplum is transcribed in the appendix, No. 36. To tackle this piece will be particularly rewarding for the student because he will encounter it again in the later course of this study in the form of two derivative motets, *Quant revient — L'autre jor — Flos filius* (Facs. 54, p. 273) and *Candida virginitas — Flos filius* (Facs. 57, p. 285).

Notation of the Upper Parts. The following examples are given in order to clarify certain peculiarities of the writing of the upper parts. A clausula *Et gaudebit* from W_1 (p. 45) is interesting as an illustration of the comparatively high degree of rhythmic freedom—within the bounds of modal meter, of course—which could be expressed by the rather primitive means of modal notation:

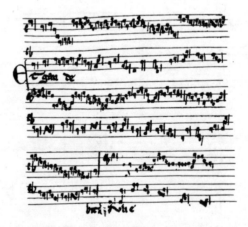

In the tenor, the liturgical melody *Et gaudebit* (from the *Alleluia, Non vos relinquam;* see *Gr. Rom.* 268) appears twice, the repetition beginning with the fourth ordo of the second staff of the tenor. The rhythm of the tenor obviously is IIc of the above tabulation. With a transcription of the tenor as a basis to start with, the interpretation of the duplum presents few difficulties if the principles of consonance are observed. In the first half of the piece the rhythm is that of the first mode with *extensio modi* being used frequently. The single notes always indicate *L*. Beginning after the first division stroke of the second line the writing of ligatures, *1 3 3* . . . would seem to indicate the third mode, that is, a change from the trochaic to the iambic rhythm. Since, however, the fundamental rhythm does not change within a clausula (see p. 237), the *ternariae* represent *extensio*-patterns of the first mode. In the tenor, the group of three single notes which closes the first representation of the liturgical melody (third ordo of line two) signifies three *D*, not *L*. Here follows the transcription of the beginning of the second brace:

An interesting and (as far as this writer's experience goes, very exceptional) irregularity of notation occurs at the beginning of the last brace. The writing of the duplum would clearly seem to suggest the first mode, with alternating *L* and *B*. However, in order to make the passage conform with the tenor the notes must all be read as *L*, similar to those of the preceding ordo:

The arrows point to the initial notes of the two staffs which, as is frequently the case, do not sound simultaneously. The penultimate note of the tenor (*B*) must be extended to cover two measures.

It would, of course, be possible to interpret the passage under consideration as being in the first mode, if in the corresponding section of the tenor the rhythm of the fifth mode (IIc) were replaced by the doubly quick rhythm of the first mode (IIa). Although such a quickening of rhythm is not uncommonly applied to the second presentation of the liturgical melody, it would seem to be rather out of place here where it would occur only with the last few measures of the second presentation. In fact, definite proof supporting our first interpretation will be found later (p. 280).

Examples. We now turn to a consideration of Facsimile 51 which shows a number of clausulae, contained on p. 174'/175 of the Florentine Codex. (1) *Et occurrens.* The tenor (beginning with the fourth note on the staff) is written in L which appear in irregular groups ('simplex groups,' see p. 245). Groups with an uneven number of L call for an extra $\frac{3}{8}$- ($\frac{9}{8}$-) measure. Naturally in cases like this $\frac{3}{8}$-measures may well be used for the entire transcription. The duplum (beginning with the *ternaria* f-e-d) is in the first mode.

(2) *Et gaude—bit.* The entire tenor is written in the grouping /*1 1*/ *3*/, which must be read in the fifth mode (IIc). The duplum is in the first mode, with the initial *ternaria* of several ordines broken up into *1 + 2*, because of repeated tones. At the beginning of the duplum we find a single note (f) followed by a *plica* note of the same pitch, another example of the *plica duplex longa*. Several ordines (end of the second brace of the page, middle of the third brace, show the grouping *1 3 3* . . . suggestive of the third mode. Actually, they indicate *extensio*-patterns of the first mode, as in the clausula *Et gaudebit* (p. 252f). In the present case definite proof for this interpretation exists in a derivative motet, *Quant florist—Non orphanum—Gaudebit*, which is notated in the unequivocal symbols of pre-Franconian notation.[1]

The student will have already noticed that in the pieces under consideration the vertical alignment of the written characters unfortunately does not always exactly correspond to the vertical alignment of the tones which are to be simultaneously sounded. Neither do the entire lines necessarily end with simultaneous notes. For instance, in the third brace the last note of the tenor sounds, not with the last note of the duplum, but with the first note of the next line. Several measures of this piece are transcribed in the appendix, No. 37a.

[1] *Mo*, no. 42 (Rokseth, *Polyphonies*) and *Ba*, no. 67 (Aubry, *Cent motets*). It is interesting to note that in both these sources the *conjunctura quaternaria* in the second ordo of staff 5 appears, not as three shorts followed by a long (see p. 249), but as a long followed by three (in *Ba* four) shorts (see *Polyphonies* i, p. 77, staff 1, and *Cent motets* i, p. 43, staff 1: 'cum iero'). This is one of many examples indicating that at the time of the composition of the motet (1250?) the conjuncturae had lost their original meaning and were interpreted as what was suggested by their shape, that is, as a long followed by several short notes.

FACSIMILE 51

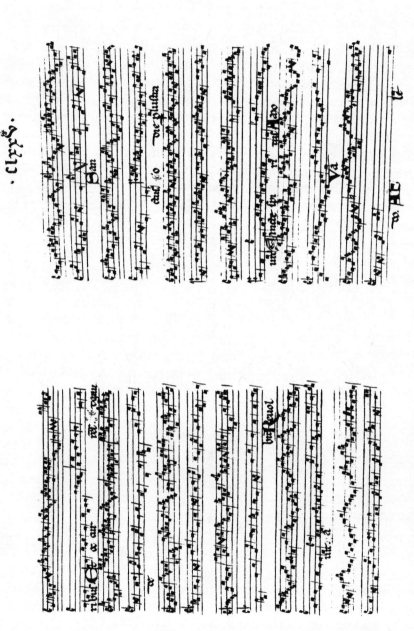

MS Florence, Biblioteca Mediocea-Laurenziana, *plut. 29.1* (13th century)
Pages 174', 175

(3) *Revolvit.* This short clausula (from the *Alleluia Angelus Domini*) has *duplex longae* in the tenor. The duplum starts with two *L*.

(4) *Ta.* The tenor has the rather unusual combination / *1* / *3* / throughout the first statement of the c.f., / *3* / in the second. The beginning is transcribed in the appendix, No. 37b.

(5) *Sanctus.* The *ternariae* of the tenor indicate the fifth mode. The duplum is in the first mode. The ternariae in the middle of several ordines always indicate *extensio modi*. The piece closes with a short *copula* whose notation suggests change from the first to the second mode, as in the almost identical *copula* of the clausula *Go* (Facs. 46, p. 229; see the remark on p. 237).

(6) *Hodie perlustra—vit.* Both duplum and tenor are in the second mode. Each ordo of the tenor consists of three perfections, corresponding to a $\frac{9}{8}$-measure. The irregular notation of the tenor to the syllables '-die perlustra-' is caused by the change of syllables, which also accounts for the numerous dashes in this passage. Actually the basic tenor rhythm, as indicated by the regular ordines, *2 3*, continues without change. The duplum is one of various examples showing that modal notation, although often proving a surprisingly pliant medium of notation for the rhythmic variants (*extensio* and *fractio*) of the first mode, is much less adapted for similar variants of the second mode. The notation of such parts often remains uncertain and doubtful in many particulars. The main guide is, as always, the principle of consonances. Occasionally the rule of corresponding ligatures (see p. 237) proves helpful in making a decision between various alternatives. See the transcription in the appendix, No. 37c.

(7) *Sancte spiritus.* The duplum begins with a single *plica* on d'. Whether the ordines of three perfections should be transcribed as two $\frac{6}{8}$-measures or as one $\frac{9}{8}$-measure, cannot be determined. At the end there is a cadential passage similar to that of *Sanctus*.

(8) *Amo.* Tenor and duplum begin with two single notes. The rhythm is similar to that of *Et occurrens*.

(9) *Vado.* The two *ternariae* at the end of the first and second ordo of the duplum evidently call for *fractio modi*.

A page similar to the one just considered is reproduced in *HdN* I, 228, and another one in *SchT*, p. 14. Both are strongly recommended for study.

We close our study of modal notation with the consideration of some clausulae showing certain notational irregularities not encountered in the previous examples. In the clausula *Mulierum* of Facsimile 52a the tenor d a a c' c' . . . appears twice (the initial d, to the syllable 'Mu-,' is omitted in the second statement), first in ternariae, then in the combination

FACSIMILES 52a, 52b

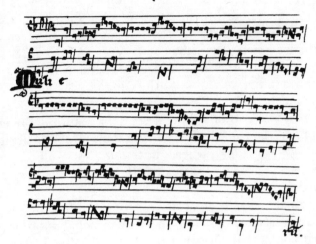

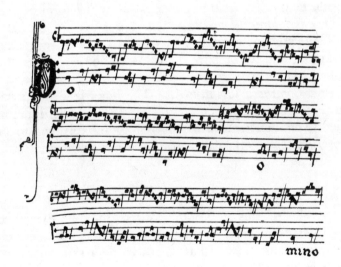

MS Florence, Biblioteca Medicea-Laurenziana, *plut. 29.1*
(13th century)
(a) From page 164; (b) From pages 88', 89

/ *1 1* / *3* /. The Ms erroneously omits two complete ordines (tenor notes: / f e f / d e c /) at the end of the first brace. They are included in the version of *W*₁, p. 45.

The great number of notes in the duplum clearly suggests the fifth mode for the entire tenor (Ic and IIc). The duplum is conspicuous for its extended use of repeated notes which, moreover, show a distinction between notes with and without the dash, or, as we may say, between *L* and *B*. Repeatedly these signs occur in the combination *L B B L* (according to *W*₁, where the *B* are written in the lozenge-shape of the later *S*, a *B* is missing at the beginning of the seventh ordo, and the fourth note of the ninth ordo should be a *L*). These groups suggest interpretation in the second mode, with alteration of the second *B*. Toward the end of the duplum (middle of the third brace) we find the characteristic ligatures of the third mode (*1 3 3* . . .), whose rhythm is closely allied with that of
* the second mode. Various passages of the piece are transcribed in the appendix, No. 38.

Facsimile 52b shows two clausulae *Domino* the first of which (designated *Do*) is an extremely difficult specimen of modal notation. The clue to its transcription is that the tenor pattern is IIb (see p. 248), and that the duplum is in the second mode, with frequent *fractio*-modifications (sixteenth-notes). Even with this information as a basis there remain many uncertainties which it would be difficult to settle definitely without some outside help. Fortunately, this exists in the form of a derivative motet, *Ne m'oubliez mie—Domino*, which is preserved in *Mo* (ed. Rokseth, No. 236). The student is advised to transcribe the piece along the lines indicated above, and to compare the transcription with that of the motet (ed. Rokseth, III, p. 60).

The second *Domino* is less difficult. The tenor is in the pattern of IIa (with the reversed arrangement, / *3* / *1 1* /), and the duplum is in the first mode. The last *ternaria* of the tenor probably has to be read as *L L L*, not *L B L*, as is the case with the other *ternariae*.

C. Syllabic Notation

The principles of this notational system may be explained in connection with Facsimile 53, containing a conductus *Hac in anni janua*. Three parts are notated on what seems to be a single staff of thirteen or more lines, but is in fact a contraction of three different staves, each with its own clef-letter c (see p. 8). Actually, all the parts move within about the same range, quite different from what the arrangement in writing suggests at first sight.

FACSIMILE 53

MS Wolfenbüttel, Herzogliche Bibliothek *677*, formerly *Helmstedt 628*
(13th century)
Page 71

The music is notated essentially in single notes, each of which belongs to a syllable of the text. Occasionally *plica* notes are used (for instance, near the beginning of the middle part), and frequently ligatures (*binariae* and *ternariae*) appear in the place of a single note. These, of course, mean that two or three tones should be sung to the syllable to which they belong.

It will easily be seen that, in each part, the number of notational signs (single notes or ligatures) corresponds with the number of syllables which, in the present case, is seven for each line of the poem:

Hac in anni janua
hoc in januario
tendamus ad ardua
virtutum subsidio.

Gaudia sunt mutua
muto facto vitio
reproborum fatua
reprobatur actio.

Following is the transcription of the beginning:

In accordance with the poetic meter of the text, the last note of each phrase has been prolonged by a pause, a procedure which is actually prescribed in notation by the 'doubled *plicas*' in the lowest part.

The last line of our facsimile is occupied by a cadential vocalisation
* (*cauda*) to the final syllable —'o'. Automatically the notation changes from syllabic to modal notation (see p. 231).

Judging from these explanations the system of syllabic notation is simplicity in itself. But this simplicity is deceptive. A transcription such as given above is only the point of departure for various considerations of a more or less controversial character, and for questions which to the present day have not been definitely answered.

The first question that arises concerns the evaluation of the groups of notes represented by the ligatures which often occur in the place of a single note. Many conductus show a considerable number of groups of

two and three notes, and often a group of two notes occurs in one part against one of three notes in another part, as repeatedly in *Hac in anni janua*. It seems highly improbable that cross rhythms such as would result from the simultaneous occurrence of two and three notes can be admitted in a period which more than any other is characterized by the rigidity of its rhythmic concepts. Proceeding from the premise that the single notes of syllabic notation represent each a *longa* (a premise which actually is the most controversial of all; see p. 262), the notes of a ligature naturally suggest interpretation according to the system of modal rhythm, based on the ternary division of the *L*. This means that the notes of a *ligatura ternaria* represent three *B* of equal value. In the case of a *ligatura binaria* either the first or the second *B* will have to be doubled, in the pattern of either the first or the second mode. Since the first mode is the much more frequent one, the former alternative appears as the more natural solution. For groups of more than three notes the rhythmic formulae given on p. 241, first illustration, under (a), may serve as a model (disregarding, of course, the final dotted quarter-note which, in syllabic notation, would be represented by a separate note). Following is a new rendition of *Hac in anni janua*, according to the
* principles just outlined:

The rhythmic interpretation of the smaller note values, as just outlined, is only one of several possibilities. Various other methods have been used in transcriptions of conductus, as appears from the table on p. 262 (all values are reduced to the same scale, *L* =quarter-note).

The interpretation, used by Wooldridge, Handschin, and Ellinwood, of the *binaria* as an iambic pattern (second mode) is suggested by the basic meaning of this ligature, that is, *B L*. In many cases this rendition seems preferable because it leads to a quicker resolution of a dissonance between the first note of the ligature and the simultaneous note of the tenor (e.g., e' - d' against d). There are, however, other instances (possibly less numerous) in which the second tone produces the dissonance (e.g., d'- e'

	binaria	ternaria	quaternaria
Coussemaker (*Histoire de l'harmonie*, Traduction, no. 23)	♩ ♪	♩ ♫	♩ ♫♫₃; ♫♫♫
Wooldridge (e.g., *OH*, 254f, 'commiserans .. considerans')	♪ ♩	♩ ♫₃	♩ ♫♫₃
Riemann (*RHdM* i. 2, p. 211)	♫	♫♫	
Handschin (in A. Einstein, *Short History of Music*, Ex. 6)	♪ ♩	♫♫	
Handschin (*ZfMW* vi, 554)	♪ ♩	♫ ♩	
occasionally	♩. ♩.	♪♪ ♩.	
Ellinwood (*MQ* xxvii, 189ff)	♪ ♩, ♪ ♩♩	♫♫	♫♫♫⁴

against d) and in which, therefore, the rhythm *L B* would give a better result from the point of view of consonance. The obvious solution, that is, to choose between both possibilities, would imply a change of modal patterns within one and the same composition which one might hesitate to admit. If such a change is ruled out, the decision in favor of the first mode becomes almost imperative, owing to the frequent occurrence in syllabic notation of *plica* notes, symbols which it is practically impossible to interpret as *B L*. (An example showing the simultaneous use of a *plica* note and a *binaria* is found at the beginning of *Hac in anni janua*, syllable 'an-'.)

While the uncertainty that exists with regard to the evaluation of the ligatures may appear as a somewhat irrelevant question of detail, a much more fundamental problem is presented by the single notes of syllabic notation. All the preceding explanations are based on the assumption that these single notes indicate values of equal length or, to put it differently, are to be read in the fifth mode. As has been previously intimated (p. 261), this theory, favored by some scholars (Wooldridge, Handschin, Reese, Ellinwood) is contested by others (Ludwig, Aubry, Gennrich, Bukofzer) who maintain that these notes actually represent alternations of longs and shorts, usually in the rhythm of the first mode. This means that modal rhythm is introduced by the single notes, not by the ligatures

which now appear only as *fractio* patterns. Here follows a 'modal' *
rendition of *Hac in anni janua*:[1]

What are the reasons in favor of this interpretation? The most obvious
argument is the versification of the text which, with its alternation of
accented and unaccented syllables, naturally suggests a conforming
alternation of long and short values. Another argument exists in the fact
that modal rhythm is, beyond doubt, required for the upper parts of the
early motets, parts which are notated in exactly the same manner as are
all the parts of the conductus (see the explanations under Motet Notation, p. 271ff; also Facsimiles 54, 55, 56). Particularly impressive is the
evidence furnished by the so-called conductus-motets (see p. 274, fn. 1),
compositions in three (or occasionally four) voices, whose upper parts
are, for all practical purposes, undistinguishable from a two- (or three-)
voice conductus, as appears from Facsimile 55 (p. 275).[2] These examples
clearly show that modal interpretation of compositions or of voice-parts
written in the uniform symbols of syllabic notation was part and parcel
of the musical practice of that time.[3]

Champions of modal interpretation have also called attention to the
fact that occasionally conductus of the period under consideration occur
in later sources in a more advanced type of notation (pre-Franconian), in
which there is a clear differentiation between *longa* and *brevis*. Following

[1] For the sake of short reference the two methods of interpretation may be designated as 'isochronous' and 'modal,' although the former also falls within the general frame work of the rhythmic modes.

[2] W_1 contains several 'conductus' (e.g., *Serena virginum*, p. 9) which actually are motets, the
tenor (in the present case, 'Manere') being omitted in this source, but found in others (e.g., *Fl*, p.
235). See *Repertorium*, p. 35 (*Serena virginum*), p. 39 (*Latex silice*), p. 40 (*Deo confitemini, Laudes
referat, Gaudeat devotio*), and p. 41 (*Qui servare*).

[3] In this connection it may be mentioned that the method of modal interpretation has also been
applied to the monophonic songs of the troubadours and trouvères, and is, at present, generally
accepted as the correct interpretation of these melodies, all of which are transmitted in syllabic
notation. See, e.g., P. Aubry, *La Rhythmique musicale des troubadours et des trouvères* (Paris, 1907);
also *HdN* i, 201ff and *AHdM* i, 189ff. It has also been used for the monophonic conductus (see
AHdM i, 187), the Spanish cantigas (*AHdM* i, 213) and, occasionally, the songs of the Minnesingers
(see *AHdM* i, 204). However, recent investigations have considerably shaken the foundation of
this theory, except in the case of the songs of the trouvères (see the author's review of H. Anglés,
La Musica de las Cantigas . . . (1943), in *Speculum*, July 1947, p. 458ff, and J. Handschin's
review of U. Sesini, *Le Melodie trobadoriche* . . . (1942), in *AM* xx, 1948, p. 62.

is the beginning of a conductus, *Crucifigat omnes*, in two versions, from W_1 (p. 71) and from the *Codex Huelgas* (p. 97):

Finally, recent investigations have brought to light the fact that in a number of conductus there exist musical relations and correspondences between the syllabic and the melismatic passages, the latter using occasionally the same music that appears at another place of the composition in syllabic form. Since there can be no doubt regarding the modal rhythm of the melismas, the obvious conclusion is that the syllabic sections are also in modal rhythm.

No doubt, these considerations constitute strong evidence in favor of

[1] See M. F. Bukofzer, 'Rhythm and Meter in the Notre-Dame Conductus' (*Bulletin of the American Musicological Association*, 1948, p. 63).

modal interpretation. The main argument against its universal acception lies in the fact that in many cases it leads to versions of a rhythmic complexity far exceeding the limitations of thirteenth century style. Such versions result in all those cases where the single notes are to a large extent replaced by ligatures, particularly if these ligatures include groups of three or more notes. Using a terminology familiar from Gregorian chant, we may distinguish between conductus in 'syllabic style' and others in 'group style.' While examples of the former type, for instance, *Crucifigat omnes* (p. 264) lend themselves very well to modal interpretation, this method leads to much less satisfactory results if applied to a conductus like *Hac in anni* (p. 259) with its numerous groups of three notes, many of which fall on the weak accent of the text, hence on the short value of the modal pattern, thus leading to a very uneven rhythmic texture. Even more awkward is the result in the case of examples showing groups of four, five, or more notes, as for instance in the three-voice conductus *Relegentur ab area* (*Fl*, p. 202′), a section of which follows on p. 266 in facsimile reproduction and two transcriptions, (a) isochronous (fifth mode), and (b) modal (first mode).

It should be noticed that the version (a) makes the rhythmic contrasts disappear to an even greater extent than the written score suggests, since it admits (and probably calls for) a certain flexibility of tempo in actual performance, including a slight prolongation of the syllables having extended groups of notes. Modal rhythm, on the other hand, by its very nature is incompatible with flexibility of tempo.

Obviously, an argument in favor of modal interpretation of conductus in group style could be established if it could be shown that the groups of notes appear preferably on the strong, that is, on the presumably longer beat. Actually this is not the case, as the examples clearly show. In some instances, however, better results can be obtained by applying another mode than the one that seems natural at first. Thus, a considerably smoother version of *Hac in anni janua* results if it is transcribed in the second mode.

In weighing all the evidence *pro* and *contra*, one will probably arrive at the conclusion that, first of all, a distinction should be made between conductus in syllabic style and conductus in group style. For the former type modal interpretation appears to be not only admissible but probably preferable. In this connection it may be noticed that the conductus-like upper structure of motets such as *Laus Domino—Eius* or *Homo quo vigeas—Et gaudebit* (Facsimiles 55, 56, pp. 275, 281) are definitely in syllabic style, and that in the Huelgas version of the *Crucifigat omnes*

(p. 264) the upper part, which contains several groups of notes, is omitted. For conductus in group style the isochronous rendition (fifth mode) appears proper, unless a modal pattern can be found which leads to a reasonably even rhythmic texture.

D. Duplum Notation

The organa dupla represent the earliest repertory of the School of Notre Dame. Their development, associated with Leoninus, the 'optimus organista' (second half of the twelfth century) forms the transition between the school of St. Martial (see p. 209ff) and the organa tripla and quadrupla of Perotinus, the 'optimus discantor.'

The notation of the organa dupla presents even greater problems than that of the conductus. While in syllabic notation at least the basic principles are obvious and incontestable, the very foundations of duplum notation are uncertain. As we shall see later, the knowledge of this system (if it ever was a 'system') was lost as early as the thirteenth century. Theorists of this period often speak of organum duplum as a miraculous thing of the past, extolling it as the most beautiful and noble kind of music, but without being able to describe it in the technical language of their day. From the historical point of view this uncertainty is readily explained by the fact that the organa dupla of the Leoninus period stand between periods representing two diametrically opposed concepts of rhythm, the free, 'Gregorian' rhythm of St. Martial and the rigid system of the rhythmic modes. Rarely in music history has a development of a half a century brought about such a radical change of methods, and the very distance between the two points makes it difficult to determine the position occupied by the organa dupla of Leoninus.

The problem presented by the notation of the organa dupla is illustrated by the *Benedicamus Domino* of Facs. 49 (p. 247). This consists of an 'organal' section, 'Benedicamus,' with long held notes in the tenor, and a clausula on 'Domino.' The latter is, of course, in modal notation and, in fact, served as an example of this system (p. 245). The former shows the characteristic traits of duplum notation, that is, ligatures and extended conjuncturas in irregular combinations which fail to suggest—let alone to indicate clearly— modal rhythm in any of its varieties. The difficulty of determining the rhythmic meaning of these signs is considerably enhanced by the fact that the tenor of these sections consists of sustained single notes, each serving as a pedal point for a great number of notes of the duplum. Thus, one of the most important clues of modal notation is missing, that is, the simple and relatively unequivocal rhythm of the tenor. Evidently, the notation of this section differs radically from that of the clausula. On the other hand, it shows an unmistakable similarity to the notation of the *Alleluia vocavit Jhesus* from the Codex Calixtinus, reproduced on Facs. 45 (p. 213), as appears, for instance, from a comparison of the second ordo on staff two of the *Benedicamus* with the third 'ordo' on staff two of the *Alleluia*. The question, then, is whether the organal section of the *Benedicamus* should be interpreted in a rhythmic style similar to that of the organa of St. Martial and Compostela, or in a more advanced style midway between free rhythm and strictly modal patterns.

As regards the interpretation in free rhythm, there are several theorists of the thirteenth century whose remarks about organum duplum (also called 'organum purum,' 'organum speciale,' 'organum proprie sumptum,' 'organum non rectum ,' 'organum per se') could be quoted as supporting evidence. Thus, Walter Odington says (*CS* i, 245b):

There is one type of organum in which only the coherence of immeasurable voice-parts (*vocum immensurabilium*) is observed, and this is called organum purum. And this is the oldest, and is in two parts only.

Anonymous of 1279 (H. Sowa, *Ein anonymer glossierter Mensuraltraktat*, p. 127):

In this chapter the author deals with organum speciale, also known as organum duplex; which, if it is found as such,[1] proceeding (*gradiens*) in its own manner, does not hesitate to transgress or interrupt the regular divisions (*regularum metas*) as distributed in a definite series of notational signs (*figurarum*) and temporal values (*temporum*), thus leading to an irregularity [which appears] upon careful observation (*irregularitas subtiliter intuenti*).

Anonymous de la Fage (De la Fage, *Essais de diphtérographie musicale*, 1864, p. 358):

In an organum the parts sound together, not by the equivalence of notes (*equalitate punctorum;* with reference to discant style), but in an infinite multiplicity and an almost miraculous flexibility.

The language of these quotations leaves little doubt that the compositions thus described were rhythmically free and unmeasured. The difficulty is that we have no way of knowing whether these descriptions refer to the organa of Leoninus as preserved in W_1 and *Fl*, or to unknown compositions of a somewhat earlier period in the development of the school of Notre Dame. It could even be argued that they refer to the organa of St. Martial, although this surmise is somewhat unlikely in view of the fact that this school was located in southern France (Limoges). It is doubtful whether, under then prevailing conditions, a provencal repertory from *ca.* 1150 was still known in Paris about 1270, the time when the above quoted theorists wrote.

[1]'per se positum;' see the explanation in fn. 1, p. 269.

Most scholars are inclined to consider the organa under consideration as examples of a more advanced rhythmic style, that is, in triple meter, but without strict modal patterns. The basis for this interpretation is provided by the fact that several of the most important theorists (all, by the way, of a somewhat earlier period than those previously quoted) expressly refer to the use of *longae* and *breves* in organum duplum. Particularly clarifying are the explanations of Johannes de Garlandia (*De Musica mensurabili positio*, c. 1250; *CS* i, 114a [some obscure or relatively irrelevant sentences are omitted]):

There are two special types of organum, *per se* and *cum alio*.[1] Organum *per se* is that which is performed in *modus rectus* or in *modus non rectus*. By *modus rectus* we mean that type of modus which is used for *discantus*. In *modus rectus longae* and *breves* are taken principally in the first mode proper (*debito modo primo et principaliter*). In *modus non rectus*, however, the *longae* and *breves* are [also] in the first mode, but incidentally (*ex contingenti*).

These remarks suggest an interpretation of organum duplum in the first mode, this mode being applied strictly in the clausulae, freely in the organal sections. Taking this rhythmic style as a basis, there arises the question as to the evaluation of the ligatures in *modus non rectus*. Judging from the relatively few transcriptions of organa dupla that have been published,[2] the guiding principle seems to be to interpret each ligature in its basic meaning, that is, the *binaria* as *B L*, the *ternaria* as *L B L*, and the ligatures with more than three notes as *fractio*-modifications of the ternaria,[3] all normally in the first mode, but occasionally (in spite of Garlandia's statement) with changes into the second mode. However, an examination of the available transcriptions shows that the ligatures are often interpreted differently, in order to obtain a smoother

---

[1]The most likely explanation of these terms is that *per se* means 'in two parts' (organum duplum), *cum alio*, 'with a third part' (organum triplum).

[2]*Judea et Jherusalem: OH*, 188ff (facsimile); *RHdM*, i.2, 156; Handschin, in *ZfMW* x, 15; Sowa, in *Ein . . . Mensuraltraktat*, p. XXXVIII. —*Hec dies: AHdM* i, 217 (Ludwig); H. Besseler, *Musik des Mittelalters und der Renaissance* (1931), p. 99f (facsimile); A. T. Davison and W. Apel, *Historical Anthology of Music* i (1946), No. 29. —*Alleluia Pascha nostrum:* Ludwig, in *ZfMW* v, 448. —*Crucifixus in carne:* Handschin, in *AfMW* vii, 161. —*Propter veritatem:* H. Anglès, *El Codex musical de Las Huelgas* (1931), ii, No. 47. —*Tanquam sponsus: OH*, 195. —*Virgo Dei genetrix: OH*, 201. —*Benedicamus Domino:* Davison-Apel, *Anthology*, No. 28c.

Special studies of organum duplum are found in *OH*, pp. 175–187, and in Sowa, *Ein . . . Mensuraltraktat*, pp. XXVII–XXXIX.

[3]Anon. VII (*CS* i, 381a): 'And be it known that any ligature with more than three notes should be reduced to a *ternaria*.' Similarly Anon. IV (*CS* i, 341b: 'Omnis figura ligata') with reference to the 'libris antiquorum . . . in tempore Perotini Magistri.'

result. As an illustration there follows a transcription of the beginning of the *Benedicamus Domino* (Facsimile 49, p. 247). In the main text an attempt has been made to follow the above rules, while the small notes illustrate modifications such as are found in modern transcriptions.[1]

Obviously, this method of transcription (if it can be called a method) is very unsatisfactory. It leaves so much room for arbitrariness that one might hesitate to accept it as the final answer to our problem. Possibly a clue toward a more satisfactory solution exists in certain statements made by several thirteenth-century theorists which deserve more careful attention than has been given them so far. These statements all emphasize the importance of consonance and dissonance as a regulating factor in the organa dupla. Joh. Garlandia, after his remarks about *modus rectus* and *modus non rectus* (see p. 269) continues as follows:

> The *longae* and *breves* are recognized as follows: through consonance, through the form of notes (*figura*) and through [the rule of] the penultimate. Hence the rule: Whatever occurs by virtue of consonance, is considered as *longa*. Another rule: Whatever has the form of a *longa*, is long. . . . Another rule: Whatever occurs before a long pause or before a perfect consonance, is considered as long.

Similar rules are given by Franco (*CS* i, 134f). By far the clearest and most detailed explanation, however, is found in Anon. IV (*CS* i, 362ff). Essentially he tells us that the consonances are unison, octave, fourth, fifth, major and minor third, and that in every ligature a note is long if it is in consonance with the tenor, short, if in dissonance. According to these principles, one and the same combination of ligatures is to be read in a different rhythm, depending upon the pitch of the tenor note:

Additional rules are that each penultimate note before a rest is long, and that the *currentes* always descend quickly, but are preceded by a long note.

---

[1] The transcriptions by Riemann should be disregarded.

As appears from the above illustration and even more so from the practical application of these rules, they entail the abandoning of triple meter as the basic rhythm. Long and short notes follow in free succession, leading to a rhythmic style very similar to the one that has long been considered by many scholars[1] as the correct interpretation of Gregorian chant. Very likely, the 'principle of consonance' would not apply to passages written in regular groups of ligatures, such as the ordo immediately after 'ne' in the *Benedicamus*. These then, together with the clausulae, would indicate the intrusion of modal rhythm into polyphonic music, and would make the organa dupla of Leoninus to appear as a plausible link between those of St. Martial and the organa tripla of Perotinus.[2] Following is a new transcription of the *Benedicamus*.

E. MOTET NOTATION

As has been pointed out in our brief historical survey of the forms of the early thirteenth century, the motet originated around 1225 by the addition of a full text to the upper parts of the clausulae. Concomitant with this change are two important notational innovations. the transition from melismatic to syllabic notation in the texted parts; and the abandoning of score arrangement for arrangement in single parts, a method of writing which was to last continuously in ensemble music until the advent of the seventeenth century.[3]

The main sources of the early motet are the Florentine Codex (*Fl*) and the Codex Wolfenbüttel *1099* (*W₂*), both of which contain numerous motets in separate fascicles. Additional sources are the manuscripts Brit. Mus. *Eg. 2615* (*LoA*), Paris, B. N. *frc. 844* (Chansonnier Roy, *R*), and Paris, *B. N. 12615* (Chansonnier Noailles, *N*).[4] From the notational point of view, these sources are clearly marked off from the well-known later collections of Montpellier, Bamberg, etc., by the fact that, as is the

[1] The so-called 'mensuralists,' Dechevrens, Wagner, Dom Jeannin, Bonvin, Jammers (see G. Reese, *Music in the Middle Ages*, p. 143; *Harvard Dictionary of Music*, p. 309a).

[2] For a detailed study of this question see W. Apel, 'From St. Martial to Notre Dame' (*Journal of the American Musicological Society*, vol. ii, No. 3, 1949).

[3] The only exceptions to the universal adoption of part arrangement for the writing down of ensemble music are certain conductus-like pieces encountered in English MSS of the fourteenth and fifteenth century. See, e.g., H. E. Wooldridge, *Early English Harmony* 1, plates XVI, LVII, and the explanations on the Old Hall MS, p. 364.

[4] The main contents of the last two MSS are monophonic melodies of the troubadours and trouvères.

case in the entire field of square notation, only one character exists for the single note, that is to say, there is as yet no notational differentiation between the *longa* and the *brevis*.

Facsimile 54 shows a number of motets from the Chansonnier Roy. The music is arranged in two columns. On the left-side column, after the closing portion of a motet beginning on the preceding page, there follows a texted duplum (or, as it is called, motetus): *Hui main au dolz mois de mai*, at the end of which the tenor *Hec dies* is written. The almost spectacular incongruity between the length of the two parts sufficiently explains why score arrangement is abandoned. It would have been a waste of the valuable parchment to assign full staves for the few notes of the tenor, to say nothing of the difficulty of aligning vertically the compact ligatures of the tenor and the widely spaced notes of the motetus.

After this two-voice motet there follows in the manuscript a texted part, *Quant revient et foille et flors*, without tenor, and a part, *L'autre jor m'en alai par un destor*, at the end of which there is the tenor *Flos filius*. Together they form a three-voice motet which may be studied here.

The writing of the tenor shows the familiar features of modal notation. After two singles notes, there follow eleven ordines written (normally) *3 2*, which evidently are in the first mode. As each ordo contains three perfections (*secundus ordo*) the question as to the length of the closing rests arises: (a) $\frac{6}{8}$| ♩ ♪ ♩ ♩ | ♩. ≸. | ; (b) $\frac{9}{8}$| ♩ ♪ ♩ ♩ ♪ ≸ | . The context of the other parts readily shows that (b) is correct, and that the $\frac{6}{8}$-meter must be abandoned for $\frac{9}{8}$-meter, except for the first ordo.

The notation of the upper parts (the duplum *L'autre jor* may be considered first) in no way differs from the syllabic notation of the conductus. However, it goes without saying that the rhythm of these voices must be accommodated to the modal rhythm of the tenor. Most frequently the upper parts show the regular alternation long-short of the first mode. The value of the ligatures depends, of course, upon whether they take the place of a *L* or of a *B*. The following transcription of the beginning serves as an illustration:

FLOS FILIUS

FACSIMILE 54

Chansonnier Roy
Paris, Bibliothèque Nationale *frç. 844* (13th century)
Pages 206'

This is the place to refer the reader back to the three-voiced clausula *Flos filius* from Facsimile 46 (p. 229), which is the model for the present motet, the music being identical save in a few minor details. It is interesting to note in this case, as in many similar ones, that the earlier notation is considerably more precise and unequivocal than the later system (see also *Homo quo*, p. 279). Not until the introduction of the pre-Franconian system did this situation change (see p. 284).

Another example illustrating the principles of motet notation is the motet *Laus domino—Eius* of Facsimile 55. This piece belongs to a special class of motets the superstructure of which consists of two or occasionally three parts with the same text, notated in the score-arrangement of conductus.[1] The determination of the rhythm of the tenor as well as of the upper parts proves more difficult here than with the previous example. To start with, a clue may be gained from a rough calculation of the number of notes contained in the different parts. Since there are 30 notes of the tenor against 79 notes of the duplum (or triplum), the ratio is almost 1:3, so that, in the average, three notes of the duplum will be placed against one of the tenor. This result suggests that the single notes of the tenor are *duplex longae*, and that the rhythm of the texted parts is the third mode. The latter conjecture is supported by a consideration of the text whose accents naturally conform with this rhythm: Láus dominó resonét omniúm jubiló. As has been remarked by J. Beck (*Die Melodien der Troubadours*, Strassburg, 1908), a frequent occurrence of trisyllables in Latin texts usually indicates the third mode.

Once these results are obtained, the actual transcription presents no real problems. The transcription of the last ordo is given in the appendix, No. 39. An emendation is necessary for the close of the triplum.

It should be observed, however, that many motets of the period under consideration present even greater difficulties than the above two examples may lead the student to expect. These difficulties are generally due to one of the two following factors: either the inadequacy of the syllabic notation for the clear indication of rhythmic modifications of the modal patterns; or else the obscure and corrupt writing of the tenors.

The latter fault occurs particularly in the two chansonniers *R* and *N*. The motet *Hui main—Hec dies* of Facsimile 54 is an example in point, though one of relatively minor difficulty. The ligatures of the tenor fail to suggest any of the modal schemes. Under such circumstances, the

---

[1] In view of the fact that such 'conductus-motets,' as one may call them, occur in great number in the sources of Notre Dame (*Fl*, *Ma*, W_2) but are absent in the later MSS (Montpellier, Bamberg), they must be considered the earliest type of motets. See F. Ludwig in *AHdM* 1, p. 236.

MS Wolfenbüttel, Herzogliche Bibliothek *1206*, formerly *Helmstedt 1099* (13th century)
Pages 126', 127

clue for the solution must be sought for in the upper part, the text of

which suggests the first mode:

Hui main au dolz mois de mai

A consideration of the consonances readily shows that the notes of the

tenor are plain *L:*

However, a satisfactory rendition of the remaining portion of the motet
is not possible without some emendations.   In order to check the correctness of the tenor one will, of course, revert to its plainsong, which is the
beginning of the gradual *Hec dies* (see *Gr. Rom.* p. 221).   A comparison
shows that the authentic melody is correctly given in the ordines 1 — 4
of our tenor, except for a final note a which is missing:

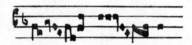

The ordines 5 — 7 of the tenor of our motet repeat the plainsong, but
less accurately.   We find five repetitions of the tone c, as against the
correct number four; furthermore, three tones, g-a-a, are missing at the
end.   Assuming, then, that the deviations of our MS are clerical errors,
we arrive at a tenor which can be satisfactorily combined with the duplum, as is shown in the appendix, No. 40.

It is interesting to note that there exists another version of the same motet in the
Codex Montpellier, no. 184 (f. 234′ of the original), which is notated in the much more
definite symbols of the pre-Franconian notation, that is, with a clear distinction of *L* and
B in the duplum and with single *L* in the tenor.   A comparison shows that the two dupla
are practically identical.   The tenor, however, represents an interesting 'secularization' of
the liturgical melody, in a form reminiscent of and apparently derived from that of the
mediaeval rondeau: A A A B A (A includes the first eight notes; B the following eight
notes; the last two, or three, notes, g-a-[a], are missing).   Actually, this secularized
tenor combines much more easily with the duplum than the 'authentic' tenor of our
motet[1]—a fact which may make one suspicious as to whether the latter may not, after
all, be the result of a fundamental error on the part of a scribe.   The only reason against
this conjecture is the fact that the tenor of the Chansonnier Roy with its simple repetition
of the plainsong follows a common practice of the early thirteenth century, whereas the
more complicated rondeau-like structure of the tenor from the Codex Montpellier suggests
a later date, and one which is probably too late for our source.   At any rate, a comparison

[1] See the transcription in Y. Rokseth, *Polyphonies du xiiie siècle*, III, 8.

of the two versions throws an interesting light upon the adaptability of the thirteenth century technique of composition.

Still more irregular and obscure is the notation of the tenors in the Chansonnier Noailles.[1] Below is a reproduction of the upper part of page 191' of this manuscript (the first staff is from the bottom of p. 191):

The first piece contains few notational difficulties. Its chief interest lies in its formal structure, which shows a liturgical tenor of strictly binary form (the melody *Quia concupivit rex* appears twice, with a different ending for the second time) combined with an asymmetrical motetus written in the shortened form a A a b A B of the rondeau (A is the melody to the text 'C'est la jus par desous l'olive,' B that to the words 'or charoles'). The notation of the tenor suggests the first mode, with *extensio modi* in the ordines containing only two notes (3, 10, 11, 13), and with the ordines 2 and 9 containing three perfections ($\frac{9}{8}$-meter). In order to make the upper part fit, an extra rest of one *L* must be inserted in the tenor between the first and the second statement of the melody (end of the seventh ordo). The rhythm of the upper voice is less clearly in-

[1] See *Repertorium*, p. 285-287 (N).

dicated.   Following is a transcription of the sections A and B of the
rondeau which will enable the reader to piece the fragments of this interesting quodlibet together:

The upper parts of the next pieces in our reproduction are merely short
refrains, combined with liturgical tenors. Possibly they represent
abridged versions of rondeaus of which only the sections A and B are
notated.   In spite of their brevity the rhythmic interpretation of these
miniature pieces presents great difficulty.   The following transcriptions
are offered with due reservation:

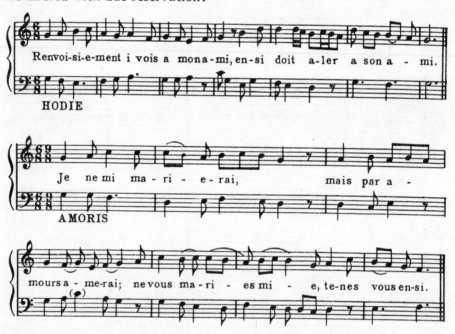

The problematic character of these pieces clearly appears from a comparison of the above transcriptions with those contained in F. Gennrich's
philological publication, *Rondeaux, Virelais und Balladen*, vol. II (Göt-
tingen, 1927).[1]   His rendition of *Renvoisiement* is shown on page 279.
Apparently, Gennrich's basis of interpretation is the declamation of the
text, and in this respect his rendition is a model of correctness.   How-

[1] See pp. 21, 22 of the publication.   The rondeau *C'est la jus* is transcribed in vol. I, p. 21 of the
same publication (Dresden, 1921).   Another motet from Noailles is reproduced in *HdN* I, 227.
Wolf's transcription may be compared with that by Gennrich (vol. I, p. 18).

Ren-voi-si-e-ment i vois a mon a-mi, en-si doit on a-ler a son a - mi.

HODIE

ever, one is entitled to question how strictly applicable to thirteenth century music modern principles of correct declamation may be. From the
notational point of view as well as from a consideration of the consonances his renditions are certainly open to objections.

As a final example, the motet *Homo quo vigeas—Et gaudebit* from W_2
may be considered. Its beginning is found on Facsimile 55, the completion on Facsimile 56. Although it follows immediately upon the
motet *Laus domino—Eius* and is very similar to this in appearance, it
presents quite a different problem. A comparatively simple question is
that as to the mode of the tenor. A calculation of the type suggested
previously is scarcely necessary in order to show that the fifth mode (IIc
of the tabulation p. 248) is correct (the tenor begins on staff 7 of the
right-hand column of Facs. 56, with the notes f-g, and continues
underneath on the eighth staff). The real problem of the piece lies in
the coordination of the upper parts to the tenor. The student is strongly
advised to try his hand on this, if only for the sake of the experience thus
gained. Even the most persevering efforts, however, will result in failure, judging from this writer's experience.[1] In fact, the problem would
be hopeless were it not for the fact that there exists a related piece the
rhythm of which is more clearly expressed in its notation, namely, the
clausula from which the motet in question is derived. This clausula, a
two-voiced setting of the liturgical tenor *Et gaudebit*, has been studied
previously (p. 252f). A glance at our reproduction shows the identity of
its parts with the tenor and duplum of the motet. All we have to do is
to underlay the text and to add the triplum in the same rhythm as the
duplum.[2]

There are, of course, certain variants between the two dupla. Most of
them need not be mentioned here, since they are rather obvious and in-
consequential. Only towards the end of the piece does the duplum of

[1] I am indebted to Mr Lincoln B. Spiess for his calling my attention to this interesting specimen.

[2] This is another example showing that modal notation is clearer than motet notation (see p. 274).
If no clausula exists, one will have to resort more or less to experimentation, in which case the principles outlined in Ludwig's *Repertorium*, p. 52ff, will prove helpful.

the motet vary considerably from that of the clausula, owing to the introduction of two notes for one [(a) clausula; (b) motet]:

The final passage of the motet, beginning with the words 'hac in via militans,' constitutes the proof previously alluded to (p. 254), that the corresponding passage of the duplum of the clausula is not in the first mode—strongly suggested by the notation—but in the fifth.

The addition of the triplum of the motet, although without any difficulties from the notational point of view, raises a stylistic problem, on account of the rather strong dissonances which result. Combinations such as f-c'-e', b -f'-c', g-d'-a (the tones are named in the order tenor—duplum—triplum) occur repeatedly on the first beat of the measure. Theorists of the period accounted for such discords and admitted them as being composed of two consonant intervals. For instance, the e' of the first chord was considered legitimate because it formed a consonance with the c' of the duplum, though not with the f of the tenor. A closer study of the piece shows that the tenor and duplum, i.e., the original clausula, as well as the duplum and triplum, i.e., the conductus-like superstructure, each form a pair of strictly consonant voices, whereas the combination of all three parts produces the above-mentioned dissonant chords.

FACSIMILE 56

MS Wolfenbüttel, Herzogliche Bibliothek *1206*, formerly *Helmstedt 1099* (13th century)
Pages 127', 128

IV. PRE-FRANCONIAN NOTATION

THE NOTATION of the thirteenth century, if compared with that of other periods of equal duration, exhibits a unique picture of great changes and rapid development. Every two or three decades new ideas of form and style appeared which necessitated the introduction of corresponding notational innovations. Thus the system of square notation was soon followed by another which we shall call pre-Franconian notation. It may be considered as falling approximately between the years 1225 and 1260.

The transition from square notation to pre-Franconian notation may be briefly summarized in the statement that the number of notational signs is increased and, consequently, the ambiguity of the interpretation of the signs is lessened. The rhythmic modes remain the basis of music and of notation, but they are more freely used, more clearly expressed, and better distinguished from one another. In fact, it is not until this period that all the modes are used equally, whereas in the sources of square notation two modes prevail: the first mode in the upper parts and the fifth mode in the tenors.

The following are the chief characteristics of the new system:

1. Notational distinction between *longa* and *brevis*.
2. Introduction of the *semibrevis*.
3. Introduction of ligatures *sine proprietate*, *sine perfectione* and *cum opposita proprietate*.
4. Change from the *divisio modi* to rests of different lengths.
5. Establishment of the *brevis* as the musical beat.

The first four points will be dealt with in the subsequent study of the sources of pre-Franconian notation. As regards the final point, the reader is referred to the general explanations given in the chapter on French Notation (p. 341 ff). Here it will suffice to say that, henceforth, a reduction in the ratio of one to eight will be used instead of the former reduction one to sixteen, so that the B becomes the quarter-note of the transcription. Properly speaking, this scale of reduction should be applied only to those motets which are written in the 'tempus medium legitimum' of Anon. IV, that is the motets in which groups of two to three smaller notes (*semibreves*) are used in the place of a B, while motets lacking these groups are in the older 'tempus minimum' and therefore should be transcribed in the scale of reduction that has been used for the pieces of the previous period. However, such a procedure would bring about a rather undesirable discrepancy which it has been deemed better to avoid. The thirteenth century term for the duration of the *B* is *tempus*,[1] a term which has remained associated with the *B* throughout the ensuing development of mensural notation, although changing its connotation from the temporal to the mensural (*tempus perfectum, tempus imperfectum*).

The pre-Franconian notation—and, as a consequence, all the later systems—developed from the motet notation of the preceding period, a circumstance easily explained by the fact that of all the forms of this period only the motet survived. Whereas, apart from the special type of the primitive conductus-motet (see p. 274), the motets of the School of Notre Dame had been mostly in two voice-parts, now the three-voice motet becomes the normal type. Its parts show rhythmical as well as textual independence, a feature clearly distinguishing this motet from the three-voice conductus-motet in which the two upper parts have identical rhythm and text.

The increased number of independent parts as well as the increase in length of all the parts lead to new methods of allotting them on the page. The following sketches show the typical arrangements either on two opposite pages, or else on one page:

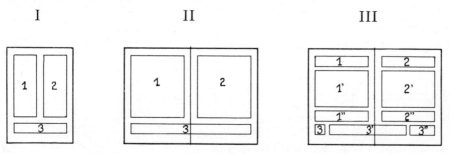

I   II   III

1: triplum; 2: duplum (motetus); 3: tenor

The advantage of these arrangements is that they make it possible for three singers to read their parts simultaneously from the same page. If a motet covers several pages the parts are always so written that the singers arrive simultaneously at the end of their parts, immediately before the page is turned. The third of the above drawings illustrates the arrangement used with shorter pieces. Such a page may contain the end

---

[1] For instance, Joh. de Garlandia (*CS* I, 97): 'Recta brevis est que unum tempus continet.'

of a motet A (1, 2, 3), a complete motet B (1', 2', 3'), and the beginning of another one, C (1", 2", 3").

Before turning to a study of the two main sources of pre-Franconian notation, the Codex Montpellier and the Codex Bamberg—both compiled towards the end of the thirteenth century, an example from the MS Brit. Mus. *Add. 30091* may be considered, a source which, although less well-known, is important because the date of the MS (*ca.* 1275?) is much closer to that of the compositions contained therein than is the case with the MSS Bamberg and Montpellier. In this source, the above-described arrangement of the parts, which makes it possible to use the manuscript for practical performance, is not yet observed. For instance, p. 1 of the MS contains, after a complete motet *O Maria—Nostrum*, the beginning of the duplum of a motet *Candida—Flos filius*, while the rest of the duplum and the entire tenor follow on the reverse side of p. 1.

Facsimile 57 shows these two pages (1 and 1'). The most striking feature of the notation, if compared with that of the motets considered previously, is the clear indication of the rhythm of the upper part, by means of *L* and *B*. The advance thus achieved becomes particularly apparent by a comparison of the motet *Candida—Flos filius* with the motet *Quant revient—L'autre jor—Flos filius* from the Chansonnier *Roy*, (Facsimile 54; p. 273), the duplum and tenor of which are identical with the two parts of the piece reproduced on Facsimile 57. It will be recalled that the motet from *Roy*, in turn, comes from the three-part clausula *Flos filius*, reproduced on Facsimile 46 (p. 229). Thus, these examples show one and the same composition in three different stages of elaboration and of notation.

A. THE CODEX MONTPELLIER, FASC. II-VI.

The Codex Montpellier (Montpellier, Faculté des Médecins *H 196*; abbreviated *Mo*) is the most extensive and most important source for the thirteenth century motet. It has been the object of repeated investigation. E. Coussemaker, in his *L'Art harmonique aux xiie et xiiie siècles* (Paris, 1865) was the first to call attention to its importance, including in that book reproductions and transcriptions of fifty pieces. This publication was the basis of further studies by O. Koller ('Der Liederkodex von Montpellier,' *VfMW*, iv) and by F. Ludwig ('Studien über die Geschichte der mehrstimmigen Musik im Mittelalter,' *SIMG*, v), who offered criticism of Coussemaker's explanations and transcriptions, as well as of Koller's theory regarding the dates of the various fascicles. Recently the entire codex has been published in facsimile and transcrip-

FACSIMILE 57

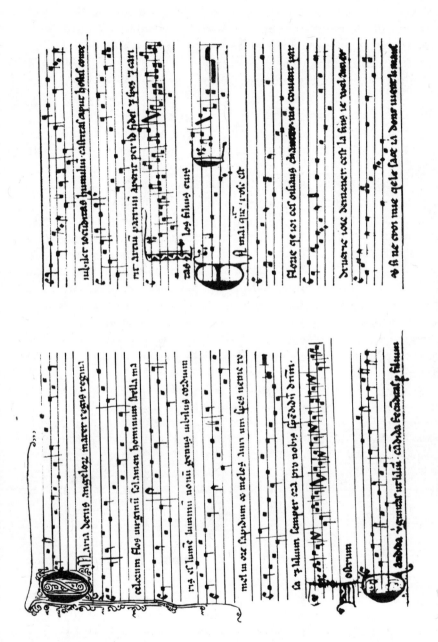

London, British Museum *Add. 30091* (13th century)
Pages 1, 1'

tion, with a commentary, by Y. Rokseth under the title: *Polyphonies du xiiie siècle*, 4 vols. (Paris, 1936-39).

The codex contains 345 compositions which are arranged in eight fascicles, according to types. Fascicle I contains organa and conductus from the Notre Dame period; II contains 17 four-voices motets; III contains 11 three-voice motets with Latin *motetus* and French *triplum*, as well as 4 two-voice Latin motets; IV contains 22 three-voice Latin motets; V contains 9 hockets and 104 three-voice motets which have, with few exceptions, French texts in both upper parts; VI contains 75 two-voice French motets; VII contains 39 three-voice motets of various kinds; and VIII contains a conductus and 42 three-voice motets of various kinds.

The first fascicle may be excluded from the following study since it contains organa written in modal notation (arrangement in score, ligatures in the upper voices). The fascicles II to VI, which represent a unified whole, comprise the most extensive collection of motets of the middle of the thirteenth century; they are written in pre-Franconian notation throughout. The last two fascicles are evidently a later addition, as may be seen from the following considerations: (1) the handwriting is of a different, more decorative character; (2) the systematic arrangement to be found in the fascicles I to VI is not carried out; (3) Franconian notation is used exclusively, along with certain even later elements of notation, which are associated with Petrus de Cruce (see p. 318 ff).

Our immediate concern is with the fascicles II to VI; first we shall treat the notation of the tenors, then that of the texted parts.

Notation of the Tenors. The notation of the tenors (*notatio sine litera*) in *Mo II-VI* shows no fundamental advance over that in the earlier sources. The same combinations of ligatures and single notes occur, the groupings I and II of our previous survey (p. 248) still being by far the most frequent. The only difference to be noted lies in the clearer distinction in the writing of the single signs, for which three shapes are now available: ■ *brevis* (B), ¶ *longa* (L), and ¶ *duplex longa* (D). The most frequent form is, of course, that which signifies the L.

The following tabulation gives a survey of the most common types of tenor-writing.[1] The figures in the column to the right indicate the number of times each combination occurs in the fascicles II-VI. The tabulation takes note only of those instances in which the type in ques-

---

[1] A complete tabulation of the tenors of *Mo* is given in Rokseth's publication, vl. iv.

tion is continued strictly, or with minor deviations only, throughout
the course of the piece.

	Symbol	Example	Number
I.	$\lvert 3 \rvert$	[♫]	69
II.	$\lvert 1\,1 \mid 3 \rvert$	[♫] [♫]	59
III.	$\lvert 3\,2 \ldots 2 \rvert$	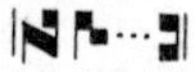 [♫]	21
IV.	$\lvert 2\,2 \ldots 3 \rvert$	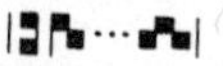 [♫]	16
V.	$\lvert 1\,3 \ldots 3 \rvert$	 [♫]	2
VI.	$\lvert 1\,1\,1 \rvert$	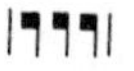 [♫]	10
VII.	$\lvert 1\,1 \ldots 1 \rvert$	 [♫]	11

What rhythms are represented by these types? In the case of the
types III to VII the situation is clear and unequivocal. Type III represents the first mode, type IV the second, type V the third and type
VI the fifth mode in the first ordo. Type VII belongs also to the fifth
mode, yet includes ordines of various length. Types I and II offer more
difficulty since they are used to represent various modes, as we already
know from our study of square notation (p. 248). Of the 69 examples of
type I we find:

Type I:

	Mode		Number	
(Ia)	First:	 [♩ ♩♩ ♩ 𝄽]	15	(e.g., nos. 58, 101, 221, 226)
(Ib)	Second:	 [♩♩♩ ♩𝄽𝄽]	17	(e.g., nos. 37, 59, 102, 220)
(Ic)	Fifth:	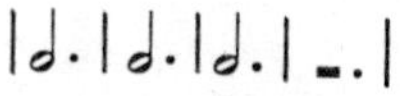 [♩.♩.♩. _.]	37	(e.g., nos. 41, 57, 107, 227)

Type II represents a similar situation as appears from the following
survey:

Type II:

	Mode		Number	
(IIa)	First:	 [♩.♩𝄽♩ ♩♩♩𝄽]	22	(e.g., nos. 24, 43, 141, 240)
(IIb)	Second:	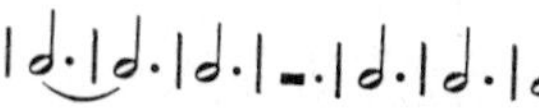 [♩.♩𝄽𝄽♩♩♩𝄽𝄽]	20	(e.g., nos. 64, 94, 142, 239)
(IIc)	Fifth:	[♩.♩.♩._.♩.♩.♩._.]	17	(e.g., nos. 23, 42, 135, 241)

The ambiguity of these two types raises the question of how one may arrive at a correct interpretation in a given case. Here a consideration of various other notational features will prove decisive. Frequently a clue is provided by that deviation of writing which arises from repeated tones (unison) and which, as in modal notation, necessitates the splitting of the ligatures. If, in such a case, a *ternaria* is replaced by a *B* followed by a *binaria*, the second mode is intended; if it is written as a *L* followed by a *binaria*, the first or fifth mode is clearly indicated:

$$\textbf{♩♪} = |\,♩♩\,♩|\,♩ \quad |; \textbf{♩♪} = |\,♩\ ♩|\,♩ \quad | \text{ or } |\,♩.\,|\,♩.\,|\,♩.\,|$$

Other useful clues are derived from a consideration of the upper voices, regarding both length and rhythm. As a matter of fact, since the fifth mode produces exactly twice the number of measures as the first or the second mode, one can sometimes find out, by simply estimating the number of measures of an upper voice, whether the fifth mode or one of the two others comes into question. Frequently the rhythm of the upper voices provides the clue to that of the tenor. In fact, a rhythmic relationship often exists, particularly between the tenor and duplum. This relationship is explained and described by Anon. VII as 'convenientia modorum,' i.e., rhythmic conformity of the modes (*CS* I, 379). For instance, the first and fifth mode combine well together, as do the second and third, or third and fifth:

  Mode 1 and 5   Mode 2 and 3   Mode 3 and 5

| $\,♩♩\,♩♩\,♩♩\,♩♩\,♩\,|$ | $\,♩♩♩\,♩♩♩\,♩♩♩\,♩\,|$ | $\,♩.\,♩♩♩\,♩.\,♩♩\,♩\,|$ |
| $\,♩.\,\,♩.\,\,♩.\,\,♩.\,|$ | $\,♩.\,\,♩♩♩\,♩.\,\,♩♩♩\,|$ | $\,♩.\,♩.\,\,♩.\,♩.\,\,|$ |

The first and second, however, will never be found simultaneously in the same motet, nor will the first and the third. Therefore, if the second (or third) mode is indicated in one of the upper parts, the first mode is not likely to occur in the tenor. Another point which must be mentioned here is the use of the *duplex longa* (*D*) which appears in the example II of our table. One would naturally expect the shape of this note to be a reliable means of distinction between the fifth mode on the one hand and the first and second mode on the other, since only in the former case does the initial note actually have the value of a *D*. Unfortunately, this is not the case. The slightly lengthened form of the initial note is found in all three modes. This statement is true particularly for the first two fascicles; in the later fascicles one can more clearly detect the attempt of the scribe to differentiate between the first (or second) and the fifth mode by distinguishing between the *L* and the *D*.

Examples. The above explanations may be illustrated by a few examples. Facsimile 58[1] contains a three-voice motet *Ave beatissima—Ave Maria—Johanne*, and the beginning of a three-voice motet *Salve virgo—Ave lux—Neuma*. The tenor *Neuma* (as much of it as is written on this page) consists of six *ternariae* and one *binaria*. In the first or second mode this would lead to $6 \times 2 + 1 = 13$ measures ($\frac{3}{4}$ each). In the fifth mode, however, there would be $6 \times 4 + 2 = 26$ measures of the same length. A superficial examination of the upper voices tells us at once that they are much longer than thirteen measures, since fifteen *L* alone appear in the triplum, to say nothing of the many *B*. Therefore the tenor must be in the fifth mode.

To follow out a similar process in the case of the first motet of our facsimile, *Johanne*, may present more difficulty to the novice. However, he may base his estimate on the fact that as a rule a single line of a triplum or duplum contains an average of eight perfections. Thus, we arrive at a total of approximately forty measures ($\frac{3}{4}$) for the entire piece. Since the tenor contains 22 groups of *ternaria*, only the first or the second mode are possible.

In the present instance this method of reckoning is not really necessary, since the use of the *B* as an initial note of a split ligature plainly points to the second mode (see the first ordo, above the initial letter, as well as the ordines 9 and 15).

A comparison of the two tenors shows that the division strokes of *Neuma* are somewhat longer than those of *Johanne*, probably corresponding to the longer rests of the fifth mode as compared to those of the second mode. Unfortunately, unlike the Bamberg Codex (see p. 302), this distinction, which would provide a simple clue to the determination of the mode, is not carried out consistently in the codex under consideration.

Finally, the tenor of the motet *Diex je—Amors qui ma—Et super* (Facsimile 59) may be studied. The first three *L* of the lowest line of the page belong to the preceding motet, together with the top lines on the left- and right-hand pages. The tenor of our motet begins with ten *ternaria*-ordines; at the end the notation shows a greater variety of combinations. The appearance of two ordines each containing three *L* (beginning of the right-hand page) might suggest that the whole tenor is in the fifth mode. In such a case, however, it would be hard to explain why these two ordines are not written in ligature, as are the others. Moreover, a quick calculation shows that the assumption in favor of the fifth mode for the whole tenor would produce more than 70 measures,

[1] The original pagination means: $4 \times 20 + 14 = 94$.

a greater number than that of the upper parts (40-50 measures). One
must assume therefore that the tenor is in the first mode (the second
mode is excluded, cf. the unison writing in the ordines 3, 5, 8), with the
rhythm changing twice to what seems to be the fifth mode, but what
more correctly should be considered an *extensio* variety of the first mode.
Following is a transcription of the second half of the tenor, beginning
on p. 142 of the original:

Besides the more or less regular tenors given in the above table, there
exist, naturally, a great number which show a free rhythm in triple
meter.   Below is an example:

In seculum (f. 231):

This tenor is in the second mode, as appears from the unison-writing.
As with the tenor *Et super*, groups of three *L* are interspersed, causing
extensio modi.   It should be noted that, according to strict theory, the
last of these single notes should be a *B*, as the *divisio modi* takes two
tempora in the second mode.   Rather than to reduce the *L* to a *B*, we
prefer to consider this tenor as an argument against too strict an interpretation of the *divisio modi* (see p. 299).   Besides the short strokes the
tenor contains several dashes which extend through the entire staff.
This is the so-called *finis punctorum* which indicates a rest in the value
of a perfect *L* (three *tempora*).   Below is the transcription of the beginning and the end of the tenor:

Duple Meter.   A unique specimen is the tenor of the motet no. 164,

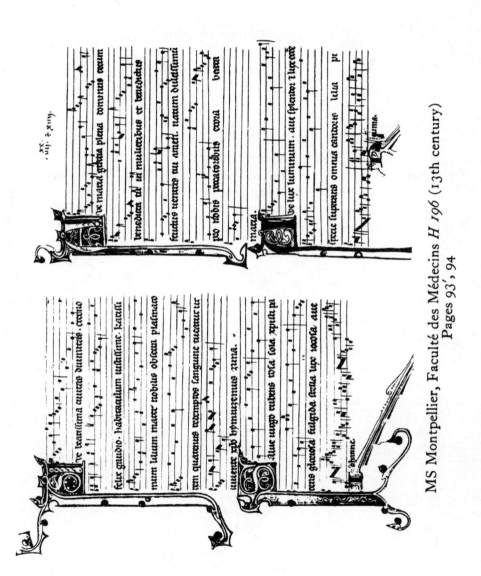

MS Montpellier, Faculté des Médecins *H 196* (13th century)
Pages 93', 94

Je ne puis—Flor de lis—Douce dame, which is notated entirely in *B:*

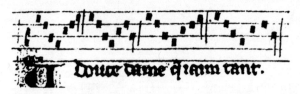

This tenor not only represents the sole example in the tenors under consideration of what seems to be the sixth mode, but—still more re-markable—it is the first example of binary rhythm or duple meter.   In fact, the *B* are not to be arranged, as they should be in the sixth mode, in groups of three: |♩♪♪|♪♪♪|♪♩| but in groups of two:|♩♪♪|♪♪♪♪|♩'| , as the context of the upper voices clearly indicates.   This piece is there-fore our first example of what was called later *modus imperfectus.*

Compositions like this (we shall encounter several more in the Bamberg Codex) are indicative of an innovation in the musical thought of the thirteenth century, indeed of a real revolution, the magnitude of which we today can scarcely appreciate.   There is an interesting remark in Magister Lambert's (Pseudo-Aristotle) treatise which not only refers to this innovation but also indicates the strength of the opposition it met (*CS* I, 271 a):

> Unde considerandum est, quando [longa] imperfecta fieri nequit nisi medi-ante brevi sequente, seu precedente, quoniam longa et brevis, et e converso, semper unam perfectionem faciunt.   Unde si querat aliquis utrum possit fieri modus sive cantus naturalis de omnibus imperfectis sicut fit de omni-bus perfectis; responsio cum probatione, quod non, cum puras imperfectas nemo pronunciare possit.

From this it appears that an imperfect *longa* can be executed only in con-nection with a following or preceding *brevis*, since a *longa* and a *brevis* (or a *brevis* and a *longa*) together always complete a perfection.   Therefore, if someone were to ask whether a mode or a natural song can be formed by imperfect *longae* exclusively just in the same way as it can be formed by perfect *longae*, the approved answer is: no; since nobody can sing a succession of pure imperfect *longae.*

Indeed, to the mind brought up in the tradition of the early thirteenth century, music in duple meter must have appeared to be something quite obviously impossible, being based upon a rhythm which had 'beginning and middle,' but no 'ending,' an 'imperfect' rhythm in the true meaning of the word.   However, evolution did not stop because of such scholastic thought.   Here was the first impulse of the movement

FACSIMILE 59

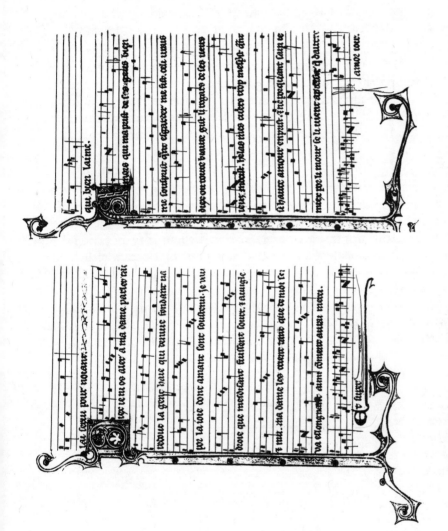

MS Montpellier, Faculté des Médecins *H 196* (13th century)
Pages 141, 142

which shattered the 'classical' system of the six modes and led to the teaching of the fourteenth and fifteenth centuries, which recognized only two modes—the *modus perfectus* and the *modus imperfectus* (see p. 99). As a matter of fact, by the year 1300 the characteristic distinctions between the six modes had become so irrelevant that they all appeared essentially the same—that is, as subtypes of one single mode, in which the *L* was equal to three *B*, the *modus perfectus*. In addition to this the *modus imperfectus* appeared, first as the equal, but soon as the predominant.[1] It is not without interest to notice the striking similarity of this development to the change from the system of the church modes to the later major and minor. Again in this case we find, although several centuries later, the same transition from many modes to two, from varied to limited tonal resources.

Notation of the Upper Voices. The pre-Franconian notation of the upper voices (*notatio cum litera,* syllabic notation) shows a considerably greater advance over the previous system than does the notation of the tenors. Whereas in the syllabic notation of the conductus and of the early motets, the upper parts are written without any notational distinction between longs and breves, we now find the rhythm clearly indicated by means of two different signs, the *L* with a tail, and the *B* without a tail. The evaluation of these signs is governed by the principles of *modus perfectus*, practically the same principles which are known to us from the consideration of *tempus perfectum* and *prolatio perfecta* in white notation. As a curiosity, we quote here the rhymed hexameters of Magister Lambert (*CS* 1, 270, 271):

> Ante vero longam, tria tempora longa fatetur
> Si brevis addatur, duo tempora longa meretur.
>
> Inter perfectas si bis brevis una locetur
> Temporis unius fit prima, secunda dupletur.

Therefore:

1. *L* before *L* is perfect
2. *L* is imperfected by a following (or preceding) *B*
3. If two *B* are found between two *L*, the second *B* is doubled.

---

[1] This change has been studied by A. Michalitschke in his *Theorie des Modus*, Regensburg, 1923, p. 80 ff. Unfortunately, this little book is written in an almost unintelligible, over-ripe and artificial type of prose, and is overloaded with that 'weltanschauliche Vertiefung' and 'schicksalhafte Verknüpfung' typical of the German post-war literature.

Magister Lambert gives further rules for three, four, and five *B* between two *L*. These may be illustrated by the following examples:

The little stroke which appears in the last two examples no longer indicates a rest (*divisio modi*), but serves to mark off perfections. It is supplanted later by the *punctus divisionis*.

As regards the application of these rules to the sources under consideration, there are rather frequent violations of the first rule. One finds numerous cases in which the third mode is written as follows: . However, the correct manner of writing occurs too: .

Besides the *L* and *B*, the *S* appears as a new type of note in the manuscript under consideration. It never occurs, however, as an isolated note but always in groups of two or three which are equal in value to a *B*. The principle of replacing a *B* by a group of smaller values was called 'equipollentia' (equivalence). The appearance of the *S* in groups of two and of three raises the question as to the values to be assigned to them in modern transcription. From the modern standpoint the simplest solution would be to transcribe a group of two *S* as two eighth-notes ( ), and a group of three *S* as triplets ( ). As a matter of fact, this method has been adopted in some recent publications, e.g., in the transcriptions given by Rokseth. However, it seems very doubtful whether conflicting rhythms such as would result from this interpretation, are in conformity with the rather rigid concepts of mensuration in this period.[1] Barring this possibility there remains a choice of two interpretations, one of which is based on a ternary division of the *B*, the other on a binary:

	2 *S*	3 *S*
B as ternary:		
B as binary:		

The fact that groups of two *S* are by far the more frequent (especially when one includes the instances in which they are indicated by *ligatura*

---

[1] Examples are not infrequent in which a group of two *S* and one of three *S* appear simultaneously in different voices, as, e.g., at the beginning of the motet *Portare* from *Ba*, Facsimile 60.

cum opposita proprietate) points to the binary interpretation as the most likely one. Moreover, the name *semi* (*-brevis*) indicates in itself that the B was originally divided into two equal halves.[1] If this view is accepted, Franco of Cologne's reiterated statement demanding the ternary division of the B (see p. 311) would represent, not a confirmation of a traditional practice, but a deliberate deviation from it. This interpretation would certainly be in keeping with the fact that most of his rules are of a decidedly novel character, intended to establish a new practice. A final argument in favor of the binary division can be derived from the fact that, in the pre-Franconian sources, groups of three *S* are practically always written in a *conjunctura*-like formation: ◆◆ . Hence, our binary interpretation of such a group would be in accordance with the principle that in a *conjunctura* the last note is the longest of all. Naturally, all these arguments do not constitute a clear proof. Throughout the thirteenth century, the evaluation of the *S* was a flexible and controversial matter, as may well be expected to be the case, considering their shortness of duration.[2]

Ligatures. The ligatures which appear in the texted parts have the same function as in the conductus and early motets, that is, to introduce two or three notes in the place of one. However, their rhythmic meaning is more clearly indicated by the introduction of those varieties which are known as *sine proprietate*, *sine perfectione*, and *cum opposita proprietate* (*c.o.p.*). As for the metrical value of these new types, it appears that we are in a transitional stage between the great ambiguity of square notation and the unequivocal exactitude of the Franconian system. It would be a futile task, we believe, to work out a set of rules for the various types of ligatures and *conjuncturae* used in the period. Instead, the following table may be given which will provide the clearest insight into the prevailing relations. It will be noticed that the value of most of these signs depends upon the value of the neighboring notes, i.e., whether the ligature in question stands in place of a perfect *L* (3 *tempora*), an imperfect *L* (2 *tempora*) or a *B* (1 *tempus*):

---

[1] Both Franco (*CS* I, 136) and Anon. VII (*CS* I, 381) explain *semis* as 'quod est dimidium' (that which is the half), and Dietricus writes: 'semibreve, quia duo talia cum tanta celeritate proferuntur sicut unum breve recte scriptum' (semibreve, because two of them are sung in the same speed as one ordinary breve). On the other hand, Magister Lambert (*CS* I, 270) explains *semis* as meaning the same as imperfect: 'semis, sema, semum, quod est imperfectum.' This etymology, however, aside from being doubtful on philological grounds, certainly cannot be considered a satisfactory explanation of the word *semibrevis* since the idea of an imperfect *brevis* did not arise until half a century later, at the earliest.

[2] See p. 320 ff.

Type	Forms	Value		
		1 tp.	2 tp.	3 tp.
2	♩ ♩	–	♩ ♩	♩♩ (♩♩)
2ˢ	♩ ♩	–	♩ ♩	–
ˢ2	♩ ♩	–	–	♩ ♩
°2	♩ ♩	♫	–	–
3	(♩♩) ♩ ♩ ♩	–	♫♩	♩♩♩ (♫ ♩)
3ˢ	♩ ♩ ♩ ♩	–	♫♩	♩♩♩
°3	♩ ♩ ♩♩	–	♫ ♩	–
4	♩♩ ♩♩ ♩♩ ♩♩ ♩♩ ♩♩	–	(♫ ♫)	♫♩♩ ♩♫♩

In this table the following abbreviations are used for a short and simple designation of the ligatures:

2, 3: lig. *cum proprietate* and *cum perfectione*

2ˢ, 3ˢ: lig. *cum proprietate* and *sine perfectione*

ˢ2, ˢ3: lig. *sine proprietate* and *cum perfectione*

°2, °3: lig. *cum opposita proprietate*

From this survey it will be seen that the various forms of *binaria* ligatures are already quite clearly differentiated from one another, while no such distinction is to be found with the *ternaria* or *quaternaria* forms. The peculiar form of the *ˢ2* is worthy of note. It appears only in the Montpellier Codex and was later discarded (see the Franconian form on p. 313; for a similar form in white notation, see p. 93). The forms ♦♦♦ and ♦♦♦ are easily confused, since often the square notes are not clearly written. Furthermore the following frequent form, ▰♦♦ , must be distinguished from that of a descending *quaternaria;* it represents the con-

nection of a *L* with a descending *ternaria* and has the following value:
|♩.|♫ ♩| (cf. *Mo*, no. 119, p. 163/4).

Plica. The *plica* also undergoes a remarkable change of form and
meaning. *Plica*-ligatures, so common in square notation, now occur in-
frequently. Instead, single *plica* notes appear in great number and constitute an important element in notation up to the time of the *Ars Nova*.
By the theorists they were considered an integral part of the system and
were grouped at the very beginning of the explanations together with the
simple forms. Thus Joh. de Garlandia says (*CS* 1, 177b):

> Longarum triplex est modus: quia quedam est longa recta, quedam duplex longa, que-
> dam plica longa. . . Similiter brevium triplex est modus. Quedam dicitur recta brevis,
> quedam semibrevis, quedam plica brevis.

> There are three kinds of *longa:* the normal *longa,* the *duplex longa,* and the *plica longa.*
> In the same way, there are three kinds of *brevis:* the normal *brevis,* the *semibrevis,* and the
> *plica brevis.*

As may be seen from these remarks, one must distinguish between two
kinds of *plica* notes, the *plica longa* and the *plica brevis*. The forms of
the *plica longa* have a short stroke on the left and a long stroke on the
right side; in the ascending form the stroke on the left side is sometimes
missing. The forms of the *plica brevis* have the longer stroke on the left,
or else the strokes are practically of equal length:

	Descending	Ascending
Plica longa	╕	╘ ╛
Plica brevis	╒ ╕	╘ ╛

The rules of Magister Lambert previously mentioned (p. 227) are valid
for the measuring of the *plica longa*. This is therefore to be transcribed
either as ♩♩ or as ♩♩ , according to whether it stands for a *longa perfecta* or a *longa imperfecta*. Nothing is said by that theorist regarding
the value of the *plica brevis*, i.e., about the measuring of its principal and
auxiliary note. According to our above explanations of the *semibreves*,
the most natural interpretation would be as two equal (eighth) notes.
The *plica brevis*, then, differs from two *S* written out or from an *²2* only
in its peculiar mode of performance, which Magister Lambert describes
as 'compositio epiglottis cum repercussione gutturis.'

Examples. We shall now consider a few examples in the study of which
further details will come to light. The first example is the motet *Salve
virgo—Ave lux—Neuma,* the tenor of which we have already considered

(Facsimile 58). The third mode is easily recognizable in the two upper voices. Occasionally the related second mode enters (e.g., triplum, first line, 'sola christi'). Whether one should interpret the various *ternariae* as three equal quarter-notes or as two eighths followed by a half-note is difficult to decide. Since the latter version would fit the iambic rhythm of the third and the second mode somewhat better we shall choose it in this instance. The long strokes indicate rests of the value of a perfect *L.* At the beginning of the second line of the duplum a short stroke appears which represents a *B*-rest. Immediately following that there is an even smaller stroke which is not a rest but the *punctus divisionis* in its older form. It prevents the preceding *L* from becoming imperfect. The beginning of the motet is transcribed in the appendix, No. 41.

The other piece of the same facsimile may serve as the second example. We have already seen that the second mode prevails in the tenor (p. 289). Therefore, one may assume that iambic rhythm appears also in the upper voices. This is especially clear in the triplum:

The short stroke after the *quaternaria* will have to be interpreted as an eighth rest, as indicated above. In the remainder of the triplum the following details may be noticed: the two *binariae* at the beginning of the second line are each *B B*, since they and another *B* complete a perfection; the note above 'gau-' is a *plica brevis*, as is also that above 'ha(bitaculum)'; two syllables later appears the short *conjunctura* , which is not to be confused with the form   at the end of this ordo; in the last line one finds again the $2^s = B B$, as well as various forms of *ternaria*, all signifying *B B B.* It is noteworthy that the final note of the ordines is nearly always written as a *L* (with a slightly shorter stroke than a *L* appearing within an ordo), although the second mode should properly end with a *B.* Apparently this final tone is meant to be held somewhat longer than a strict correspondence to the modal rhythm would demand. The same type of a *L* appears also in the fifth ordo of the tenor. Whether one should transcribe this note as |♩♪| or as |♩♪♪| is difficult to say. A compromise would be |♩.♪|; this, however, is perhaps too fastidious. We shall choose the version with the half-note in order to follow the original as closely as possible.[1]

---

[1] Rokseth's publication holds to the strict modal interpretation, which also has its justification. In any case, the performance of motets in the second mode should avoid that cut-up rendition which is suggested by the use of two quarter-note rests in modern transcription.

The duplum of this motet begins with a *plica longa perfecta* 'cum repercussione' (see p. 238). As regards the *B* above 'ma(ria),' there may at first be some doubt as to whether it makes a perfection with the preceding or the following *conjunctura ternaria*. The context of the voices leads one to a decision in favor of the latter.

In the fourth line the relationship of the voices shows that the *binaria* on 'ex(ora)' is perfect (*B − L*). As a result the *ternaria* on '(exor)a' which follows immediately is rendered imperfect by the preceding *B*.

The close of the motet displays a peculiarity which may be seen in numerous compositions of the codex—namely, a sort of ritardando which is fully written out in notes. Following is a transcription of the last ordo (the tenor begins with the last note of the third from last *ternaria*):

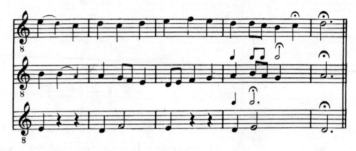

(Note: We have interpreted the last *ternaria* of the fourth line as °3.)

It appears that the triplum is one note too long as compared with the other voices. Apparently the motetus and tenor are supposed to follow the triplum freely. In the tenor this is indicated by the use of a somewhat lengthened note in the middle of the last ligature. Naturally, a certain liberty must be admitted in the interpretation and transcription of such irregularities. We suggest using a $\frac{4}{4}$-measure for all the parts.[1] The transcription of the beginning is given in the appendix, No. 42.

The motet of Facsimile 59 is a more difficult example. We have already considered the tenor which is in the first mode, with groups of perfect *L* interspersed at the end (p. 289 f). In transcribing the upper voices one will do well to begin with the duplum (right-hand page), the rhythm of which is clearer.

The *ternaria* at the very beginning, on 'qui,' is to be interpreted as °3, since otherwise its value would be too great to complete a perfection.

---

[1] In Rokseth's edition the transcription of these final cadenzas is always carried out strictly in $\frac{3}{4}$-time and is marked 'ritardando.' This seems to us to leave a great deal too much freedom to the players and singers of today. One can imagine what performers who do not know the original notation might do with such a ritardando.

The first note of the next ordo, on 'de,' is a *plica longa imperfecta*. Following is the beginning of the motetus in transcription:

In front of the last note of the first line there appears a flat (B-flat) which is repeated at the beginning of the next line. The fifth character of the third line is a *plica longa (imperfecta)*, the last character of the same line is a *plica brevis*. The ordo which begins in the middle of the fifth staff ends exceptionally with a *B* instead of a *L*. Toward the end of this staff is another *ternaria* meaning ⁰3. The close of the motetus is found at the end of the bottom line.

Let us turn now to the transcription of the triplum, the beginning of which is as follows:

The last note of the first line is an ascending *plica longa*, which is imperfected by the first *B* of the second staff. The *quaternaria* on 're(dout)'

must be reduced to two beats: ♩♪♩ ♩♩♩ ♩

The *quaternaria* in the third staff (on '-mant'), on the other hand, contains three beats; as an exception, however, it begins with an up-beat: ♫|♩♩. The last note of the fifth line is a poorly written *plica longa*—not a *plica brevis*. The *ternaria* at the beginning of the next staff, on 'es-(longuant),' is again ⁰3. At the close is another written-out ritardando which again is best transcribed in $\frac{4}{4}$ time:

In the appendix, No. 43, the transcription of the middle section is given (beginning with the third staff of the triplum; with 'li regars' in the duplum; and with the eighth *ternaria* in the tenor). It contains some bold appoggiaturas.

B. The Codex Bamberg

The Codex Bamberg (Bamberg, *Ed. iv. 6*, abbreviated *Ba*) contains 100 motets in its main section; with the exception of no. 92 (four voices with two tenors) all are for three voices. An appendix, written in the same hand, contains three additional motet-like pieces and a few compositions without text (*In seculum longum, In seculum viellatoris*, etc.) notated in score in the older manner.

The arrangement of the voices is that indicated by the first sketch on p. 283, i.e., with all the parts written on the same page. Three motets (nos. 52, 53, 54, pp. 31'-34) are arranged in a peculiar manner, namely, in three parallel columns of equal width on one page. This arrangement is explained by the fact that in these pieces the tenor also bears a text. Therefore all the voices require approximately the same space.

The notation of *Ba* is, in principle, the same as that of *Mo* ii-vi. However, considerable progress in the direction of clarity and exactness is evidenced in various particulars. Owing to this progress the pieces of *Ba* are far easier to understand and to transcribe than those treated in the previous chapters. Perhaps the most important innovation consists in the fixing of exact values for the *divisio modi* or, as it may hereafter be called, for the rest. Indeed, this sign is no longer a stroke of indefinite length, drawn carelessly through the staff, but is written very accurately and appears in four different lengths, namely:

$\frac{1}{2}$ *tempus* (*S*)   1 *tempus* (*B*)   2 *tempora* (*L* imp.)   3 *tempora* (*L* perf.)

Example (*In seculum breve*, *Ba*, p. 64):

This manner of writing the rests is in keeping with the teaching of Magister Lambert (*CS* i, 278), while Joh. de Garlandia, although probably somewhat earlier in point of time, already uses the Franconian system of rests in which the *B*-rest covers only one space, the imperfect *L*-rest two, and the perfect *L*-rest three (*CS* i, 104a). It may be noted that the notation of *Ba* corresponds in almost all details (especially in regard to ligatures) to the system described in the little-known but very important treatise by Dietricus.[1]

---

[1] Dietricus' presentation is distinguished by unusual clarity and conciseness. Cf. H. Mueller, *Eine Abhandlung über Mensuralmusik in der Karlsruher Handschrift St. Peter pergamen. 29a* (Leipzig, 1886).

Notation of the Tenors. Even though the tenors of *Ba* employ the same ligatures and combinations as *Mo* II-VI, the rhythmic relations are much easier to discover, since the rests make clear at once the prevailing mode. Indeed, the second of the above rests (1 *tempus*) indicates the first mode, the third type (2 *tempora*) the second mode, and the fourth type (3 *tempora*) the third or fifth. Three examples may serve to illustrate:

1. *Victime*, p. 46[1]

2. *Pro patribus*, p. 56

3. *Brumans est mors*, p. 20′

The first example is *L B L /* . . . , the second *B L B /* . . . , the third *L B B L /* . . . .

A confusion of the fifth mode with one of the others is all the less likely since the fifth mode is regularly written entirely in *L*, i.e., without ligatures. The second mode is distinguished from the others not only by the use of the 2-*tempora* rest, but also by the persistent use of ˢ*3*-ligatures, to denote *B L B* (see the tenor *Pro patribus*). The tenor *Optatur* (p. 57′) reproduced below shows the use of ˢ*2* in the meaning of *L B* (the reverse of *2*) as well as that of *3*ˢ in the meaning of *B B B*. It may be noticed that in *Ba* the shape of the ˢ*2* is that of the Franconian system (and of all the ensuing periods), whereas in *Mo* a peculiar form is used (p. 297). At the beginning of the third ordo of the example the form *2*ˢ is used in the meaning of *B B*.

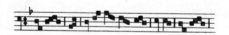

It does not seem necessary to treat the ligatures of *Ba* systematically, since on the one hand their meaning becomes easily clear from the context, and on the other the principles involved give way very shortly to the Franconian system.

As a curiosity we mention two tenors which are written in *modus imperfectus*, namely *Proh dolor* (p. 19 , no. 35) and *Aptatur* (p. 54′, no. 86).

---

[1] The page references are to the facsimile volume (vol. 1) of P. Aubry's *Cent motets du xiiie siècle*; see the survey of source material, p. 201 ff.

Proh dolor

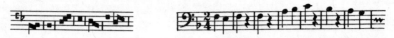

Notation of the Upper Voices. The *notatio cum litera* of *Ba* scarcely differs from that of *Mo* II-VI. However, the clearer writing does much to make the transcription easier; and even more does the fact that in *Ba* any given staff of the triplum is always composed of the same number of bars and beats as the adjoining, i.e., corresponding staff of the motetus. This means that the initial as well as the final notes of two such staves sound simultaneously. Since these staves are rather short, a great number of points of coincidence are provided by the observation of this fact.

Single *semibreves*, that is, those which are sung to separate syllables, occur, as in *Mo*, only in groups of two. Groups of three *S* occur also, but these are always sung to one syllable and therefore are written in the form of a *conjunctura*. As has been explained previously (p. 296), this usage supports our theory that in pre-Franconian notation the *B* is binary, not ternary. Therefore: ♦♦ = ♩♩ ; ♦♦♦ = ♩♩♩ .

The writing of the descending *ternaria* as a *conjunctura*, ♦♦♦ , which occurs so frequently in *Mo* II-VI, is not to be found in *Ba*. In its place one finds frequently the form ♦♦ (Facs. 60, right column, beginning of line 5), which always means °*3*: ♫♩ . This notational variant is of interest since it evidences the tendency towards identifying the diamond shaped characters of the *conjuncturae* with the *S*, a significance which, as we know, they did not have originally. It should be noted that the symbol in question represents exactly twice the value of ♦♦♦ = ♫♩ .

Facsimile 60 shows a motet *Mou[l]t me fu grief—Robins m'aimme—Portare*. In spite of its apparent plainsong derivation, the tenor has the structure of a secular song. It consists of two short melodies, A (from c′ to f) and B (from a to c′) which are repeated according to the scheme: A B A′ A B A B (A′ denotes the first half of A). This scheme is an incomplete variant of the form of the thirteenth-century rondeau: A B a A a b A B. Tenors 'ad modum rondelli' are not infrequent in the sources of the late thirteenth century.[1] A fourteenth century example is G. de Machaut's motet *Trop plus—Biauté parée—Je ne suis*, which is reproduced in *SchT*, p. 23. Here, the tenor consists of two short melodies A, ('Je—amie'), and B, ('mais—amis'), which are to be repeated according to the full scheme of the rondeau.

[1] See the reference to such a motet from *Mo*, p. 276.

MS Bamberg, Bibliothek, *Ed IV 6* (13th century)
Page 52'

C. THE CODICES TORINO AND HUELGAS

The Torino Codex (Torino, Bibl. Reale *Var. N. 42*), which has been little investigated, shows a striking resemblance to *Ba* in its notational *details as well as in its graphological appearance. The most important difference exhibited by our Facsimile 61 is the Franconian writing of the rests. Evidently, the rests covering two spaces equal two *B*, as against one in the Bamberg Codex. The transcription presents no difficulties.

The Codex Huelgas, which has recently been published in full by H. Anglès (*El Codex musical de las Huelgas*) contains a very motley repertoire, including monophonic chants as well as various types of polyphonic music among which are the earliest known settings of the ordinary of the mass (two-voiced *Kyries*, etc. in conductus style). The notation, too, is anything but uniform and suggests a scribe who was not too well informed in this matter. It is scarcely worthwhile to point out the many peculiarities of notation to be found here. Perhaps the most interesting notational detail is the writing of the ligatures of the tenors. The forms used here show the attempt to clarify the meaning of the ligatures, and may be regarded as indicative of a transitional stage between the purely 'modal' forms of pre-Franconian notation and those introduced by Franco. The following reproduction, showing the beginning of one and the same tenor *Alleluia* from (a) Bamberg (p. 59') and (b) Huelgas (p. 106) illustrates this point:

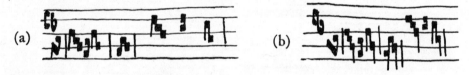

In Franco's system, the dashes at the end of the descending ligatures would have to be omitted.

A comparison between Huelgas and Bamberg (or Montpellier) also reveals interesting examples of 'transmutatio,' i.e., rewriting of motet in a different mode (see p. 246, footnote). For instance, the motet *In omni fratre tuo*—(tenor), which is notated in Huelgas (p. 96/96') in the third mode, occurs in Bamberg (p. 27 ff, *Mout me grief—In omni fratre—In seculum*) in the shortened rhythm of the sixth mode, i.e., with /L B B L/ replaced by /B B B B/.

Finally, brief mention may be made of the *semibreves caudatae* which occur on several pages of the MS. They are, without doubt, not a feature of the original writing but represent the attempt made by a later hand to remodel the thirteenth century notation according to the prin-

FACSIMILE 61

MS Torino, Biblioteca Reale *mss. varii 42* (13th century)
Page 40

ciples of the early fourteenth century. The following reproduction (from

p. 106′) serves as an illustration:[1]

For a more detailed study of the MS the reader is referred to the above-mentioned publication which also contains numerous transcriptions from W_1 and *Fl.* It must be mentioned, however, that Anglès' versions are not always convincing. Perhaps the most striking example is his rendering of an *Et in terra pax* (Facsimile 62), in which the clear rhythmic meaning of the notational characters is completely disregarded. Here follows the beginning of Anglès' version (a) together with what undoubt-.
* edly must be considered the correct transcription (b):

(a)

(b)

Another point is Anglès' inconsistency in transcribing pieces written in the third mode (/L B B L/). Whereas the motets, p. 113, 114, 114′, are transcribed in modal meter ($L = 3\ B$), duple meter (*modus imperfectus*, $L = 2\ B$) is used for the above-mentioned motet on p. 96/96′ as well as for another one on p. 87. Possibly, a reason for this procedure is given in the introductory volume (I) which, unfortunately, is written in the Catalan language.

[1] For a similar case of greater interest, see the explanations on the *Roman de Fauvel*, p. 325 ff.

Codex Huelgas
Monastery Las Huelgas, near Burgos (13th century)
Page 4'

V. FRANCONIAN NOTATION

A. The Franconian System

AROUND 1260 there occur those decisive changes in notation which by all subsequent writers are coupled with the name of Franco. Apparently two men, both bearing this name, lived at the same time and accomplished much the same thing—a Franco of Paris and a Franco of Cologne. They are mentioned in the important historical account of Anon. IV *(CS* 1, 342a) as 'Franco primus et alter Magister Franco de Colonia.' The title 'primus' as applied to the Parisian Franco may best be construed as meaning earlier, elder. It cannot be accepted as an estimate of value, since by far the most important of the various Franconian treatises—the *Ars cantus mensurabilis (CS* 1, 117) was written by Franco of Cologne.

Since the principles evolved during this period form the basis of notation until the sixteenth century, and in some respects up to our own time, they will be given here rather completely but in as concise a form as possible. In general it may be said that Franco introduced no new signs of notation. For that reason his achievement was all the greater: the building, out of the equivocal symbols inherited from a previous age, of a system which for the first time was free of ambiguity.

Single notes. Franco enumerates the following 'figurae simplices' (*tp* = *tempus*):

	Longa		Brevis		Semibrevis	
Duplex	perfecta	imperfecta	recta	altera	major	minor
¶	¶	¶	■	■	◆	◆
6 *tp*	3 *tp*	2 *tp*	1 *tp*	2 *tp*	$\frac{2}{3}$ *tp*	$\frac{1}{3}$ *tp*

The rules ('ordinatio figurarum'), which concern the various combinations of *L* and *B*, are virtually those which we already know from the treatise of Magister Lambert (p. 294). Briefly summarized they run as follows:

A *L* is perfect if followed by another *L*, or by two or three *B*. If it is followed by one or by more than three *B*, then the first *B* imperfects the *L* and the remainder are grouped together in groups of three (perfections). If in such a case two *B* are left over, alteration of the second occurs; if

310

only one remains, it imperfects the following *L*. If an exceptional grouping is desired, the 'signum perfectionis' in the form of a short stroke ('tractulus') is used.

Of the greatest importance is the principle, expressed several times, that the same rules govern the relation between the *B* and the *S*: 'et nota hoc idem esse judicium de brevibus et semibrevibus' (note that the same principles are valid for the *B* and the *S*); or 'de semibrevibus autem et brevibus idem est judicium in regulis prius dictis' (the rules just given apply equally to the *B* and the *S*; see *CS* 1, 119 and 122).

Here the *S* is recognized for the first time as an independent note value which theoretically may occur in any number and combination. Moreover, the relationship between the *B* and the *S* is governed by the same principle of ternary mensuration which forms the basis of the relationship between the *L* and the *B*. In fourteenth century terminology, in addition to *modus perfectus* there now exists *tempus perfectum*. It will be noticed that this principle differs from that prevailing in pre-Franconian notation where the mensuration of the *B* is binary.

The rests of Franco's system are those known to us from white notation: the *B*-rest covers one space, the *L*-rest two or three spaces, according to whether it is imperfect or perfect. His writing and evaluation of the *plicas* show no difference from the system that has been previously explained (p. 298).

It must be noted, however, that the practical sources of the late thirteenth century are much more conservative with regard to the use of *semibreves* than one might expect on the basis of Franco's statement; nor is it likely that Franco himself was aiming at a complete analogy between the use of *L* and *B* on the one hand, and between the *B* and *S* on the other, an achievement which did not take place until the *Ars Nova* (Philippe de Vitry). There are at least two important differences between the use of *B* and that of *S*. The first difference is the fact that a single *S* never occurs, in other words, the *B* is never imperfected by a preceding or following *S*. The second difference consists in the fact that groups of more than three *S*, which appear occasionally in the later motets of the period, call for a particular interpretation different from that to be applied to groups of *B*. According to Franco they are to be arranged in pairs with alteration or, if they are uneven in number, in pairs with a final group of three, for instance:[1]

---

[1] Pieces of the Franconian period are usually transcribed in $\frac{3}{4}$-meter with eighth-note triplets. Since, however, the ternary measurement of the *B* (quarter-note) is an integral feature of the Franconian notation, a rendering in $\frac{9}{8}$-meter ([III, 3]) is at least equally appropriate.

Examples of these Franconian 'chains of *S*' (as one might call them in contrast to the later 'groups of *S*' of Petrus de Cruce) are not very frequent in practical sources. We may well understand that they attained little practical importance since they offered no possibility for rhythmical variety within a series of *S*. Apparently another device had to be introduced in order to allow for combinations such as *B SSS SS B* or *B SS SSS SS B*. This advance in the notation of the smaller values was made by a younger contemporary of Franco, namely, Petrus de Cruce. It will be discussed later (see p. 318 ff).

Ligatures. Franco's principles in the writing and the evaluation of ligatures are virtually the same as those which we already know from white notation. It may not be superfluous, however, to summarize them once more with special emphasis on the historical point of view.

The fundamental dictum is contained in the following sentence (*CS* 1, 124):

> Item ligaturarum alia cum proprietate, alia sine, alia cum opposita proprietate. Et hoc est a parte principii ligature; a parte autem finis, alia cum perfectione, alia sine. Et nota istas differentias essentiales esse et specificas istis ligaturis.

> Furthermore there are ligatures *cum proprietate, sine proprietate* and *cum opposita proprietate*. These characteristics refer to the initial note of the ligature. As for the final note, a ligature may be *cum perfectione* or *sine perfectione*. These differences are real and specific properties of the ligatures.

This sentence contains two new thoughts of great importance: first, that *proprietas* has to do exclusively with the *initialis*, and *perfectio* exclusively with the *finalis* of a ligature; second, that these features are essential and characteristic, in other words, that they fully and unambiguously determine the value of the ligature which no longer depends upon the context (i.e., on the mode or the value of the neighbouring notes). The practical realization of these principles was achieved by the establishment of the following rules:

The *initialis* is *B* in a lig. *cum propr.*; *L* in a lig. *sine propr.*
The *finalis* is *L* in a lig. *cum perf.*; *B* in a lig. *sine perf.*
The first two notes are *S* each in a lig. *cum opp. propr.*
These rules are supplemented by the following statement:

> A parte autem medii ligaturarum nulla essentialis differentia invenitur. . . . Per quod patet, positionem illorum esse falsam qui ponunt in ternaria aliqua mediam esse longam, in omnibus autem aliis fore brevem.

> As for the middle notes of a ligature, there is no difference between them.

. . . Therefore it is obvious that they commit an error who maintain that in a certain *ternaria* the middle note is an *L*, but in all the others a *B*.

Indeed, according to Franco all middle notes are always *B*.

The indication in writing of the various types of *proprietas* and *perfectio* is governed by principles explained below by means of two tables, the second of which also includes some modifications to be found in sources of the fourteenth century:

	WRITTEN		VALUE
	ascending	descending	
cum propr:	initialis without stroke	initialis with stroke ·	initialis *B*
sine propr:	initialis with stroke	initialis without stroke	initialis *L*
cum perf:	finalis turned toward left	finalis square	finalis *L*
sine perf:	finalis turned toward right	finalis oblique	finalis *B*
opp. propr:	initialis with upward stroke	initialis with upward stroke	first and second notes *S*

BINARIA

type	/	\	value
2	(b)		B L
s2	(a) (a) (b)		L L
2s			B B
s2s	(a) (a)		L B
°2			S S
—	—		

TERNARIA

type	/	\	∧	∨	value
3	(b)			(b)	B B L
s3	(a) (a) (b)		(a) (a)	(b)	L B L
3s					B B B
s3s	(a) (a)		(a) (a)		L B B
°3		(b)			(b)	S S L
°3s					S S B

Remarks:

(a) Franco mentions two manners of indicating *sine proprietate* for an ascending ligature, that is, with the dash to the left or to the right side of the initial note. The second, which he calls 'magis proprium,' was the only one to survive after 1300.

(b) In earlier times this form expressed the *binaria (ternaria) plicata* (see p. 236), and Franco mentions it as still having this meaning (*CS* I, 125b). However, as the *plica* ligatures continued more and more to lose their former importance, this character was adopted in place of the older form of the ascending ligature *cum perfectione*, probably because this is awkward to write when the lines of the staff are close together. The downward stroke at the end of a ligature thus changes its meaning from that of a *plica*-stroke to the sign of a *longa*. The new form appears (beside the older form) as early as the Codex Huelgas.

A comparison of this table with that of the pre-Franconian ligatures, given on p. 297, shows that the system has been broadened by the introduction of ligatures *sine proprietate* and *sine perfectione* ($^s2^s$, $^s3^s$), as well as of ligatures *cum opposita proprietate* and *sine perfectione* ($^o3^s$).

The progress made by the Franconian system of ligatures over that of the pre-Franconian period is apparent from a comparison of Franco's teaching with that of Dietricus which, as we have said, corresponds to the notation of the Bamberg codex. According to Dietricus, the *ternaria cum proprietate* is *L B L* (first mode), the *ternaria sine proprietate* is *B L B* (second mode). The transition from this purely modal interpretation to that of Franco may be glimpsed in Dietricus' remark that under certain circumstances the *ternaria cum proprietate* is *B B L*, namely when a *L* precedes (third mode). Franco's contribution consisted in making this last interpretation the exclusive one. As a result, all ligatures *cum proprietate* (*binaria* and *ternaria*) begin with a *B*. Therefore Franco could make the decisive statement that the quality *cum proprietate* did not concern the entire ligature but only its *initialis*. And herein lies the chief difference between his system and all the earlier ones. Once this step was taken, it was a simple matter to relegate the quality *cum perfectione* to the last note, which, of course, had to have the value of a *L* in order to complete a *perfectio* with the initial *B* (in the *binaria*). Having assigned *proprietas* to the *initialis* and *perfectio* to the *finalis*, all the possibilities of differentiation were exhausted. The middle notes, therefore, had to have a value independent of these distinctions: 'A parte autem medii ligaturarum nulla essentialis differentia invenitur.' In order to illustrate the difference between the Franconian and the pre-Franconian systems, we give here a table of the chief modes in both notations.

	I	II	III	V
Pre-Franconian:	3 2 2	2 2 3	*L* 3 3 3	3 (*L L L*)
Franconian:	^{s}3 2 2	2 2 2 *B*	*L* 3 3 3 (^{s}4 3 3)	*L L L*

In the first mode a ʼ*3* must be used since the initial note is a *L*. In the second mode the *3* must be divided, since a *media* can never be a *L*. The third mode needs no modification; however, Franco prefers a ʼ*4* in place of *L* + *3*, following the principle: *ligare quantum possibile est* ('to use ligatures as much as possible'). In the fifth mode ligatures cannot be used: 'vehementer errant qui tres longas aliqua occasione, ut in tenoribus, ad invicem ligant' (he makes a serious mistake who, under any circumstances—e.g., in tenors—writes three *L* in ligature). We have seen that this older manner of writing was virtually abandoned even before Franco.

Examples. Compositions written according to the principles of Franco occur, though sparingly, in the fascicles VII and VIII of *Mo*, in the Codex Torino, in Paris, Bibl. Nat. *f. fr. 146* (*Roman de Fauvel*), and a few other MSS of the late thirteenth and early fourteenth centuries. A motet *Huic ut—Huic ut*—(tenor) (Facsimile 63) may be studied as a first example. The tenor begins in the middle of the staff, after the empty interspace. It is written in the first mode: ʼ*3 2 2* . . . The last ordo is identical with the first and, in fact, is written out only in order to indicate that the entire melody must be repeated until the upper voices have finished (four times; the motet closes on the next page of the Ms).

The motetus (right-hand column) starts with an extended vocalization on the syllable 'Hu-', and continues with seven lines of music to which a full text is underlaid ('huic ut . . . mira potentia'). Exactly the same two passages occur in the triplum, but in reversed order, resulting in *Stimmtausch* (interchange of parts). Both parts continue with a vocalization on (potenti) 'a-', in which groups of *S*-(*S*) frequently sound against groups of (*S*)-*S* in the other part, leading to hocket effects. The *S*-rests [(*S*)] are written as small dashes irregularly placed below, above, or across a staff line. The strictly Franconian interpretation of this motet would make it necessary to double the *S*-rests in the groups S-(*S*). In order to avoid this rather awkward consequence, it may be better to transcribe groups of two *S* as equal notes.

In the appendix, No. 44, are shown the beginning of the first and of the third section in transcription.

Facsimile 64 illustrates the use of the Franconian 'chains of *S*.' The *S* appear always in even number, that is, in groups of two, four, six etc. According to the above principles, they are to be arranged in pairs. The tenor *Aptatur* is written entirely in *ternariae sine perfectione*, each of which equals *B B B*. Since each ligature is followed by a *B*-rest, groups

MS Montpellier, Faculté des Médecins *H 196* (13th century)
Pages 393', 394

FACSIMILE 64

MS Montpellier, Faculté des Médecins *H 196* (13th century)
Pages 311', 312

of four *B* result which obviously indicate *modus imperfectus*. Here is the beginning of the duplum in transcription:

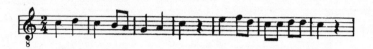

B. The Innovations of Petrus de Cruce

As mentioned above, compositions in true Franconian notation are rather scarce. The greatest shortcoming of Franco's system was the lack of rhythmic variety in the realm of the small values, and it was in this matter that new contributions were soon made. Important progress was made by Petrus de Cruce (*ca.* 1280?) who actually inaugurated a new trend in thirteenth century music and notation. Since the notational devices introduced by him are sharply distinguished from Franco's principles it seems appropriate to refer to them by a special name, i.e., Petronian notation.

Petrus de Cruce's innovations are often mentioned by theorists of the early fourteenth century. Robertus de Handlo, after explaining the Franconian principles of *semibreves*-notation, continues (*CS* i, 387):

> Securius tamen et verius . . . addatur punctus inter duas et duas vel inter tres et tres. . . . ut ponit Petrus de Cruce

> For the sake of greater accuracy and truth . . . a *punctus* should be added, between two and two, or three and three *S*, . . . as is done by Petrus de Cruce.

Jacobus of Liége, in *Speculum Musicae*, says (*CS* ii, 401 a):

> Petrus de Cruce primo incipit ponere quatuor semibreves pro tempore perfecto

> Petrus de Cruce was the first to introduce four *S* within the span of a perfect *tempus*.

According to the first writer, Petrus de Cruce introduced the *punctus divisionis* in order to mark off groups of *S* neighbouring on other similar groups. Thus, combinations such as *B SS.SSS.SS.SSS.SS B*, which are not possible in Franconian notation, could easily be formed. This innovation, however, was only the point of departure for another one of greater significance, namely, the introduction of four, five, six or seven *S* in the place of a *B* (*perfecta*). In *Montpellier* vii, viii are found a number of motets which embody this innovation (e.g., nos. 253, 254, 255,

262, 289, 293, 297, 298, 299, 317, 332 etc.). A famous motet by Petrus de Cruce, *Aucun ont trouvé chant*, the beginning of which is cited by various theorists, may serve as an example (Facsimile 65). The tenor *Annun(ciavit)* is in groups of three (perfect) *L* throughout. The motetus is notated chiefly in *L* and *B*, with occasional groups of three *S* in *conjunctura*, and of two *S* in *ligatura c.o.p.* The triplum, however, displays a remarkable advance in rhythm. It is written chiefly in *S* which appear in groups from two to seven. The beginning or the end of a group is indicated either by a longer note (*L*, *B*) or an equivalent rest, by a ligature, or by the *punctus divisionis*. Two *S*, written as a *binaria c.o.p.*, do not combine with preceding or following *S*, but occupy the value of a *B* by themselves. Disregarding, for the moment, the question of the rhythmic organization within a group of *S*, the following transcription of the beginning results:

Obviously, the replacement of a *B* by more than three notes results in practice in the introduction of values smaller than the *S*, i.e., the *minima* (or even the *semiminima*). However, in the Petronian teaching and notation these smaller values still appear under the guise and under the name of *semibrevis*, and a considerable time elapsed before the *M* was recognized *de jure* as an independent type of note.

The main problem presented by the groups of more than three *S*, characteristic of Petronian notation, is that of the metrical values within such a group, i.e., the question whether they simply indicate notes of equal duration, or whether they call for some sort of rhythmic organization similar to that of a series of *S* in Franconian notation. This problem may be illustrated by two transcriptions of the beginning of our motet: (a), Coussemaker, *L'Art harmonique*, no. XI; (b), Wolf in *GdM* III, no. 1, and in *HdN* I, 266 (see p. 320).

Both Coussemaker and Wolf interpret the *S*-groups on the basis of strict triple meter or, in fourteenth century terminology, of *tempus perfectum* (*B* = 3 *S*). Furthermore, Wolf applies *prolatio perfecta* and introduces an iambic grouping (alteration) which is similar to that called for by the Franconian 'chains of *S*.'

These two versions may be compared with the preliminary transcrip-

The small notes indicate the rhythm in the reduced note values used in the present study.

tion given above which conforms with the transcription given by F. Ludwig (*AHdM* I, 254).[1]

The question as to which interpretation is correct is certainly not an easy one to answer.[2] In three treatises of the mid-fourteenth century— namely, Theodoricus de Campo, Anon. III, and Anon. IV of the third volume of Coussemaker's *Scriptores*—one finds explanations which would seem to support the theory of a strictly measured interpretation of the groups of *S*. These writers deal chiefly with the notation of the *Ars Nova*, which is distinguished from the notation under consideration by the use of the so-called *semibreves signatae, semibreves caudatae,* or *semibreves cum proprietate,* i.e., special types of *S*.characterized by an upward or a downward dash: ⬧ *semibrevis maior;* ◆ *semibrevis minor;* ⬧ *semibrevis minima* or, briefly, *minima*. The same writers, however, expressly refer to earlier practice and give as its chief characteristic the failure to distinguish between these forms and the use of the *punctus divisionis*. They also give detailed explanations regarding the values of the various notes within a group of *S* which are not *signatae*. It will suffice to illustrate their principles by the following table:

	Tempus perfectum		Tempus imperfectum	
2S	♪ ♩		♫	
3S	♫♩		♫♩ (3)	or: ♫♩ (3)
4S	♫♫ (3)	or: ♫♫ (3)	♫♫ (3 3)	or: ♫♫ (3 3)
5S	♫♫♩ (3 3)	or: ♫♫♩ (3 3)	♫♫♩ (3 3)	or: ♫♫♩ (3 3)

---

[1] Still another interpretation is used in Rokseth's transcription, *Polyphonies,* III, 81 ff.

[2] This problem has been studied particularly by J. Wolf in *GdM* I, 7 and 21, and in *HdN* I, 264. His explanations in *GdM* (1904) are based largely upon the theory that, in the late thirteenth century, Italian music and notation was sufficiently developed to exercise a strong influence upon French

FACSIMILE 65

MS Montpellier, Faculté des Médecins *H 196* (13th century)
Pages 278, 278'

These detailed explanations, made with reference to an earlier practice, seem to support the interpretation by Coussemaker and especially that of Wolf. The only remaining problem, then; would be the question as to which of the two mensurations mentioned by the theorists should be applied, *tempus perfectum* or *tempus imperfectum*, and whether trochaic. or iambic rhythm should be preferred for the notes in *prolatio perfecta*.

It would be lost labor to search for an answer to these questions. Indeed, the very futility of this task raises suspicion as to the admissibility of the whole issue. Fortunately, another theorist—and one of much greater weight and authority—namely, the author of the *Speculum musicae*,[1] comes to our assistance. In his extensive and unusually informative explanations he repeatedly touches upon the problem of the *semibreves*. The following remarks are especially clarifying (*CS* II, 429):

> Quod si moderni multis distinctionibus, multis nominationibus utantur in semibrevibus, quidquid sit de figuris antiqui, quantum ad rem, uti videntur pluribus. Nam cum pro eodem et equali tempore, pro brevi recto importato, nunc duas semibreves ponerent inequales; nunc tres equales, nunc quatuor, quinque, sex, septem, octo vel novem, cum duas ponebant, vocari ille poterant semibreves secunde, . . . ; cum tres semibreves tertie . . . ; cum quatuor semibreves quarte . . . ; cum quinque semibreves quinte, . . . cum novem, semibreves none. Cum tot distinctionibus in semibrevibus uterentur, numquam eas in figuris distinxerunt, numquam eas caudaverunt, et tamen eas sufficienter ab invicem per puncta diviserunt.

The modern musicians use numerous distinctions and names for the *semibreves*. Whatever variety there may be in shapes, the old masters in reality

---

music. This theory is untenable, as has been shown by F. Ludwig (*AfMW* v, 289) and H. Besseler (*AfMW* vii, 177). In particular, Ludwig has shown that the date 1274 for Marchettus de Padua's *Lucidarium*, which was a cornerstone of Wolf's conclusions (see *GdM* i, 16), is erroneous, being at least fifty years too early. In his *HdN* (1913) Wolf has quite rightly given up the idea of an Italian influence upon the notation of the early French *Ars Nova*. Instead, he gives a detailed account of the information contained in the writings of Walter Odington, Johannes Hanboy, Robertus de Handlo, Joh. de Garlandia the younger, W. de Doncastre, Robert Trowell and other theorists of the period of transition from the *Ars Antiqua* to the *Ars Nova*. It has not been deemed necessary to dwell here upon this subject as our knowledge about it is practically limited to its theoretical aspect which has been fully expounded by Wolf.

[1] The *Speculum musicae* is not only by far the most extensive treatise on medieval music, but also the most penetrating and informative one. Only the last two of its seven books have been published, (*CS.* II, 191-433). In Coussemaker's *Scriptores* as well as in many books of more recent date the *Speculum* has been attributed to Johannes de Muris; however, H. Besseler has shown that this theory is untenable (*AfMW* vii, 180 ff). The author of this treatise is one Jacobus who probably lived in Liège. At any rate, the author of the *Speculum* was an extremely conservative musician, whereas Johannes de Muris was a close friend of Philippe de Vitry's and an ardent champion of the *Ars Nova*.

had a larger variety. For one and the same *tempus*, namely, that of the *brevis recta*, they used two *semibreves* unequal in value, or three, four, five, six, seven, eight and nine equal *semibreves*. Thus, in the case of two *semibreves*, one might speak of *semibreves secundae*, . . . ; in the case of three, of *semibreves tertiae* . . . ; in the case of four, of *semibreves quartae;* in the case of five, of *semibreves quintae* . . . in the case of nine, of *semibreves nonae*. Although they used such a variety of *semibreves*, they never distinguished them in shape, never provided them with dashes; yet, nonetheless, they discriminated them from one another sufficiently by *puncta*.

In order to attach the proper importance to these remarks one must realize that the whole extensive treatise of Jacobus is designed to show the superiority of the *Ars Vetus* over the modernistic innovations of the *Ars Nova*. In the present case, he justifiably points out that the apparently revolutionary changes introduced by the 'modern' composers (de Vitry, Johannes de Muris) actually are not an enrichment, but rather an impoverishment in comparison to the varieties of rhythm possible in the late thirteenth century. First, he calls attention to the fact that the introduction of the *minima* (or, in other words, of *tempus* with *prolatio*) amounts to nothing but the expression of the old rhythms and values by other signs. This statement becomes clearer upon realizing that the introduction of the apparently smaller notes was accompanied by a lengthening, in fact, an exact triplication of the duration of the B and L, as will be seen subsequently. Thus, there is no difference *ad rem* between the 'modernistic' ♦♩ or ●♦ and the 'old-fashioned' ♩▪ . After having demonstrated this the author of the *Speculum* justly points out that the followers of Franco, first among them Petrus de Cruce, actually succeeded in introducing into music and notation a variety of metrical values not to be found in the practice of the *Ars Nova*. As a matter of fact the introduction of the Petronian groups of more than three S not only leads to values resulting from a repeated bipartition and tripartition ($\frac{1}{6}$, $\frac{1}{9}$ B), but also means the creation of essentially new fractions such as $\frac{1}{4}$, $\frac{1}{5}$, $\frac{1}{7}$, and $\frac{1}{8}$ of a B (*semibreves quartae, quintae, septimae, octavae*).

Jacobus' explanations, if viewed in the light of this general situation, are perfectly clear and unambiguous. It appears, therefore, that the Petronian groups of S must be interpreted according to the following scheme:

B	$2S$	$3S$	$4S$	$5S$	$6S$	$7S$

A correct transcription of the beginning of the motet is given in the appendix, No. 45. A comparison of this transcription with those of Coussemaker and Wolf immediately shows that the question of tempo, and consequently that of the proper scale of reduction, plays a decisive rôle in this matter, as it also does in many others. Indeed, a great number of misinterpretations and controversies could have been avoided if this point of view had been properly considered. The transcriptions in Coussemaker and in Wolf's *GdM* illustrate the complete neglect of this viewpoint, a neglect which is a common characteristic of almost all the earlier editors (except H. Riemann); indeed, under the pretext of 'scientific exactness' it still continues to exert its detrimental influence in many recent editions of early music. The transcription in Wolf's *HdN* (p. 266) shows a better understanding of this matter, since the reduction there chosen suggests a tempo in which the beat falls on the *S*. However, although the problem has at least been faced, it is not answered correctly. There is sufficient evidence to show that throughout the *Ars Antiqua*, to which no doubt Petrus de Cruce still belongs, the normal musical pulse is represented not by the *S* but by the *B*, except for the earliest period (School of Notre Dame) in which it is represented by the *L*. Ample proof of this exists in the repeated remarks of the author of the *Speculum musicae*, who always extols Petrus as one of the great masters of his beloved *ars veterum*, and who on the other hand is one of the many theorists to inform us about the fact that in the old art the beat (*tempus*) was represented by the *B* in contrast to the modern art (*Ars Nova*) in which it falls on the *S*. If, then, a composition of this period is sung in its proper speed (▪-♩- M.M. 60-70), it becomes immediately clear that no differentiations of temporal values are possible within a group containing four, five, or more *S*. Such groups are performed either as quick coloraturas or else, if underlaid with a full text, like rapid speech not dissimilar to Italian parlando or an English patter song.

In the light of these considerations it appears that the explanations of Theodoricus de Campo and the various anonymi mentioned above represent the attempt, made in the second half of the fourteenth century, to interpret the notation of the Petronian period according to the concepts of speed and rhythm which prevailed in their day. Some people went even farther and changed the notation of the earlier MSS by adding upward or downward dashes to those *semibreves* which they considered to be shorter or longer than the others. There exist at least two MSS in which these attempts at remodelling have left traces. One of these, the Codex Huelgas, has already been briefly discussed. The other, which is the more interesting and more important one, is the so-called *Roman de Fauvel*.

C. The Roman de Fauvel

This MS (Paris, Bibl. Nat. *f. fr. 146*), which contains motets and mono- *
phonic songs inserted in a continuous narrative[1] and which was completed in 1314, represents the last extant document of the *Ars Antiqua*.
Its chief notational interest lies in the fact that, in addition to the plain
S, so-called *semibreves signatae* or *caudatae* occur, i.e., *S* with a downward
or upward tail or with other characteristics designed to indicate differentiation of values within the realm of the smaller notes. For instance,
the combination ♦♦♦ would indicate that the first note is longer than
the second, and this (in turn) is longer than the third. The exact interpretation, of course, would still depend on the mensuration, i.e., on
tempus and *prolatio*. In the above example the following renditions
would seem to be possible:

[3, 3]: 9/16 | 𝅘𝅥𝅭 𝅘𝅥𝅮𝅘𝅥𝅮 | [2, 3]: 6/16 | 𝅘𝅥𝅭 𝅘𝅥𝅮𝅘𝅥𝅮 | [2, 2]: 4/16 | 𝅘𝅥 𝅘𝅥𝅭𝅘𝅥𝅮 |

B = 𝅘𝅥 :   B = 𝅘𝅥𝅭 .   B = 𝅘𝅥

Like the plain *S* of the Petronian motets the *semibreves caudatae* of the
Roman de Fauvel have been the subject of divergent interpretations and
controversial utterances on the part of various scholars such as Coussemaker, Wolf, and Ludwig. But once more, as in the previous case, the
whole issue is futile. An examination of the MS shows easily that none
of the indications of *semibreves signatae* are part of the original writing,
but that all are later additions. In fact, they appear as extremely short
dashes, timidly and furtively drawn, which in many cases are clearly out
of the center of the note (see the illustration p. 326).

The unauthentic quality of the *semibreves signatae* in the *Roman de
Fauvel* is particularly evident in the case of the form with an upward
dash, the *semibrevis minima* (the *minima* of the later system). The presence of these forms in the piece *Quare fremuerunt* (f.1; see the reproduction
on p. 326) has led J. Wolf to a rendition in *tempus perfectum cum prolatione perfecta* (GdM III, No. 4), whereas F. Ludwig, in his criticism of
Wolf's publication (*SIMG* VI, 624) advocates the application of *tempus
imperfectum cum prolatione perfecta*. Actually, in this case the controversy is particularly futile, not only because the '*minima*'-strokes are
barely visible and are used without any consistency (cf. the beginning of
the second and the end of the third staff), but also because the piece in
question, which appears on the first page, is the only composition of the
whole codex to show these pseudo-*minimae*. The conclusion is inevit-

---

[1] See the list of contents in *GdM* I, 40 ff.

Quare fremuerunt (Tenor enlarged)

able that a revisor of the manuscript tried to remodel it after the principles of *Ars Nova* style and notation, but soon gave up, becoming aware of the futility of his task.   He was more persistent in the application of the downward dash which appears throughout the manuscript, apparently indicating *semibreves* of a somewhat longer value (*semibrevis major*). However, a glance at our Facsimile 67 (e.g., left and right column, staff 8) will readily show that they bear the same appearance of being a later emendation as the upward dashes mentioned previously.   The final conclusion, then, is that this MS was originally written in true Petronian notation and that, in all probability, its groups of *S* must be interpreted according to the principles set forth above.

   The application of this theory to the *Quare fremuerunt* leads to the following transcription, to which for the sake of comparison two other interpretations have been added, one (a) according to J. Wolf (see *GdM* III, p. 8), the other (b) according to F. Ludwig (see *SIMG* VI, p. 625):

We now turn to a more general discussion of the notation of the polyphonic compositions of the *Roman de Fauvel*.

The Tenors; Modus and Maximodus.   The notation of the tenors follows the Franconian principles, as is illustrated in the following two examples, both of which are in *modus perfectus:*
Fur non venit (f. 7):

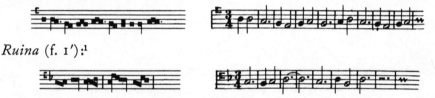

Ruina (f. 1′):[1]

The *modus imperfectus* is much more frequent now than in the earlier sources.   Sometimes it is explicitly indicated as in the motet *Nulla pestis* (f. 3), the tenor of which bears the inscription 'Vergente ex imperfectis' (i.e., tenor *Vergente* performed with imperfect *L*).[2]   In this case the remark would appear to be superfluous since the use of *L*-rests covering two spaces unmistakably points to imperfect *modus:*

The situation is less clear in the case of the tenor *Displicebat* of the motet *Quasi non ministerium* (f. 6′),[3] where there is no such remark nor

[1] See *GdM* II, 6.
[2] See *HdN* I, 281.
[3] See *GdM* II, 10.

any rest.   Here it is the duplum and triplum from which the correct mensuration, namely *modus imperfectus*, must be derived:

Imperfect *modus* is particularly frequent in the tenors written without ligatures.   Among nine tenors of this type four are in perfect *modus* and five in imperfect, namely, *Superne matris* (f. 2), *Imperfecte canite* (f. 13), *Heu me tristis* (f. 30), *Merito hec patimur* (f. 42), and *Alleluia benedictus* (f. 43).   The last-named tenor is reproduced on Facsimile 66.   Following is the beginning of the transcription:

This tenor is also indicative of another broadening of the system of mensurations.   While in the earlier sources the combination of the *longa* and the *duplex longa*—or, as it was called in the fourteenth century, *maxima (Mx)*— always leads to groups of two *L*, e.g.: /*Mx/L L/Mx/L L/ Mx/* (see the tenors *Ruina* and *Vergente*), in the present example there result groups equalling three *L*:/*L Mx/L Mx/L (L) (L)/*.   In this may be seen the germ of the *modus maximarum (maximodus*, see p. 124) which became of practical application in the motets of the early *Ars Nova* and of Machaut, and which was perpetuated in the theoretical writings of the fifteenth to the seventeenth centuries.   Like any of the other mensurations the *maximodus* was either perfect or imperfect.   It must be noticed, however, that the *Mx* itself was never admitted to be ternary; it was only the grouping of the *L*'s—with or without the binary *Mx*— which caused the *maximodus* to be either perfect or imperfect by implication.

Whenever the *maximodus* is clearly perceptible in a composition it should be indicated in the transcription by heavier bar-lines or some similar means.   In the above transcription of the *Alleluia*-tenor, such bar-lines should appear, then, after every three measures.   Another possibility would be to combine three $\frac{2}{4}$-measures into one $\frac{3}{2}$-measure.

Red Notes.   In the *Roman de Fauvel* are found the earliest examples of red notes which are used to signify transition from *modus perfectus* to *modus imperfectus* in the tenor.[1]   They occur in two motets one of
* which, *Garrit gallus—In nova fert*, is reproduced on Facsimile 67.   That the black and red notes have the meaning just indicated appears from

---

[1] In Aubry's facsimile edition of the *Roman de Fauvel* the red notes appear as ordinary black notes. Thus an important feature of the notation is obscured.

FACSIMILE 66

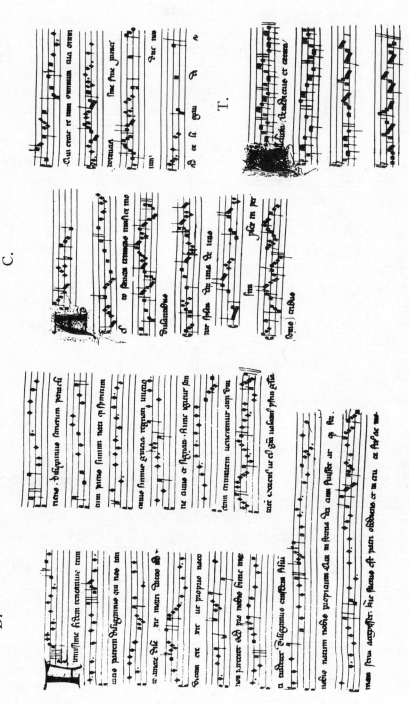

Roman de Fauvel
Paris, Bibliothèque Nationale *fonds fre. 146 (ca.* 1310)
From pages 43, 43'

the length of the rests which cover three spaces in the passages written in black notes, two in those notated in red ones:

This tenor is also remarkable as one of the earliest examples of that fourteenth century extension of the modal scheme which is known as isorhythmic construction (isorhythmic motet). In fact, the elaborate rhythm of the above passage appears three times in succession, much in the same way as, in a thirteenth century motet, the simple scheme of a modal pattern is repeated a number of times.

Notation of the Upper Parts. The *S*-groups of the upper parts have already been discussed. Normally they will have to be interpreted on the basis of the scheme worked out for the Petronian groups in the Codex Montpellier. In two motets, *Servant regem—Rex regum—O Philippe* (p. 10-12) and *Detractor est—Qui secuntur—Verbum iniquum* (p. 4), one finds two small dashes, similar to the *S*-rests of *Mo*, written before the first notes of the parts, e.g. (see *GdM* II, p. 6 and 13):

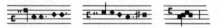

Since real rests cannot be meant here, J. Wolf (*GdM* I, 57) interprets these signs as indicating *tempus imperfectum* in contradistinction to the *tempus perfectum* prevailing normally. This plausible interpretation would mean that in these pieces groups of two and of three *S* must be read in binary meter as follows: ♦♦ = ♫ ; ♦♦♦ = ♩♫ . The rhythm of the more numerous groups of *S* naturally remains unaltered. Binary mensuration of the *B* may also be preferred in pieces which, although not marked in the above manner, show a distinct prevalence of groups of two *S*. An example is the motet *Firmissime—Adesto—Alleluia benedictus* (Facsimile 66),[1] in the upper parts of which groups of two and four *S* are much more numerous than groups of three. As a matter of fact, in this case we possess definite evidence in the following remark of Philippe de Vitry, made in his *Ars nova* (*CS* III, 20; see also *GdM* I, 47):

Modus imperfectus et tempus imperfectum continentur in Adesto, quia ibi duo tempora pro perfectione qualibet accipiuntur et quodlibet tempus non partitur nisi in duas partes aequales semibreves

---

[1] The queer appearance of our Facsimile is explained as the result of its having been pieced together from different pages of the MS.

FACSIMILE 67

Roman de Fauvel
Paris, Bibliothèque Nationale *fonds frç. 146 (ca.* 1310)
Page 44'

Modus imperfectus as well as *tempus imperfectum* are found in the motet *Adesto,* because two *tempora* (i.e., *breves*) are contained in a perfection (i.e., *longa*), and because each *tempus* (i.e., *brevis*) is divided only in two equal *semibreves.*

Naturally, there are quite a number of motets in which a decision is difficult, if not impossible, to reach. It would seem that the blame for this must be laid, not upon our lack of knowledge, but upon the vagueness of early fourteenth century musicians themselves in the matter of the small note values. Much in the same way as the organa dupla of Leoninus form the transition between the plainsong-like rhythm of St. Martial and the modal meter of the thirteenth century, so the motets of the *Roman de Fauvel* indicate the gradual change to the new rhythmic concepts of the *Ars Nova.* In both cases, the intrinsically transitional character of the period forestalls any attempts to arrive at 'the correct solution.' In both cases it seems advisable to incline to the less rigid notions of the earlier period rather than to the more strictly regulated principles of the development to come. It is particularly this general consideration which causes us to pass over the hair-splittings encountered in the treatises of the fourteenth century (as well as in modern writings)—mindful of the wise remark which was made by a contemporary with a view to this particular situation and which appears as a motto on the dedication page of the present book.

Semibreves Signatae. This remark applies particularly to the *semibreves signatae (caudatae)* which have already been discussed briefly. That the strokes are later additions there can be no doubt. Whether they represent an authentic clarification of the original intentions or an unauthentic remodelling of the rhythm according to principles of a later period remains to some extent an open question. The following points, however, should be observed, in view of the great importance which J. Wolf, F. Ludwig, and others have attached to these signs:

(1) The *semibrevis minima* (with an upward stroke) appears only in one short piece (*Quare fremuerunt*) on the first page. It is clearly a subsequent addition to which no importance whatsoever need be attached. (2) The *semibrevis maior* (with a downward dash) occurs only in groups of two or three *S,* never of four or more. This fact clearly supports our former contention that the groups of four or more *S* must, at any event, be read in the Petronian style as groups of equal notes. (3) The *semibrevis maior* appears only in the following two combinations: ♦♦♦ ; ♦♦ . Both are capable of being interpreted in *tempus perfectum* (a) as well as

in *tempus imperfectum* (b), as appears from the following table which
may serve as a basis for the transcription of the upper parts:

Conjunctura and Plica. If several *S* are to be sung to the same syllable,
they are naturally grouped closely together, as for instance at the beginning of the duplum of Facsimile 67 (*In nova fert*). These groups, of
course, have nothing to do with the old *conjunctura* to which they bear a
certain resemblance in appearance. More closely related to the *conjunctura* is the following character, ⌐, which occurs quite frequently, e.g.,
at the beginning of the duplum *Adesto* of Facsimile 66. This sign takes
the place of a *L*, usually an imperfect one, the only question being as to
whether it indicates a long note followed by two short ones (a), or the
inverse rhythm (b), conforming with that of the old *conjunctura*:

	Tp. pf.	Tp. impf.
(a)	$\frac{6}{8}$ ♩. ♪♩ |	$\frac{2}{4}$ ♩ ♫ |
(b)	$\frac{6}{8}$ ♪♩ ♩. |	$\frac{2}{4}$ ♫ ♩ |

J. Wolf, in *GdM* I, 52, admits both versions, but in his transcriptions
from the *Roman de Fauvel* (*GdM* III, nos. 2-10) always uses (a). Ludwig,
in *SIMG* VI, p. 627, criticizes this method, contending that the character
must be read in the old manner. His view is strongly supported by the
following passage from the motet *Favellandi vicium* (p. 1 of the original;
see the reproduction in *GdM* II, no. II, third staff), in which the version
(b) certainly deserves preference on account of the better consonance *
with the tenor:

The *Roman de Fauvel* shows a striking increase of the *plica*, shortly before its final disappearance in polyphonic music. The shapes are the

familiar ones of the *plica longa* and the *plica brevis* in their ascending and descending varieties. The ascending *plica longa* usually has only a long dash to its right side, the short dash to the left being missing. Nothing need be added to our previous explanations on the *plica*, as far as the questions of pitch and performance are concerned. As regards the temporal value allotted to the *plica*-tone, all theorists of the early fourteenth century agree that it is reduced to a short passing tone, immediately before the following note. This meaning is clearly expressed in the following remark of Hieronymus de Moravia in his explanations on 'flores,' i.e., ornamentations (*CS* I, 91):

> . . . sed flores subitos, non alia quam plica longa. Inter quam et immediate sequentem note brevissime ponuntur ob armonie decorem.

The *flos subitus* (rapid ornamentation) is nothing but the *plica longa*. A very short note is placed between this and the following note, for greater refinement of the sound.

More concrete and, hence, more useful for our purpose, are the explanations of Marchettus de Padua (*Pomerium*, see *GS* III, 181), according to which the *plica*'s are to be executed as follows:

Examples. (1) *Quare fremuerunt* (p. 326). The problem of the *semibreves*, ordinary as well as *signatae*, has already been fully discussed (p. 325). The *modus* is perfect, as appears from the fact that on the second staff there is a group of nine *B* (or their equivalents) between two *L*. In contradiction to the rules of Franco the former of these two *L* (last note of the first staff) remains perfect. As a matter of fact, imperfection of this note would entail alteration of the last *B*, a procedure which is impossible since a group of four *S* occurs instead of this *B*. For the same reason the initial *L* (*longa plicata*) as well as all the other *L* of the piece remain perfect, except those which are followed by a single *B*-rest (e.g., the last note of the second staff).

An interesting feature of this piece is its conductus-like texture, the tenor being in almost exactly the same rhythm as the upper part. It clearly foreshadows the 'ornamented conductus style' of Italian fourteenth century music.

Another point of interest offered by this piece is its form which is that

of the French ballade, namely, A A B. The repetition of the first section
(A) is fully written out in the discant where it begins with the third line.
In the tenor, however, A is written only once and, therefore, must be repeated, as is indicated by the rest-like dash after the first *L* of staff seven.
Moreover, there is a different ending for the *prima volta* and the *seconda
volta* or, as it was called then, for *ouvert* and *clos*. In repeating the section one has to continue after the *brevis* e-flat not with the group d-e-d-c
—d, but with the group d-e-d-b—c.[1] See the complete transcription in
GdM III, 8.

(2) *Firmissime—Adesto—Alleluia benedictus* (Facsimile 66). As we
already learned (pp. 328 and 330), this motet is in imperfect *modus* and
tempus, with perfect *maximodus* [*III*, II, 2], a mensuration the modern
equivalent of which is $\frac{2}{4}$-meter with groups of three measures each (or $\frac{3}{2}$-
meter). The upper parts contain various instructive examples of *con-
junctura* (first staff of the duplum), *plica longa* (same staff) and *plica
brevis* (second staff). The fifth staff of the *triplum* shows a *plica longa*
and a *plica brevis* in succession. The character above 'ut' on the fourth
staff of the triplum, however, is not a *conjunctura*, but a *L* followed by a
group of four *S*. Below is a transcription of the beginning of the motet:

(3) *Garrit gallus—In nova fert* (Facsimile 67). The tenor, with its
alteration of black and red notes, that is, of *modus perfectus* ($\frac{3}{4}$) and
modus imperfectus ($\frac{2}{4}$), has already been discussed (p. 328). As regards
the upper voices, the foremost question is whether to interpret them in
tempus perfectum or in *tempus imperfectum*. Since groups of two, three,
and four *S* are freely mingled, it is impossible, we believe, to arrive at a
definite conclusion from internal evidence. It is only on the basis of
certain general considerations that preference may be given to *tempus
perfectum*. These considerations are chiefly based upon the fact the

[1] See the explanation of *ouvert* and *clos*, p. 349 ff.

Franconian teaching established the ternary division of the *B* as the **only** possible one and that, therefore, a deviation from this scheme may **not** reasonably be assumed unless it is clearly indicated. The very fact **that** with two or three motets of our MS such an indication is given (see **p.** 330) is a strong argument in favor of the assumption that these are the exceptions from the rule, as may also be those motets in which groups of two *S* appear in the majority. As there is no such evidence in the present composition we prefer to transcribe it in *tempus perfectum* (see appendix, No. 46). However, for the sake of instruction, a rendering in *tempus imperfectum* has also been indicated.

Another problem presented by this piece is that of the evaluation of the various *L* in the duplum and triplum. The context shows that some of them equal two *B*, others three, although the notation fails to indicate any such distinction between perfect and imperfect values. One might expect to find a clue to this problem in the mensuration of the tenor which constantly alternates between *modus perfectus* and *modus imperfectus*, the obvious assumption being that the upper voices would follow the same scheme. This, however, is not the case. Nor can the upper parts be interpreted throughout in either of the two modes. In several places their notation indicates groupings which differ from those of the tenor, as, e.g., at the end of the first staff of the duplum (text: '[for]mas draco'), where a ternary *L* (imperfected by a *B*-rest) is followed by two binary *L*, whereas the simultaneous passage of the tenor begins with two binary *L* and ends with a ternary *L* (see the transcription of the beginning, appendix, No. 46). The tenor, as written, covers only one half of the motet; it must be repeated in its entire length.

A feature worth noticing is the peculiar underlaying of the text which results in the most absurd declamation to be imagined. Students of the humanities will notice particularly—and, no doubt, with horror—the alteration of Ovid's elegant hexameter (the words *In nova fert animus* are the beginning of Ovid's *Metamorphoses*) into a distorted stammering which is one of the most striking illustrations of the indifference of mediaeval composers in the underlaying of text.

For further studies of the *Roman de Fauvel* the reader is referred to the reproductions and transcriptions in *GdM* II, III, nos. 2-10, and in *HdN* I, p. 279. Since Wolf's transcriptions are based on principles which have been partly rejected in our previous explanations, some indications are given below as to what we consider to be a more appropriate rendering:[1]

[1] 1: *GdM*, no. 2 (ending); 2: *GdM*, no. 6; 3: *GdM*, no. 7; 4: *GdM*, no. 10; 5: *HdN* I, p. 279.

All these examples are taken from the tripla of the motets. The versions (a) and (b) illustrate the application of *tempus perfectum* or *tempus imperfectum*. The small notes above the staff refer to the variants indicated by the *semibreves signatae*.

VI. FRENCH NOTATION

A. The Innovations of the Ars Nova

THE CHIEF contribution of Franconian notation was the establishment of clear and unequivocal relationships in the notes of larger values, the *longa* and *brevis*. In this respect Franco arrived at definite results which were taken over essentially unaltered by later centuries.

Concerning the smaller values, however, the chief problems had still to be solved. Here Franco took only the first steps, when he introduced groups of two or three *semibreves* in place of a *brevis*. With the innovations of Petrus de Cruce notes smaller than the *semibrevis* were admitted *de facto*, although they had still to be recognized *de jure* and to be expressed clearly in notation.

In the *Roman de Fauvel* we have found evidence of a first attempt towards the differentiation of small values, namely, the addition (by a later scribe) of a downward or an upward stem for values larger or smaller than the normal *S*. Apparently, numerous other forms were invented around the turn of the century, for, as Walter Odington says, 'There are as many inventors of new signs as there are scribes';[1] and Jacobus of Liege complains 'And thus in this matter as well as in others, everybody disapproved of what the other did.' He continues however: 'Most of them agree in that they distinguish the *semibrevis minima* by an upward stroke.'[2]

As a matter of fact, the *semibrevis minima* or, as it was later called, the *minima* (M) is the only form which found acceptance in French practice and consequently in the mensural notation of later periods. The following remark from Anon. I of *CS* III (p.336) clarifies its origin: 'The minim

* was invented in Navarre and was sanctioned and used by Philippe de Vitry, the finest figure of the entire musical world.'[3]

---

[1] See *HdN* I, 271.

[2] *CS* II, 409a.

[3] According to Johannes Hanboys (*CS* I, 424) the 'inventor' of the *minima* and of the *semibreves signatae* in general was the younger Johannes de Garlandia who flourished around 1300, and who was an important link between Petrus de Cruce and Philippe de Vitry. The kingdom of Navarre, situated north and south of the Pyrenees, was one of the most important cultural centers of the thirteenth century. From 1201-1255 it was ruled by Thibaut, Roy de Navarre, who was one of the foremost trouvères and after whom the *Chansonnier Roy* was named.

Philippe de Vitry, whom we now encounter for the first time, is the leading personality in the development of French notation of the fourteenth century. Even if he did not invent *minima*, he played an important part, if not the decisive rôle, in its adoption as a basic element of the new notation and of the new rhythm. For it is a new rhythm which makes its appearance in the works of the *Ars Nova*. In this respect the following remark from the *Speculum musicae* is informative (*CS* II, 417 b):

. . . antiqui . . . habebant pro consuetudine primam minus, secundam magis tenere, motu forte ex imitatione nature que fortior est in fine quam in principio. Dicunt autem moderni istud non esse necessarium cum e converso possit fieri, scilicet quod prima semibrevis amplius teneatur quam secunda, sicut ipsi nunc observant; . . . dicunt etiam quod non oportet ut ars semper naturam imitet.

. . . the old masters always made the first [*semibrevis*] shorter, the second longer, a rhythm full of strength and harmonizing with nature which is always stronger at the end than at the beginning. The modern musicians, however, maintain that this is not obligatory and that it may be done in the opposite way, namely, with the first being longer than the second, as they actually do it nowadays . . . They also say that it is not necessary for art always to follow nature.

These words are, indeed, a very apt description of that fundamental change by which European music for the first time ceased to aim at being the image of divine law and nature, and began to turn to emotionalism and refinement as sources of artistic inspiration.[1]

With the introduction of the *S* as an independent, and of the *M* as a

---

[1] In putting the blame for the change from 'naturalness' to 'artificiality' at the door of the 'moderni,' Jacobus was either insufficiently informed or, more likely, forgetful of the fact that these modernistic tendencies had made their appearance in a considerably earlier period. Already in the anonymous treatise from 1279 (edited by Sowa, p. 51) we find the following interesting remark: 'Sed figura binaria per oppositum figurata recte brevi proportionaliter equipollet, ergo frustra in ea inequalia habenda, quod verum est. De quorum dispositione contingit similariter dubitarem eo quod quidam dicunt in illa figura minorem semibrevem procedere et maiorem sussequi vel paritus e converso promutua cantantium voluntate. Et isti opinioni videtur maxima pars canentium adhere' ('The *ligatura binaria c.o.p.* equals a *brevis recta* [i.e., not altered]; therefore its parts must be performed unequally, as is the truth. At the same time, however, one may be doubtful about their order, since certain authorities say that in this ligature the shorter value proceeds and the larger one follows, or just as well the other way around, according to the pleasure of the singers. It seems that the majority of the singers share this opinion'). Although this remark clearly confirms our contention that in the notation of the late 13th century a group of two *S* must be read in ternary rhythm, it simultaneously introduces another element of choice into the interpretation of the music of this period. On the basis of the date of the above treatise, the option between the iambic and trochaic reading of a group of two *S* would apply to all pieces written in Petronian notation, including those from the *Roman de Fauvel* (see e.g., p. 337, no. 3).

new note value, *prolatio* appears in addition to *tempus* and *modus*. It may be well to note here that the term *prolatio* originally was used in a broad sense, namely, as a general expression for any variety of mensura-
* tion. Johannes de Muris, for instance, begins his *Libellus cantus men-surabilis* by saying: 'There are five elements of *prolatio*, namely, *maxima*, *longa*, *brevis*, *semibrevis* and *minima*.' Nevertheless he uses the same term in the more restricted sense as well:' . . . the *semibrevis* equals three *minimas* in the *prolatio maior* (i.e., perfecta), two in the *prolatio minor* (i.e., imperfecta).[1] Still another meaning is encountered in the 'quatre prolacions' which are mentioned by various writers as an invention of Philippe de Vitry,[2] and which are identical with the four combinations of *tempus* and *prolatio*. Anon. VI (*CS* i, 369) describes the same combinations as four different types of *breves* namely: *brevis perfecte perfecta* ([3, 3]), *brevis imperfecte perfecta* ([3, 2]), *brevis perfecte imperfecta* ([2, 3]), and *brevis imperfecte imperfecta* ([2, 2]).

This leads us to a second important advance made by Vitry, namely, the *de jure* recognition of the equality of perfect and imperfect mensura-tion. The Franconian system rests entirely on perfect mensuration. We have seen, however, that imperfect *modus* already appears in some of the motets of the Montpellier and of the Bamberg codices, and more frequently in the *Roman de Fauvel*. Once more—as in the case of the *minima*—all that was necessary was to recognize and legitimatize an accomplished fact. This is credited to Vitry, who not only considered perfect and imperfect *modus* as having equal rights, but also applied the same dichotomy to *tempus* and *prolatio*, each of which might be either perfect or imperfect. Another innovation of Vitry which, however, was not readily accepted by his contemporaries, was the use of signs to indi-cate mensuration. He introduced the circle and the semicircle for *tempus perfectum* and *tempus imperfectum* respectively. The *modus* can be recognized by the rests, the *modus perfectus* being indicated by the 'pausa triorum temporum' and the *modus imperfectus* by the 'pausa quarum quelibet valet duo tempora.' None of these signs were adopted in common use before the fifteenth century.

It should be noted that *prolatio* and the metric combinations resulting from it are not yet treated in the *Ars Nova* in the same systematic fashion as the combinations of *tempus* and *modus*. They appear instead under the guise of various species or modifications of *tempus*. According to Vitry *tempus perfectum* can be *minimum*, *medium*, and *majus*, while

---

[1] *CS* iii, 46, 47.
[2] *Règles de la seconde rectorique*; cf. *GdM* i, 65, also *AHdM* i, 265.

tempus imperfectum may be *minimum* or *majus*. The *tempus perfectum minimum* is nothing but the Franconian *metrum* ('tempus minimum posuit Franco'). It actually means *tempus perfectum* without *prolatio*, i.e., with only three (or, occasionally, four) notes to the *B*, but with the *modus* (*perfectus* or *imperfectus*) as an additional factor of mensuration. The other four kinds of *tempus* prove to be identical with the above-mentioned 'quatre prolacions' or, in other words, with the four combinations of *tempus* and *prolatio*:[1]

Tempus perfectum			Tempus imperfectum	
Minimum	Medium	Majus	Minimum	Majus
[III, 3], [II, 3]	[3, 2]	[3, 3]	[2, 2]	[2, 3]

A further important characteristic of the new epoch is the lengthening in duration of the large values which occurred automatically as the result of the introduction of smaller values. Anon. I speaks of this when, looking back at the Franconian (Petronian?) period, he says: 'At that time the *longa* and the *brevis* were sung as quickly as is the *tempus imperfectum* today.'[2] Jacobus of Liege speaks even more clearly of this matter in his *Speculum musicae*. Chapter XVII of Book VII, entitled 'Antiquorum excusatio et dictorum suorum expositio' (*CS* II, 400) contains so many interesting remarks that we quote it in translation at considerable length, particularly since it has not yet received sufficient attention in modern publications:

> In order to understand better the old musicians and their rules, one should notice that a double or triple mensuration of the *longa*, *brevis* and *semibrevis* exists—that is, a quick ('cita'), a slow ('morosa') and a medium ('media'). This is pointed out also by the moderns. One of them says this: one can sing in three different ways—'tractim,' 'velociter,' and 'medie'; however,

[1] Vitry's reason for distinguishing these five types of *tempus* shows that even this progressive thinker occasionally inclined toward mediaeval scholasticism (*CS* III, 22, 'Et sic apparet . .'): 'And thus it appears that the perfect [*tempus*] is divided into three kinds of prolation just as the perfect [*brevis*] consists of three *semibreves*; and that the imperfect [*tempus*] is of two kinds, corresponding to the fact that the imperfect [*brevis*] contains only two *semibreves*.'

[2] 'Tunc pronunciabantur longa et brevis ita velociter ut nunc tempus imperfectum' (*CS* III, 362). J. Wolf (*GdM* I, 67) maintains, probably rightly, that it should read *tempus perfectum* instead of *tempus imperfectum*. No less definite and conclusive is the statement by Hieronymus de Moravia (*CS* I, 90): 'Nota longa, in cantu ecclesiastico sumpta, habet et habere debet duo tempora modernorum. resolvendo vero sex tempora antiquorum.' Later on he speaks of 'unius temporis modernorum, sed trium temporum antiquorum.'

the notation remains the same in each case.   Another, in limiting himself
to *tempus perfectum*, says: *tempus perfectum* may be of three kinds, namely,
'minimum,' 'medium' and 'maius.'

Here one must know that when the ancients say that *tempus perfectum*
cannot be divided into more than three *semibreves*, they presuppose the
quick mensuration ('cita mensuratio'), as is confirmed by a contemporary
scholar with reference to Franco. . . . In reality, the *semibrevis* is to Franco
the same as the *minima* or 'athoma' is to the moderns, being the ninth part
of the *brevis* and in general considered indivisible.

When the ancients said that the perfect *brevis* can be divided into three
semibreves and not into more, they referred to the customary practice [in
performance] of their time, particularly in the motets. . . . I say particularly in the motets; for if we speak of the hocket . . . the perfect *brevis*
had here such a quick mensuration that one could hardly place three *semibreves* in place of it.   Here . . . one can really speak not of a quick mensuration but rather of a very quick one ('citissima'), since there the perfect
brevis does not last any longer than the *semibrevis minima* [i.e., the *minima*]
does today.

Modern musicians on the contrary frequently employ a slow mensuration.   In reality, in modern writing the third part of the *brevis perfecta*
lasts as long as the *brevis perfecta* was formerly . . . and the *brevis perfecta* is worth as much as the *longa* was formerly. . . .

Thus it is that they [the moderns] attribute to the *semibrevis* . . .
exactly that which is the property of the *brevis*—namely, to be divisible—
and also many other properties which do not belong to it.   In this way
they follow certain [musicians] who attribute to themselves the honor of
inventing [the small note values] although the ancients had already used
the quick mensuration in motets and also the very quick one in the double
hocket.   However, they too have made use occasionally of the slow or
moderate manner ('morosam et mediam'), in which more than three *semibreves* are used in place of the perfect *tempus*.   That eminent composer
Petrus de Cruce . . . made the beginning when he set four *semibreves* for
the perfect *tempus*.

By these remarks the conservative author seeks to defend the doctrine
of Franco, according to which the *S* is the smallest note value ('indivisi-
bilis') against the modern champions of the *M*.   He shows that the *M*
really represents nothing new; its smaller value is only an illusion since
it is compensated in practice by a general tempo three times as slow as
formerly.   Expressed in modern terms the whole change simply amounts
to this: the same tempo is no longer expressed as allegro in half-notes but
as andante in quarter-notes.

A study of the organa and motets from 1200 to 1350 shows that there
occurred four definite changes in the duration of the note values, changes

which, however, entail only two really different tempi, as appears from
the following table:

$$t$$

Perotinus:	D	$= 40$	$L =$	80	$B =$	240
Franco:	L	$= 40$	$B =$	120	$S =$	360
Petrus de Cruce:	L	$= 27$	$B =$	80	$S =$	240
Vitry:	B (pf.)	$= 40$	$S =$	120	$M =$	360
Machaut:	B (pf.)	$= 27$	$S =$	80	$M =$	240

The column marked t represents the *tactus* (beat).[1]

It follows that there occurred twice an almost exact triplication of the
note values, without a real change of tempo, the temporal value M.M. 80
being represented by the L, B, and S around 1225, 1275, and 1350 respectively. A really different tempo, however, is found in the Franconian
motets, and recurs in the early *Ars Nova* (Vitry). It appears that the
terms 'velociter,' 'medie,' and tractim' can be interpreted as indicating
the values M.M. 120, 80, and 40 for the B. The former duration is the
'minimum in plenitudine vocis' of Joh. de Garlandia (*CS* I, 97).

From the point of view of our present study the important conclusion
is that the actual tempo of an *Ars Nova* motet was the same as that of a
Franconian motet; the notation was simply made in smaller values, the
speed of S MMM S S now being the same as that of the former B SSS
B B. This means that, once more, we have to change our scale of reduction, rendering the S by the quarter-notes of modern notation. This
leads to a transcription in *semibrevis*-beat which, as we know, persisted
throughout the fifteenth century.

B. The Notation in the Works of Machaut

The establishment of perfect and imperfect mensuration in the three
degrees of *modus*, *tempus* and *prolatio*, together with the application of the
Franconian principles of perfection, imperfection and alteration to each
of these degrees, led to a notational system which is essentially identical
with that known to us from our study of white notation. In fact, white

---

[1] This table may be compared with that given by H. Besseler in *AfMW* VIII, 212 and reproduced in
G. Reese, *Music in the Middle Ages*, p. 333. It will be seen that our tempi differ from his indication
chiefly in the case of the motets of Petrus de Cruce for which Besseler suggests a considerably slower
tempo (M.M. 54). It goes without saying that our above metronome marks are deliberately
'standardized' and, therefore, should not be taken too literally. They are intended to show not
only that there existed only two different tempi in the period under consideration but, in addition,
that these two tempi are related to each other. As a matter of fact, three quarter notes in M.M. 120
are equal in duration to two quarter notes in M.M. 80. It appears that, for instance, Franco's
tempo results by dividing the D of the Perotinus tempo in three, instead of two, parts.

notation is, in principle as well as in most details, nothing but a graphological modification of the fourteenth century French notation, with white shapes used instead of the black ones. Therefore few explanations are necessary in addition to those given previously.

The earliest source of fourteenth century French notation is the MS Ivrea.[1] Its notational features are practically the same as those of the various MSS containing the works of Machaut (1300-1377), to which the subsequent explanations chiefly refer.

Imperfection and Alteration. Whereas in the thirteenth century these devices were limited to the *L* and *B*, they can now be applied in any perfect degree. In addition to the *imperfectio ad totum* (*L* – *B*; *B* – *S*; *S* – *M*), the *imperfectio ad partem* is used (*L* – *S*; *B* – *M*), and theorists hastened to expand this scheme by the addition of *imperfectio ad partem remotam* and *partes remotas* (*Mx* – *S*; *L* – *M*), as well as of *imperfectio ad partem remotissimam* and *partes remotissimas* (*Mx* – *M*).[2] They take a particular delight in constructing tricky examples showing the combination of imperfection and alteration.[3] As a curiosity the following example from Tunstede (*CS* IV, 270; see also *GdM* I, 129) may be cited:

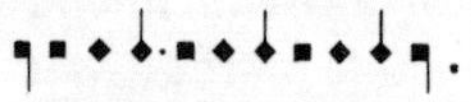

Here the mensuration is [III, 3, *3*]. The *punctus* indicates the end of a group of notes equal to a perfect *L*. The *L* itself is imperfected by a *B* which in turn is imperfected by a *S* which again is imperfected by a *M*. A second group of the same value is contained between the *punctus* and the final *L*. In order to reach the value of three *B* or nine *S*, one must double the value of the second *B* (alteration). However, both the *B recta* and the *B altera* are imperfected by the group *S* – *M* which follows each of them. Here is the transcription:

Needless to say, no such tricks occur in the musical sources. Their difficulty lies in clerical errors or inaccuracies rather than in deliberate intricacies of notation. Most frequently the complications are caused by the lack of a *punctus divisionis* which would be necessary or at least helpful in clarifying the situation. Below are two examples from Machaut's Mass. In (a) the normal grouping of the four *B* between the two *L*

[1] See the description by H. Besseler in *AfMW* VII, 174.

[2] See p. 112.

[3] See p. 122.

would be 1 + 3; however, the context shows that they have to be divided as follows: 3 + 1 (imperfection of the following, instead of the preceding *L*). Example (b) shows a similar case of seven *B* which, according to the context, must be grouped 3 + 3 + 1, instead of 1 + 3 + 3. In both cases, a *punctus divisionis* after the first *L* would have been sufficient fully to clarify the rhythm:[1]

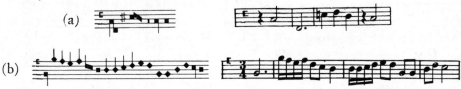

(a) cf. *GdM* II, 29, staff 5; (b) cf. *GdM* II, 35, staff 8.

An interesting license of Machaut is illustrated by the following examples of *imperfectio ad partem:*

[III, 2]: ♩◆-³⁄₂|♩♩♩| [3, 2]: ■♩-³⁄₄|♩♩♩|

Such use of imperfection does not correspond to strict theory, according to which imperfection may be caused only by a note which belongs to a perfect mensuration or, in modern terms, which is one-third of the next higher value. In the above examples, however, the 'imperfecting' note is one-half of the next higher degree. As a matter of fact, an example like the above is extremely rare in the sources of mensural notation. It seems that Machaut alone was open-minded enough to transgress the theoretical limitations and to admit a freer, yet perfectly logical and simple use of imperfection.[2] Two examples from the ballade *De petit po* are quoted by Wolf in *GdM* I, 171 (without indication of the MS source):

---

[1] In these two examples our thirteenth century scheme of transcription (*B* = quarter-note) is used because the entire mass is evidently written in *brevis*-beat. This fact is one of the various features proving that Machaut's mass is one of his earliest works, possibly written under the immediate influence of the mass of Tournay (see G. Reese, *Music in the Middle Ages*, p. 356). There should be an end to the story, inaugurated by Kiesewetter one hundred years ago and still repeated in modern books, that Machaut's mass was written for the coronation of Charles V in 1364.

[2] Machaut was known among his contemporaries for his freedom in the treatment of established principles of notation, as we know from his contemporary Johannes de Muris (see *GdM* I, 170). It is interesting to recall in this connection Glarean's similar remark about Josquin de Près, two hundred years later (see p. 108, footnote 2).

The following passage from the ballade *Plourez dames* (beginning of the contra) illustrates the use of imperfection in [3, 3]:

The first three *puncti* mark off groups totalling the value of a perfect *B*. The second and the third *B* are reduced by *imperfectio ad partes* from nine *S* to the minimum number of four *S*. The next perfection would seem to include the group *MBM*, after which there is another *punctus*. Actually, however, this group has the total value, not of nine *S*, but only of six, the three missing *S* being supplied by the two following *M* (with alteration). A similar group occurs at the end of the passage (for the complete piece, see *GdM* II, no. xxv):

Determination of the Mensuration.   In the sources of the French *Ars Nova* the note values *Mx, L, B, S,* and *M* are used in the various combinations of *modus, tempus,* and *prolatio.* However, the mensuration is almost never indicated by signs but must be derived from the context.[1]   Herein lies the chief difficulty presented to the novice by the works of Machaut.

In his *Geschichte der Mensuralnotation* J. Wolf has treated the subject of the determination of the mensuration in a special chapter (*GdM* I, 150), containing 34 rules by means of which this problem is to be solved. F. Ludwig (*SIMG* VI, 607) criticises this procedure as unnecessarily complicated and recommends that one rely chiefly on the musical sense of the composition or the part—that is, he should recognize the mensuration from the rhythmical nature of the entire melody rather than from single details.   In particular, he points out that in many cases the mensuration is indicated in the original MSS by the writing of notes in groups (e.g., groups of three *S* written close together would indicate *tempus perfectum,* etc.) and regrets that this important detail of notation is obscured in Wolf's reproductions (*GdM* II).

Ludwig's advice is thoroughly justified and we repeat here the sugges-

---

[1] Such time signatures are mentioned by nearly all the theorists of the fourteenth century; see the comprehensive table in *GdM* I 101. The absence of such signs in most of the compositions is all the more striking when one considers that Jacobus, the champion of the *Ars Antiqua*, bitterly complains about their use (*CS* II 431: 'Haec et multa alia ponunt moderni. . . .').

tion given previously that one try to sing short sections of each voice before attempting to transcribe it. On the other hand, however, some of the rules given by Wolf prove to be useful and indeed necessary. Below is a presentation of these rules condensed and put into different order:

1. Rests. The rests are the surest and most valuable aid in recognizing the mensuration. The rest of three *tempora* ☰ unequivocally indicates *modus perfectus* (III), while the combination ☰ invariably indicates *modus imperfectus* (II). A single rest of two *tempora* may occur in both *modi*; obviously however in III it must always be accompanied by a preceding or following *B*: ☰ ☰ . If it should appear between two *L*, the *modus* is imperfect: ☰ . Also two successive binary rests indicate II: ☰ , since in III the same duration would be expressed by ☰ .

As regards the *tempus* (or *prolatio*), a clue is frequently found in the writing of two successive *S* (or *M*) rests. Such rests occur either on the same line of the staff, ☰ , or on two different lines, ☰ , according to whether they belong to the same or two different groups of two or three *S* (or *M*). Whereas the latter way of writing can be used in either perfect or imperfect mensuration, the former will be found only if the *tempus* (or *prolatio*) is perfect. As a matter of fact, in imperfect mensuration two such rests would occupy a full group of two *S* (or *M*) and, therefore, will have to be replaced by a *B* (or *S*) rest. It follows, that two *S* (or *M*) rests written on the same line indicate *tempus perfectum* (or *prolatio perfecta*).

2. Notes. A generally trustworthy indication of perfect mensuration is found in the occurrence of groups of three notes of the same kind between two of the next higher value, e.g.:

III: ◗▪▪▪▪◖ ; 3: ▪◆◆◆◆▪ ; 3: ◆♩♩♩♩◆ .

Of course, such a combination may occur in imperfect mensuration as well, namely, as a syncopated rhythm: ▪◆◆◆▪ = |♩|♩♩|♩|♩♩|♩ . However, in this case a fourth note of the same value will always be found in close proximity which will complete the gap left by the syncopation. Syncopation is very frequent in the French *Ars Nova* and may easily obscure the mensuration. The more frequently combinations such as *B SSS B* (*S MMM S*) appear, the more likely they are to indicate perfect mensuration. Similar deductions may be made from the appearance of an isolated note between two others of the next higher value. Persistent alternation of *B* and *S* (or *S* and *M*) generally indicates that the *tempus* (or *prolatio*) is perfect: ■◆■◆■◆ (3); ◆♩◆♩◆♩ (3). Again, however, the possibility of syncopation has to be taken into account:

◆♩◆♩◆♩◆♩◆ = $\frac{2}{4}$ |♩♫|♫♩|♪♩♪|♩ .

Frequent groups of two point to imperfect mensuration, although they may also occur in perfect mensuration, with alteration of the second note. The conclusion in favor of imperfect mensuration becomes more binding if the last note of such a group is replaced by its 'valor,' i.e., by smaller notes of the same value, since in such a case alteration is impossible. However, a combination such as *B S MM B* is also possible in *tempus perfectum* if both *imperfectio a parte post* and *imperfectio a parte ante* are applied: ■◆♩♩■ = $\frac{3}{4}$ |♩♩|♫♩| .

3. Dots. Here we must recall the statement previously made (p. 116 f) that there are in reality only two kinds of *puncti*—the *punctus divisionis* in perfect mensuration, and the *punctus additionis* in imperfect mensuration. The latter demands the presence of a note of the next smaller value to supply the missing part of the beat. Therefore, if such a note is not present (either following immediately or in close proximity) the dot must be a *punctus divisionis* and therefore points to perfect mensuration.

4. Red notes. In this period, red notes (which, by the way, appear only in tenors) have the same significance as blackened notes have in white notation: three red notes are equal to two black ones (*proportio sesquialtera*, or *hemiolia*). Although in white notation blackening (coloration) is used in both perfect and imperfect mensuration, in early fourteenth century music the use of red notes occurs chiefly, if not exclusively, in perfect mensuration, which is thus temporarily changed into imperfect mensuration. As we have seen previously (p. 131), coloration of *breves* (for instance) causes a change not only in the *tempus* but also in the *modus*. The appearance of red *B* points therefore not only to *tempus perfectum* but also to *modus imperfectus* in the black notes. The passages notated in red (reproduced below as white notes) are then in *tempus imperfectum* and *modus perfectus*: ■◆◆◆□□□ = $\frac{3}{4}$ |♩·|♩♩♩|$\frac{3}{2}$ ♩♩♩| .

It is scarcely possible to give more detailed information on this subject, since everything depends upon the context. In this connection it should be noted that many of the rules given by Wolf are by no means as infallible as he suggests. As an example we may take the rule I, 7 of his list, according to which *modus perfectus* is understood 'wenn hinter drei breves sich ein Punkt befindet': ■◆◆·· . This conclusion is by no means certain. If a *S* were to follow the dot, the dot might then be a *punctus additionis* and the *modus* might be imperfect: ▪▪▪·♦=|♩|♩|♩|♩♩| . Also rule 8 of the same group ('wenn die einer longa folgende longa einen Punkt hat') is incorrect; ❡❡· may mean |o·|o·| as well as |o|o|♩ (with a following *B*).

It should be noticed that several compositions of Machaut display a mixture of mensurations, another feature illustrating his free treatment of the theoretical rules. For instance, in his rondeau *Rose lis*, passages such as those given under (a) clearly point to [3, 2], while others such as under (b) no less definitely suggest [2, 3]:

Obviously, the rhythm changes here from one mensuration to the other, e.g.:

For more details, see *GdM* i, 168, and F. Ludwig, *Guillaume de Machaut, Musikalische Werke* (Leipzig, 1926), i, 60.

Ouvert and Clos. Finally, the problem presented by the repetition of sections in the secular forms of the fourteenth century (ballade, rondeau, virelai) must be briefly considered. The ballade, for instance, consists of two sections, the first of which is provided with two lines of text and must be repeated, so that the form A A B results. The repeated section usually has two different endings which are sometimes designated *ouvert* and *clos* and which correspond to our *prima volta* and *seconda volta*. However, these cadential passages are not as clearly marked off as they are in modern music and, therefore, demand special attention.

The ballade *De petit po* may be considered as a first example. Following is a reproduction (from MS Paris, B.N. *frç. 9221*) of the passage near the end of section A, beginning with simultaneous notes (the mensuration is [3, 2]):

In each voice, the end of A (*prima volta*) is indicated by a single long stroke, whereas the *seconda volta* group extends from this stroke to the double stroke, after which the second section *B* begins. This *clos* group, of course, is not meant to follow after the last note of the *ouvert* group, but to be sung in place of a corresponding part of the *prima volta*.   The main question, then, is to decide at which point to leave the *ouvert* and substitute the *clos* group.   It is in their failure to indicate this point that the manuscripts of this period differ from modern practice.   The situation is usually made clear to some extent by the fact that the *clos* group at its beginning repeats one or several notes of the *ouvert* group; therefore, the initial notes of the *clos* group serve as a clue as to where the *ouvert* group starts.[1]   Here follows the transcription of the passage:

It must be noticed, however, that this is an exceptionally simple example for two reasons: first, because, in each single voice, the *clos* group has the same length as the corresponding *ouvert* group; second, because the length of these groups is the same in all three voices.   Neither regularity is requisite or even usual.   The following passage from the ballade *S'amours ne fait* (see *GdM* II, no. XXIII) may serve as an illustration:

In the discant, the lines of demarcation appear as short strokes which, having the shape of *B* rests, may easily mislead the novice.   The *clos* group of the discant includes three *B* and the final *L* (the mensuration is [2, 3]), while the *ouvert* group, beginning with the same two notes as the *clos* group, includes only two *B* and the final *L*.   Similarly, the tenor has five notes (four *B* and one *L*) in the *clos* group, but only four (three *B* and one *L*) in the *ouvert* group which, of course, opens with the second note of the ligature.   It appears not only that within each part are the

---

[1] Another clue is provided by the distribution of the second line of text.   However, owing to the habitual carelessness of the scribes in the underlaying of the text, these indications cannot always be relied upon.

two groups unequal in length, but also that there is a 'vertical' variation from one part to the other:

	Ouvert	*Clos*
Cantus:	$2\,B + L$	$3\,B + L$
Tenor:	$3\,B + L$	$4\,B + L$

It is particularly this vertical variation which calls for attention. It implies that the performers of the two parts must change from their *ouvert* group to their *clos* group at different times. Although, from the point of view of part-performance, this is a perfectly legitimate procedure (it is obviously dictated by the desire to make the endings as short as possible), it causes some inconvenience if a transcription in score is to be made. Here the *clos* group must be filled out with certain notes which do not appear in the original. These are indicated in brackets in the subsequent transcriptions. Asterisks are added to show the places in the original notation where the singer must leap to the *clos* group.

Naturally, the first measure of the *seconda volta* may be omitted in the final draft, as it happens to be identical with the corresponding measure of the *prima volta*. In this case, the signs 1 and 2 must be shifted forward by one measure.

An example showing a different 'jumping-off place' in each of its three parts is furnished by the ballade *Ploures dames*. Below is a reproduction of the passage in question:

In the discant and contra, the end of the *prima volta* is indicated by a small stroke in the shape of a *B* rest, while a sign x indicates the corresponding place of the tenor. It appears that in this example the strokes

have the meaning of real rests; they are the equivalent of the group of
the tenor between the *L* and the asterisk.[1] The only clue for the
'jumping-off place' in each part is found in the fact that the initial note
(or notes) of the *seconda volta* reiterate the corresponding notes of the
prima volta. Thus, the *S* on e' in the discant refers back to the final *L*
on e', while in the lower parts the indication is a good deal clearer on
account of the fact that a small group of notes, identical in pitches as
well as in values, is reiterated. In the above example these points of
reference are marked by the letters a and b. It is important to notice
that in the score the relative position of the signs b for the *seconda volta*
always conforms to that of the signs a for the *prima volta*. This observation provides a helpful cue as to where to start with the *clos*-endings of
the different voice parts. In the present example the *clos*-ending of the
contra starts one measure, that of the discant two measures after that of
the tenor. The empty measures (two in the superius, one in the contra)
must be filled in with the notes found in the corresponding measures of
the *prima volta*.

Examples.   We turn now to the consideration of several compositions by
Machaut.   Facsimile 68 shows a two-part ballade *Ne pensez pas*. The
frequent groups *S – M* indicate *prolatio perfecta*, as do still more clearly
the two *M* rests followed by a third *M* near the beginning of the second
staff. As to the *tempus*, the two *S* rests in the first staff (second half)
following the *S* over the syllable '-e' point to *tempus perfectum*. The
mensuration [3, 3] is also implied by the group of notes found between
the first *L* of the cantus (syllable 'pas') and the next *B*.

   This piece illustrates the difficulties brought about by the too sparing
use of the *punctus divisionis* in Machaut's works. Actually, this sign is
all the more necessary here, since in the present mensuration the *B* can
be reduced by various degrees of imperfection from its normal value of
nine *M* to as little as four *M* (see p. 122). However, the correct group-

---

[1] The transcription of this passage in *GdM* III, 69 is not quite correct.

FACSIMILE 68

MS Paris, Bibliothèque Nationale *frç. 1584 (ca.* 1375)
From page 459'

ing is rarely indicated by a *punctus divisionis*, but must be determined by other considerations. For instance, in the group to the value of six (perfect) *S* right after the first *B* of the discant, the 'Franconian' grouping $6 = 1 + 3 + 2$ (involving imperfection and alteration) is impossible because the last *S* is replaced by the combination $S + M$ which, of course, cannot undergo alteration. The proper grouping therefore is $6 = 3 + 3$, so that the initial *B* remains perfect. In the group of nine *S* to the text: 'vous ne pen-' (fourth staff) the desired grouping $9 = 3 + 3 + 3$ is suggested by the writing of the notes in close groups, a feature which frequently provides a helpful clue. However, the second *B* on staff 3 remains perfect although it is written close to a *S* and *M*. In all cases of doubt, the correct values must be derived from the context.

The *clos* group of the discant (syllable 'foy') includes only one *L*, that of the tenor a *S* and *B* in addition to a *L*, so that some notes must be inserted in the discant. Unfortunately, the writing gives no clear indication as to the place where one has to make the jump to the *clos* group or, in other words, where the *ouvert* group begins. Below are two transcriptions which illustrate the situation. The second is that given by F. Ludwig (*Machaut*, 1, 9). The first seems preferable not only from the musical point of view, but particularly with regard to the underlaying of the text. In fact, in Ludwig's transcription the place of the syllable 'foy' is willfully changed.[1]

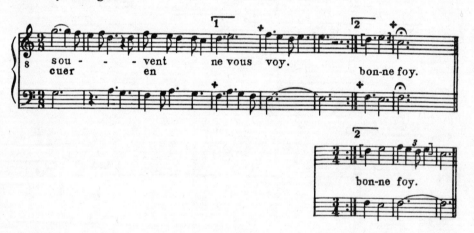

The two sharps on the fourth staff refer to the note f, not g. The form of the piece is that of a ballade, i.e., A A B, the first section being repeated. The beginning is transcribed in the appendix, No. 47.

[1] It may be remarked here that F. Ludwig, in his edition of Machaut, practically always interprets adjacent notes of equal pitch as tied notes, by connecting them with a dotted tie. We cannot see any justification for this procedure.

The two-part ballade *Dous amis* of Facsimile 69 has the less usual form A A B B, both sections being repeated. Since it includes several *L* (see also the first two ligatures of the tenor) the mensuration involves not only *tempus* and *prolatio*, but also *modus*. The combination *B L B L B* at the beginning of the tenor strongly suggests *modus perfectus*, as does also the corresponding passage of the discant. The groups of smaller notes, such as *S M M*, or *M M M M*, clearly point to imperfect *tempus* and *prolatio*. The mensuration is, therefore, [III, 2, 2]. However, the *modus* is not always strictly observed. For instance, the tenor for section A includes 31 *B* prior to the final note of the *ouvert* group, that is, prior to the last note of staff 4—which by the way, should properly be written as a *L* (see the last note of the *clos* group). This number is one too many to fill in perfections of three *B* each, so that one measure must be expanded to include four half-notes, as indicated below. It may be noticed that this change of meter would be unnecessary if the *punctus divisionis* after the first *ternaria* of the tenor were considered as a clerical error; in fact, the corresponding note of the *cantus* (*L* over '-plaint'; this *L* is written with an upward stem which, however, does not have the meaning of a *plica*) has no dot. If this conjecture is adopted, the two *L* would be imperfected by the following *B*, a procedure which would reduce the number of *B* to 30 (see below, version (a)).

A similar case of irregular measures occurs in the second section which contains 28 *B* before the final note. As before, this number can be reduced to 27 if the *punctus divisionis* after the third *L* of the tenor is disregarded (once more, the corresponding *L* of the discant—end of the second staff—has no *punctus*). The student is advised to make two transcriptions and to compare them, not only from the notational point of view, but also from that of the musical phrase.[1]

In both sections A and B the *clos* groups of the tenor (beginning of staff 5 and end of staff 6) include 3 *B* before the final note, while the corresponding groups of the discant (second staff, middle, between the two

---

[1] F. Ludwig's transcription (*Machaut* 1, 5) introduces numerous changes of meter ($\frac{3}{2}$, $\frac{4}{2}$, $\frac{2}{2}$) which are not indicated in the original notation and which, from the point of view of the musical phrase, are frequently not convincing. The same remark applies to many of his transcriptions.

pseudo *B*-rests,[1] and a similar group at the end of staff 3) include notes
of the value of only one *B* before the final note. Hence, notes to the
value of two *B* must be supplied in the transcription of the discant. It
may be noted that the final notes of the various sections are written always as *B* in the discant, whereas in the tenor they are written partly as
B, partly as *L*. In any case, their duration is not exactly determined,
so that a fermata sign would properly indicate their character.

The sign before the *B* in the middle of the first staff is a ♭. At the end of the second
staff one finds a sharp for the *L* on g, a sign which probably is not valid for the following
M on the same pitch, since otherwise a chromatic progression g♯, a, b♭ would result.

Finally, a three-part ballade *Biaute qui toutes autres* (Facsimile 70)
may be studied, which is particularly interesting because it is one of the
earliest compositions to show the use of Vitry's signs ○C (see the
tenor). The tenor starts out in [3, 2] which is the normal mensuration
of the whole piece, but changes three times to [2, 2]. The first and the
third sections in [2, 2] are lengthy examples of syncopation, in the scheme
S B B B . . . B B S. The sign C makes all these *B* binary whereas
under the sign ○ they would be ternary. Other manuscripts indicate
the binary value of these *B* by the use of red notes (e.g., Paris, B.N. *frç.*
1586) or white notes (Paris, B.N. *frç. 1585*): ○■C⊤■■■■■♦♦○■ =

Below is a transcription of the beginning of the tenor:

The transcription of the other parts presents no difficulties. The second *B* of the contratenor is perfect, as is suggested, in a vague manner,
by the arrangement of the subsequent *S* in ligatures *c.o.p.* In fact, it is
more natural for such a ligature to be placed within one perfection; however, this is by no means a universal usage.

In Machaut's motets it is principally the tenors which show notational
features of interest. Many of them are 'isorhythmic,' that is, they repeat several times a long and elaborate rhythmic pattern called *talea*.
This principle of rhythmic reiteration is evidently a continuation and

---

[1] I.e., the two dashes which look exactly like *B*-rests, but actually are lines of demarcation.

FACSIMILE 69

MS Paris, Bibliothèque Nationale *frç. 1584 (ca.* 1375)
From page 456[']

development of the modal patterns of the thirteenth century. Just as in the Franconian motets the liturgical tenor was forced to conform, for example, to the rhythmic scheme of the first ordo of the third mode |♩.|♩♩|♩.|-.|, so we find here schemes of longer extension and of freer design, as for example in the motet *He mors-Quare non sum* in which each *talea* comprises eleven *L* (see below, A, B, C). Another principle of construction to be found in nearly all the motets of Machaut is the writing in two sections (I, II), the second of which repeats the tenor of the first in diminution.[1] Thus, our tenor continues (after a fourth incomplete *talea* D) with three groups a, b, c, each of which includes eleven *B*, replacing each note of the first section by its half:

As appears from the rests, the tenor is in *modus imperfectus*, i.e., with the *L* equal to two *B*. The *tempus* and *prolatio* which, of course, must be determined from the upper parts, is [2, 3], so that each *B* occupies one $\frac{6}{8}$-measure, each *L* two, each *Mx* four:

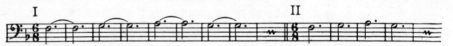

In section II the grouping of notes and rests suggests phrases of three measures each or, in other words, *modus perfectus* (see *GdM* II, no. xiv).

A more complicated structure is found in the four-voiced motet *Felix virgo—Inviolata—Ad te suspiramus—*(contratenor), the tenor and contra of which are reproduced on page 360.

The motet begins with a long 'Introitus' which, in the two lower parts, includes eight rests each of the value of a perfect *L* and notes to the value of six perfect *L*. The double bar after this indicates the beginning of the main portion which shows alternation of groups of black and red notes in both parts. As is indicated by the inscription 'Nigre sunt perfecte, et rubee imperfecte,' the black notes are in perfect mensuration, i.e., perfect *modus*, the red ones in imperfect. Each black *L*, therefore, equals three *B*, each red *L* two. Of particular interest is the fact that the black and red notes do not appear simultaneously in both parts, but in alternation. As a matter of fact, the initial group of the tenor (after the Introi-

---

[1] The cantus firmus melody itself is called *color*. See G. Reese, *Music in the Middle Ages*, 339.

FACSIMILE 70

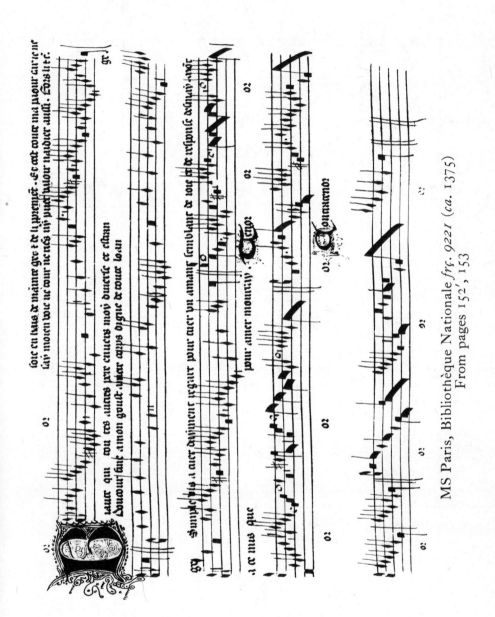

MS Paris, Bibliothèque Nationale *fr̄. 9221 (ca. 1375)*
From pages 152, 153

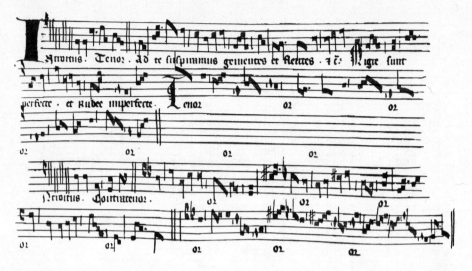

tus) includes six perfect *L*, equal to eighteen *B*, while the initial group of
the contra includes nine imperfect *L* which also equal eighteen *B*. This
scheme of alternation continues throughout the entire motet. As usual
with Machaut, the tenor and contra are repeated in the diminution.
The beginning of this final section is indicated in the contra by three long
'bar-lines' (not rests) although a similar sign is missing in the tenor. As
can be seen from the identical succession of pitches, as well as from the use
of smaller values (*S*), the diminution section begins after the first quaternaria of staff 2. Here the black and red notes indicate perfect or imperfect *tempus*, so that six black *B* or nine red *B* are equal to eighteen *S*.

The upper parts (not reproduced here, but to be found in *GdM* II, 24-
27) are in [2, *3*], that is, in $\frac{6}{8}$-meter with imperfect *modus* (binary *L*)
throughout. For simplicity's sake this meter has been disregarded in
the subsequent transcription (see p. 361) in which the *B* are rendered
as plain half-notes (instead of dotted half-notes), each of which equals a
$\frac{6}{8}$-measure of the upper parts. They are grouped in $\frac{3}{2}$- or $\frac{2}{2}$-measures,
according to the mensuration indicated by the black or red notes. The
small notes on top of the staff indicate the rhythm of the discant (D).

C. The Notation of the Later Sources

The French notation just described, which on account of its clarity
and simplicity may be regarded as the classical notation of the Middle
Ages, persisted with but slight modification through the first half of the
fifteenth century. Indeed, in a sense it continued to exist much longer,
since the white mensural notation is its direct continuation, with the
black notes supplanted by white ones. Aside from the manuscripts

containing the works of Machaut, the preserved repertory of fourteenth
century pieces written in French notation is rather limited, as appears
from the list given on p. 202. Additional material for the study of this
period is available in the reproductions, contained in *SchT*, p. 80-82, of
the fragment Bern, Bibl. Bongarsiana *Ms. A 421*. The study of these
facsimiles is strongly recommended. The beginning of the cantus of
the ballade *Il n'est si grand possession* (p. 82) illustrates a very free
application of the principle of imperfection:

The initial *L* is reduced here by the following *M*, although the mensuration of the piece is imperfect in all degrees ([II, 2, 2]):

Similar cases are cited in *GdM* 1, 183 and 323.

The fifteenth century sources of French notation (see the list, p. 202) show an increased use of red notes which now appear in all the parts. They usually occur in groups of three *B* or three *S*, that is, in the familiar combinations of coloration (three red notes equal to two black ones). Aside from these groups one finds single red *M* which have the meaning of an *Sm*. A three-voiced *Kyrie* and *Christe* from Cambrai *Ms. 6* may serve as an illustration (Facsimile 71; in the original the discant is written on p. 4′, the tenor and contra on p. 5; the red notes are reproduced here as white shapes). The discant of the *Kyrie* contains several red *Sm*, the contra red *Sm* as well as coloration-groups. The second red ligature of the contra (*L-B*) appears in syncopated position, being inserted between the second and third of a group of six *M*. Similar examples have been encountered in our study of pieces from the MS Canonici (p. 133, 134) which is only slightly later than the MS Cambrai. As will be seen later, this use of syncopation is only a modest reminiscence of those rhythmic complexities of the late fourteenth century which will be treated in our last chapter (Mannered Notation). Here follows the beginning of the contra in transcription:

The *Christe* is written in *tempus imperfectum diminutum*, that is, in about twice its apparent speed. The beat falls here on the *B* which, therefore, must be transcribed as a quarter note. It should be noted that this section contains no *Sm* which here would be too rapid to be performed.[1]

The same notational methods occur in other manuscripts of the period, such as Rome, Vat. *urb. lat. 1411* (see the examples in *GdM* i, 193); Munich, *mus. ms. 3192* (*GdM* i, 194, 195); Bologna, Lic. mus. *cod. 37* H. E. Wooldridge, *Early English Harmony*, pl. 49–60; *GdM* i, 198); Bologna, Bibl. Univ. *2216* (*GdM* i, 199 ff); Oxford, *Selden B 26* (facsimile reproduction in J. Stainer, *Early Bodleian Music*, i, pl. 37–97 and 109; see *GdM* i, 368 ff); and the Old Hall Manuscript (ed. by A. Ramsbotham and H. B. Collins, 3 vls., Westminster, 1935-38; see *GdM* i, 373 ff),—the last two of English origin. The reproductions given in *GdM* ii, nos. XXX—XXXVII provide additional material for the study of the notation of the Dufay period. Regarding no. XXXVI (Dufay) it may be mentioned that the section 'Qui ipsa . . . dubitationem' (p. 57), marked 'faulx bourdon,' calls for the addition of a third part which is a

[1] See footnote of p. 193.

FACSIMILE 71

MS Cambrai, Bibliothèque Communale *Ms. 6* (*ca.* 1425)
From pages 4′, 5

fourth below the written discant throughout (J. Wolf's transcription, vol. iii, p. 87–88 gives only the two notated parts).[1] The section 'Quamvis benedixeris' (p. 59) is also in "faulx bourdon," with two notated parts. Unfortunately, the lower part is missing in the source used by Wolf. It may be noticed that the transcriptions of pieces from Bologna, *cod. 37*, which are given in vol. II of *Early English Harmony*, contain numerous errors. These are due chiefly to a failure to realize the correct meaning of alteration and of the red notes (compare, e.g., the facsimiles pl. 51, 52 of vol. I with the transcription in vol. II, p. 120).

Owing to its notational peculiarities, the Old Hall MS, which was written in the first half of the fifteenth century, deserves a few explanatory remarks. The most striking feature is the extensive use of score arrangement, a method of writing which, as has been stated previously (see p. 271) was generally abandoned after the school of Notre Dame and which was not readmitted for the writing down of ensemble music until the early seventeenth century. Its use in the Old Hall MS is, no doubt, a feature of typically English conservatism, similar in nature to those which have been observed in our study of English keyboard music of the sixteenth century (see p. 8 ff). The score arrangement is used for all the pieces which are written in the conductus style of the thirteenth century, i.e., with similar rhythm in all the parts. For an example see the frontispiece of vol. III of Ramsbotham's publication. On staves 8, 10, and 11 of this facsimile there occur examples of a rare ligature to which reference has been made in footnote 1 of p. 90.

Facsimile 72 shows a page from the Old Hall MS containing a *Et in terra* by J. Tyes. The notation is without problems, except for the question of the temporal relationship between the sections in ₵ and in C which alternate several times. This question, however, is clearly answered by the tenor which shows black notes for the former sections, red notes for the latter. It follows that the B of C is two-thirds of the B under ₵, or in other words, that the M have equal duration throughout the piece. Therefore, a transcription in $\frac{6}{8}$-meter alternating with $\frac{4}{8}$-$(\frac{2}{4})$

* meter results, with the eighth-note unchanged.

An understanding of the examples in *GdM* I, 374 ff., illustrating the use of red and white notes in the Old Hall MS will be facilitated by the remark that in the examples la) and lb) we have *color prolationis*, in those under 2a) and 2b), *color temporis*. The former indicates the change from [2, *3*] to [*3*, 2], the latter from [II, 3] to [III, 2]. The examples 3a), 3b), 4a) show the use of white or red M in the meaning of a Sm, a practice

---

[1] See the explanations on improvised fauxbourdon (*supra librum*) in H. Riemann, *Geschichte der Musiktheorie*, Leipzig, 1898, p. 142 ff. Also M. Bukofzer, *Geschichte des Englischen Diskants*, 1936.

FACSIMILE 72

Old Hall MS
Old Hall, Catholic College of St. Edmund (*ca.* 1425)
Page 15

which was already observed in our previous facsimile. The MS contains several pieces in which this meaning of coloration, that is, halving of the normal value, is applied to whole passages written in *B*, *S*, and *M*. The following reproduction (beginning of an *Et in terra* by Pycard, p. 21' of the MS) illustrates this usage:

Here the white *B*, *S*, and *M* are identical in value with the black *S*, *M*, and *Sm* respectively.[1]

Although the majority of the pieces in the Old Hall MS are written in the simple French notation, there are a number which present considerable problems, some of which are mentioned in the introductory notes to vol. III (pp. xxi ff and xxvi ff) of the modern publication. Here we must confine ourselves to an example illustrating the canon-technique of the tenors. Below is the tenor of a motet by Sturgeon *Salve mater Domini —Salve templum gratiae—In nomine Domini* (p. 92 of the MS), which in the modern publication (vol. III, xxviii) is described as 'particularly puzzling':

This, indeed, it is, and it goes without saying that with a tenor like this all hopes to arrive at a solution by deduction exclusively must be abandoned. Only through an experimental procedure, following the completion of the upper parts which are free from notational problems, will the puzzle presented by the tenor be solved. While this practical goal has been fully achieved by the editor of the Old Hall MS (see vol. III, 51), his explanation of the enigma is not satisfactory. First of all, it must be mentioned that the original contains a clerical error: the last two of the mensuration signs should appear in the reverse order. Only by this assumption does the table of values, given by Collins, become understandable. In order to obtain an insight into the construction of this tenor it is best to begin with the sign ○, indicating *tempus perfectum*. Here it must

[1] See the complete transcription in vol. I, p. 76 ff of the publication.

be noticed, that in this tenor, as in many others of the Old Hall MS and of other English sources of the fifteenth and sixteenth century, the *modus* is usually understood to be perfect.[1] Thus, the actual mensuration is [III, 3], leading to groups of three $\frac{3}{4}$-measures in the transcription. Considering now the first group of black values: $(S).(S) (B) B L (S) (S)$, it appears that the whole group contains notes to the equivalent of two perfect L, the first of which is replaced by a group of two B, with alteration of the second B. The resulting larger values, however, are imperfected by the S-rests through a very peculiar process which can only be understood if the *punctus* at the beginning is interpreted as a *punctus syncopationis*, calling for an imaginary bar-line after the first quarter-rest.[2] To explain the situation from the point of view of the singer, the *punctus* directs to count, not 1 2 3 , 4 5 6 , 7 8 9 , 1 2 . . 9 (two L of nine S each), but: 1 ; 1 2 3, . . . 9, 1 2 3, . . 8. Once this meaning of the dot is understood, the rest is relatively simple. In the first of the two groups: $(S) (B) B$, the second B must altered, but also imperfected by the (S), since the B-rest cannot be imperfected. Therefore, the signs have the values of 1, 3, and 5 S respectively. The total value of the second group, $L (S) (S)$, is reduced from nine to eight by the syncopation. The two final S-rests reduce the L from eight to six S. Following is the transcription of the black notes:

The red notes indicate change from perfect to imperfect *tempus*. Since the *modus* remains perfect, the B must be altered, leading to the values of 2, 4, and 6 S for $(B) B L$. There follows a second *talea* in the same notation and rhythm.

The first presentation of the tenor, in ⊙ , is, of course, the exact triplication of the above values, owing to the augmenting character of the *prolatio perfecta*. Each S of the *integer valor* becomes a perfect B. A correct evaluation of the second representation, in ℂ , is obtained if each S of the *integer valor* is read as an imperfect B; thus all the values of the above transcription are to be doubled. This, of course, is not the correct meaning of this mensuration in which, properly speaking, no imperfection of a B by a S would be possible. It is only here, then, that we must admit a fault in what otherwise may be termed a perfect example of fifteenth century notational arithmetic,—higher arithmetic, to be sure. ∗

[1] In the example under consideration this is expressly indicated by the remark 'De modo perfecto.'
[2] See the detailed explanation of syncopation, p. 395 ff.

VII. ITALIAN NOTATION

A. THE ORIGIN OF ITALIAN NOTATION

WHILE the French music of the fourteenth century represents for us the result of a long development, the characteristics of which we can recognize in all their essential points, the evolution leading to the Italian *Ars Nova* is veiled in obscurity. That there was in Italy an activity in the field of part music as early as the thirteenth century can scarcely be doubted for several reasons. First, the earliest preserved Italian compositions, dating from the mid-fourteenth century (Jacopo da Bologna, Giovanni da Cascia) by no means bear the stamp of a first attempt, but rather exhibit remarkable traits of individuality and perfection. To be sure, the term individuality should not be construed to suggest complete freedom from outside influence. Such influence can clearly be seen in the fact that the style of early Italian polyphony is obviously derived from the *conductus* style of the French *Ars Antiqua*, and that there exist French models for the *caccia* which, for a long time, has been considered a purely native type of Italian music.[1] However, these facts do not invalidate the above statement, but only show that Italian music must have had sufficient time to develop those indigenous traits which distinguish the earliest preserved examples from those of contemporary French music.

More definite evidence of the origins of Italian polyphonic music is to be found in the field of musical theory, that is, in the *Pomerium musicae mensuratae* of Marchettus de Padua. This important treatise, which was written nearly simultaneously with Vitry's *Ars nova (ca.* 1325),[2]

---

[1] See the French *chace* from the MS Paris, B. N. *Coll. de Pic. 67* which has been reproduced by H. Besseler in *AfMW* VII 251 f.

[2] Marchettus de Padua is also the author of a treatise *Lucidarium musicae planae (GS* III 64-121) which deals in a well-known manner with the intervals, ecclesiastical modes, etc. The dates of these two MSS have been the subject of extended controversies, chiefly between J. Wolf and F. Ludwig. Regarding the date of the *Lucidarium*, see p. 320, footnote 2. The *Pomerium* was written after 1309, since it is dedicated to king Robert of Sicily who ascended to the throne in this year. J. Wolf gives 1309 as the exact date of the treatise (*GdM* I 26; *HdN* I 277). Again this date is perhaps a decade or two too early. In fact, in the above mentioned comparison ('De distantia et differentia cantandi de tempore imperfecto inter Gallicos et Italicos, et qui rationabilibius cantant') Marchettus refers to the *tempus imperfectum*, the *semibrevis maior, minor*, and *minima*, to the use of *semibreves caudatae* to a 'tertia divisio temporis' (i.e., to notes equivalent to a *semiminima*), and to other devices of fourteenth century French notation which are not likely to have been fully developed, much less to have become known outside of France before 1320 at the earliest.

contains a detailed description of the principles of Italian notation and, in addition, an interesting comparison between this system and the French one, the latter being recognized as superior (*GS* III, 175). Evidently, at this time Italian notation was already sufficiently developed to be codified and discussed.

Finally, notational as well as stylistic features of Italian music rather definitely point to the late thirteenth century as the period when the Italian tradition branched off from the French. The Italian system of notation obviously rests upon the basis created by Petrus de Cruce. Indeed, while his fundamental principles of notation, the grouping of several *S* to the value of a *B*, and the consistent use of the *punctus divisionis* for the marking off of these groups, were soon abandoned in France in favor of principles derived from the Franconian theory (*tempus, prolatio,* imperfection, alteration, etc.), they were kept up and developed in Italy. Actually, the Italian notation is but a modification of the Petronian system, a modification characterized by the introduction of numerous special shapes of *semibreves* (*semibreves signatae, caudatae*) against which French and English theorists of the time frequently raised their voices in protest.

Needless to say, the close alliance of the notational systems is paralleled by one of the musical styles. The rapid parlando declamation of the Petronian school was adopted by the Italians and was developed into a highly decorated style which frequently reminds one of the coloraturas of seventeenth century Italian arias. In fact, if viewed in the light of general music history, the Petronian parlando appears to be so much closer to the Italian than to the French idiom that one is almost tempted to reverse the usual assumption, by venturing the conjecture that Petrus was not a Frenchman[1] whose ideas spread to Italy, but an Italian who came ∗ to Paris and introduced into the French motet certain features of a native thirteenth century Italian music all other traces of which are lost.

B. The Principles of Italian Notation

The explanation of the Italian notation by Marchettus is scarcely suitable to serve as the starting point for our study. His thought processes are overladen with scholastic arguments and lengthy elaborations which are not conducive to an understanding of the essential points. His factual information corresponds only in a general way to the notation

---

[1] The much-used version Pierre de la Croix is, of course, an arbitrary Frenchification introduced probably by Coussemaker but still retained in recent publications. Perhaps we may have the pleasure, before long, of reading in German books about an illustrous predecessor of 'Peter vom Kreuz,' named 'Franz von Köln.'

used in the documents and is in many particulars more complicated and less definite than actual practice. Since, moreover, his teachings have already been given in detail by J. Wolf (*GdM* 1, 28), we shall resort to Marchettus only for the rudiments and the terminology, drawing our presentation chiefly from the actual documents.

Divisiones. The Italian system of notation rests entirely upon the Petronian idea of the *B* as the fundamental unit. Whereas, in French notation, the *B* may be shortened or lengthened by imperfection and alteration, in the Italian system it is an unalterable value. The smaller notes always appear in groups each of which takes the place of a *B*. The marking off of such groups is effected in exactly the same way as in the system of Petrus de Cruce, namely, either by a *B* or *L*, or by a *B-* or *L*-rest, by a ligature (generally a *binaria c. o. p.*), or in the majority of cases by the *punctus divisionis*. An example follows:

Here nine groups (measures), each having the value of a *B*, are easily recognizable. The only remaining problem, then, is the determination of the rhythm within such groups. For this purpose a great variety of signs, so-called *semibreves signatae* or *caudatae*, were introduced, some of which are shown in the above example.

The division of the *B* into smaller values does not depend, as with the French, upon *tempus* and *prolatio* but upon the so-called *divisiones* which, to a certain extent, can be considered ready-made combinations of *tempus* and *prolatio*. These *divisiones* are distinguished according to the number of parts into which the *B* is broken, and appear in three different degrees, namely, as *prima*, *secunda* and *tertia divisio*. In each degree, two or three notes can appear in the place of one of the preceding degree:

divisio prima:	binaria	·	ternaria
	2		3

divisio secunda:	quaternaria	senaria imp.	senaria perf.	novenaria
	4	6	6	9

divisio tertia:	octonaria		duodenaria
	8		12

The two *divisiones primae* are of only theoretical importance. The others are indicated by letters as follows:

.q.: quaternaria; .i.: senaria imperfecta; .p.: senaria perfecta; .n.: novenaria; .o.: octonaria; .d.: duodenaria.

By representing the *B* as a half-note, or a dotted half-note, we arrive at the following schemes of transcription:

Apparently, the four *divisiones secundae* are equivalent to the four combinations of *tempus* and *prolatio* (Vitry's 'quatre prolacions').

Note Forms. Within this general frame the notational fixation of rhythm is governed by the following principles:

1. If in a *B*-group the full number of notes demanded by the *divisio* is present (i.e., four notes in *.q.*, six notes in *.i.* or *.p.*, etc.), each of them is represented by a *semibrevis* with an upward stem or, as we might call it, by a *M*. This means, therefore, that the value of an *M* fluctuates between $\frac{1}{4}$ *B* and $\frac{1}{12}$ *B*, according to the prevailing *divisio*. However, it must be noted that within a given *divisio* the value of the *M* is constant, that is, it is always worth that part of the *B* which is demanded by the *divisio*.

2. If in any (*secunda* or *tertia*) *divisio* the slower rhythm of any preceding *divisio* (*prima* or *secunda*) is to be expressed, the plain *S* is used. In the four *divisiones secundae*, in which there is only one preceding *divisio*, this principle leads to the same manner of writing as is used in French notation:

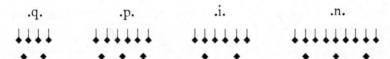

However, something essentially different results in the case of the two *divisiones tertiae*, in which there are two degrees of slower rhythm, both of which are represented by *S:*

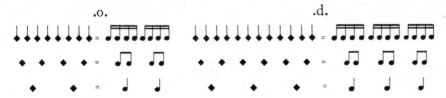

3. If in any *divisio S* are used in smaller number than that of the normal groupings indicated under (2), the last of these *S* will be lengthened. This principle, which obviously is rooted in the alteration of French notation, leads to the following combinations:

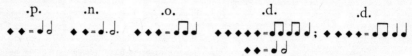

The resulting rhythm is a rhythm in which the longer notes appear at the end of the group, and is called *via naturae* (in the natural way).

4. If a rhythm is to be expressed in which the larger values are found at the beginning or in the middle of the group, this must be represented by the *S major:* ↑ . These rhythmic formations are called *via artis* (in the artificial way). Here are some typical examples:

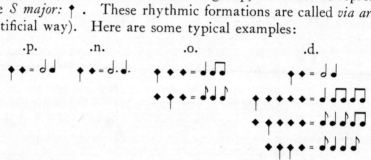

5. In the *divisiones* .*q*., .*p*., .*o*., and .*d*. each *S* can be replaced by two *M*. Examples:

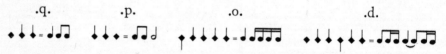

6. In the *divisiones* .*i*. and .*n*. each *S* can be replaced by three *M* or by the group *S-M*. Examples:

7. In each *divisio* two *Sm* may occur in place of one *M*. Examples:

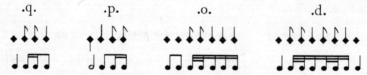

8. In *.q.*, *.p.*, *.o.* and *.d.* (cf. no. 5) triplets are often found in the place of two *M*. These are indicated by the form: ⸶ . Examples:

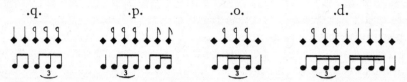

It must be noted that the flagged notes of nos. 7 and 8 are often used with the meaning exchanged, that of no. 7 for triplets, and that of no. 8 for the *Sm*. There even are pieces in which one and the same shape serves both purposes, the proper interpretation for a particular passage being easily recognizable from the number (two or three) in which they occur.

9. In the same *divisiones*, the value of three *M* is represented by the sign ✦ . This is equivalent to the dotted *S* (*punctus additionis*) of French notation. Examples:

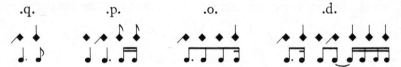

This form is found also in *.n.*, especially in syncopated rhythm, for the sake of clarity. The normal *S* will then have the value of two *M*. Example: ✦✦✦✦✦ = ♩.♩♪♫♫ .

10. The value of three *Sm* or, in other words, of a dotted *M*, is indicated by the sign ✦ . Examples:

From these explanations it is apparent that the signs in Italian notation are of two types, those which have an unalterable value within a given *divisio*, and those whose value is variable within a given *divisio*, depending upon the other notes found in the group. The signs of the first type are ♦; ♦=⅔♦; ♦=½♦; ✦=3♦; ♦=³⁄₂♦ , whereas the *S* and the *S major* are the signs of the second type. The following example shows that, in *.d.*, the value of the *S* may vary from an eighth-note to a half-note: ✦✦✦✦✦✦✦✦♭■ =|♫♫♫♫|♩♩♩|♩♩|♩.|. Usually, the determination of the value of these variable signs is without difficulty. In the case of complicated combinations, especially in the .*d*., the advice given by J. Wolf (*GdM* 1, 284) is useful: first of all subtract from the *B* the fixed values, and then determine the alterable notes from what is left. For example, in the following group, .*d*. ♪↓↓↓↓↓♦♦ , the two first notes require four *M*, the next three two *M*. In order to complete the *duodenaria*, the remaining two *S* must comprise the value of six *M*. Since they would normally yield only four *M* the value of the last *S* must be doubled *via naturae:* ♫♪ ♫♫♪ ♪ .

˙C. ˙Examples of Italian Notation

The sources which are available for the study of Italian notation are indicated in the general list of manuscripts, p. 203.[1] Except for the MS Rossi, which is of a slightly earlier date and which will be considered separately (p. 382), these sources form a unit, musically as well as notationally. As a matter of fact, they have many pieces in common,[2] and the same notational methods are found in each of these five codices. This is not to say that all the pieces are written in one and the same system of notation. On the contrary, the large repertory contained in these books falls into three distinct classes: French notation, Italian notation, and a mixed type. The first class comprises chiefly the pieces with French text. The second group generally coincides with the repertory of the representatives of the early Italian school, such as Giovanni da Cascia, Jacopo da Bologna, and Giovanni da Florentia (active *ca.* 1350). The number of the pieces in this group is relatively small. The majority of the Italian pieces are compositions of the later Italian school (second half of the fourteenth century) of which Francesco Landini (1325-1397), Laurentius de Florentia, Bartolinus de Padua, Paolo tenorista are members. These pieces are generally written in a notational system combining French and Italian elements ('mixed notation'). Finally, about a dozen of pieces in *It* and *Rei* belong to a notational type of considerable complexity which is called in this book 'mannered notation.'

Facsimile 73 contains a three-voiced piece by Jacopo da Bologna which may serve as a first illustration of Italian notation. The simultaneous use of different texts (Aquil' al tera ferma—Ucel' di dio—Creatura gentil) probably points to an influence of the French motet. The com-

---

[1] In the subsequent explanations the abbreviations: *Panc, Brit, It, Sq,* and *Rei* are used for the MSS 2-5 listed on p. 203 under Italian Notation.

[2] See the lists of contents in *GdM* 1 pp. 233 ff, 245 ff, 252 ff, 261 ff, and 269 ff. Corrections of these lists have been given by F. Ludwig in *SIMG* VI, 613-616.

FACSIMILE 73

MS Paris, Bibliothèque Nationale *ital. 568 (ca. 1400)*
Pages 2', 3

position falls into two sections the first of which is obviously in *octonaria*.
Typical combinations are:

[musical notation example]

In the second section (La el parere—La vidi—La el imagin) the
divisio changes to *senaria perfecta*. This change of rhythm, which is a
typical feature of the fourteenth century madrigal, raises the question as
to the time relationship between the two sections. Considering the
fundamental rôle which the B plays in Italian notation, one is naturally
inclined to consider this note as the common unit of time and, therefore,
to attribute to a group of six M in *senaria* the same duration as to a group
of eight M in *octonaria*. This theory, however, does not agree with the
explanation of Marchettus who in his *Pomerium* repeatedly maintains
that the *B perfecta* has a longer duration than the *B imperfecta* (GS III,
172). If he is to be trusted, the S, rather than the B, must be considered
the unchangeable unit of time measurement. In the present case this
would mean that the temporal relationship between the two sections is
as follows: [musical notation]; not: [musical notation]
Although this result would seem to be acceptable from the musical point
of view, the general principle expressed by Marchettus is clearly contra-
dicted by a composition to be considered later (Facsimile 75) in which
the B has the same value in four different *divisiones*.

The beginnings of the two sections are transcribed in the appendix,
No. 48. A reproduction of the same composition from *Sq* is given in
SchT, p. 79. The other composition of our facsimile (p. 3, *Fortune*) will
be studied later (see p. 400).

Facsimile 74, containing a two-voiced [*P*]*erche cançato e'l mondo* by
Bartolinus de Padua is a slightly more complicated example of Italian
notation. The *divisio* is not indicated at the beginning, but can easily
be derived from a group such as the one beginning over the syllable '-che,'
which consists of nine M, one of which is replaced by two Sm. With the
syllable 'Non' near the beginning of the second line the meter changes to
duodenaria (.*d*.) and returns later to *novenaria* (.*n*.), on the syllable '-mi-.'
The latter *divisio* persists throughout the second section of the piece
('Che . . . amara').

This piece, which no doubt belongs to a later period, is remarkable for
its unusual display of syncopated rhythms. In order to express them

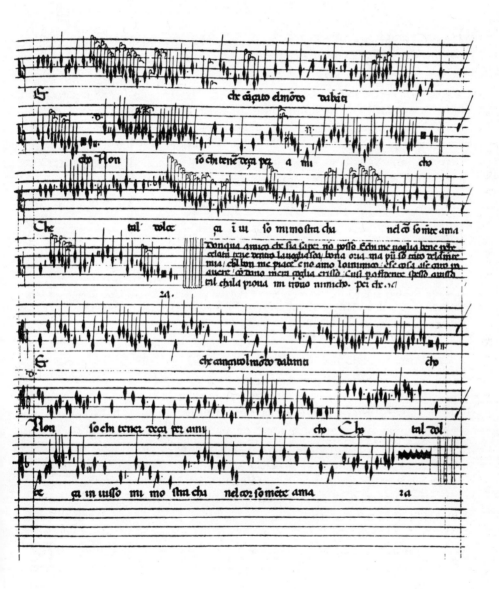

MS Paris, Bibliothèque Nationale *nouv. acq. frç. 6771 (ca. 1400)*
Page 117

clearly, a distinction is made between a binary S, ◆ , and a ternary S, ◢ (see p. 373, rule 9), for instance (first line, after 'mondo'):

However in groups with plain unsyncopated rhythm this distinction is not observed, e.g., in the initial group, the first two S of which are ternary whereas the third, written in the same shape, is binary.

In contrast to the distinction between two types of S, one and the same sign is used for the binary and for the ternary S rest. For instance, the rest in the last group of the first line equals two M, whereas those placed at the end of the first and the second section have the value of three M, which, of course, is the normal one in .n.. The sign after the first note of the fourth group is a Sm rest.

The piece is written with a B-flat in the upper part and an E-flat in the lower part, probably in conformity with the average range of the two voices. It goes without saying that the E-flat of the tenor entails the use of a B-flat wherever this degree occurs. In the discant the E is normally natural, as appears particularly from the beginning of the second section (third staff). However, for the conclusion of the piece, a flatted E is required from both the harmonic and melodic point of view. This change of tonality is probably indicated by the (misplaced) flat on the third staff, over 'dolce' (the same shape for the flat is used in the signature of the last staff). The penultimate note of the first staff is A, not G. In the second group of the *novenaria* passage near the end of the first section ('- mi - cho') a binary S, on D, is missing after the first M, as appears from a comparison with the notation in Sq. See the appendix, No. 49.

The three-voiced *Benedicamus Domino* of Facsimile 75 is interesting not only because it uses four *divisiones* (.o., .s i., .p., and .q.), but also because of the notation of the tenor. This part contains, in addition to ordinary ligatures and single L, certain *conjunctura*-like characters which are very unusual in the polyphonic music of the fourteenth century, and which actually have no place in the Franconian system of ligatures. The explanation lies in the fact that the entire tenor is not written in mensural signs but in the characters of plainsong notation, which, although similar in appearance, have an entirely different significance. In their original form as neumes they indicated, of course, the unmeasured rhythm of Gregorian Chant. However, in the thirteenth century, the Gregorian tradition was lost, and plainsong was interpreted as consisting of notes of equal duration (hence the name 'cantus planus,' in contradistinction to 'cantus mensuratus'). It is in this meaning that the 'Roman chorale notes' (i.e., the Roman, not the Gothic, thirteenth century modification of the neumes) were occasionally adopted for the writing down of liturgical tenors of polyphonic compositions. In such tenors, which,

FACSIMILE 75

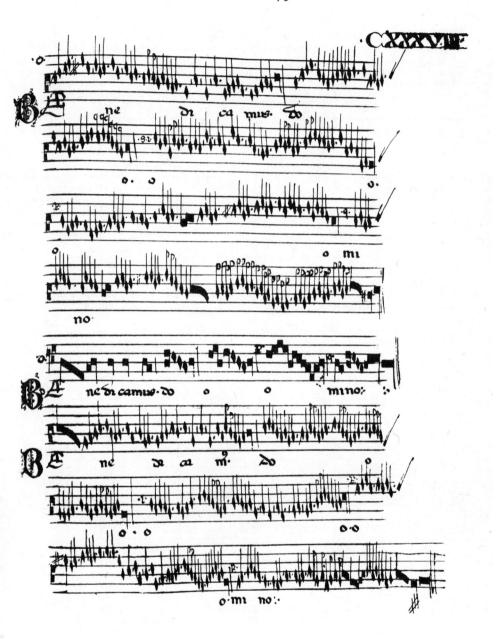

MS Paris, Bibliothèque Nationale *ital. 568* (*ca.* 1400)
Page 138

by the way, are encountered also in manuscripts of the fifteenth and sixteenth century (for an example see *HdN* 1, 404), each note always has the
value of a *B*, regardless of its shape. The unalterable value of the notes
of the tenor entails, of course, equal duration of the *B* in the different
divisiones of the discant and contra, a fact which is in opposition to
* Marchettus' statement regarding the duration of the *B* (see p. 376).

The piece presents no difficulties except for the end of the last section
which is in *quaternaria*. The last group of the discant includes four *Sm*
and two *S*, instead of four *Sm* and two *M*. This manner of writing is all
the more irregular since the two *S* are written in ligature which, according to a fundamental principle of Italian notation, always occupies for
itself the place of a *B*. Still more corrupt is the notation of the contra.
The letter *.p.*, given at the beginning of the section 'mi-no' is a clerical
error since the grouping clearly indicates *quaternaria*. Beginning with
the third ligature (*c.o.p.*), some sort of *diminutio dupla* (halving of the
values) must be conjectured, in order to arrive at a satisfactory result:[1]

Although the above reference to *diminutio dupla* is merely conjectural,
there is sufficient evidence to show that Italians as a matter of fact were
quite familiar with the idea of halved values or of doubled speed. Following is the beginning of Jacopo da Bononia's madrigal *Un bel sparver*
in two versions, (a) from *Rei*, p. 4, and (b) from *Sq*, p. 91:

(a)

---

[1] For another emendation see *GdM* III, 118.

(b)

Apparently (a) is written in *quaternaria*, whereas for (b) *octonaria* is indicated at the beginning and clearly expressed in the notation. By adhering strictly to the general principles of Italian notation the following two transcriptions would result:

(a)

(b)

Which of these two versions requires modification in order to make it conform with the other is easy to decide if our general principles of tempo transcription are born in mind. If, as always, the quarter-note is taken to represent the beat, it appears that only version (b) leads to a musically sound result. In other words, version (b) conforms with the general fourteenth century practice of having the beat represented by the *S*, whereas (a) uses the *B* for the beat and hence must be considered as written in diminution.

These explanations will suffice to demonstrate the character of the Italian notation and to show that, in spite of a somewhat confusing variety of notational symbols, it surpasses all the other systems in simplicity, chiefly on account of the persistent use of what are the equivalents of bar-lines. This feature and the rhythmic regularity of Italian fourteenth century music make it easy to clarify notational details of minor importance which are occasionally encountered, such as special signs of rare occurrence, or minor deviations from the general principles. We refrain from further discussion of these details, since additional information as well as numerous examples are available in *HdN* I, 293 ff., *GdM* I, 274 ff., *CdM* II, nos. 38-51, 53-58, 60-62, and *SchT*, pp. 77-79.

D. THE EARLY STAGE OF ITALIAN NOTATION

In conclusion, we may add a few remarks regarding the early history of Italian notation, or, in other words, regarding the transition from the Petronian notation of the late thirteenth century to the Italian notation of the mid-fourteenth century. Obviously, the most striking difference is the use of the *semibreves caudatae* in the latter, instead of the plain *S* in the former. Although such a development is quite natural, it is somewhat surprising to see that it went as far as the expulsion of the plain *S* from its dominant position and its replacement by the *semibrevis minima* or, in other words, by the *M*. In fact, the fundamental rhythm of the *divisiones quaternaria, senaria, novenaria*, etc. is expressed in Italian notation by four, six, nine, etc. *M*, whereas, in the Petronian system, the corresponding signs have the form of simple *S* (see the reference to *semibreves quartae, quintae, sextae*, etc., p. 323). It is natural therefore to suppose that there was an early stage of Italian notation in which the plain *S* still held its former place of importance.

There exists, in fact, a manuscript which illustrates such a usage, namely the MS Rome, Vat. *Rossi 215*.[1] This interesting source, which probably enables us to trace back the documented history of Italian polyphonic music to the first quarter of the fourteenth century, is written in a notation which actually forms a link between the Petronian system and the fully developed Italian notation. Our Facsimile 76 shows a three-voiced caccia *Or qua conpagni*,[2] in two canonic parts (for the imitating voice, only the beginning and the end are notated, top of the right-hand page) and an accompanying tenor. The *divisio* is indicated by the
* letters *.sg.* which evidently signify *senaria* (the literal meaning of the letter *g* is unknown to this writer). In fact, groups of six notes can be seen at the beginning of the discant, on the seventh staff of this part, and in the final passage of the canonic voice. Downward tails and upward tails are sparingly added to the notes, indicating larger or smaller values, according to the principles expounded in connection with the *Roman de Fauvel*. That the *senaria* is imperfect may be concluded from the frequent occurrence of groups of two *S* (particularly in the tenor) and of four *S*. A rhythmic evaluation of the various combinations is not without its difficulties. Without attempting to prove our conclusions we submit them in a table reproduced on page 384.

It is interesting to note that the rhythms *via naturae* absolutely con-

---

[1] See the study by J. Wolf in *Jahrbuch der Musikbibliothek Peters* 45, 1938.

[2] I am indebted for this photography to Mr W. Th. Marrocco, whose *Fourteenth-Century Italian Cacce* (1942) contains transcriptions of all the Italian caccias.

FACSIMILE 76

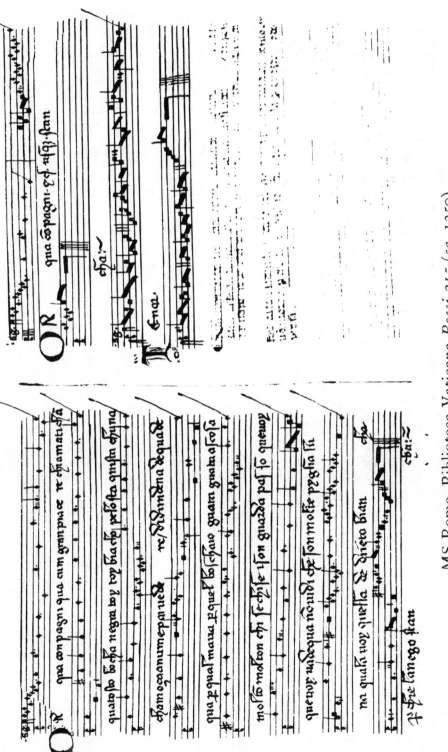

MS Rome, Biblioteca Vaticana *Rossi 215* (*ca.* 1350)
Pages 19', 20

Via naturae   Via artis

♦ ♦   = ♩. ♩.   ↑ ♦   = ♩. ♩ ♪

♦ ♦ ♦   = ♩. ♩ ♪   ♦ ↓ ♦   = ♩ ♪ ♩. (♩. ♪ ♩ ?)

♦ ♦ ♦ ♦ = ♩ ♪ ♩ ♪   ↓ ♦ ↓ ♦ = ♪ ♩ ♪ ♩

♦ ♦ ♦ ♦ ♦ ♦ = ♫♫ ♫♫   ♦ ♦ ↓ ♦ = ♫♫ ♪ ♩

tradict the teaching of Marchettus and other fourteenth century theorists, according to which the longer values appear at the end of the group.
For instance, in a group of three *S* the values would follow exactly in the
reverse order of those indicated above (see *GdM* i, 30, or *HdN* i, 288, under *divisio senaria imperfecta*).   This is but another evidence of the uncertainty in the evaluation of the small notes which prevailed around
1300 (see p. 339).   In fairness to the theorists it should be mentioned
that they were by no means unaware of this situation, as appears from
various remarks in which the singer is given a choice between the trochaic and the iambic rhythm (Theodoricus de Campo, *CS* iii, 185).

The initial character of the canonic parts and the tenor is a *B plicata*.   The rest near
the middle of the eighth staff should be a *B* rest.   The second note of the *ternaria* near
the end of staff 6 (syllable 'l'u-') is probably a clerical error and should read c, instead
of d.   The concluding passage for the imitating voice is to be used instead of the passage
of the *dux* beginning with the *ternaria* to the syllable 'stan-'.   A transcription of the
beginning of the caccia is given in the appendix, No. 50.

We may now refer the reader back to a piece which has been briefly
discussed near the beginning of this book, that is, the example of the
earliest organ tablature to be found in the Robertsbridge Codex (reproduction p. 38).   Indeed the upper part of this piece is written in exactly
the same type of 'primitive' Italian notation—a fact which would seem
to allow for some doubt regarding the supposedly English origin of this
manuscript and its contents (another suspicious detail is the rather un-
English name Petrone to be found at the beginning of the piece).   The
divisio is, as can easily be seen, *quaternaria*.   Musical considerations
show that this *quaternaria* is in diminution, similar to what we found in
the Reina version of *Un bel sparver* (p. 380).   In other words the *B* represents not the measure, but the beat.   As a rule, three *B* form a rhythmic group (*modus perfectus*), so that a transcription in $\frac{3}{4}$-meter results.

VIII. MIXED NOTATION

A. General Characterization

THE most characteristic feature of the Italian notation is the consistent use of the *punctus divisionis* with the same meaning as the modern bar-line. Considering the progressive character of this principle one is rather surprised to see it disappear after a short period without leaving any traces in the notation of the ensuing centuries. The reason for this disappearance, however, is not difficult to find. The bar-line means a great simplification but also a decided limitation of rhythm, unless it is accompanied by the use of the tie for syncopated effects. As a matter of fact, there was no place in Italian notation, and consequently in Italian music of the fourteenth century, for syncopation from one measure to another; the entire display of rhythmic imagination is an unfolding of the possibilities within a measure and nothing more. In other words, the rhythm of the early Italian school is merely a more decorated variety of the rhythmic structure of the compositions of the *Ars Antiqua*, particularly of the conductus. When, after 1350, Italian composers came into contact with contemporary French music, they soon became aware of the limitations of their style and hastened to introduce into their music the newly won achievements of the French *Ars Nova*. The adoption of the rhythmic innovations of Philippe de Vitry and Guillaume de Machaut made it necessary to give up the principles of Italian notation. A new notational system evolved which was essentially French in character, but which retained certain features of the earlier Italian system. This notation which, for want of a better name, is called here 'mixed notation,' differs from the pure Italian notation chiefly in the abandonment of the *punctus divisionis* as a regular device of barring, and differs from the pure French notation by the continued use of some of the Italian shapes of notes.

It goes without saying that this characterization should not be interpreted too rigidly. The term mixed notation is introduced here chiefly for purposes of general classification, without making special claim to historic significance. This writer is fully aware of the fact that what he calls mixed notation is a rather loose aggregate of various notational elements differing from each other as to localities and periods. However, our very incomplete knowledge of the state of affairs in the late four-teenth century renders futile all attempts towards a more thorough classification of the subject.

The sources for the study of mixed notation are the same which served as a basis of our discussions of the Italian notation. By far the greater part of the Italian music of the fourteenth century is written in this system, particularly the compositions of the later school, including practically all those of Francesco Landini.

B. EXAMPLES OF MIXED NOTATION

As a first example we choose a composition of the earlier school, Giovanni de Florentia's madrigal *Naschoso el viso* (Facsimile 77), which illustrates the transition from the pure Italian notation to the system under consideration. The Italian *divisiones* are still indicated by the letters *.n., .q., .i., .p.,* but the *punctus divisionis* is never used. Instead, the dot appears as a *punctus additionis*, a practice to which the pure Italian system had been thoroughly opposed. No less 'un-Italian' is the use of a dotted *L* in the tenor (first note of the initial ligature, and various single *L*) which, as can easily be seen, are perfect *L* in *modus perfectus*. Similarly, a passage like that which follows the first ligature of the tenor (single *S* and syncopated *B*) is impossible in Italian notation. As a matter of fact, the beginning of the piece may be transcribed with the least difficulty as an example of French notation, in [III, 2, 2]:

It may also, however, be considered as being written in a free, 'Frenchified' *quaternaria*, in which the *puncti divisionis* are missing and the *B* occasionally occur in syncopation:

Italian notation is more clearly suggested by the passage 'me guardava' (end of the second staff) where the letter *.n.* calls for *novenaria*, i.e., for nine *M* to be placed against a *B* of the tenor. Unfortunately this obvi-

FACSIMILE 77

MS Florence, Biblioteca Nazionale *Panciatichi 26 (ca. 1375)*
Pages 49', 50

ous interpretation turns out to be incorrect, as appears from the following transcription:

A correct transcription is obtained if each group of nine notes is spread over three *B*, in some sort of threefold augmentation, as follows:

Obviously, this means that the nine notes of the *.n.* are equal, not to a *B*, but to a (perfect) *L*. In other words, the *novenaria* is not, as is the normal case, a *divisio* of the *B*, but a *divisio* of the *L*. From a study of the whole piece it appears that *.n.* and *.i.* are treated as *divisiones* of the *L*, whereas *.q.* and *.p.* are *divisiones* of the *B* as usual. In *GdM* I, 315 ff., J. Wolf has mentioned various examples of the same kind.

A truer understanding of this practice will be obtained if our previous remarks regarding the use of diminution in Italian notation are recalled. Once more it appears that a clear insight into such problems cannot be gained without the question of tempo being taken into consideration. Obviously, the above interpretation, although it leads to a correct alignment of the parts, suggests a tempo which is much too slow. The fault of our transcription lies in the fact that the *quaternaria* of the beginning has been taken to indicate normal tempo (*integer valor*, in the language of the fifteenth century) and that, as a consequence, the *novenaria* has been interpreted as augmentation. Actually, the reverse interpretation is correct. The *.n.* is in *integer valor*, and the *.q.* in diminution, so that the transcription given on page 389 results.

The correctness of this rendition is confirmed by a comparison of our facsimile with the version of *Sq* which follows the familiar principles of Italian notation (see *GdM* II, no. xxxix):

The reason why another method of writing is chosen in our manuscript

is not difficult to find. Obviously, the idea was to avoid the *duodenaria*, the most complex of all the *divisiones*, and to express its rhythm and tempo by the *quaternaria*, performed in three-times the normal speed:

(a) *.q.* in normal tempo   (b) *.q.* three times as quick

Evidently, (b) is identical with *duodenaria*.

The principles to be observed in the transcription of this piece and of others written in a similar way may be summarized as follows: The *divisiones* with 'prolatio perfecta,' that is, *.n.* and *.i.*, are in *integer valor*, those with 'prolatio imperfecta,' that is, *.q.* and *.p.*, in diminution. Their exact metrical relationship appears from the following table in which a horizontal bracket is used to indicate the *tactus*, i.e., the common unit of time:

It will be noticed that the *B* (represented in each case by a whole measure), has the duration of a quarter-note in *.q.*, a dotted quarter-note in *.p.*, a half-note in *.i.*, and a dotted half-note in *.n.* .

A sign indicating *quaternaria* is missing at the beginning of the third staff, syllable 'So-'. The second section of the piece, from 'Qual'era' is transcribed in the appendix, No. 51. It may be noticed that in *Sq* this entire section is a tone higher (see *GdM* II, no. xxxix).

The musical form of the piece is that of the fourteenth century madrigal which usually agrees with that of the French ballade: A A B. Section A includes three lines of the poem:

> Naschoso el viso stavam fralle fronde
> D'un bel giardino appresso a me guardava
> Sopr' una fonte dove si pescava,

section B, the so-called *ritornello* (indicated in the original by the letter *R*), the two concluding lines:

> Qual era scalza e qual com'ella nacque
> Piu non vo' dir quanto quel di mi piacque.

The text for the repetition of A, before the *ritornello*, is given at the end of the music:

> E vidi donne vermigliette e bionde
> Leggiadre al modo che solean leguane
> Trovarsi al boscio e quando alle fontane
> (Qual era. . .)

The second piece of the same facsimile, Francesco Landini's ballata *Chol gli ochi*, is a more typical example of mixed notation. The basic mensuration is the French [3, 2], as appears clearly from the tenor (bottom of left-hand page). Aside from the occurrence of the Italian triplet-*minima* (see discant, third staff), the most striking feature is the ample use of white notes as well, with exactly the same meaning: ♦♦♦♦♦♦♦= $\frac{3}{4}$ ♩ ♫♩ ♫♩ . The transcription presents no difficulties.

For the correct underlaying of the text it is important to know that the ballata, which is the Italian counterpart of the French virelai (not of the ballade!) consists of two sections of music, A and B, which are repeated as follows: A b b a A.[1] The general disposition of the text is indicated below:

> A:　*Chol gli occhi . . . sospiro*
> b:　Questo fo . . . sentir mi fay
> b:　[E tu sempre . . . cio fu may]
> a:　[Dunque singnor . . . in martiro]
> A:　*Chol gli occhi . . . sospiro*

The text of the lines in brackets is given at the end of the music in the original.

Facsimile 78 contains a ballata *Se pronto* by 'Magister Franciscus Caecus Horghanista de Florentia' (the first three words are found on the opposite page of the MS), i.e., by Francesco Landini. The mensuration is [2, 2] (.*q*.), as appears, e.g., from the beginning of the tenor. The white notes appear in different degrees and relationships. A single group of three white *M* stands in the place of two black *M* and thus occupies half of a $\frac{2}{4}$-measure. A group of three white *S* or their equivalent in other values (e.g., *B MM*), on the other hand, comprises a whole measure

---

[1] See p. 151 f.

FACSIMILE 78

Codex Squarcialupi
Florence, Biblioteca Medicea-Laurenziana *Pal. 87 (ca.* 1400)
Page 170

and brings about a temporary change from *quaternaria* to *senaria perfecta*, which may be most clearly indicated by triplets of quarter-notes. In the middle of staff 5 we find a group of three white *B* which naturally occupy two $\frac{2}{4}$- or one $\frac{4}{4}$-measure (half-note triplets). The following schematic example clarifies the meaning of the three varieties of coloration:

[musical notation example]

The beginning of the ballata is transcribed in the appendix, No. 52.[1]

A more complicated specimen of mixed notation is Landini's three-voiced ballata *Nessun ponga speranza*, which is preserved in four manuscripts.[2] Our facsimile (no. 79) is from the Codex Squarcialupi.

The beginning clearly shows *senaria* rhythm (cf. the group between the first and the second *B*). That one is here dealing with *senaria imperfecta*, [2, 3], is apparent in the writing of the next group (after the second *B*) in which two groups to the value of three *M* each are clearly discernable. The white *B* and *S* which follow indicate, according to the principles of coloration, the transition to *senaria perfecta*, [3, 2]. Toward the end of the staff two white *B* appear in succession, followed by two groups of four black *M* each. Evidently, the *divisio* changes here from *senaria* to *quaternaria*, a change which, in the transcription, is expressed by a transition from $\frac{6}{8}$ (or $\frac{3}{4}$) to $\frac{2}{4}$, with the quarter note unchanged in duration. Similar passages in *quaternaria* are found later (end of the first section), and it is for these that the *punctus divisionis* is reserved.

Later in the course of this piece there frequently occurs a double-stemmed note form (beginning of the third staff) which such theorists as Anon. III (*CS* III, 373) and Theodoricus de Campo (*CS* III, 186) call a *dragma*. It is used in various connotations by theorists as well as composers.[3] In the present case it has the value of two *M*, and is thus equal in duration to the white *S*. In fact, either the white form or the *dragma* occurs here to represent the same rhythmic relationships, in the *quaternaria* as well as in the *senaria*:

Quaternaria: *[musical notation]*　Senaria perfecta: *[musical notation]*

For the transcription of the beginning (discant), see the appendix, No. 53.

---

[1] In L. Ellinwood, *The Works of Francesco Landini* (Cambridge 1939), p. 157, a rather arbitrary rendition in *senaria imperfecta* ($\frac{6}{4}$-meter), is given, the white notes being considered as indicating the normal mensuration, and the black notes as being equal to dotted white notes.

[2] *Sq*, 162'; *Panc*, 40; *It*, 11; *Brit*, 75.'

[3] See the table on p. 405.

FACSIMILE 79

Codex Squarcialupi
Florence, Biblioteca Medicea-Laurenziana *Pal. 87 (ca. 1400)*
Page 162′

Occasionally, one encounters still other notational characters in the pieces of the Italian composers of the late fourteenth century, particularly in those of Paolo tenorista. Following is the beginning of his three-voiced ballata *Amor da po che tu ti maravigli* (It, p. 79'/80):

The tenor clearly indicates *tempus perfectum*. In the contra, the shape ↓ occurs repeatedly in groups of four. Apparently it is used here in the meaning of a *Sm*, not of a triplet-note (see the remark p. 373, under no. 8). The note ↓ has the value of three *Sm*, that is, of a dotted *M*. The three white notes with the flag to the right side are, of course, triplets. As can easily be seen, they take the place of one *M*: ♪♪♪ = ↓ . In turning to the discant we find a double-stemmed white note which always appears together with one of the white triplet-notes and which, therefore, evidently equals two of these: ♪♪♪ = ♪♪ = ↓ . Following is the transcription of the beginning of this part:

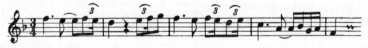

The pieces to the study of which we shall turn presently are still more 'French' in their notation, particularly by reason of the extended use of syncopation to be found in them. Since this device, which plays a still greater part in mannered notation, presents considerable difficulty to the modern reader, a detailed study is given below.

C. SYNCOPATION

The earliest mention of syncopation occurs in the writings of Philippe de Vitry (*Ars perfecta in musica Magistri Phillipoti de Vitriaco, CS* III, 28) and of Johannes de Muris (*Libellus cantus mensurabilis secundum Johannem de Muris, CS* III, 46). Their explanations are almost identical, namely (see *CS* III, 34 and 56):

> Sincopa est divisio cujuscumque figure ad partes separatas que ad invicem reducuntur perfectiones numerando.

> Syncopation is the division of a note into separate parts which are connected with each other by counting perfections.

This means that the parts of a given note (for example, the three *M* contained in a perfect *S*) do not appear in immediate succession, but are separated from each other by larger values, such as a perfect *S* or *B*. Indeed, if in the combination |♫♩·| the dotted quarter-note is placed after either the first or the second of the eighth-notes, syncopation results: |♪♪♪♫|;|♫♪♪| . Naturally, the eighth-notes may be separated also by longer groups of inserted values, e.g.:

As appears from the above-cited explanation of Vitry and Muris, syncopation was originally limited to perfect mensuration. However, Muris mentions the possibility of using it also in imperfect mensuration, for instance:

In turning to a consideration of how syncopation was expressed in mensural notation, it may first be noticed that there is no difficulty at all if the mensuration (more properly the *prolatio*) is imperfect. One simply has to write the shorter and longer values in their desired order, e.g.:

The student will recall that this kind of syncopation is very frequent in the compositions of the Flemish masters, from Ockeghem to Lassus.

The setting down of syncopation becomes considerably more complicated in *prolatio perfecta*, which prevails in almost all the pieces of the late fourteenth century. The following example, showing the same values in normal (a) and in syncopated (b) position, will illustrate the difficulty:

(a)   c♩♦♦♦♦•••   (b)   c♦♦♦♦♦♦♦

It appears that, according to the fundamental principles of mensural notation, the writing (b) by no means indicates the intended rhythm, but has to be read by applying alteration and imperfection, as follows: |♪♩♩.|♩.♩♪| In order to guarantee a syncopated execution dots preventing alteration and imperfection must be added, as follows:♩.♩•••.♩. |♪♪♩.♩.♩♪| . In reality, these dots are nothing but the ordinary *puncti divisionis*. However, because of their special function and their appearance at other points than the beginning or exact middle of a measure they are usually called *punctus syncopationis, demonstrationis,* or *reductionis.* The number of the dots required to guarantee syncopation varies. In most instances two are sufficient to bring about the intended effect, as appears from the following example (all the examples considered here are in [2, 3]):

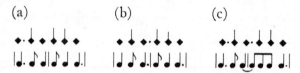

(a)   (b)   (c)

Only the version (c) is in syncopation. Here the first dot prevents the initial *S* from being imperfected, and the second has a similar effect upon the second *S*.

The following example shows another combination:

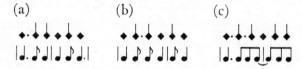

(a)   (b)   (c)

Again, the first dot in (c) prevents imperfection of the initial *S*, while the second prohibits the use of alteration for the pair of *M*. In a case like this, where there happens to be only one note between the two dots, these are frequently written so close to each other that they look like a peculiar sign of syncopation, in the shape of a 'pair of dots': ♩ . J. Wolf in his explanations on this matter (*HdN* I, 343) repeatedly speaks of the 'Punktpaar' as a somewhat mysterious sign of syncopation. Although the *Punktpaar* does indicate syncopation, a clear understanding of its meaning and function can only be gained if it is understood as consisting of two different *puncti divisionis* each of which serves its own purpose. Generally speaking, the function of the dots is negative, namely, to obviate the application of imperfection and of alteration.

As a further illustration of the principles of syncopation there follow a number of examples, all in [3, 3], found in fourteenth century treatises.[1] In the study of such examples, it is frequently helpful to identify the 'partes separatas' which must be referred to each other 'perfectiones numerando' (see the definition of syncopation, p. 395):

1. *Ars perfecta in musica* (*CS* III, 31):

As none of the *B* may be imperfected, we have to look for values which complete the isolated *S* into a perfection. These values are the *S* rest

and the group of three *M:*

2. *Philippi de Vitriaco Liber musicalium* (*CS* III, 44):

The two dots, one on each side of the *M*, prevent this note from being connected through imperfection to either the preceding *B* or the following *S*. Here again, two other values must be found which will complete a perfect group. Evidently, these are the second and the last *M* of the

example:

It must be noted that in syncopation the general rules of perfection and imperfection are valid, particularly the rule 'similis ante similem perfecta.' In the present case, the first three of the four *S* in ligature *c.o.p.* are necessarily perfect, and only the last *S* could be imperfected by the following *M*. Since this is not intended, a dot should appear after this *S*, rather than after the *M*. However, the latter manner of writing is sufficiently clear; the dot, then, indicates the end of a measure or, in other words, the return to normal meter and accent.

[1] For a detailed discussion of the syncopation as explained in the theoretical sources, see *GdM* I, 132-141.

3. Johannes Verulus, *Liber de musica* (CS III, 161, 165, 161, 159):

(a)   (b)   (c)   (d)

In (a) the *M* must be connected with the last *S*, as the two preceding *S* are both perfect. In this example the dots are not necessary, since the first and the second *S* are already perfect. In (b) the second *M* makes a perfection with the last *S*, as the penultimate *S* is necessarily perfect. In (c) both *S* are perfect; since there are only two *M* in the group, the second must be altered. In (d) the perfect *S* and the *M* take the place of four *M*; thus, only five *M* are left (by imperfection) for the *B*.

We now turn to the study of compositions involving syncopation. Facsimile 80 shows a three-voiced *Benche partito* by Dom. Paolo [tenorista]. The mensuration is obviously [2, *3*]. The tenor presents no difficulty and may be transcribed first. Near the beginning of the discant, four dots appear in close succession, all of which serve to clarify the syncopated rhythm of the passage beginning with the syllable 'par(ti'): *S M.M.M S M.M.M* (*M*) (*M*). The first of these dots is a normal *punctus divisionis*, since it occurs exactly in the middle of a ($^6_8$-) measure. The second is a *punctus divisionis* in irregular position or, in other words, a *punctus syncopationis*; it prohibits the alteration of the third *M* and, at the same time, indicates imperfection *a.p.a.* for the subsequent *S*. The other two dots would not seem to be absolutely necessary. They are added merely for the sake of clarity, the third obviating alteration for the subsequent *M* and the fourth indicating return to the normal beat (*punctus divisionis*):

It may be noticed that the next passage in syncopation (shortly before the syllable '-a') uses only three dots for the same rhythm.

Another example of syncopated notation is found in the final passages of the first and second section of the contra: *S.*(*M*) (*M*) *S S.M.L* . Here, the two *M*-rests together with the penultimate *M* form a perfection which is interrupted by two perfect *S*. In the corresponding passage of the second section there is only one dot, instead of three. As a matter of fact, only this second dot is indispensable; the first is desirable for the

Facsimile 80

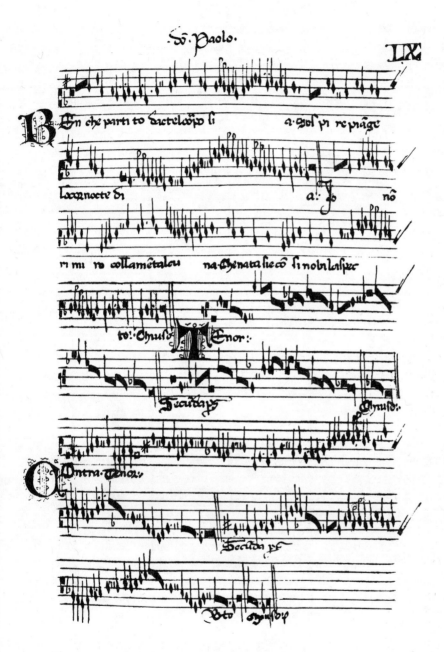

MS Paris, Bibliothèque Nationale *ital. 568* (*ca.* 1400)
Page 84

sake of clarity (preventing imperfection of the preceding *S*), and the last is superfluous.

The *dragma* which occurs in the discant and in the tenor is the equivalent of an imperfect *S* (two *M*). When this shape occurs in groups of three (e.g., beginning of the last staff), it temporarily introduces [3, *2*], while single *dragmas* usually serve to express syncopation. Particularly informative is the combination *Dr S.M* near the middle of the seventh staff, in which a binary *S* is followed by a ternary *S*, the measure being completed by a *M*.

The sharp immediately after the initial *B* of the contra probably refers to c' rather than to b. The signatures (B-flat for the entire discant and for sections of the tenor and contra) as well as the accidentals (C-sharp at the beginning of the contra, B-natural at the beginning of its second section, E-flat in the closing passages of the tenor) are a reliable indication of the tonality of the piece. Only in two places of the contra is a conjecture necessary, namely for the two *dragmas* on B, which must be read as B-flats, and for the end of staff 7 where the previous B-flat must be suspended for the last three notes on B. The fact that a *seconda volta* (chiuso) is provided for the Secunda Pars shows that this composition is a ballata. The first section is transcribed in the appendix, No. 54.

The two-voice *Fortune* of Facsimile 73 serves as another example of syncopation. This is one of the few pieces in the sources under consideration to show the familiar signs of mensuration, the whole and the semicircle. However, in the fourteenth century, the meaning of these signs frequently differs from the established practice of the fifteenth and sixteenth centuries and, therefore, must be verified in each case. In the present piece the full circle denotes [3, *2*], as is easily seen from the tenor. The reversed semicircle, however, signifies, not diminution, but [2, *3*], a meaning which is most clearly indicated in the Secunda Pars of the tenor.

The upper part is conspicuous for the frequent use of single white notes. The value of these notes is the same which they possess in ordinary coloration-groups, i.e., two-thirds of that of the black shapes. Thus, the white *B* equals four *M*, the white *S* two. The first section of the discant is interesting because it includes examples of syncopation in [3, *2*], which are much rarer than those in [2, *3*]. The initial passage shows a perfection consisting of a black *S* and a white *B* inserted between the third and the fourth of four *M*: |♩ ♫♫♩|♩♩♪|♩.| . Actually, the white form of the *B* is not really necessary here; if the note were black, it would be reduced to its imperfect value by the preceding *S*. Towards the middle of the line, one finds two *M* rests in succession which normally ought to be written as one *S* rest. The idea may have been to facilitate the reading of the syncopation, by suggesting counting *M*, rather than *S*. The various dots placed after a *S* are, of course, *puncti additionis*. The fourth note from the end of the first staff is a *M* (not a *S*) which completes the syncopation inaugurated by the dotted *S* of the first ligature *c.o.p.*

In the Secunda Pars, there follows after the initial *B* a passage in which white and black *S* alternate, so that groups equalling five *M*, or in modern notes, ⅝-measures, result. We see no reason why this clear and definite rhythm should be obscured by forcing it into the scheme of ⅝-meter, a procedure which would result in a complicated succession of tied notes. Of course, the use of ⅝-meter in the upper part against ⅝-meter in the tenor is likely to cause grave disturbance to the eye of the modern reader. However, it must be remembered that we are concerned here with chamber music of a truly polyphonic nature, a type of music which allows for a much greater rhythmic independence of the parts than piano music or orchestral music. As a matter of fact, nothing is more obstructive to an understanding of fourteenth and fifteenth century polyphony (or, by the way, to the introduction of true polyphony into modern music) than that concept of rhythm which is embodied in the person of the orchestral conductor who directs all the players with one unifying beat. Of course, early polyphonic music is also based upon a common unit of time, without which, needless to say, ensemble performance is impossible; however, this unit is not necessarily the beat (quarter-note), but frequently a smaller value (eighth-note, *M*), which may be grouped in different numbers in the different parts. Following is a 'polyrhythmic' transcription of the beginning of the Secunda Pars.

This passage shows that in fourteenth century notation syncopation could be expressed, not only by means of the *punctus syncopationis*, but also by the intercalation of notational characters denoting irregular values, such as the white *S* in the above example. More complicated examples of both methods will be encountered in our study of mannered notation.

IX. MANNERED NOTATION

A. General Characterization

TOWARD the end of the fourteenth century the evolution of notation led to a phase of unparalleled complication and intricacy.
Musicians, no longer satisfied with the rhythmic subtleties of the *Ars
Nova*, began to indulge in complicated rhythmic tricks and in the invention of highly involved methods of notating them. It is in this period that
musical notation far exceeds its natural limitations as a servant to music,
but rather becomes its master, a goal in itself and an arena for intellectual sophistries. In this period, we find not only black, white and (filled)
red notes, but also hollow red notes, as well as notes which are half red
and half white, or half red and half black, and many special forms derived from or similar to those of Italian notation. Here for the first time
we find use made of canons, i.e., written prescriptions which explain the
meaning of the notes 'sub obscuritate quadam.' Here we find compositions written in the form of a circle or a heart, again an indication of the
strong hold upon the imagination of the composer that the purely man-
ual business of writing exercised in those days. Frequently these elaborations of notation are mere tricks of affected erudition, since the effects
desired could be represented in much simpler ways. In other cases they
are indispensable, leading then to a product of such rhythmical complexity that the modern reader may doubt whether an actual performance
was ever possible or intended. Regardless of their artistic value, these
'pathological cases' are of particular interest to the student of notation.
Each of them calls for separate examination and presents problems which
are not easily solved. Thus they form a fitting conclusion of our study,
as the 'gradus ad Parnassum,' the 'études transcendentales' of notation.

Once more, as in the introduction to the previous chapter, we wish to
point out that our classification and terminology are based primarily on
principles of methodical study and of instruction. Terms such as 'mixed
notation' and 'mannered notation' are introduced here chiefly because
they permit us to arrange conveniently and appropriately the material
which we have to present. Whether, in addition, they have a historical
significance is quite a different question and one which, as has been remarked already, we are not in the position to answer definitely, owing to

the very rudimentary state of our knowledge of music history between Machaut and Dufay. There can be little doubt that the systems described in this book as French notation, mixed notation, and mannered notation were in use simultaneously around 1400. The problem presented by the most striking contrast between the classical simplicity of French notation, the motley appearance of mixed notation, and the highly involved character of mannered notation may perhaps be accounted for by differences of localities or schools. Tentatively, one is tempted to locate the first in northern France (Cambrai, Paris), the third in southern France (Dijon, the capital of Burgundy), and the second in northern Italy and the bordering provinces of the two countries. However, as far as the two latter systems are concerned, no clear line of demarcation is possible, either geographically or notationally. Regarding the geographical (or national) point of view, it may be noticed that of the two main sources of mannered notation, one, the Codex Chantilly, is entirely French, while the other, the Codex Modena, includes chiefly pieces by Italian composers, many of which, however, have French texts.[1] As regards the notational characteristics, the border lines are even more blurred. For instance, to classify the piece *Fortune* of the previous chapter as an example of mixed notation, rather than of mannered notation,
* is rather arbitrary.

Our statements regarding the highly involved and affected character of the notation under discussion should not lead the reader to conclude that the music itself is just as artificial. As a matter of fact, although our incomplete knowledge of the musical situation around 1400 makes it difficult to generalize, there are a number of pieces which are quite remarkable for their musical qualities and charm.

The most extensive sources for mannered notation are the Chantilly and Modena MSS just mentioned. However, pieces of this type also occur in MS Florence, *Panc. 26* (here only two, on p. 16′,17, evidently written in a later hand), in MSS Paris, B.N. *ital. 568*, and *f.fr. 6771*, and in MS Torino, Bibl. Naz. *J. II. 9* (see *HdN* 1, 368). Although, as has been previously remarked, each example of mannered notation presents its own and individual problems, it will be useful to discuss briefly a few general points.

B. Principal Features

Signs of Mensuration. Signs of mensuration are still of rare occurrence. Their absence presents, in many cases, considerable difficulties which are

---

[1] See the lists of contents in *GdM* 1, 328 ff., and 336 ff. Corrections of these lists have been given by F. Ludwig in *SIMG* VI, pp. 611, 616.

increased by the frequent use of syncopation and other irregular groupings. But even if signs of mensuration are given, they cannot always be
relied upon to have their familiar significance. As far as the present
author's experience goes, the signs O ¢ ⊙ always have their usual
meaning. However, the semicircle and the reversed semicircle, C Ɔ , *
are very inconsistently used. The former may indicate [2, *2*], but is also
found to indicate [2, *3*], and [2, *2*] in *diminutio simplex*. Exactly the
same three meanings occur with the reversed semicircle, which frequently
signifies *tempus imperfectum diminutum*, but is also used as a sign for
[2, *2*] or for [2, *3*].

Special Notes. A great variety of *semibreves caudatae* occur in the sources
under consideration. Some of the more common ones are shown in the
table below, the data of which cannot, of course, be applied indiscriminately. As will be seen, some of these shapes are used with different
meanings even in one and the same composition.

♩	♩	♩♩♩	♩	♩♩♩	♩	♩	♩
2 M (79, 80)	3 M (82)	$\frac{3}{2}$ M (A, L)	$\frac{3}{2}$ M (W₄)	$\frac{1}{2}$ M (87, W₁)	$\frac{4}{3}$ M (W₄)	$\frac{5}{2}$ M (L)	$\frac{3}{4}$ M (L)
$\frac{3}{2}$ M (82, 83, 86)	2 M (F)						
$\frac{4}{3}$ M (83)	$\frac{9}{4}$ M (R)						
1 M (W₁)							
$\frac{1}{3}$ M (H)							
$\frac{4}{9}$ M (GdM, no. 66)							

The numbers 79, etc. refer to the Facsimiles; W₁, etc., to the pieces from Wolf's *GdM*
discussed on p. 426ff. A = *Amor da po*, p. 394. F = *Á qui fortune* (*Mod*, 19′). H = *Il
n'est nul hom* (*Ch*, 38′). L = *Le grant desir* (*Mod*, 46; see W. Apel, *French Secular Music
of the Late Fourteenth Century* [*FSM*], No. 2). R = *En remirant* (*Mod*. 34′; see *FSM*,
No. 59). See also the tables in *GdM* i, 302, and in *FSM*, 'The Notation'.

Coloration. The ample use of red notes in the codices Modena, Chantilly and Torino bestows upon these a special character of decorativeness
and complexity. There is, of course, no essential difference between the
red notes encountered in these sources and the white ones used in others.
For instance, Anthonello de Caserta's *Biaute parfaite* (Facsimile 86)
occurs in the Codex Modena (*La beaute parfaite*, p. 14) with red notes
instead of the white ones used in the Codex Reina. The following explanations, therefore, apply equally to red and to white notes, unless
there is a remark to the contrary

1. Normal coloration, i.e., groups of three red notes (or their equivalent) equalling two black ones. This device, being identical with the
coloration of white notation, does not need further explanation. It
occurs in [3, *2*] (three red B) and, most frequently, in [2, *3*] (three red *S*);

also, occasionally, with triplet-effect, in [2, 2] (three red *S*, see *GdM* I, 345, d; or, three red *M*, see *GdM* I, 345, e).

2. Syncopated and incomplete coloration. By these terms, we refer to a variety, frequently encountered in the manuscripts under consideration, of the normal type in which the red notes essentially retain their normal meaning, but appear in groups of less than three. In many cases, complementary notes will be found shortly after, in the typical manner of fourteenth century syncopation, e.g.:

There are also examples showing a dovetailed arrangement of incomplete groups of black and red notes, e.g.:

In cases in which there are not sufficient red notes to complete a full group of coloration one has to consider these notes separately. In [2, 3], the only mensuration which concerns us here, we have the following values:

$$■ = 4M \qquad ◆ = 2M \qquad ↓ = M$$

as against:　　$$■ = 6M \qquad ◆ = 3M \qquad ↓ = M$$

Examples:

3. Red notes indicating dotted values. Although coloration usually diminishes the value of a note (by one third), it is occasionally used in an opposite meaning, signifying an increase by one half, that is, synonymous with a dotted note. Naturally, this type of coloration can only be applied to imperfect notes. For instance, in [2, 2] a single red *B* is likely to represent a dotted *B*, and a red *S* in the meaning of a dotted *S* may occur in [2, 2] or in [3, 2]. The following examples will help to clarify the meaning of 'reversed coloration,' as we may call it:

(a) [2, 2]:

(b) [3, 2]:

(c) [2, 3]:

4. Red notes indicating halved values. This meaning of coloration occurs only with the *M*, the red *M* thus being used instead of the *Sm*.

These red (or white) *Sm* are very frequent in the early fifteenth century sources of French notation, as has already been observed (p. 362).

5. Hollow red notes. These characters—for which there is obviously no equivalent in white shapes—usually serve to introduce binary groups instead of the ternary groups of *prolatio perfecta*. Depending upon whether the *S* or the *M* is considered, the relationship to the normal characters is either 2:1, or 4:3 :

C. EXAMPLES

We turn now to the consideration of a number of examples of man-nered notation.

1. Pa[olo tenorista], *Amor tu solo 'l sai* (Facsimile 81). The most striking feature of this three-voice ballata (discant on left-hand page; texted tenor and untexted contra on right-hand page) is the use of red notes, *B* and *S*, which appear either singly or in groups of two, never in the normal grouping of three notes. Their meaning depends upon the mensuration, the determination of which, in turn, is not without difficul-ty. Only with the contra is a sign of mensuration given, calling for [3, 2]. Here the red *B* indicate the imperfect, instead of the perfect value and therefore equal four *M* instead of six. With the red *S* the situation is different, since the black *S* is already imperfect. The red *S*, therefore, indicate 'reversed coloration' or, in other words, dotted values.

The application of the same methods to the discant fails to lead to a satisfactory result. Actually, this part is in [2, 2], as appears most clearly from the group of eight *M* on the first staff (syllable 'sa—[y]'), a combina-tion which virtually excludes the possibility of perfect mensuration in *tempus* as well as in *prolatio*. Here, then, the red *B* as well as the red *S* signify dotted values. The notation of the tenor gives hardly any clue regarding its mensuration. One must, therefore, resort to experimenta-tion. Such a procedure, however, will not result satisfactorily, unless it is realized that the two texted parts must be read in *diminutio dupla*. In-deed the direction is found written with the contra 'ut jacet et aliud per medium,' i.e., '[contra tenor] as it stands, but the other parts in halved values.' According to this canon each *B* of the texted parts equals one *S* of the contra. On the basis of this direction the tenor will be found to be in [2, 2].

Although *tempus perfectum* is expressly indicated for the contra, its rhytnmic design as such shows but little evidence of ternary meter. In fact, the principles of alteration, perfection, and imperfection cannot be applied without taking regard of the free metrical structure. To a certain extent this is indicated by *puncti divisionis* in displaced positions (*puncti syncopationis*). For instance, the first *punctus* appears after 19 *S* (the half-red ligature is a *binaria*). Therefore one extra beat ($19 = 6 \times 3 + 1$) must be interpolated in order to get the two ensuing *S* into the proper position as a group of alteration.

A similar situation occurs in the middle of staff 6, where the consistent use of $\frac{3}{4}$-meter would cause the *S*-rest (after the single red *S*) to fall on the first beat, thus leading to alteration for the ensuing *S*. Actually this *S* is not altered. In order to guarantee correct reading, a *punctus syncopationis* should appear before the red *S* (or, at least, before the first black *S* thereafter). The following figure shows the rhythmic structure of the passage, starting with the first single *B* of the staff:

The *S* on c′ appearing above the word 'Ut' should probably be on d′, and the black *B* on c′ appearing below this word may be read as a. See the appendix, No. 55.

2. *Je la remire sans mesure* (Facsimile 82). The basic mensuration * of this textless (instrumental?) piece is [3, 2], as appears from the use of two *S* rests in succession, at the beginning of the discant as well as throughout the tenor. However, [2, 2] is introduced frequently by the semicircle. Several times the latter sign is followed by a group of three *B*, which evidently take the place of two perfect *B*. The resulting rhythm is the same as that usually indicated by coloration. In the transcription three $\frac{2}{4}$-measures may be combined into one $\frac{3}{2}$-measure. Of special interest are the passages in which the mensuration changes with each single note, as in the middle of the second staff. This passage falls into three groups, each of which consists of an imperfect *L*, a perfect *B*, and an imperfect *B*, in the value respectively of 4, 3, and 2 *S*. Together, they fill in three $\frac{3}{4}$-measures in syncopation: .

Finally, the semicircle is also used in connection with two special signs, the *semibrevis* with a downward stem (*S maior*, see p. 332), and the double-stemmed *semibrevis* (*dragma*, see p. 392), both of which have occurred already in our previous studies. However, they have a different meaning here. The former character has the value of a dotted *S*, (3 *M*, dotted quarter-note), and the latter is half of the former ($\frac{3}{2}$ *M*, dotted eighth-note). A rendering of these values in $\frac{2}{4}$-meter is somewhat awkward. Their significance is more easily grasped if they are interpreted as duplet formations in $\frac{3}{4}$-meter (see p. 410). It follows, then, that, in spite of the changes in mensuration, triple meter can be maintained throughout the piece (a full circle is missing after the *ternaria* on the first staff).

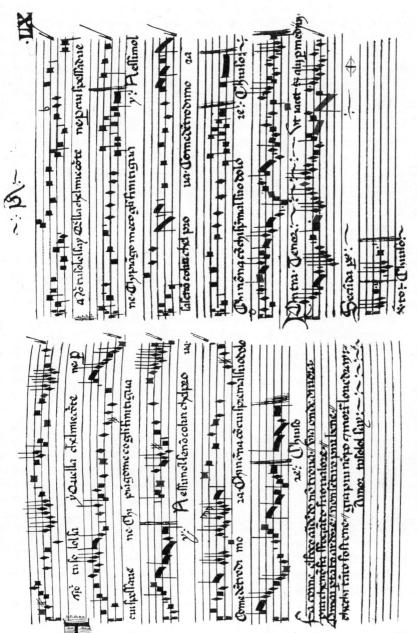

MS Paris, Bibliothèque Nationale *ital.* 568 (*ca.* 1400)
Pages 73', 74

The beginning of the discant contains an example of syncopation in
[3, 2]. Another example, including the *Punktpaar*, occurs near the beginning of the second staff. As always each dot has its own significance:
the first prevents the preceding *B* from being imperfected, whereas the
second prohibits the use of alteration. Each of the following *B* is perfect, since another *B* follows immediately, while the last *B* is rendered
perfect by the third dot.

The fourth *S maior* of the group in staff 4, over 'Je la remire,' should be c′, not a.
The correct reading is found in both other sources, *ital. 568* (p. 126′/127) and *f. fr. 6771*
(p. 80), which, however, contain several other errors. For the three main cadences of the
discant sharps are given which, although evidently not a part of the original writing,
probably are of sufficiently early date to be considered as authentic. No editorial accidentals are needed, not even for the last f (*S maior*) on staff 5, although it occurs almost
simultaneously with a c-sharp in the discant. The beginning of the first and second
section is transcribed in the appendix, No. 56. Our transcriptions are designed to clarify
the notational peculiarities of the compositions. For a final rendition it may be preferable to make a homorhythmic score, in equal measures, indicating the original rhythm
in small notes on top of the staves.

On the bottom of the page one finds a two-voice rondeau *Se vous n'estes* which is a
composition by Machaut (see F. Ludwig, *Machaut, Werke*, 1, 56). This is one of the few
compositions contained in the Machaut MS of the Pierpont Morgan Library, New York
(*MS no. 396*, f. 214v).

3. *Je ne puis avoir* (Facsimile 83). The notational methods used in
this piece are nearly the same as those encountered in the previous example.[1] The chief difference is the use of the reversed semicircle for the
passages written with the *semibreves signatae* (*S maior* and *dragma*), for
instance, those above 'puis avoir.' Actually, there is no diminution to
be applied to these passages, the notes having exactly the same value as
they had in *Je la remire* under the simple semicircle. The notation used
in the present case is apparently a confusion of two different methods to
bring about the same rhythm, one by the *S maior* in *tempus imperfectum*,
the other by the *B* in *tempus imperfectum diminutum:*○▪C♦♦ = ○▪◗▪▪ =
¾|♩.|♩♩| . Occasionally, there occur groups of three red *dragmas* which,

---

[1] In the original nearly all the signs of mensuration are written in red. It has not been deemed
necessary to preserve this peculiarity in our facsimile.

FACSIMILE 82

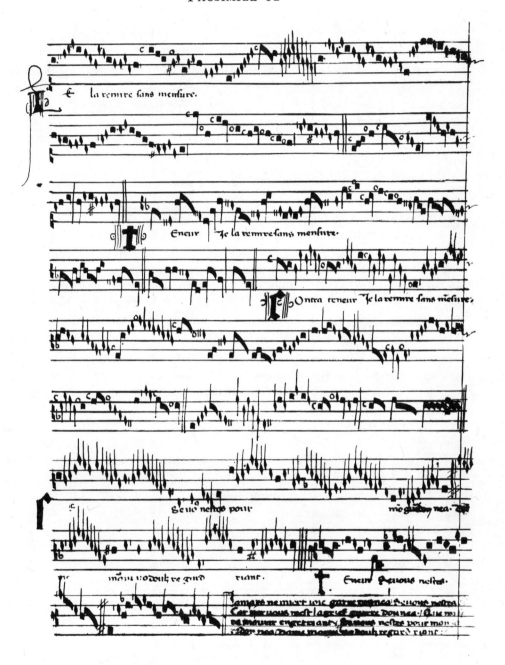

MS Modena, Biblioteca Estense *L. 568* (*ca.* 1400)
Page 34

as can easily be seen, take the place of two black ones, thus introducing triplet groups among the duplets (see the transcription below).

Only once is the reversed semicircle used in its proper meaning, that is, in the group after the *binaria* near the beginning of the third staff. This group consists of two plain *S* preceded by three *dragmas* which take the place of another pair of *S*. Thus, the whole group comprises notes to the value of two *B* (four *S*) in *tempus diminutum*, or of one *B* of the *integer valor*. The rhythm of this group is identical with that expressed elsewhere (near the end of the second staff) by three red and two black *dragmas*:

It appears that in this piece one and the same note, the *dragma*, is used in two different meanings, either in the value of $\frac{2}{3}$ *M* or of $\frac{4}{3}$ *M*.

The red *S* (in ligature *c.o.p.*) near the beginning of the second staff are 'reversed coloration'; each of them equals a dotted *S* or in other words, a *S maior*. In the middle of the third staff, the first note after the *punctus* above the syllable 'sou'- is a *S*, not a *M* (correct in Modena). On the last staff, the third *L* from the end is imperfected by both *S*. The dot does not indicate the end of a perfection, but serves to prevent alteration of the two *S*. The end of the second section affords another example of a *clos* (and, consequently, an *ouvert*), the length of which is different in each part. As a matter of fact, the *clos* group comprises five, six and eight *B* ($\frac{3}{4}$-measures) in the discant, contra, and tenor respectively. This passage is also remarkable for the bold treatment of dissonances.

Special mention must be made of two ligatures in the tenor (fifth and thirteenth ligature on the fifth staff) which show the extremely rare use of oblique writing for an ascending ligature.[1] In the late fifteenth century these shapes became the issue of a heated controversy between theorists (see p. 90, footnote). In the present piece, the ascending *binaria* with a downward tail has the value *B B* (not *L B*), in conformity with the view held by Tinctoris.

The piece has a rather unusual signature, a B-flat in the discant, and an E-flat in each of the lower parts. Properly, the lower parts should have a B-flat in addition to the E-flat. The reason for the omission probably lies in the fact that the lower parts reach the B only a few times, whereas the E lies within their normal compass. The form of the composition is that of the virelai, as can readily be seen from the fact that the second section is underlaid with two lines of text, whereas in a ballade the first section has two
* lines of text (see, e.g., Facsimiles 68, 70). The structure of the virelai (and of the

---

[1] Disregarding, of course, ligatures *c.o.p.*

FACSIMILE 83

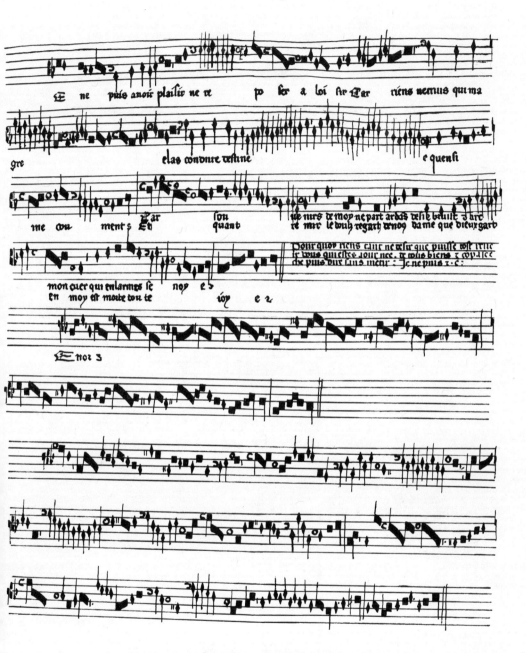

MS Chantilly, Musée Condé *1047* (*ca.* 1400)
Page 24

Italian ballata) is A b b a A. The second line of text for the section a is given after the music. The following scheme clarifies the underlaying of the complete text:

A	b	b	a	A
Je ne ..	Car son ..	Et quant ..	Pour quoy ..	*Je ne*

The beginning and the end of the discant are transcribed in the appendix, No. 57.

4. Anthonellus, *Dame gentil* (Facsimile 84). This piece shows interesting examples of syncopation, particularly in the discant. The mensuration is [2, *3*], as appears from a glance at the lower parts; in fact, as has already been remarked, the great majority of the compositions of the late fourteenth century are written in this mensuration. The dot after the initial *B* is both a *punctus divisionis* and a *punctus additionis;* not only does it prevent the *B* from being imperfected by the following *M*, but it actually increases its value from six *M* to nine *M*. The subsequent passage in syncopation begins with two *M*, between which there is a dot preventing the application of alteration. Thus, each *M* equals one eighth-note of the transcription. The first of the two *S* in ligature *c.o.p.* is, of course, perfect (three eighth-notes) because it is followed by another *S*. The second *S*, however, is imperfected a *parte post*, and so are the two following *B*, each of which is reduced to five eighth-notes by the following *M*. The third *S* (on d) is perfect by virtue of the *punctus* following it:

Although this transcription gives the correct rhythm, yet it obscures to a certain extent the real nature of fourteenth century syncopation which is quite different in character and meaning from that of more recent periods. It suggests that type of syncopation which is most clearly expressed in jazz music, and which may be explained as an omission of the strong beat within an unchanged meter. The aesthetic significance of this rhythmic peculiarity is that of an unexpected loss of balance, of a sudden shock, which momentarily upsets our rhythmic security. Fourteenth century syncopation, needless to say, is far from having this character. It can be most properly described as a temporary displacement, rather than an omission, of the strong beat. Thus, it is much closer in nature to that more recent type of syncopation which is frequently encountered in the works of contemporary composers, such as Hindemith or Stravinsky. The difference between the two interpretations appears from the following example in which one and the same rhythm is notated in two ways, one indicating 'elision,' the other 'displacement':

FACSIMILE 84

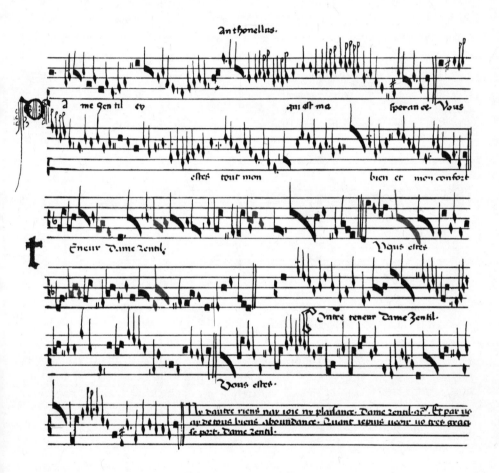

MS Modena, Biblioteca Estense *L. 568* (*ca.* 1400)
From page 38′

The initial passage from *Dame gentil* is a typical example of fourteenth century 'displacement of bar-lines.' Indeed, if an imaginary bar-line is drawn after the second *M*, there results a series of normal perfections to the value of three *B*. Below is a 'displacement' rendition of the passage, together with still another method of writing which, although quite unfamiliar in appearance, actually is particularly well suited for our purpose, because it makes clear not only the displacement of the bar-lines but also the 'insertion' character of fourteenth century syncopation which causes the accent to return to its normal position after a shorter or longer stretch of syncopation:

Another interesting passage in syncopation starts with the *M*-rest after the four *M*: (*M*) *B B S.M S S.M*. All the *B* and *S* are perfect, either because they are followed by another perfect note or by a *punctus perfectionis* (in correct writing, there probably should also be a *punctus perfectionis* after the second *B*). Another perfection is formed by the three *M* which, however, are separated from each other by the insertion of longer values (see Philippe de Vitry's explanation of syncopation, p. 395). The following rendering clarifies the rhythmic construction of the passage:

An unusually long passage in syncopation starts with the first *S* on the second staff. This *S* is preceded by a *M*-rest which falls on the first beat of the measure. However, the dot after the *S* prevents it from being imperfected by the preceding rest. Then begins a long passage in the normal rhythm of [2, 3] ($\frac{6}{8}$), in which the principles of perfection, imperfection, and alteration apply as usual; however, the whole passage is removed by one eighth-note from the normal accent and barring. After six and a half measures, the barring is brought back to normal by the two *M* which are separated by a dot (in order to prevent alteration).

Various other instances of this method occur in the piece, for example, at the very beginning of the contra. Aside from this passage, the two lower parts present no difficulty, the red notes of the tenor being normal coloration. As a matter of fact, there is such a striking difference of rhythmic and notational complexity between the discant and the lower parts, particularly the tenor, that one gets the impression of a composition written for a 'syncopation virtuoso' and two accompanists of average musical intelligence. There exist a great number of pieces of this type in the sources under consideration.

A correct transcription of the discant will be facilitated by the remark that the two closely grouped *M*-rests that appear twice on the first and three times on the second staff each time stand at the beginning of a perfection (that is, of a full or of a half measure), thus causing the ensuing note to appear in displaced position.

The form of *Dame gentil* is that of the rondeau: A B a A a b A B (see p. 140), as appears from the reiteration of the refrain 'Dame gentil' in the text given at the end of the music. The complete underlaying of the words is as follows:

A		B	
1.4.7.	*Dame gentil . . . spérance*	2.8.	*Vous estes . . . confort*
3.	Ny d'autre . . . playsance	6.	Quant ie puis . . . port
5.	Et pour vous . . . aboundance		

The first section is transcribed in the appendix, No. 58.

5. *Tout houme veut* (Facsimile 85). This is a three-voice ballade, the *Abgesang*[1] of which falls into two sections, one to the text 'Car celui—oublier' (second staff), the other to the text 'Sans—entreprendie' (third staff). The tenor, written in plain [2, 3] with normal groups of coloration presents no difficulty, aside from the careless writing.[2] The contra shows similar features of notation and, in addition, a few relatively simple and short passages in syncopation, e.g., immediately after the first group in coloration. Both parts contain many instructive examples of alteration.

As in the previous piece, the discant is a part for the 'syncopation (or notation) virtuoso.' It contains two particularly interesting passages in

---

[1] We borrow the terms *Stollen* and *Abgesang* for the first and second section of the ballade from the German counterpart of this form, the *Bar* of the Minnesinger and Meistersinger. See the description in R. Wagner's *Meistersinger*, act I, 3 (Kothner: 'Ein jedes Meistergesanges Bar . . .').

[2] In the photographic reproductions of the Codex Torino which have been available for the present study, the indication of the red notes is frequently very poor, so that in some places conjectures have been necessary.

syncopation, the first beginning immediately after the initial *B* (here, the *M*-rest, the subsequent *M*, and the final *M* on c form the perfection which is interrupted by five *S*), the other starting with the *M* on g after the *S*-rest in the middle of the first staff (here the perfection is formed by the initial *M*, the second *M* on e after the red ligature, and the *M* on c). The reversed semicircle indicates that type of *proportio dupla* which also prevails in the earliest sources of white notation (see p. 151), and which serves to introduce duplets, two *S* of the proportion being equal to one (ternary) *S* of the *integer valor*. In the passage marked $\frac{3}{2}$, three *S* are equal to two normal *S*. The *prolatio* is here perfect, so that groups of nine *M* result, each of which takes the place of a group of six *M* in the *integer valor*. The passage at the end of the third staff (after the *binaria*) reads g e f d g b d' c' a (the final character of the staff is the *custos* which merely anticipates the first note of the next staff).

The section A (*Stollen*) of the discant is transcribed in the appendix, No. 59.

6. [*B*]*iaute parfaite* (Facsimile 86). The entire tenor is in [2, *3*], as appears from the frequent groups of two *M*-rests followed by a single *M*. In the contra, however, the *prolatio* is normally imperfect, as is suggested by the occurrence of dotted *S* in succession, since otherwise the dots would be unnecessary. As for the *tempus*, the music itself fails to lead to a decision between *tempus imperfectum* and *tempus perfectum*. Notational considerations suggest [2, *2*] as the intended mensuration, the main point in evidence being the *B*-rest near the beginning of staff 6, which must be binary, not ternary. For the first section of the Secunda Pars (*Abgesang*), [3, *2*] is introduced by the full circle, while for its second section the mensuration changes back to [2, *2*]. It must be noticed, however, that throughout the contra the mensurations have a notational rather than a musical significance. Although they correctly indicate the values of the notes and rests (*B* and *S*), they fail to express the prevailing rhythm. This is particularly true for the sections notated in [2, *2*] which, from the musical point of view, suggest a free alternation of
* measures or passages in $\frac{2}{4}$, $\frac{3}{4}$, and $\frac{6}{8}$.

In the discant, the normal mensuration is [2, *3*], on the basis of the same evidence as in the tenor. The initial passage is in syncopation; in fact, the first dot is not, as one might believe at first sight, meant to mark off a perfection (which would lead to alteration of the second *M*), but is a *punctus syncopationis* which indicates the beginning of displaced barring. The *B*, being followed by an *S*, retains its full value of six *M*, while the *S* itself is imperfected by the following *M*. The two *M* placed between the second dot and the *B* do not undergo alteration, any more

FACSIMILE 85

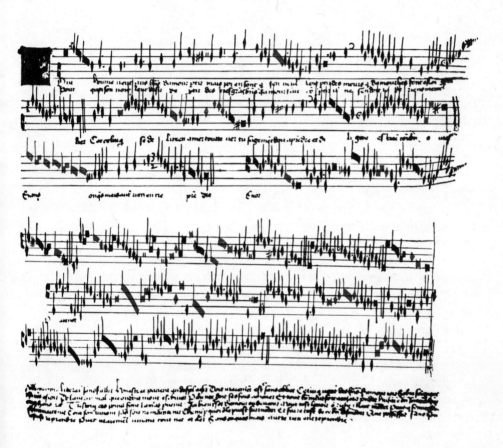

MS Torino, Biblioteca Nazionale *J. II. 9* (*ca.* 1400)
From pages 134', 135

than those at the beginning of the piece.   The fourth dot is similar in
function to the second, while the fifth, as usual, prohibits the use of alteration for the last two *M*.   A transcription according to the idea of broken-
up perfections and displaced bar-lines readily clarifies the rhythmic
structure:

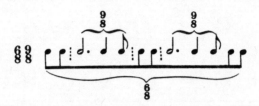

In the first section of the *Abgesang* ('Je ne puis—endurer') syncopation is
effected by the use of special note values, the white *S* and the *dragma*.
The former sign equals 2 *M*, the latter 1½ *M*.   At the beginning of the
second section ('Puis') a sign indicating [2, 2] is missing.   As in the corres
ponding section of the contra, this sign has only notational significance, a
rendering in ² and ³ being musically appropriate.

The use of the white notes in the discant is very peculiar.   According
to the normal mensuration [2, *3*] one might expect to find three white *S*
taking the place of two black ones.   Actually, however, the *S* remains
unchanged; the coloration applies to the *M*, with which it indicates the
transition from groups of three to groups of two, i.e., to dotted *M* or duplets.   Therefore, this is a case of 'reversed coloration' of the type illustrated by the example (c) given under no. 3 (p. 406).   In order to clarify
the difference between the two interpretations, it may be observed that
both lead to the same mensuration [3, *2*] for the group of white notes, in
conformity with what is indicated in the original.   However, although
in normal coloration this group, which comprises 6 white *S*, would be
equal to 4 black *S* and, therefore, would fill in two ⁶₈-measures, it actually
is equal to 6 black *S* and, consequently, takes the place of three such
measures.[1]

The interpretation of 'reversed coloration of the *M*' applies to the first
and to the second passage of white notes.   However, the next passage of
white notes is in 'normal coloration of the *S*,' with triplets introduced by
the *prolatio perfecta*.   With the subsequent groups and with the single
white notes the situation is much simpler, because they include only *S*,
no *M*.   Here the prevailing mensuration unequivocally indicates which
* type of coloration is meant in each case.

---

[1] See the erroneous transcription in *GdM* I, 344, where the group of red notes (the passage is copied
from the MS Modena) occupies two, instead of three, normal measures.

FACSIMILE 86

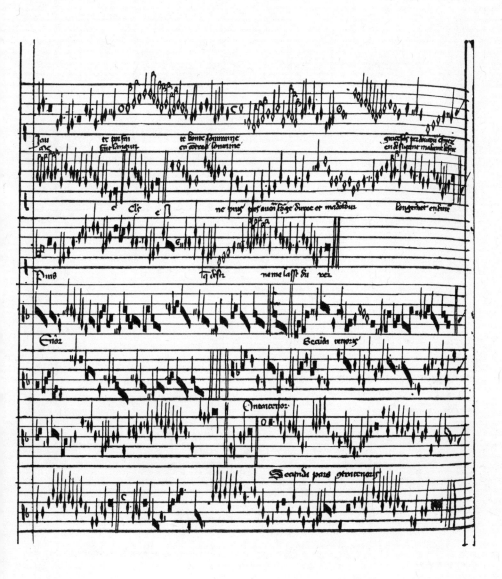

MS Paris, Bibliothèque Nationale *nouv. acq. frç. 6771 (ca.* 1400)
Page 46

The following errors or inaccuracies of writing may be noticed. Discant: A semicircle is missing at the beginning of staff 3. Contra: (1) After the 13th note (dotted *S* on d′) three notes *M M M* on d′, g, d′ are missing (correct in Codex Modena); (2) in the last *binaria* of staff 5, only the *finalis* is dotted, not the *initialis*; (3) the last *M* on this staff is g, not a; (4) in the final section (staff 7) the 14th note (*S* on g) should be dotted; the 21st note (*M* on d′) should be c′; the 25th note (*M* on g′) should be a′.

The first section of the piece is transcribed in the appendix, No. 66

7. Jacopinus Selesses, *En attendant esperance* (Facsimile 87). The basic mensuration of this three-voice ballade[1] is [2, *3*] in all the parts. The tenor is free from rhythmic complications and, therefore, provides a basis (a very desirable one, indeed) for the interpretation of the other parts. In the contra we find filled red notes which have the usual meaning of coloration (red *B* = 4 *M*, red *S* = 2 *M*; red *M* = 1 *M*). The value of the hollow red *M* can easily be derived from the fact that they appear in groups of eight (or sixteen, see the group beginning at the end of staff 8). Four of these notes are equal to a *S*, thus introducing quadruplets instead of the ternary groups of the *prolatio perfecta*. In the discant, we find three new forms in addition to those encountered in the contra: ⧫ (a), ⧫ (b), and ⧫ (c)[2]. These shapes are used in a very inconsistent and confusing manner. In a way, they all indicate one and the same rhythm, that is, triplets instead of two notes of the quadruplets indicated by the hollow red notes. On the other hand, however, the form (b) is also used with a totally different meaning, that is, equal itself to two of these quadruplet-notes. The only clue as to which interpretation applies in a given case is found in the grouping of these notes. The passage towards the end of the first staff, after the syllable 'a—(voir)' serves as an illustration; it shows the identity in meaning of the forms (a) and (b), as well as the two different meanings of (b):

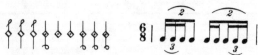

In the middle of the staff three, we find exactly the same rhythm, with the form (c) used for the triplets.[3]

The discant contains several interesting and complicated examples of syncopation. Instead of dots (*punctus syncopationis*), red notes are used

---

[1] The figure 4 given in *GdM* 1, 337 for the number of parts of this piece is erroneous.

[2] The form (a) is hollow black, the other two (characterized here by a dot) are hollow red in the original.

[3] The present writer has made numerous, but futile, efforts to arrive at an interpretation which would make the meaning of these characters less equivocal. A comparison with the version in the Chantilly Codex has proved of no help since the writing there differs in many particulars.

FACSIMILE 87

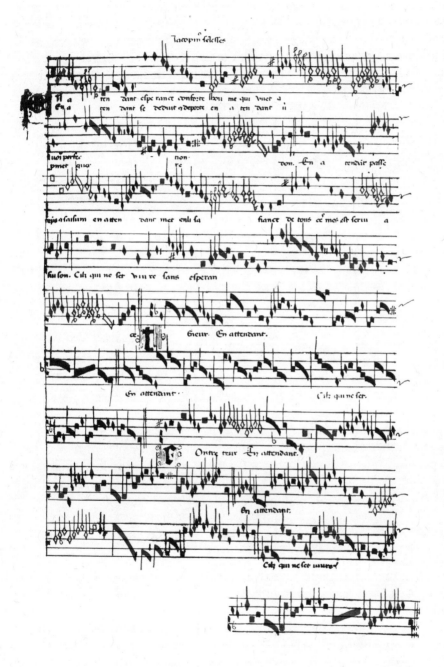

MS Modena, Biblioteca Estense *L. 568* (*ca.* 1400)
Page 39′ and part of page 40.

to introduce and to indicate irregular grouping. For instance, in the initial passage, the black *B*, *S*, and *M* always designate full perfections, while the red *S* and *M* occur in groups of the value of 4 *M*, 2 *M*, 4 *M*, and *I M* which, together with a *M*-rest, add up to 12 *M*, that is, to two complete $\frac{6}{8}$-measures. There is no mensural interdependence between the black and the red notes; that is, in spite of subsequent or preceding red notes, the initial *B* remains perfect and the two black *M* form a group of alteration, as if they were separated from the red notes by a dot. With an example of this type our method of transcribing syncopation proves particularly suitable and natural: one simply has to write the black notes with an upward stem, the red notes with a downward stem, as follows (the group with the *semibreves caudatae* is treated as a 'black' group, because it fills in a full perfection of $\frac{3}{8}$):

In the next group, to the words 'esperance conforte,' the red notes from two complete $\frac{3}{4}$-groups, *S S MM S S S*. The second of these, however, is broken up by the insertion of a black *M* which imperfects (by remote control) the black *B*, reducing this to five *M*.

The subsequent passage, 'l'houme qui vuet,' shows a group of three black *S* interspersed between a group of hollow red *M*, four of which equal in value three black *M*. Since the inserted groups appear after two of these red notes, a shift to the value of $1\frac{1}{2}$ *M* results:

The contra of this composition is almost as full of intricate rhythms as is the discant. Right at the beginning we find a passage consisting of split groups of black as well as red notes:

A different example of syncopation occurs immediately after the first group of hollow red notes (middle of staff 7). Here a single *M*-rest (which falls on the first beat of a measure) is followed by the combination *S S S S B*. Syncopated rhythm results here from the fact that the rule 'similis ante similem perfecta' prevents imperfection of the first three *S*. With the next *M*-rest of the contra another passage of syncopation starts in a similar way. Here the question of when and how to return to normal barring is more difficult. The simplest solution would be to use the first black *S* after the red notes for this purpose. The *M*-rest at the end of staff 2 presents quite a problem. It can only be retained if its value is subtracted from the two subsequent hollow red *B*, making each of these $\frac{5}{2}$ *M*.

In the appendix, No. 61, a transcription of the first section of the discant is given. In order to facilitate orientation, the normal bar-lines as they occur throughout the tenor, have been indicated above the staff. The entire composition is transcribed (from Modena) in W. Apel, *French Secular Music of the Late Fourteenth Century*, No. 23.

8. Baude Cordier, *Belle bonne* (Facsimile 88). After the intellectual labour and the rhythmic intricacies of the foregoing examples, our last facsimile, the 'Musical Heart' from the Codex Chantilly will be greeted with relief. Its relatively simple notation and rhythm characterize it as an example of a slightly later period than that to which the previous pieces belong. This assumption is corroborated by the mensuration ∗ [3, 2], the typical meter of the Dufay period, as well as by the fact that the *prolatio perfecta*, which is repeatedly introduced in the discant and tenor, has the same meaning it normally has in white notation, namely, three-fold augmentation, with the *M* equalling the *S* of the *integer valor*. This fact is all the more remarkable since this interpretation was not unanimously adopted until the later part of the fifteenth century (see p. 164 ff).

Coloration is used in three different degrees: in the discant we find groups of three red *M* in the place of two black *M* (triplet coloration) as well as three red *B* in the place of two black *B* (courante coloration, owing to the perfect value of the black *B*); the contra shows groups of three red *S* in the place of two black (perfect) *S*, values which, owing to the augmenting character of [2, 3] are identical with those of the red *B* in [3, 2] (or, more properly speaking, in [II, 3]).

The white notes in the middle of the first staff indicate *diminutio dupla* within the augmentation of the *prolatio perfecta*. Therefore, two white *S* equal one black *S* of the augmentation or, one *B* of the *integer valor*. The figure 3 to be found near the end of this staff indicates *proportio tripla* within the augmentation: three *M* equal one *M* of the augmentation or, one *S* of the *integer valor*. The rhythm of this group is actually the same as that indicated previously by the red notes. In a way the *proportio tripla* cancels the augmentation of the *prolatio perfecta*, since the three (perfect) *S* of this group consume the same time as three (imperfect) *S* of the *integer valor*. As a matter of fact, the subsequent group of white notes is in *integer valor*, two white *S* being equal to a normal black *S*. The sign ⊖ at the end of this staff indicates (or confirms) the return to normal *tempus perfectum*. In spite of the dash the sign has no proportional meaning. The explanation of this uncommon usage probably lies in the fact that this sign serves here merely as a time-signature which is understood at the beginning of all the parts. It would then merely indicate an increased speed (S = M.M. 96) which is actually necessary for the performance (see p. 193). At the end of the second staff we find a rare instance of augmenting proportion: the sign $\frac{8}{9}$ indicates that the subsequent eight notes are equal to the nine notes of the preceding passage marked 3.

H. Riemann, in *RHdM* i. ii, 354, has given a transcription of this piece with a D-major signature and with an occasional introduction of G-sharp, a procedure which he considers justified by the fact that in a few places a (non-cadential) C-sharp and F-sharp are indicated in the original. Needless to say, this theory is wholly without foundation. In reality no editorial accidentals are required, if the C-sharp near the end of the first staff of the contra is considered to have prolonged validity until the end of the staff. Only in the cadences is the use of leading-tones (*subsemitonium* for the octave as well as for the fifth) admissible (see the explanations on this question, p. 106). The beginning of the piece, which is interesting on account of the initial imitation, is transcribed in the appendix, No. 62).

D. Discussion of Examples from Other Publications

We close our study of mannered notation with a consideration of some pieces which have been given in other books (chiefly in J. Wolf's *Geschichte der Mensuralnotation*), to which the reader is referred for the reproductions as well as for the complete transcriptions. It is hoped that our explanations will help the reader to understand more clearly the problems presented by these pieces.

1. Guido, *Dieux gart* (*GdM* ii, no. LXIV). In this piece, as in many compositions of the late fourteenth and early fifteenth centuries, the determination of the mensuration is difficult because the basic meter is obscured by the frequent use of syncopation (most of the *puncti* are *puncti divisionis* in displaced position, i.e., *puncti syncopationis*). Nonetheless, upon closer examination one finds various features indicating [2, 3], for instance, groups of two S (*tempus imperfectum*) in the tenor, and numerous groups $S - M$ (*prolatio perfecta*) in the discant.

The red notes indicate normal coloration or, if they appear singly, a loss of one-third (S = 2 M, B = 4 M). Two forms, namely ♩ and ♩ are used indiscriminately for the value of half an M (*Sm;* cf. the begin-

FACSIMILE 88

MS Chantilly, Musée Condé *1047* (*ca.* 1400)
Page 11′

ning of staff 1 with that of staff 4). On page 114, the combination ♦♦♦♦

appears several times. The value of this whole group is a perfect
S, as can easily be seen. Obviously, the note ♦ is worth two ♪, so
that the following rhythm results: ♪♪♪♪(= ♩.) . Thus, the form ♦ has
the same value as the simple *M* ♩ . Probably the use of the above manner of writing, instead of ♩♪♩♪ , is meant to indicate the change of the
ternary *S* (*prolatio perfecta*) into a binary *S*, or, in other words, the introduction of two groups of triplets: ♪♪♪ instead of syncopation:
♪♪♪♪ .

In this ballade there are various interesting examples of syncopation.
As explained above, the meaning of the *punctus syncopationis* is to indicate an imaginary displacement of bar lines and, consequently, to prevent
the use of alteration and imperfection, such as would normally apply.
For instance, disregarding the *punctus*, the beginning of the discant
would have to be read as follows:

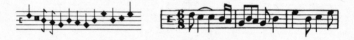

However, the *punctus* (*syncopationis*) after the fifth note indicates the
beginning of an imaginary ⁶⁄₈-measure immediately after the first note (*M*)
of a normal measure. Thus, instead of a group of five *M*, which would
call for alteration of the last *M*, we have a group of four *M* which calls
for imperfection (*a.p.a.*) of the *S*. At the end of the passage there appears a group of four *Sm* (equalling two *M*), complementing the single
M which served to introduce the syncopation:

2. Jo. Cunelier, *Se Galaas* (*GdM* 1, no. LXV). The mensuration is
[2, *3*], as is readily apparent from an examination of the contratenor.
The filled red notes have the normal meaning. In fact, the whole second part of the composition ('Dont doit . . . devise') is written in red
notes throughout and, therefore, is in [*3*, 2]. The hollow red notes indi-

cate, as usually, *diminutio dupla,* two of these *S* being equal to one normal *S*.

The bow-like signs above the first notes of the third part ('febus . . .') are fermatas, such as appear very frequently in the documents of the fifteenth century (Dufay etc.), under various forms, for instance: ∴ (cf. *GdM* ii, 132, 133; also *HdN* i, 385). Immediately after these fermatas we find groups of white notes (*S* and *M*) in the contra against black *S* and *M* in the other voices. They are used here with a special meaning, namely, to indicate *diminutio dupla* in *prolatio perfecta.* Thus two groups, ○♩○♩ , are equal in value to one group ♩♩ :

3. **Conraaus de Pistoria,** *Veri almi pastoris* (*GdM* ii, No. LXVII) The tenor and contra clearly indicate [2, 3] and, indeed, fit together satisfactorily. However, if one tries to apply the same mensuration to the discant, impossible results are obtained, as appears from the following tentative sketch:

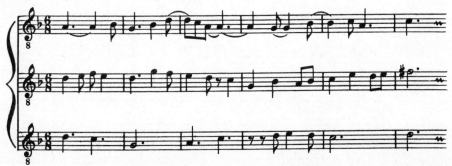

In reality, this composition is one of those examples in which different mensurations are called for in the different voices without signs to indicate the fact. The mensuration of the discant is [2, 2], with the *M* as the common duration-value in all the voices. The single red notes, then, do not indicate a decrease, but rather an increase in value, namely, dotted notes (reversed coloration). The beginning of the transcription is given on page 430.

It is, of course, possible, to write the top voice in $\frac{6}{8}$-meter also (see *GdM* iii, p. 161); however, it seems to us that in so doing a particular characteristic of rhythm and phrasing is lost, to say nothing of the complete obscuring of the notation which results from such a method.

4. **Bartholomeus de Bononia,** *Que pena* (*GdM* ii, no. LXVIII). In

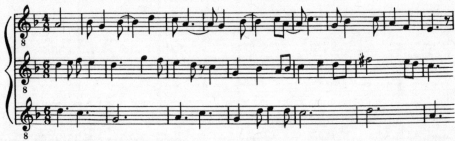

this composition all the parts are in [3, 2]. In the tenor we find single
red S as well as groups of three white S with a downward stem. The
former indicate reversed coloration (dotted values), the latter normal
coloration, that is, three *S* in the place of two normal *S*. Since the mensuration is *tempus perfectum*, there results an unusual rhythmic pattern
involving triplets in the place of two notes of a $\frac{3}{4}$-measure. In an earlier
discussion (p. 158, below middle) this rhythm has been characterized as
being 'of purely hypothetical significance,' a characterization which is
correct for the period to which these explanations referred. In the late
fourteenth century, however, such a rhythm appears as a relatively mild
manifestation of the prevailing tendencies.

If several such groups of three white *S caudatae* appear in succession,
as for instance in the discant, p. 123, st. 7, it is advisable temporarily
to change from $\frac{3}{4}$-measures to $\frac{2}{4}$-measures, in order to avoid artificial
syncopation:

Coincident with this passage is one of similar design in the contra (p.
125, st. 5). This starts with a dotted *S caudata*, a form which, as a simple
calculation shows, has the same value as a normal black *S* ($\frac{2}{3} + \frac{1}{3} = 1$).
Therefore the triplets of the contra appear in syncopated shifting against
those of the discant. Toward the end of this passage we find the very
unusual form of a *B caudata*, to the value of two of the *S caudatae*. Here
follows a transcription of this interesting passage (p. 431, top).

The white *B* which appear twice in the discant (staff 5, 6) have the
usual meaning. Each of them has the value of two *S*. Finally, in the contra there is peculiar form, ♪ (♪ in Wolf's reproduction), which equals
a dotted *M*.

Aside from these special signs frequent use is made of proportions which
are indicated by the figures 2 and 3. Their meaning is explained at the end
of the music by a 'Canon virilarie' (canon of the virelai), according to
which 2 calls for *proportio dupla* and 3 for *proportio hemiolia* (*sesqui-*

altera). Under the former proportion 2 *M* take the place of one normal *M* (or 6 *S* the place of three normal *S*), while under the latter three *M* (or *S* + *M*) are worth two *M* of the *integer valor*, so that triplets of eighth-notes result (middle of staff 4):

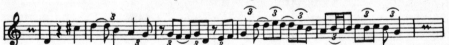

In two places of the discant, on staff 1 and staff 6, the combination *B S* appears as a part of a *sesquialtera* group. This *hemiolia temporis*, as it may be called in distinction from the *hemiolia prolationis*, *S M*, introduces the same rhythmic patterns which is expressed by the groups of three white *S caudatae*, that is, triplets for two quarter-notes of the $\frac{3}{4}$-measure. Here is a transcription of the passage on staff 1:

In the *sesquialtera* passage of the contra, p. 125, st. 5/6, a *S* (possibly on c') seems to be missing between the ligature and the final *M*. This conjecture would make it possible to read the end of this passage in conformity with all the other passages of this type, that is, in binary values (such as are customary for passages in coloration). Otherwise the ending of this passage (starting with the fifth note before the circle) would have to be read in perfect mensuration, applying alteration and imperfection (see the rendition in *GdM* iii, p. 166, syst. 4, meas. 3).

5. Magister Zacharias, *Sumite karissimi* (*GdM*i, no. LXX). This

piece may be said to represent the acme of rhythmic intricacy in the entire history of music.   Not unreasonably F. Ludwig disposes of it as a
'Schulbeispiel ohne Bedeutung' (*SIMG* VI).   Nonetheless, it is interesting from the notational point of view, and its rhythmic oddities, at least,
throw an interesting light upon the mentality of the period.

The notes appearing in this piece, as well as the mensuration, are the
same as in the preceding example.   The eccentric feature of the present
selection, however, is the excessive use of 'displaced barring.'   Time and
again an existing mensuration is not carried on to the end of the normal
measure, but stops somewhere in the middle of the measure and is followed by a long passage in a different meter, at the end of which the interrupted measure is completed.   We have repeatedly illustrated this
principle of fourteenth century syncopation in the previous discussions.
However, in the present case, it leads to formations far more complicated
than usual.   As a matter of fact, the rhythmic intricacies of this piece
are so involved that a satisfactory rendition in the normal notation of the
present day is not possible.   J. Wolf, in his transcription (*GdM* III, 168),
resorts to a method which is arithmetically correct, but which does not
reveal an insight into the rhythmic construction.   It seems to us that
only our method of 'displaced bar-lines' leads to a result which is, if not
wholly satisfactory, at least clarifying and instructive.   The first section
is transcribed in the appendix, No. 63.   Of particular interest is the passage at the end of the first staff, beginning with the red *B* on 'de re-
(mulo),' in which two syncopations of the above-described type overlap.

6. *Patrem omnipotentem* (Old Hall MS).   This interesting specimen,
which illustrates the spread of mannered notation to England, has been
reproduced in facsimile in A. Ramsbotham, *The Old Hall Manuscript*, vol.
III, after p. xxiv, and has been transcribed in vol. II, p. 101-113 of the same
publication.[1]   Although the transcription is essentially correct, it frequently obscures the notational features of the original, particularly by
the choice of the same meter and the same barring for all the parts, a
procedure which may find some justification in the primarily practical purpose of the publication.   Since, moreover, the explanations
given in vol. II, p. ix-xii, do not cover all the points of interest, there follows a concise study of the piece which, it is hoped, will enable the reader
to make a transcription of his own, according to the principles set forth
in the present book.

The piece is written in three parts, discant, contra and tenor.   However, the discant itself is a three-voice canon, so that the number of parts

---

[1] The transcription of this piece is chiefly the work of H. B. Collins who has been particularly
ingenious in the emendations of the missing notes of the discant.

actually is five. The notation is in black, red, and blue notes. Their meaning as well as that of the various signs of mensuration is explained in a *canon* (see the reproduction, p. 101 of vol. 11). Instead of a literal translation, there follows below a summary of its main contents in a different order, corresponding to that of the subsequent explanations:

The tenor and the contra are in [2, *3*] (*de tempore imperfecto perfecti*) with the red notes indicating [*3*, *2*] (*proportio sesquialtera*, that means: three red [imperfect] *S* equal to two black [perfect] *S*).

The discant yields three parts, I, II, III. They are in different mensurations which also vary from one section to another, as follows:

	'Before the *figura*'[a]			'After the *figura*'		
	Black	Red	Blue	Black	Red	Hollow red
I.	[II, 2, *2*]	[*3, 3*][b]	[*3, 2*] *dim.*[d]	[*2, 3*]	[*3, 2*][e]	3*B* = 2*B*
II.	[III, 3, *2*]	[*2, 3*]	[*3, 2*] *dim.*[d]	[*2, 3*]	[*3, 2*][e]	2*B* = 1*B*
III.	[III, 3, *3*]	[*2, 2*][e]	[*3, 2*] *dim.*[d]	[*2, 3*]	[*3, 2*][e]	3*B* = 1*B*

Annotations: (a) The *figura* mentioned in the *canon* is the sign of *prolatio perfecta* in the middle of the eighth staff.   (b) In the *canon*, this mensuration is explained as *proportio dupla sesquiquarta*, that is, proportion in the ratio of nine to four. Actually, no proportional reduction in this ratio or in any other takes place; the term merely refers to the fact there are now groups of nine *M* ([3, *3*]) instead of the previous groups of four *M* ([2, *2*]), with the *M* unaltered in value.   (c) This mensuration is described in the *canon* as *proportio dupla sesquinona*. This designation is a blunder from the point of view of terminology as well as of notation. It should read *proportio subdupla sesquiquarta*, i.e., the ratio of four to nine (the version *sesquinona* has probably been caused by the fact that here the figure nine appears in the denominator); regarding its notational meaning, the explanation given under (b) applies in the reverse.   (d) The *diminutio* of the blue notes is properly referred to in the *canon* as *proportio dupla*.   (e) This mensuration is explained as *proportio sesquialtera*, a designation which correctly, though not very clearly, indicates the fact that in [*3, 2*] three (imperfect) *S* are equal to two (perfect) *S* in the mensuration [2, *3*] of the black notes.

On the basis of these explanations, the actual transcription may progress as follows:

a.   The tenor is in [2, *3*] throughout with normal groups of coloration. Its transcription in $\frac{6}{8}$ with interspersed measures of $\frac{3}{4}$ and $\frac{3}{2}$ presents no difficulties.

b.   The contra is in the same basic meter, but involves much greater problems.   In a way, it is the most difficult of all the parts.   In addition to normal groups of coloration, red notes are used singly or in groups of other than three notes.   In the sections in [2, *3*] they represent the following values:

$$\underset{\text{1 } M}{\mathord{\text{♩}}} \qquad \underset{\text{2 } M}{\mathord{\diamond}} \qquad \underset{\text{4 } M}{\mathord{\square}} \qquad \underset{\text{5 } M}{\mathord{\blacksquare}} \qquad \underset{\text{8 } M}{\mathord{\text{⌐}}} \qquad \underset{\text{10 } M}{\mathord{\text{◼⌐}}}$$

(Here, as in all subsequent explanations, *M* is the black *M* as it prevails throughout the tenor).   The black-red oblique ligature on staff 3 equals two black-red *B* of the value of 5 *M* each, like the preceding ligature in square shape.   The red *B* rest on the same staff has the value of 4 *M*. The red *L* after the black-red ligatures is reduced to 7 *M* by the subsequent *M*.   The meaning of the blue *S* rests on staff 2 is obscure.   As is suggested by the sign ⊙ , the total value of a black-red *B* and the subsequent blue rest is nine *M*.   If, as may reasonably be assumed, the note retains its value of 5 *M*, the rest would equal 4 *M* (in Collins' transcription, p. 105, the distribution 6 + 3 has been adopted).

In the section marked ⊙ which begins at the end of the third staff, the red *B* equals in value, of course, 6 *M*, since the value of the black is here 9 *M*.   The correct rendering of this section is made difficult not only by a clerical error (the first note of staff 4 is a red *S*, not a *B*), but also by a very tricky meaning which attaches to the black notes.   As a matter of fact, one may wonder why, at the beginning of staff 4, a black *S* and *M* are used without any apparent reason, since the same rhythm could be expressed by the corresponding red notes.   The explanation is that these black notes must be mentally combined with the next group of black notes (*M B M*) in such a way that they participate in the imperfection of this *B*.   Actually, this *B* has not the value of seven (9 − 2), but only of four (9 − 2 − 3) *M*.

In the subsequent section marked ᴄ   (middle of staff 4) the black and red notes exchange their meaning, not, as Collins surmises, by virtue of an 'obscure sign' (see p. 109, footnote 2), but simply because in this mensuration the red notes always indicate 'reversed coloration,' i.e., dotted values.   Here, then, the red *M*, *S*, and *B* (also the red *B*-rest) have the value of $1\frac{1}{2}$, 3, and 6 *M* respectively.   The flagged notes at the end of this staff are, of course, *Sm*, two of which equal one red *M*.

At the beginning of staff 5, the sign ꜰ appears in red.   This means that now the red notes are the normal mensuration ([2, *3*]), and that the black notes are 'coloration,' with three black *S* equalling two red ones.

It must be noticed, however, that here the black *S* are perfect, i.e., equal to three black *M*, not to two, as would normally be the case. Therefore, the passages containing *M* introduce triplet-groups into the $\frac{3}{4}$-measures of the 'coloration.' The black *S*-rest near the beginning of staff 5 should be red.

The notation of the short passage marked by a red ○ (middle of staff 6) is very problematic. Instead of Collins' emendation (see p. 112, footnote) we suggest interpreting the red notes in [*3*, 2], and the black notes in the same mensuration, but augmented in the ratio of 3:4, so that three black *S* consume the same time as four red *S*. If, in addition, the red-black *S* of the ligature are interpreted as dotted (red) *S*, a satisfactory transcription results which fits very well with the other parts. The final section in ₵ needs no explanation. The *dragma* is, as in previous examples, one-half of the (perfect) *S*.

c. As for the three renditions of the discant, only a few remarks need to be added to the explanations given in the *canon*. The initial letter P has been removed and has been clumsily replaced, so that notes at the beginning of the first three staves are misplaced or missing. For these gaps, Collins has furnished ingenious and convincing conjectures. According to him, the first two notes of staff must be one third higher (a′ a′), while the notes a a c (values: *B M M*) and f′ g′ g′ f′ g′ g′ a′ (values: red *S S S M S M S*) must be added at the beginning of the two following staves (see p. 102, meas. 5; p. 103, meas. 12). Collins has also shown that the parts II and III start canonically, each with a full measures ($\frac{3}{4}$ and $\frac{9}{8}$) rest. These two parts are designated in the *canon* as being in *modus perfectus*. This statement refers particularly to the *L* at the end of the first staff which must be interpreted as perfect in both parts, taking the place of three $\frac{3}{4}$- or $\frac{9}{8}$-measures. Collins fails to observe this fact in his transcription of III (see the correct rendering in the appendix, No. 64 b).

In the passage of red notes immediately after the 'figura' (middle of staff 8) the fifth note should probably be a *M*, not a *S*. This conjecture allows for an interpretation in simple coloration, while Collins' version (p. 113, meas. 2) is somewhat forced. The beginning of the piece as well as several sections thereof are transcribed in the appendix, No. 64.

COMMENTARY

P. xx. Score arrangement survived in English sources through the middle of the fifteenth century (see p. 271, fn. 3; also p. 364). In a recent article, 'The Music of the Old Hall Manuscript' (*MQ* xxxiv, p. 512), M. F. Bukofzer called attention (p. 515) to a four-voice Gloria and a four-voice Agnus 'written in a most peculiar manner: three voices in score and one voice separately.'

P. xxii. 'Music written in part-arrangement is ensemble music.' The only exception known to this writer are the organ compositions by Michael Praetorius which are included in the parts books of the *Hymnodia Sionia* (1611) and *Musae Sioniae VII* (1609), with the remark: 'pro organicis: sine textu.' The obvious reason for this procedure is that it would have been technically unfeasable to include keyboard scores in a publication issued as separate part books. In a 'Nota' Praetorius says that an organist wanting to use these compositions may transcribe them 'aus den Noten in die Tabulatur' (see K. Matthei, *Michael Praetorius, Sämtliche Orgelwerke*, 1930; preface by W. Gurlitt, p. 17b). In other words, the actual playing was, of course, from a score, not from the separate parts.

P. 3. Due to the recent discovery (or, rather, rediscovery) of the Codex Faenza the use of this method can be traced back to the late fourteenth century. See D. Plamenac, in *Journal of the American Musicological Society*, IV, 179 (facsimiles opp. p. 192).

P. 6. The flag-like sign in syst. 3, meas. 1 of Facs. 2 is a *Sm-* rest.

P. 10. A transcription of the music preceding the *II. Versus* will be facilitated by the remark that the obscure sign at the beginning of the third measure is a 3, indicating triplets, and that the black *S* and *M* at the beginning of staff 4 are equivalent to a dotted *M* and a *Sm* (*minor color*, see p. 128).

P. 14. The second rest on the first staff of Facs. 5 (near the end of the line) is a *M-* rest.

P. 16. The little curve appearing in Facs. 6, staff 1, near end of meas. 2 (and elsewhere) is a tie.

P. 19. To the list should be added the recently discovered *Libro di ricercate a quattro voci di Rocco Rodio . . .*, Naples, 1575.

P. 26. The second piece of Facs. 7, *Creature*, is in four parts, the third of which is generally the lowest and is, therefore, best transcribed as the bass. In meas. 2 of the first and of the second brace the quick notes of the *altus* should be read an octave higher than written.

P. 30. In the group of letters: c h c h a g (near the end of the second system) the dash indicating the higher octave should extend only over the c and h. In Kotter's tablature as well as in most of the later German tablatures the higher octave starts with h. See *WoHN* ii, pp. 23 and 29.

P. 32. The indication of octaves seems to be rather irregular. Sometimes the b and h below middle c are written with, and sometimes without a dash. Moser's transcription of *In dulci jubilo* contains several errors, owing mostly to a confusion of the letters e and c. The bass part in meas. 2 should be exactly like that in meas. 5.

P. 34. Since these *intonazioni* are ascribed to Giov. Gabrieli in the original publication of 1593, they must be assumed to be his.

P. 44. The short strokes appearing in the upper part of the *Praeambulum bonum super C* are not rests but *puncti divisiones* such as were regularly used in the Italian notation of the fourteenth century. There are many details suggesting a connection between German organ music of the fifteenth and Italian music of the fourteenth century. The lower part is notated exclusively in *B*, often written with elongated heads. The tails attached to two of the *B* are signs of chromatic alteration (b-flat, e-flat).

P. 47. Following are additional suggestions for emendations. Brace 1, meas. last: second note a *M*; brace 5, meas. 2: the dragma takes the place of a *M*; brace 7 (p. 77), meas. 2: the fifth note is a *S*; brace 7, meas. last: the last four notes are a *Sm* each; brace 8, meas. 2: the third note is a *M*; brace 9, meas. 4: the third note is a (dotted) *M*.

P. 49. The sign in Facs. 16, brace 4, upper part, middle, after 10 9 8 is a rest (*M*). The single dot is the rhythmic sign for the minim. The letters D. and M. at the left side mean *Destra* (right) and *Manca* (left).

P. 50. Henestrosa's book has been published by H. Anglés, *La Musica en la corte de Carlos V* (Barcelona, 1944), and that of Araujo by S. Kastner, *Libro de tientos . . . compuesto por Francisco Correa de Arauxo* (Barcelona, 1948). The Spanish keyboard tablature persisted until 1700, e.g., in a Portuguese Ms 'Libro de cyfra . . . ' of the Municipal Library of Porto (see S. Kastner, *Carlos de Seixas* [1947?], p. 26).

P. 62. The dots placed below some of the figures are signs for fingering (index finger).

P. 71. The student will readily notice that in this piece the bass strings are tuned in D major: G-F#-E-D-C#. See the subsequent remarks about *scordatura*. In Gaultier's Ms these changes of tuning are not expressly indicated, but are implied by the grouping of the pieces in suite-like formations under headings such as 'Mode Dorien,' 'Mode Sous-Dorien,' etc. Our piece belongs to the 'Mode Dorien,' which, according to the system then in vogue, is the equivalent of our C major (see *Harvard Dictionary of Music*, s.v. 'Church Modes,' end of III). In Gaultier's collection, however, most of the 'modes' appear in transposition, for instance, the 'Mode Dorien' as D major.

P. 72. No. 76 of *Schrifttafeln* shows the use of stopped bass strings, indicated by the letters b and d (instead of a).

P. 77. The little vertical dashes attached to some of the rhythmic signs indicate the use of the index finger, while those without this dash indicate the thumb.

P. 85. Other early organa written in staffles neumes are found in manuscripts from Chartres, Fleury, Einsiedeln, etc.

P. 96. The use of a whole circle for 'perfect', and of a half circle for 'imperfect' is plausible enough, and the indication of the same qualities by means of a dot would seem to be hardly less plausible, through the coordination: presence = perfect, absence = imperfect. Actually, the latter explanation is wrong. Originally, that is, in the fourteenth century, *prolatio perfecta* was indicated by three dots (perfect = three), *prolatio imperfecta* by two. This method occurs in some Italian sources of c. 1400 (see *WoGMi*, p. 96, 322). Some time later the number was reduced to two for *perfecta* and one for *imperfecta*. An example of this practice exists in a late-fourteenth- century ballade, 'Ung lion say' (see W. Apel, 'The French Secular Music of the Late Fourteenth Century,' *AM* xviii/xix, p. 22). Finally, the number of dots was reduced to one and none respectively.

P. 102. Recent studies of the problem of partial (or, as it is also called, 'conflicting') signatures are: E. E. Lowinsky, 'The Functions of Conflicting Signatures in Early Polyphonic Music' (*MQ* xxxi, p. 227) and M. Johnson, 'A Study of Conflicting Key-Signatures in Francesco Landini' (*Hamline Studies in Musicology*, vol. ii, 1947). Specialized studies like the latter are much needed in order to get more definite results.

P. 104. The MS contains a few errors which we leave for the student to find.

P. 112. According to strict theory this example is wrong, since imperfection is caused here by a note which forms part of a binary group (2 $M = S$), while properly it can be caused only by a note forming part of a ternary group (such as the S in the preceding examples). Correct examples of *imperfectio ad partem remotam* would be:

However, as early as the fourteenth century composers admitted imperfection by a note of a binary group (see the remark on p. 345). On the other hand, it is interesting to notice that the application of the above rule automatically leads to the correct reading of the passage from Pierre de la Rue's *Missa L'homme armé* discussed on p. 112. Here the imperfection is caused, not *ad partem remotam* by the M, but *ad partem propinquam* by two M, that is, the *valor* of a S.

P. 118. M. Bukofzer, in an interesting article, 'The Beginnings of Polyphonic Choral Music' (*Papers of the American Musicological Society*, Annual Meeting, 1940) has pointed out (p. 33) that simultaneous rests are a frequent and characteristic trait of duo sections in English compositions of the fifteenth century. The tenth note on staff 2 of the *recto*-page of Facs. 24 should be a M.

P. 122. Facs. 30 is a section from the Credo of Ockeghem's *Missa L'Homme armé*. At the beginning of the tenor part of the Credo the canonic inscription, 'descendendo in dyapente' is given (see *Johannes Ockeghem, Sämtliche Werke*, ed. by Plamenac, vol. i, p. XXXVa). This accounts for the seemingly faulty pitch.

P. 124. Yet in other words: the equivalent of a *maximodus perfectus* is always represented by a group such as L L L (3+3+3), or Mx L (6+3), never by a single Mx (9).

P. 134. Numerous examples of split groups of coloration in [2, 3] occur in Ockeghem's *Missa Prolationum*, a complete facsimile of which is given in *Johannes Ockeghem, Collected Works* (ed. by Plamenac), vol. ii, plates II–IX (e.g., pl. VI, Contra, first line, starting with the last black ligature,

S S, which is completed by the first *S* of the next ligature). The facsimiles of this publication (subsequently referred to as *Ockeghem* ii) provide most valuable material for the study of the more complicated aspects of White Notation.

P. 136. Mr Bukofzer has identified this composition as Bedingham's *Mon seul plaisir* (after Ms Oporto *714*).

P. 138. See the remark to p. 122.

P. 148. Regarding the proportional signs used in the subsequent explanation see the Commentary to p. 155.

P. 152. The following corrections of Stainer's transcription are suggested. The *S* on a', middle of first staff (above the word *orgoglio*) should be perfect, as is indicated by the dot. This means that the last of the three ensuing *M* goes to the next measure, imperfecting the *B*. This version not only is notationally correct, but also makes much better musical sense. In the three-note ligature near the beginning of the contra the initial *S* remains perfect in spite of the preceding *M*- rest, since it is followed by another *S*, and it is this second *S* which is imperfected by the *M*- rest. This method of producing syncopation occurs frequently in the sources of the late fourteenth century (see p. 395ff). Possibly the passage near the end of the first staff of the contra should be interpreted in a similar way, that is, with the *M*- rest imperfecting, not the preceding *S*, but the second *S* of the ensuing ligature (as in our transcription, No. 20). In the 'clus'- section of the contra the eighth note (omitted by Stainer) should probably be a *M* (once more imperfecting the second-next *S*).

P. 155. Very likely the solution (or, at least, a partial clarification) of the intriguing problem presented by *tempus perfectum diminutum* exists in the fact that a distinction must be made between the signs O 2 and ⊕, to the effect that the former indicates notated [III,2], the latter, notated [II,3]. Hence, the former sign calls for a rendition in $^3/_4$ (as in the example (b) of p. 154), the latter for one in $^3/_8$ or, if two perfections are combined, in $^6/_8$ (as under (a) of the same page). A good illustration of this practice is found on pl. XIII of *Ockeghem* ii, containing the *Rex gloriae* of the Requiem. Here the entire *cantus* and *bassus* are notated in O 2, while a section of the contra (beginning near the end of the third staff) is notated in ⊕ . Under the former sign we find groups of three imperfect *B* to the equivalent of a perfect *L*; under the latter groups of three (imperfect) *S* to the equivalent of a perfect *B*.   Isaac also seems to have followed this practice.   The student may compare the example quoted on p. 154 (from *De radice Jesse*, Facs. 38, p. 173) with his *Dico ego* (Facs. 37, p. 174; discussed on p. 170).   The question would certainly be worthy of further investigation.

If the above theory is confirmed, our general explanations given on pp. 148 to 150 would be correct only if the sign ϕ is replaced everywhere by the sign O 2.

P. 163, top.   For a transcription of the whole example it is advisable to use irregular measures in the tenor as well.

P. 163, bottom.   It is entirely possible that the time signatures in this source and in others of the period still retain to a certain extent their proportional meaning, serving to regulate the tempo (see p. 188ff).

P. 164.   Two other early examples of this practice exist in *Helas merci* and *A qui fortune* by Matheus de Perusio, who flourished in the first two decades of the fifteenth century.   They are transcribed (from the Codex Modena) in W. Apel, *French Secular Music of the Late Fourteenth Century* (1949).

P. 167.   While Ockeghem's *Missa L'Homme armé* is an example of the later practice, his *Missa Prolationum* is based on the earlier interpretation of *prolatio perfecta* (see below, remark to p. 181).   The 'Exemplum Quinti Toni Johannis Ockegem' reproduced on p. 167 is taken from the *Missa Prolationum*.   Therefore our remarks regarding 'lack of correctness in late documents' and Seb. Heyden's failure 'to use the signs correctly' are without foundation, all the more since Heyden in connection with this and other examples from the *Missa Prolationum* expressly says that this use of the 'signa integra' (i e., of the signs of *prolatio perfecta* without the sign of diminution) is 'contra artem ac usum aliorum,' ascribing it to scribal error (see *Ockeghem* ii, p. XXIII).   Another very interesting example of this type is the *Quam olim Abrahae* from Ockeghem's Requiem (*Ockeghem* ii, pl. XIV).

P. 168.   As is explained in the commentary to p. 155, the sign used in this example indicates notated [II, 3], actual [2, 3], so that a transcription in 6/8 appears proper.

P. 170.   See the commentary to p. 155.

P. 172.   Possibly they are a late remnant of the 'reversed coloration' which is often found in the sources of Mannered Notation (see p. 406, par. 3). If so, they would suggest perfect B, resulting in a shift of accent from $\acute{B}\ \acute{S}S\ \acute{B}$ to $\acute{B}S\ \acute{S}B$ (i.e., from $^3/_4$ to $^6/_8$).

P. 176. See the commentary to p. 155.

P. 179. It will be noticed that our two renditions (p. 178 bottom and p. 179 top) show yet another inconsistency in the reading of the discant, that is in the two passages marked $\supset$ ($^2/_4$ meter), the first of which is transcribed in: S = eight-note, the second in: S = sixteenth-note or, in the final rendition on p. 179, in sixteenth and thirty-second notes respectively. It is possible to avoid this inconsistency by doubling all the values of second passage (spreading this passage over two, instead of one, $^6/_8$-measures of the contra, but only by the admission of another inconsistency of the same nature, that is in the two passages marked $\emptyset$, the second of which (beginning at the end of our transcription) would then have to be rendered in half the values used for the first (initial measures of the transcription). The former of these alternatives (used in our transcription) is, no doubt, preferable on stylistic grounds, as it results in a much smoother counterpoint. By the way, *exent* means not 'exhausted' but 'superior' or 'outstanding', a designation equally not devoid of significance.

P. 181. This composition is the final *Agnus Dei* from La Rue's *Missa L'Homme armé*. Ample additional material for the study of mensuration canons as well as other devices of White Notation exists in the facsimile reproduction of Ockeghem's *Missa prolationum* which are given in *Ockeghem* ii, plates II to IX. A brief explanation of the notational principles of this work is given on p. XX of the publication In the title of this famous composition the term *prolationes* is used in the older sense of the word (Philippe de Vitry, see p. 340), synonymous with what we call mensurations. Each of the four voice parts is written in a different mensuration, the two upper parts forming a canon in [2,2] and [3,2], the two lower ones a canon in [2,3] and [3,3]. The relationship between imperfect and perfect prolation is based on the equality of the M, in conformity with the older practice recommended by Tinctoris (see p. 166; also commentary to p. 167).

P. 184. In the bass part the fourth note from the end of the second staff should be a Sm. On the third staff there are three groups of two F. In each group the second of these F should be a Sm.

P. 186.   The solution is correct, as is confirmed by the recent publication of the piece in S. Clercx, *Johannes Ciconia* (1960), vol. ii, No. 22 (based on Bologna, Lic. mus. *Q 15, olim Cod. 37*).   In the Tenor the last pair of 'rests' is actually the sign for repeat and the two subsequent *L* are the beginning of the *Amen* which is omitted in the three other parts.   In Bologna the first of the two long ligatures is separated after its sixth note, the second after its fifth note, whereby both of these notes automatically become *L*.

P. 202.   Regarding doubts as to the existence of a 'younger Johannes de Garlandia' see G. Reese, *Music in the Middle Ages* (1940), p. 287, fn. 42.

P. 206.   It may be noticed that the intervallic indications of this example are in contradiction to the principle, stated in the *Musica Enchiriadis*, that the fundamental *vox principalis* (in the present case, the second voice from below) cannot be chromatically altered.   The adoption of this principle would mean that the second and fourth parts are to be read with F-natural, the other two with B-flat.

P. 207. For a photographic reproduction of the original, together with more detailed explanations see W. Apel, "The Earliest Polyphonic Composition . . . " (*Revue Belge de Musicologie* x, 1956, p. 129).

P. 208.   P. Wagner, in *AMW* vi, p. 405, fn. 2, gives a plausible explanation of this sign, saying that it is 'the *oriscus* or *strophicus* well known from neumatic notation, that is, a *portamento* transition from one main note to the next, which later was performed as a simple prolongation.'

P. 212.   Goslenus (Josquelin de Vierzy) was archbishop of Soissons from 1126 to 1152.   The prevailing opinion is that the ascriptions frequently given in the *Codex Calixtinus* are fraudulent.   See G. M. Dreves, *Analecta hymnica*, xvii, p. 5; *Liber Sancti Jacobi: Codex Calixtinus* (Santiago de Compostela, 1944), iii (Estudios e Indices), p. LII, fn. 1.

P. 219, top.   Modal rhythm is clearly indicated for the clausula- sections of Leoninus' organa.   Whether the organal sections of his compositions should also be interpreted in modal meter, is still a controversial question (see p. 267ff).   The *Benedicamus Domino* of Facs. 49 (p. 247), although not necessarily by Leoninus, illustrates the style of his period.

P. 219, middle. Our distinction between these four types should not be construed as implying that they represent different systems of notation. Rather are they different manifestations of one unified system, that is, of Square Notation.

P. 222. The rules regarding the rests in the various modes are implied in the statement that the final note of a mode (or of an ordo) has the same value as the first ('. . . terminatur per eamdem quantitatem qua incipit;' Anon. IV, *CS* i, 328b). The only mode which does not conform with this rule is the fourth.

P. 223. Both Anon. IV and Joh. de Garlandia (*CS* i, 102ff) explain the imperfect modes in such detail that a few more words of explanation (and, to a certain extent, correction) seem to be in place, particularly since the descriptions given in *HdN* i, 232 and G. Reese, *Music in the Middle Ages*, p. 280 are incomplete. The imperfect modes can be defined as modes in which rests appear at regular distances in such a way that each group of notes closes with a value different from that which opens it (Garlandia, p. 97: 'modus imperfectus . . . terminatur per aliam quam per illam in qua incipit'). As an illustration there follow examples of the first and second mode:

Primus modus imperfectus

Primus ordo:

Secundus ordo:

Tertius ordo:

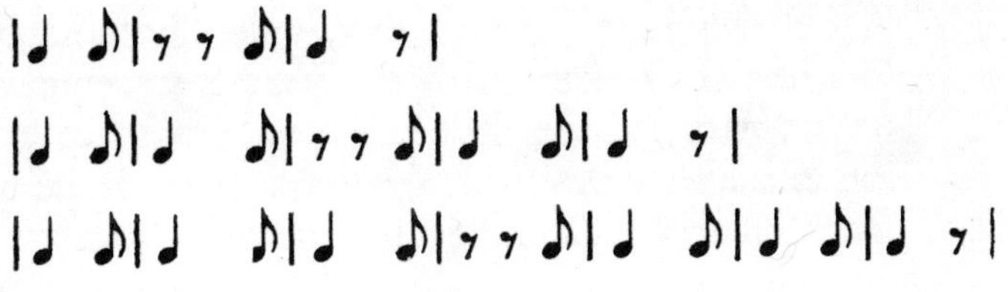

Secundus modus imperfectus

Primus ordo:

Secundus ordo:

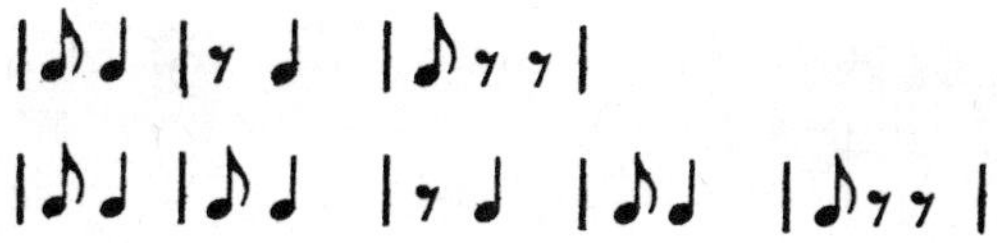

The only example I have found in the practical sources is the tenor of the motet *Se je sui—Jolietement—Omnes* (*Mo*, No. 316):

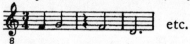 etc.

According to strict theory, however, the third measure should have a quarter note (*B*) followed by two rests.

P. 232.   An unusually clear description of the various meanings of the *pausatio* is given by Anon. IV (*CS* i, 350b): 'There is another kind of *pausatio* which seems to be a *pausatio* but actually is not, and this is called *suspirium*. It has no time value as such, but takes its time from the preceding note. This, by the way, is often done by the singers whether there is a dash (*tractus*) written or not. . . . There is yet another kind of dash found in the lower part. This is sometimes longer, sometimes shorter, and does not have a definite time value (*nullum tempus signat*). It is written because of the change of syllables (*divisio sylla-barum*) . . .'

P. 237.   'The mode never changes within the main part of a clausula.' Aside from internal evidence (writing of ligatures) this theory is supported by the fact that all clearly notated motets show uniformity of mode. Some scholars (Bukofzer) are inclined to extend this principle to the final *copulae*, preferring (in the example under consideration) a rendition in the first mode, with upbeat. Since the *copulae* were never included in the motets, it is difficult to arrive at a decision in this question.

P. 256.   At the end of the first brace the last note of the duplum coin-cides with the *initialis* of the last ligature of the tenor (as suggested by the vertical alignment), while the *finalis* of this ligature coincides with the first note of the next line of the duplum. The second section of the duplum (coincident with the second statement of the c.f. in the tenor) starts with a *D* on c'. The penultimate note of the preceding section, on g, is also a *D*. Aside from this, each single note of the duplum is a *L*, each binaria *B L*, and each ternaria *L B L*.

P. 258.   According to Mr Bukofzer this clausula should be transcribed in the first mode. In this case the *L* of the original would indicate perfect *longae*, the *B*, imperfect *longae* or *breves*.

P. 260.   There exist a number of conductus in which the *caudae* are of extraordinary dimensions, occasionally leading to an almost complete obliteration of the syllabic sections. Two such highly embellished con-ductus, *Pater noster commiserans* and *Salvatoris hodie* (the latter by

Perotinus, according to Anon. IV; see *CS* i, 342a) are reproduced in *OH* (pp. 252, 292; the transcriptions given there are not correct, particularly in the melismatic sections).

P. 261. The introduction of bar-lines is contingent on the metrical structure of the poetic text, the obvious principle being that the accented syllable should fall on the first beat. The great majority of conductus texts show the versification of *Hac in anni janua*, that is, of four trochaic feet (the last catalectic): $- \cdot - \cdot - \cdot -$. In the case of iambic feet, $\cdot - \cdot - \cdot - \cdot -$, the first syllable falls, of course, on the upbeat. An example in point is the conductus *Luto carens et latere* (W_1, p. 73):[1]

In not a few cases the versification changes within the poem, for instance from trochaic to iambic feet. An example is the conductus *Roma gaudens jubila* (W_1, p. 107). Following is the first stanza of the poem (the second stanza has identical versification), arranged in musical measures: Ro- . . . ma / gau- dens / ju- bi- / la — / Men- tis / pro- cul / nu- bi- / la Splen- / dor ex- / pel- lat / nu- bi- / la Splen- / dor pa- / cis et / glo- ri- / e Fi- / de- li- / bus Lu- / gen- ti- / bus Or- . . . / tus de / tu- o / prin- ci- / pe — /.

The dots indicate the places of melismatic passages which occur in this conductus not only at the end of the composition (as in *Hac in anni janua*), but also at the beginning of several lines.[2]

From the preceding explanations it appears that an understanding of the vers structure of the poetic texts is of great importance for the transcription of the music.[3] The great majority of conductus have trochaic or iambic feet and therefore can be rendered in two-beat measures ($\frac{6}{8}$), with or without upbeat. In the case of dactylic or anapaestic feet ($- \cdot \cdot$ or $\cdot \cdot -$) three-beat measures ($\frac{9}{8}$) would have to be used. Naturally the possibility of irregular groups must be admitted, either if the music clearly calls for a modification of the regular scheme, or if the text shows irregular versification.

Examples showing irregular versification are found particularly in the 11th fascicle of W_1 (pp. 176–197) which contains a singular repertory of

---

[1] In the transcription given by L. Ellinwood ('The Conductus,' *MQ* xxvii, p. 191) the bar-lines are wrongly placed.

[2] The entire conductus is transcribed in A. T. Davison and W. Apel, *Historical Anthology of Music*, i (1946), No. 38. For a somewhat different rendition see G. Reese, *Music in the Middle Ages* (1940), p. 309.

[3] Many of the texts of the repertory in question are reprinted in G. M. Dreves and C. Blume, *Analecta hymnica*, vols. xx, xxi, or in G. Milchsack, *Hymni et sequentiae* (1886). Nearly all of them are listed in U. Chevalier, *Repertorium hymnologicum* (1892ff). In dealing with conductus from W_1 the references given in A. Hughes, *Index to the Facsimile Edition of MS. Wolfenbüttel 677* (1939) are useful.

sequences and tropes for the Ordinary of the Mass, mostly composed in two-voice syllabic style.[1] A composition such as the *Kyrie super celos* (*W*₁, p. 177) is best transcribed without bar-lines, possible also in free rhythm rather than in modal meter.

P. 262.   There are, however, instances showing that it is advisable to approach this question with an open mind.   A particularly interesting case is the conductus *Dic Christi veritas* (*Fl*, p. 203).   At three places of the tenor, each time for the first syllable of a verse ('dic,' 'dic,' and 'u-') we find a *binaria* with a prolonged head for the *initialis*, a shape which, no doubt, is intended to indicate the rhythm *L B*, and which possibly proves *ex contrario* that the normally written *binariae* mean *B L*, an interpretation which is also strongly supported by the contrapuntal context.

As regards the groups with three or more notes, numerous mistakes have been caused by the fact that these notes occur preferably in descending motion and, consequently, appear in the misleading form of *conjuncturae* (see p. 241; also the explanations in *OH*, p. 242f). There can be hardly any doubt that the *conjuncturae* have the same rhythmic meaning as the ligatures.

P. 263.   A rendition in the second mode would lead to a more acceptable result.

P. 271.   Attention is called to the exchange of Communications between W. G. Waite and me in *JAMS* v, 272ff.   Mr. Waite's reply does not (as he hopes) "satisfy my questions."   Aside from any points of debate or disagreement I want to say that I consider my explanations not as a 'theory' (as is, to a large extent, the 'modal theory') but only as an exegesis of statements given by some of the most eminent writers of the 13th century.   Whoever finds fault with the 'principle of consonance' (and I am not entirely certain about its validity myself) will have to take it up with them.

---

[1] J. Handschin has made a plausible case for the surmise that the entire contents of this fascicle is of English origin. See his article, 'A Monument of English Mediaeval Polyphony' (*The Musical Times* lxxiii [1932], p. 510 and lxxiv [1933], p. 697).

P. 306. The codex is published in A. Auda, *Les "Motets Wallons" du manuscript de Turin, Vari 42*, 2 vols. (1953). The major part of its contents turn out to be in Franconian, partly even Petronian notation.

P. 308. Mr Anglés informs me that the reasons for his methods of transcription are set forth in his Introduction and Critical Commentary.

P. 325. Published by L. Schrade in *Polyphonic Music of the Fourteenth Century*, vol. I (1956). Concerning Schrade's interpretation of the small values see my review in *Speculum* xxxii, p. 863.

P. 328. The other is *Quomodo cantabimus*. Its tenor closes with three red *L*, each of which is perfect, while the preceding *L* are all imperfect. Thus, the red notes have here the meaning of reversed coloration (see p. 406).

P. 333. A strong argument in favor of Wolf's view is supplied by the organ arrangement of the motet *Firmissime—Adesto—Alleluia* (Facsimile 66), which exists in the Ms Brit. Mus. *Add. 28550* (Robertsbridge Codex), the earliest extant source of keyboard music (see p. 37). Here the various *conjuncturae* of the motet are reproduced in single notes which invariably show the rhythm *B SS*, not *SS B*. Following is the beginning of the organ arrangement, which may be compared with the transcription of the motet given on p. 335:

Since this organ arrangement is only about twenty years later than the *Roman de Fauvel*, it carries great weight in all the questions presented by this source. On the other hand, it carries no greater weight than older sources, such as *Mo* and *Fl*, which have several pieces in common with the *Roman de Fauvel* and which, naturally, show the older rhythm of the *conjuncturae* (see the examples in *WoGM* i, 52). The only safe conclusion is that matters were in a fluid state between 1300 and 1325.

It will be noticed that the above example also furnishes additional evidence in the question of the groups of *S*, supporting the rendition favored by F. Ludwig (see p. 327). The same rhythm is consistently used in the organ arrangement of the motet *Tribum quem* which, together with the original version from the *Roman de Fauvel*, is reproduced in *WoGM* ii, iii, No. 78.

It is not impossible that a full investigation, long overdue, of the *Roman de Fauvel* may yield more definite results for the various problems which this source presents.

P. 335.   In the discant, at the end of the second long line, notes to the value of a *L* are missing in the MS.   According to Brussels, Bibl. Roy. *Ms. 19606* the notes to be supplied are g' f'-e'-f'-e' (*B S-S-S-S*).

P. 336.   Or, very possibly, of the delight in grotesque shapes which appears so clearly in the pictorial representations of this period, for instance the gargoyles and hunchbacks that adorn the Gothic cathedrals.

P. 338.   "*In Navarino*" does not refer to the kingdom of Navarre but to the *Collegium Navarrense* of Paris, founded in 1304 by Jeanne de Navarre, wife of Philippe IV (*le Bel*).   Cf. the remarks by A. Gilles in *Revue Belge de musicologie* x, p. 150, concerning the possibility of de Vitry's association with the College either as a student or as a teacher.

P. 340.   The literal meaning of *prolatio* is 'manner of delivery.'

P. 345.   See commentary to p. 112.

P. 358.   Both sections are perfect, I in *maximodus perfectus*, II in *modus perfectus*, but with an imperfect group at the end.

P. 364.   The tenor is repeated in diminution.

P. 367.   In a recent article, 'The Music of the Old Hall Manuscript' (*MQ* xxxv, No. 1), M. F. Bukofzer makes a remark to the effect that my assumption of a clerical error in the use of the mensuration signs does not provide a satisfactory explanation (p. 49, fn. 31).   However, his criticism is evidently based on the arrangement of these signs as they occur in the original Ms, not on the exchanged order which I suggested. If the signs are arranged as I suggested, that is, ⊙ ℂ O, the values under ⊙ (that is, in the first section) *are* triple of those under O (that is, in the third section).   This little controversy is included here because it will contribute to clarify our explanations of the notation of this tenor.

As regards the duplication of values which takes place in the second section (that is, according to my theory, under the sign ℂ), a plausible explanation can be given if this section is considered in relationship not to the third section (as is done in the main text), but to the first.   In fact, the signs ⊙ and ℂ designate respectively 9 and 6 units, and therefore correctly indicate the ratio of 3 to 2 which exists between the first and the second sections.   See the table of values given in Collins' edition, vol. iii, p. XXVIII.

P. 369.   Petrus de Cruce came from Amiens in Northern France.

P. 374.   Giovanni da Cascia and Giovanni da Florentia are identical. Cascia was a little place near Florence.

P. 380.   This argument loses some of its weight in view of the fact that the *divisiones* .o., .p., and .q. are indicated in the tenor, possibly to direct the singer to use different values for the *B* in the different sections.   The sixth note from the end of the first staff in Facs. 75 should be omitted.

P. 382.   The sign .sg. means *senaria gallica*.   Marchettus de Padua in his *Pomerium musicae* (*GS* iii, p. 121ff; see also *CS* iii, p. 1ff) comments in detail upon the difference of the French and the Italian interpretation of the smaller values (i.e., groups of *S* taking the place of a *B*), and suggests using the letters *g* (*gallice*) and *y* (*ytalice*) for the purpose of distinction (*GS*, p. 175ff).   The following table illustrates the main points of his theory:

According to F. Ludwig (*Guillaume de Machaut, Musikalische Werke*, ii, p. 24b, fn. 1) the signs *g* and *y* are both found in the Rossi Codex.   I am not in the position to say whether their practical use in this source conforms with the theoretical explanation of Marchettus.   The description of the codex, given by J. Wolf in *Peters' Jahrbuch*, vol. 45, contains no information on this question.

P. 384.   The word probably means *Retrove* (not *Petrone*).

P. 404.   On the basis of recent investigations the situation can be more clearly outlined.   The system of mixed notation can, for all practical purposes, be identified with the late Italian school, while the system of mannered notation developed in France after the death of Machaut, where it was in vogue from c. 1375–1400.   The main difference between the two systems is that the Italians, in spite of all refinements, never abandoned the idea of 'measure music,' that is, of music whose rhythmic life unfolds within the limits of measures. In Italian music the measures vary, if at all, only from section to section (horizontally), never from part to part (vertically). Moreover, syncopation over the bar-line is practically non-existent in Italian music. These limitations are completely abandoned in the French music of the late fourteenth century, a music which may well be said to represent the most complete realization (in a way, the only realization in all music history) of the polyrhythmic ideal. It is probably not by chance that the polyrhythmic composition *Fortune*, which has been studied as an example of mixed notation, bears a French title. It would find its proper place among the examples of mannered notation. The manneristic school was located mainly in southern France, at the papal court of Avignon and the splendid secular courts of the Duke of Berry, of the Count of Foix, of the King of Aragon, and others. This school included, in addition to numerous Frenchmen (Solage, Senleches, Trebor and others) some composers of Italian extraction, notably Anthonellus de Caserta (a town near Naples), Philipoctus de Caserta, and Matheus de Perusio (Perugia). Philipoctus can definitely be associated with Avignon.

The decline, after 1400, of the manneristic extravagances of this school brought about a return of a simpler style. This change entailed the abandoning of mannered notation and the return to the principles of French notation.

Recent publications dealing with this period are: G. de Van, 'La Pedagogie musicale a la fin du moyen âge' (*Musica Disciplina* ii); N. Pirrotta, 'Il Codice Estense lat. 568 e la musica francese in Italia al principio del '400' (*Atti della R. Accademia di Scienze Lettere e Arti di Palermo*, serie IV, vol. V, parte II, 1944/45); W. Apel, 'The French Secular Music of the Late Fourteenth Century' (*AM* xviii/xix); W. Apel, *French Secular Music of the Late Fourteenth Century* (1949).

P. 405. For a variation in the meaning of these signs see the article in *AM* xviii/xix, p. 22. See also the commentary to p. 96.

P. 408. In two other sources, Paris, Bibl. Nat. *nouv. acq. frc. 6771*, p. 80, and Paris, Bibl. Nat. *ital. 568*, p. 126'/127, the composition appears with a text for the upper part.

P. 412. Even in those cases where the text is incomplete or missing can the form be determined from the position of the *clos-* ending. In a ballade this short group appears at the end of the first section, in a virelai at the end of the second section, while in a rondeau there is no *clos-* ending since neither of its two sections is repeated immediately. Thus it appears that *Je la remire* (Facs. 82) is a virelai.

P. 418. In examples like this may be seen the first adumbration of the modern principle of notation according to which binary values are used for the writing down of ternary (as well as binary) meter. A particularly interesting case exists in Senleches' *Je me merveil* (*Ch*, p. 44′), which is reproduced and discussed in *French Secular Music* (No. 48).

P. 420. For further clarification of the problems presented by this extremely involved specimen see *French Secular Music*, Commentary to No. 23.

P. 422. For a new attempt of evaluation, on the basis of *Ch*, see *French Secular Music*, Commentary to No. 49.

P. 425. Both the 'Musical Heart' and Cordier's equally interesting 'Musical Circle' (*Tout par compas suy composés*; facsimile in P. Aubry, *Les plus anciens monuments de la musique francaise* (1905), pl. 22; see also *RHdM*, I. ii, p. 351) are later additions to the main repertory of the Chantilly Codex, written, probably by Cordier himself, on separate front leaves.

Commentary (by A. T. D.)

Our ingenious friend, Baude Cordier
Sat him down one Saint Valentine's Day
And made him a heart
Which he sent to his tart
(Wish to hell she had thrown it away!)

INDEX

Extended discussions are indicated by figures in bold type. Musical illustrations (in original notation) are indicated by asterisks. References to modern scholars are not included if these are only named as authors of books.

Abgesang 417

Accidentals 16, 104ff; see Chromatic alteration; Musica ficta; Partial signature

Accord 71f

Adam von Fulda 90, 99

Ad organum faciendum 201, 207

Agricola, Martin 72

Al Farabi 55

Alla breve 148

Alla longa 157

Alla semibreve 148

Alleluia (Ba, Hu) *306

Alleluia vocavit Jhesus (Cod. Calixtinus) 212, *213, 267

Alleluya (St. Victor) 248, *249

Allwoode 8

Alteration 108, **112**, 122, 221, 344

A madame playsante *133

Amans ames *175

Amerus 202

Ammerbach, Nicolaus 22, 32

Amo *255, 256

Amor da po *394

Amor tu solo 407, *409

Anapaest 222

Angelica 55, 72

Anglés, H. 214, 308, 447

Anima mea 134, *135

Anonymus: A. II (*GS* i) 21; A. III (*CS* iii) 202, 320, 392; A. IV (*CS* i) 202, 218, 240, 243f, 270, 282, 310, 444, 445; A. IV (*CS* iii) 320, 392; A. V (*CS* iii) 202; A. VI (*CS* i) 340; A. VII (*CS* i) 202, 296; A. de la Fage 268; A. Sowa 202, 246, 268, 339

Anthonellus de Caserta 414, *415

Antonius de Leno 203

Apostropha 210

Apt, Codex 202

Aptatur (Ba) *303; (*Mo*) 315, *317

Aquil' al tera ferma 374, *375

Arnaldi *94

Aron, Pietro 114

Ars Antiqua 322, 324f, 385

Ars Nova 106, 311, 320, 322, 326, 332, 339, 385, 403

Aston, Hugh 8

Attaingnant, Pierre 4, 6, *7, 56, 64

Aubry, P. 241

Aucun ont trouvé—Lonc tans—Annuntiantes 319, *321

Audi filia 215

Augmentation **163**

Ave beatissima—Ave Maria—Johanne 289, *291

Ave regina 117, *119

Bacfarc, Valentin 69

Bach, J. S. 32, 33, 37, *39, 127, 132

Ballade 417

Ballata 151, 390

Bamberg, *Ed. IV. 6* 202, **302**

Bar (form) 417

Bar-line 3, 9, 16, 28, 67, 85, 101, 416

Bartholomeus de Bononia 140, *143, 429

Bartolinus de Padua 374, 376

Bass courses 69f, 72

Basse danse 67f

Beat 97, 147, 324, 343

Beck, J. 274

Bedingham 440

Beethoven 100

Belle bonne 425, *427

Belle que vous 166, *167

Bellermann, A. 87, 132

Benche partito 398, *399

Benedicamus Domino 216; (*Fl*) 245, *247, 267f, 270f, 444; (*It 568*) 378 *379

Benet, Johannes 102, *105, 106

Berlin, *Mus. Ms. Z 26* (Kleber tablature) 30. *P. 283,* see Orgelbüchlein

Bermudo, Juan 47f, *48

Bern, Bibl. Bongarsiana *Ms A 421* *361

Bernelinus 21

Besardus, Jean-Baptiste 69

Besseler, H. 102, 322, 343

Biaute parfaite 405, 418, *419

Biaute qui toutes 356, *359

Bitonality 78, 102, 104

Black notation xxii, **199**

Blackened notes, see Coloration

Blitheman, William 8

Blume, F. 67

Boethian letters 21, 208

Boethius 146

Bologna, Bibl. Univ. *2216* *94, 202, 362

Bologna, Lic. Mus *37* 94, 364

Boumgartner 22, *25

Brahms 132

Branle commun *7

Brevis 3, 87, 220, 269, 282, 370

Bruger, H. 68

Brumans est mors *303

Brumel, Antoine 158

Brussels, Bibl. Royale *MS 6428* *142; *Proportionale* (Tinctoris) 152, *153, 158, 161

Buchner, Johannes 24

Bukofzer, M. F. 230, 264, 364, 437, 440, 445, 448

Burgundian cadence 106, 117

Burgundian School 26, 106

Buxheimer Orgelbuch 22ff, *25

Buxtehude 37

Cabezon, Antonio de 50f, *53

Caccia 368

Cambrai *Ms 6* 202, 362, *363

Candida—Flos filius 252, 284, *285

Canon **179**, 403, 433

Canonic inscriptions 186f

Canonici MS, see Oxford

Cauda 260, 445

Cavazzoni, Girolamo xxi, 14

Ce ieusse fait 123, 140, *141

C'est la jus *277

Cephalicus 210, 226f

Chansonnier: Laborde *109, *130; *Noailles* 201, 271, *277; *Roy* 201, 271f, *273, 338

Chantilly, Musée Condé *1047* 91, 164, 203, 404, *413, 425, *427

Cheironomic neumes 208

Chitarrone 55

Chol gli occhi *387, 390

Choir book arrangement xx

Choralis Constantinus 168ff, *169, *171, *173, *174

Chromatic alteration 4, 6, 21f, 23, 24f, 44, 50

Ciconia, Johannes 202

Cithrinchen 55, 72

Clausula 145, 215, 217, 230, 237, 267

Clef 3, 9, 16, 107

Climacus 240

Clivis 88

Clos, see Ouvert

Codex Calixtinus 201, 212, *213, 214, 443

Coelho, Manoel Rodriguez 19

Collins, H. B. 188, 366, 432ff

Coloration 10, 12, **126**, 142, 405. See Courante-coloration, Half-coloration, Minor color, Triplet coloration, Reversed coloration

Color prolationis **127**, 138, 140

Color temporis **127**, 138, 140

Compostela, School of 212

Conductus 216, 219, **258**

Conductus-motet 263, 274

Conjunctura 224, **240**, 254, 296, 304, 333, 447

Conradus de Pistoria 429

Consonance and dissonance **244**, 270f

Convenientia modorum 288

Copula 234, 237, 248, 256, 445

Cordier, Baude 175, 425, *427

Correa de Araujo 50, 438

Corona 94

Courante coloration 14, 68, **127**, **138**

Coussemaker, E. de 262, 284, 319

Covered play 70

Creature *25, 437

Crucifigat omnes *264, 265

Crucifixus *186

Cunelier, Johannes 428

Currentes 240, 270

Custos 3, 94, 418

Dactyl 222

Dame gentil 414, *415

Dangier tu m'as 107, *109, 129

Dannemann, E. 175

Dasia notation 204, 206

De petit po *345, *349

De radice Jesse 172, *173, 441

Descendit de celis 231f, *233, 241

Detractor est—Qui secuntur—Verbum iniquum 330

Diastematic neumes 208

Dic Christi veritas 447

Dico ego 170, *174, 441

Didier le Blanc 129

Dietricus 202, 223, 296, 302, 314

Dieux gart 426f

Diex je—Amors qui m'a— Et super 289, *293

Diminutio 147, 149, 151f, 155

Discantus 218f

Discantus positio vulgaris 201, 220

Divisio modi 225, 231, 245, 282, 302

Divisiones **370**, 389

Dodekachordon 108, 180, *181

Dominicus de Feraria *143, 187

Domino *257, 258

Dona i ardenti 94, 102, *103

Dot 4, 122.   See Punctus

Dous amis 355, *357

Dragma 392, 400, 408, 412, 420

Ductia 238

Dufay, Guillaume 102, *103, 117, *119, 134, 142, *166, *194

Dunstable, John *124, *187

Duodenaria, see Divisiones

Duple meter 290

Duplex longa 224, 245f, 286, 288, 310, 328

Duplum notation 219, **267**

Dusiacki 70

Ellend du hast *45, 47

Ellinwood, L. 262

En attendant esperance 422, *423

Ensemble music xxi

Epiphonus 226

Epitrita 161

Erlangen, Univ. Bibl. *729* 40

Ersatzklausel 215

Et gaudebit (W_1) *252, 279; (F_1) 254, *255

Et in terra (Ockeghem) *167; (*Huelgas*) 308, *309; (*Old Hall*) 364, *365, *366

Et occurrens 245, 254, *255

Et resurrexit *139

Extensio modi 223, **234**

Falscher Schäffer 34, *36

Favellandi vicium *333

Felix virgo—Inviolata—Ad te suspiraamus 358, *360

Fillis sass 34, *36

Finalis 89

Finger notation 54

Finis punctorum 104, 290

Fitzwilliam Virginal Book 8

Firmissime—Adesto—Alleluia benedic-tus *329, 330, 335, 447

Florence, Bibl. Laur. *Pal. 87*, see Squarcialupi Codex

Florence, Bibl. Laur. *Plut. 29.1 (Fl)* 201, 215, 217, *229, *247, *248, *250, *251, 254, *255, *257, *266

Florence, Bibl. Naz. *Magl. xix 112 bis* *135, 191, *192

Florence, Bibl. Naz. *Panc. 26* 203, *387

Flos filius *229, 238, 251, 274, 279, 284

Flos subitus 334

Fortune *375, 400f

Fortune a bien couru 64, *65, *66

Fractio modi 223, **235**

Franco of Cologne xxii, 202, 220, 270, 296, 310ff

Franconian notation xxiii, 199, **310**

Freistimmigkeit 4

French notation 199, **338**, 404

Frescobaldi, Girolamo 67

Friderici 70

Fuenllana, Miguel de 62

Fuhrmann, Leopold 69

Fundamentum organisandi 40, 44, *45

Fur non venit *327

Fusa 3, 87

Gabrieli, Andrea (Giovanni) 34, *35

Gafurius, Franchinus 90f, 110, 116, 145, 152, *160, *162, 163

Galilei, Michelangelo 70

Garlandia, Johannes de (the elder) 202, 220, 234, 244, 269f, 283, 298, 302, 343, 444; (the younger) 202, 338, 443

Garrit gallus—In nova fert 328, *331, 335

Gaultier, Denis 70f, *73

Gennrich, F. 278

Genus (multiplex, etc.) 146

Gerle, Hans 76

Giovanni da Cascia 374

Giovanni de Florentia 374, 386, *387

Glarean, Heinrich 108, 120, 172

Glogauer Liederbuch xx

Go *229, 230, *248, *250

Gombosi, O. 61

Goslenus 212, 443

Grossbrummer 74ff

Group style 265f

Guido 426

Guido d'Arezzo xx, 21, 85

Guilelmus Monachus 145, 202

Guitar 55

Hac in anni janua 258, *259, 260ff, 265

Hadrianus, Emanuel 69

Half-coloration 142

Hamilton Codex 71, *73

Hanboys, Johannes 338

Handel 132

Handschin, J. 212, 243, 262

Heckel, Wolff 76

Hei diex—Mal latus *307

Hemiolia 131, 158, 348

He mors—Quare non sum *358

Heyden, Sebaldus (*De arte canendi*) *154, 157, 159, *160, *167, 442

Hieronimus de Moravia 334, 341

Hodie perlustravit *255, 256

Homo quo vigeas—Et gaudebit 265, *275, 279, *281

Hucbald 21, 207

Huelgas, Codex 202, *264, **306**, *309, 324

Huic ut—Huic ut 315, *316

Hui main—Hec dies 272, *273, 274

Hupfauf 78

Iambic 222, 446

Ideoque quod nascetur 168, *169

Ileborgh tablature 8, 40ff, *41

Il n'est si grand possession *361

Imperfection **107**, 122, 129; Imper-fectio ad totum, ad partes, 111, 112, 344, 439f

In campo aperto 208

In dulci jubilo *31, 32, 438

Initialis 88

In seculum (*Mo*) *290; (*Ba*) *302

Instrumental music xxi

Intavolatura 14, 16

Integer valor 52, 147ff, 388

Isaac, Heinrich 144, 168ff, *169, *171, *173, *174

Isochronous 263, 265, 266

Ivrea, Codex 202

Jacobus (of Liége) 318, 338, 340f; see *Speculum musicae*

Jacopo da Bologna 374, *375, *380

Janequin, Clément 159

Je la remire 408, *411

Je ne puis avoir 410, *413

Je ne puis—Flor de lis—Douce dame *292

Je suy exent 176,* 177

Jobin, Bernhard 76

Josquin des Près 152, *154, 180, *181

Judenkunig, Hans 76ff, *79

Judentantz, Der 78, *81

Kargel, Sixt 76

Keyboard partitura xxiv, 16

Keyboard score xxiii, 3

Keyboard tablature xxiii; German 21; Spanish 47

Kinkeldey, O. 28

Kleber, Leonhard 30

Kleinbrummer 74, 78

Kleinsaite 74, 78

Koczirz, A. 78

Koller, O. 284

Körte, O. 60f

Kotter, Hans 28f, *29

Kyrie (La Rue) *121; (Ockeghem) *165; (Obrecht) *183, *184; (*Di dadi*) *184, *186; (*MS Cambrai*) 362, *363; *Kyrie super celos* *447

La dedicasse *73

Lambert, Magister (Pseudo-Aristoteles) 202, 226f, 292ff, 296, 298, 302, 310

Landini, Francesco 374, 386, *387, 390, *391, 392, *393

Lantins, Hughe de 123, *133, 140, *141, 176ff, *177

Laudamus te *94

Laurentius de Florentia 374

Laus Domino—Eius 265, 274, *275, 279

Lautenkragen 75

Leoninus 215, 219, 245, 267, 271

Le Roi, Adrian 68

Letter notation 21f, 24, 30, 32, 34, 37f, 71, 74, 77, 207f

L'homme armé (Josquin) 180, *181; (la Rue) *112, 118, 120, *121, 180, 440, 443; (Ockeghem) *139, 163, *165, 180, 440, 442

Liber usualis 210

Lieto, Don Bartolomeo 33

Ligatures 10, **87**, **223**, 282, **296**, **312**; rules for ligatures 91; ligatura binaria, ternaria, etc., 91, 224, 241; ligatura obliqua 10, 90

Lombardic rhythm 129

London, Brit. Mus.: Keyboard scores 8; *Egerton 274* 201; *Egerton 2615* 201, *242, 271; *Add. 28550*, see Robertsbridge Codex; *Add. 29987* 203; *Add. 30091* 201, *284, *285; *Harl. 978* 238, *239, 242f

Longa 87, 220, 261, 269

Ludwig, F. 100, 209, 217, 220, 224, 230, 245, 274, 284, 322, 325, 333, 346, 354, 355, 368, 448

Lute tablatures xxiii, **54**; French **64**; German **72**; Italian and Spanish **56**

Lute ornamentations 70

Luto carens 446

Mace, Thomas 69f

Machaut, Guillaume de 99, 124, 145, 202 (Mss), **343** (Notation), *353, *357, *359, *360

Madrid, *Hn 167* 201, *240

Madrigal 390

Magi videntes *194

Magnus liber organi 200, 201, 215, 217, 230

Mandora 55, 72

Mannered notation 199, **403**

Marcantonio da Bologna 3, *5, 14

Marchettus de Padua 203, 322, 334, 368ff, 449

Maxima 87, 124, 328

Maximodus 99, **124**, 327f, 440

Mayone, Ascanio *17, 18, 48

Meane 12

Media 91

Melismatic notation 217f

Melismatic style 212, 216, 219

Mensuralists 271

Mensural notation xxii, **3**, **85**

Mensural notes 3, 87

Mensuration 3, **96**, **346**, 404f

Mensuration canon 118

Mensurstrich 101

Mertel, Elias 69

Michalitschke, A. 294

Micrologus xx, 201

Milan, Luis de 56, *57, 62, 190

Minima 3, 87, 319f, 325, 328, 338

Minor color 46, 108, 127, **128**, 136, 144

Missa: Di dadi *184; *L'homme armé*, see *L'homme armé*; *Je ne demande* *184; *O quam suavis* *188; *Prolationum* 440, 442, 443; *Si dedero* 182ff, *183, *185

Mittelbrummer 74, 78

Mittelsaite 74

Mixed notation 199, **385**, 404

Modal notation 199, 219, **220**

Modal rhythm 263, 444

Modena, Bibl. Est. *L. 471* 134, 136, 193, *194; *L. 568* 203, 404f, *411, *415, *423

Modes, rhythmic **220**; perfect, imperfect 223, 444f; rectus, non rectus 269f

Modus 98, **124**, 327; modus major, minor 98; modus perfectus, imperfectus 131, 292, 294, 303, 318, 327, 340, 347

Mon seul plaisir 440

Monsieur 136, *137, 440

Montpellier *H 159* 21; *H 196* 202, **284**, *291, *293, 315, *316, *317, *321

Mora generalis 94

Mordent 24, 30, 49

Morley, Thomas 116

Morleye, Guillaume 68

Mors *235

Motet 219, 263

Motet notation 219, **271**

Moult me fu—Robins m'aimme—Portare 304, *305

Mudarra, Alonso 66

Muffat, Georg 194

Mulierum 256, *257

Mulliner Book 8, 12, *13

Munich, *Mus. Ms. 2987* 47; *Cim. 351a* *137; *Mus. Ms. 3725*, see *Buxheimer Orgelbuch*

Muris, Johannes de 117, 145, 182, 202, 322, 340, 395

Murschhauser, Franz Xaver 163

Musica enchiriadis xx, 201, 204, *205, 443

Musica ficta 16, 104ff, 120

Musica mensurata, plana 87

Musica reservata 118

Narvaez, Luys de 66f

Naschoso el viso 386, *387

Ne pensez pas 352, *353

Nessun ponga speranza 392, *393

Neuhaus tablature 8, 40

Neumes 88, 208, 209, 212

Newsidler, Hans 56, 75ff, 78, *81; Melchior, 76‾

Niemann, W. 220, 228

Nos qui vivimus *206

Notatio cum (sine) litera 218, 286, 294, 304

Notker Labeo 21

Notre Dame, School of 201, 215, 219, 267

Notum fecit *236

Nouveau ton 70, 72

Novenaria, see Divisiones

Nulla pestis—Vergente *327, 337

Obrecht, Jacob xxi, 114, 129, 182, *183, 184, *185

Ockeghem, Johannes *139, *165, *167, 180, 440, 442, 443

Octaves, Indication of 24, 28, 30, 34, 37, 438

Octonaria, see Divisiones

Oddo of Cluny 21

Odhecaton 113, *128, 154, *155, *193

Odington, Walter 202, 220, 221, 268, 338

O dolce compagno *143, 187

Old Hall MS 91, *124, 362, 364ff, *365, *366, 432ff, 437

O Maria—Nostrum 284, *285

Opposita proprietas 10, **90**, 296f

Optatur *303

Ordo **222**

Organ tablature xxiii

Organum 208, 215; organum duplum 267ff; organum purum (etc.) 268f

Orgelbüchlein (Bach) 37, *39

Oriscus 443

Ornithoparchus, Andreas 150

Or qua conpagni 382, *383

Ouvert and clos 94, 152, 335, 349, 412

Ovid 336

Oxford, Christ Church College *MS 371* 8. Oxford, Bodleian Library: *572* 21, *205, 207f; *Can. misc. 213* *103, *119, 123, *141, *143, *175, *177

Paix, Jacob 32

Paolo Tenorista 374, *394, 398, *399, 407, *409

Paris, Bibl. Nat.: *ital. 568* 203, *375, *379, *399, *409; *lat. 11266*, 202; *lat. 15139 (St. Victor 813)* 201, 246, *249; see Chansonnier Noailles, Roy; Machaut (Mss); Reina, Codex; Roman de Fauvel; St. Martial

Part arrangement xx, 437

Part books xx

Partial signature 102, 104, 140, 378, 439

Partitura xxiii, **16**

Patrem omnipotentem 432ff

Paumann, Conrad 40, 44, *45, 74

Pausatio 445

Pavane *57, 66

Perchè cançato e'l mondo 376f, *377

Perfect, imperfect 96, 292, 439; see Tempus, Imperfection, Modes, Modus

Perfectio (in ligatures) **88**, 224, 312f

Perotinus 145, 215, 218, 267, 271, 446

Petrucci 56, 62

Petrus de Cruce 318ff, *321, 324, 369

Philippe de Vitry 202, 322, 330, 338f, 340f, 395

Piae voces 170, *171

Pierpont Morgan Library 410

Pierre de la Rue *112, 118, *121, 157, 180, *181

Pisador, Diego 56, 62, 66

Pitch notation 54

Plica **226**, 235, 260, **298**, 311, 314, **333**; p. duplex longa 230 p. -note, p. -tone, 227

Ploures dames *346, 351

Podatus 88
Porquoy je ne puis *128
Power, Leonel 134, *135
Praetorius, E. 130
Praetorius, Michael 437
Prague, Univ. Bibl. *XI E 9* 202
Preambulum 42f
Pre-Franconian notation xxiii, 199, 263, **282**
Priamel *79
Prima (seconda) volta, see Ouvert and clos
Proceleumaticus 222
Proh dolor 303f, *304
Prolatio 96, **120**, 319, 323, 340, 347, 443, 448; p. perfecta diminuta 167
Pro patribus *303
Proportional notation 145
Proportional time signature 52, **188**
Proportions 52, 62, **145**; p. dupla 147, **148**, **151**; p. tripla 62, 147, **148**, **155**; p. quadrupla 157; p. quintupla 160; p. sesquialtera 146, 157, **158**, 166, 348; p. sesquitertia 146, 160f, 166
Proportz 157
Proprietas **88**, 224, 312f
Prosdocimus de Beldemandis 145, 182, 202, 203
Pseudo-Aristoteles, see Lambert
Punctum (neume) 88, 210
Punctus: p. additionis 101, 116f, 348; p. divisionis 11, 113f, **115**, 295, 299, 318, 344, 348, 352, 369, 385, 396; p. syncopationis 367, **396**; p. alterationis, perfectionis, etc. 116
Punktpaar 397, 410
Pyrrhichius 222

Quadratnotation 217
Quant florist—Non orphanum 254
Quant revient—L'autre jor—Flos filius 252, 272, *273, 284
Quare fremuerunt 325f, *326, 334

Quasi non ministerium—Displicebat 327f, *328, 337
Quaternaria, see Ligatures, Divisiones
Quel fronte signorille *103, 134
Que pena 429ff
Quia respexit *142, 155
Quintsaite 74, 78

Ramis de Pareia 164
Redford, John 8
Red notes **328**, **348**, 356, 358, **405**; see Coloration
Reduction (of note values) 4, 6, 9, 16, 26, 30, 33, 97, 222, 282, 324, 343
Regina Clara Im Hoff 34f, *36
Regnat 250, *251
Reina, Codex 203, *377, 380, *421
Relegentur ab area 265, *266
Renvoisiement *277, 278
Repeated notes 225
Repertorium (Ludwig) 230
Resolutio 184, 186
Resonet *31, 32
Rests 3, 87, **347**, 445; see Divisio modi, Pausatio
Reversed coloration 406, 412, 420, 442
Revolvit *255, 256
Rhétorique des dieux 71, *73
Ricercare 61, 63
Riemann, H. 67, 97, 172, 187, 208, 221, 262
Rippe, Albert de 69
Robert de Handlo 202, 318
Robertsbridge Codex 22, 37, *38, 384, 447
Rokseth, Y, 286, 295, 299, 300, 320
Roma gaudens jubila 446
Roman chorale notation 88, 210, 378
Roman de Fauvel 202, 315, **325**, *326, *329, *331, 448
Rome, Bibl. Vat.: *Chigi cod. C. VIII* 234 *139, *165; *Rossi 215* 203, 374, 382, *383
Rompeltier 154, *155, *193

Rondeau 140, 276ff, 304, 417
Rore, Cipriano de 19, *127
Rose lis *349
Ruina *327
Rules of the B 104

Sachs, C. 67
Salvator withe a meane 12, *13
Salve mater—Salve templum—In nomine *366
Salve regina *27, 28
*Salve virgo—Ave lux—Neuma 289, *291,* 298
S'amours ne fait *350
Sancte spiritus 237, *255, 256
Sanctus: (Benet) 102f, *105; (Obrecht) *185; (*Fl*) 237, *255, 256
Scheidt, Samuel 19f, 22
Schering, A. 43
Schlick, Arnolt 26, *27, 56, 76
Schmid, Bernhard (the elder) 32; (the younger) 32, 33f, *35, 49
Scholia enchiriadis 21, 201, 204, *206
Schrade, L. 61
Scio cui credidi 245, 246, *249
Scordatura 71, 78, 438f
Score arrangement xx, 364, 437
Scotch snap 129
Se Galaas 428f
Se je suis—Jolietement—Omnes 445
Selesses, Jacopinus 422, *423
Semibrevis 3, 87, 295f, 304, 311, **318**; s. major 326; s. caudata (signata) 306, 320, 325, 332, 337, 369, **370**, 381, 405; s. minima, see Minima
Semifusa 3, 87
Semiminima 3, 87, 319
Senaria, see Divisiones; s. gallica 449
Se pronto 390, *391
Sesquialtera, see Proportions
Shepard 8
Short octave 47, 49, 438
Sicher, Fridolin *31, 32
Si dedero, see under *Missa*

Signum congruentiae 94, 102, 118, 167, 180
Silbenstrich 231
Simplex groups 245, 254
Sources of black notation 201ff
Speculum musicae 202, 318, 322, 339, 341
Spiess, L. 204
Spinaccino, Francesco *63
Squarcialupi Codex 203, *391, *393
Square notation xxii, 199, **215**
St. Gall, Stiftsbibliothek *530* *31, 32
St. Martial, School of xx, 201, **209**, 218f, 267, 268, 271
St. Victor 813, see under Paris
Staff 3, 6, 8, 23, 48, 69, 204
Steigleder, Ulrich 14, 22
Sthokem, Johannes *128
Stimmbücher xx
Stollen 417
Strophicus 443
Subsemitonium 120
Subtonium 120
Successive proportions *161*
Sumer is icumen in 243
Sumite karissimi 431f
Sweelinck, Jan Pieterszon 20
Syllabic notation 217, 219, **258**
Syllabic style 216f, 265f
Syncopation 14, 28, 133, 342, 347, 356, 362, 367, **395**, 414f

Ta (W₁) *235; (*Fl*) *255, 256
Tablatures, xxii, xxiii, **21, 54**
Tactus 147f, 150, 190, **191**, 343, 389
Talea 356
Tempo 4, 97, **188**, 324, 343, 388
Tempus 96, 282f, 302f, 340f; t. imperfectum **100**, 322, 330; t. perfectum **107**, 311, 319, 322, 330, 340; t. perfectum diminutum 155, 441
Tenors, Notation of **245, 286, 303, 327**
Text, Underlaying of 118

Theodoricus de Campo 202, 320, 324, 384, 392

Tie 3, 85, 385

Time signatures **188**

Tinctoris, Johannes 90f, 114, 145, *153, 156, 164, 166, 180

Titelouze, Jean 19

Tonschrift 54

Tordion 68

Torino: Bibl. Naz. *J II 9* 203, 404, 405, *419; Bibl. Reale *Var. N. 42* 202, 306, *307, 315

Tout houme veut 417, *419

Trabaci, Giov. Maria 18, 48

Transmutatio 246

Trent Codices 102, *105, *110, 114

Tribrachic 222, 446

Triplet coloration 127, 130, 138

Trochaic 222, 446

Trop plus—Biauté parée—Je ne suis 304

Tui sunt celi 8

Tuning 56f, 70f; see Scordatura

Tunstede, Simon 202, 344

Tu patris sempiternus 204, *205

Un bel sparver *380f

Unison, see Repeated notes

Upper parts, Notation of **252, 294, 304, 330**

Ursprung, O. 92

Ut tuo propitiatus 21, 201, *205, 207

Vado *255, 256

Valente, Antonio 19, 48, *51

Venegas de Henestrosa 50, 438

Veni sancte spiritus (*Old Hall MS*) *124; (*Trent Cod.*) *187

Veri almi pastoris 429

Verulus, Johannes 202, 398

Via artis (*naturae*) 372ff, 382

Victime *303

Viderunt Hemanuel 209, *211

Vieil ton 72

Vienna, Staatsbibliothek *Ms. 18491* 34, *36

Vierhebigkeit 208

Vihuela 56

Vince con lena 123, 140, *143, 151

Virdung, Sebastian 8, 26

Virelai 151, 412

Virga 88, 210

Vitry, see Philippe de Vitry

Vocalisation 219

Vocal music xxi

Vox organalis, principalis 207

Vulpius, Melchior 130

Wagner, P. 443

Warner, S. T. 117

Warsaw, Library Krasinsky *MS 52* 186

Wasielewski, J. W. 60f

Wecker, Hans Jacob 76

Weiss, Silvius Leopold 71

White mensural notation xxii, **85**

Wilkin tablature 22, 40, 43

Willaert, Adrian xxi

Winchester troper 85, 201, 208

Wir Christenleut *39

Wolf, J. 15, 40, 44, 46, 48, 55, 61, 64, 65, 72, 129, 163, 222, 228, 319, 320, 325, 330, 333, 346, 368, 374, 397, 447

Wolfenbüttel: *677* (*W₁*) 201, 217, *235, *236, *252, *259, *264, 446, *447; *1206* (*W₂*) 201, 217, 231, *233, *275, 279, *281

Wooldridge, H. E. 262

Zacharias, Magister 431

Zoppa, Alla 129

APPENDIX
TRANSCRIPTIONS

No. 1   (FACSIMILE 1)

No. 2   (FACSIMILE 2)

No. 3   (FACSIMILE 3)

No. 4   (FACSIMILE 5)

No. 5   (Facsimile 6)

No. 6   (Facsimile 7)

No. 7   (Facsimile 12)

No. 8   (Facsimile 15)

No. 9 (Facsimile 16)

No. 10 (Facsimile 20)

No. 11 (Facsimile 21)

No. 12 (Facsimile 23)

Do- na i ar-den-ti ray

T. Do- na i ar-den-ti ray

C.

No. 13 (Facsimile 25)

Dan- gier tu m'as tol-lu ma da- me

A- ve re - gi - na ce-lo- rum. a- ve

A- ve re - gi - na ce-lo- rum a- ve

A- ve re - gi - na ce-lo- rum a- ve

do- mi- na an-ge- lo-rum sal- ve ra-dix sanc-ta

do- mi- na an-ge- lo-rum sal- ve ra-dix sanc-ta

do- mi- na an-ge- lo- rum sal- ve ra-dix sanc-ta

Kyrie

Kyrie

Kyrie

Kyrie

Gia n'a-mo-ra-to el ben co- sta- re pec- to po-co a ri- guar- do

Ce ieu-sse fait ce que je pen- ce

Ce ieu-sse fait ce que je pen- ce

No. 20

e tro- var an- cor mer-ce- de chi non dis-

pe- ra al pe- ri- glio- so sco- glio.

No. 21

No. 22

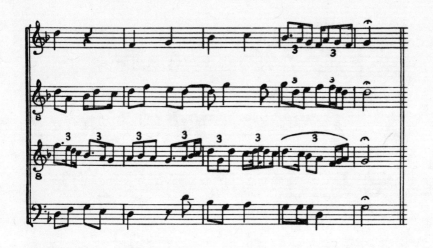

A-

mans a-

mes

se- cre-te- ment se lon- gue-

ment vo- les a- mer.

No. 26

No. 27

No. 28 (FACSIMILE 40)

Crucifixus

No. 29 (FACSIMILE 40)

Sanctus

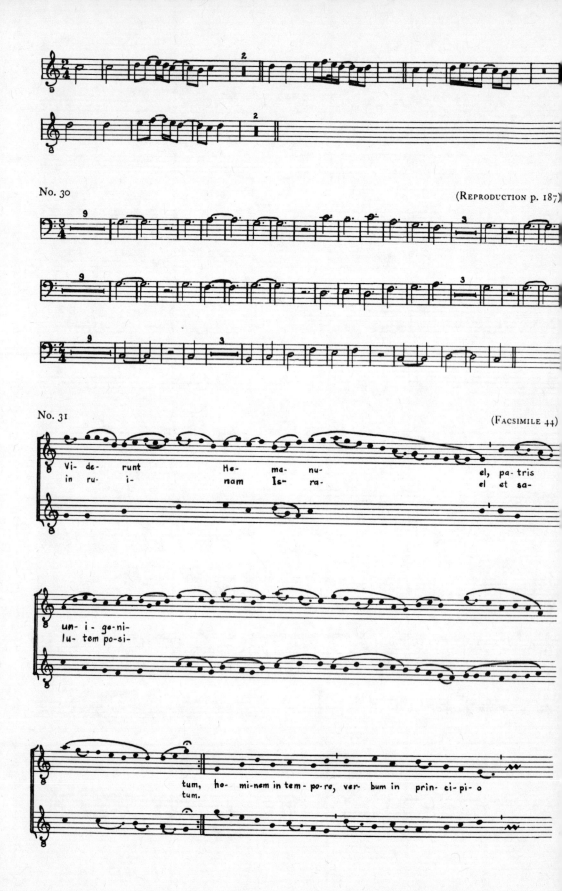

No. 30   (Reproduction p. 187)

No. 31   (Facsimile 44)

Vi- de- runt   He-   ma- nu   el, pa- tris
in ru- i-   nam Is- ra-   el et sa-

un- i - ge- ni-
lu- tem po-si-

tum, ho- mi-nem in tem- po- re, ver- bum in prin- ci- pi- o
tum.

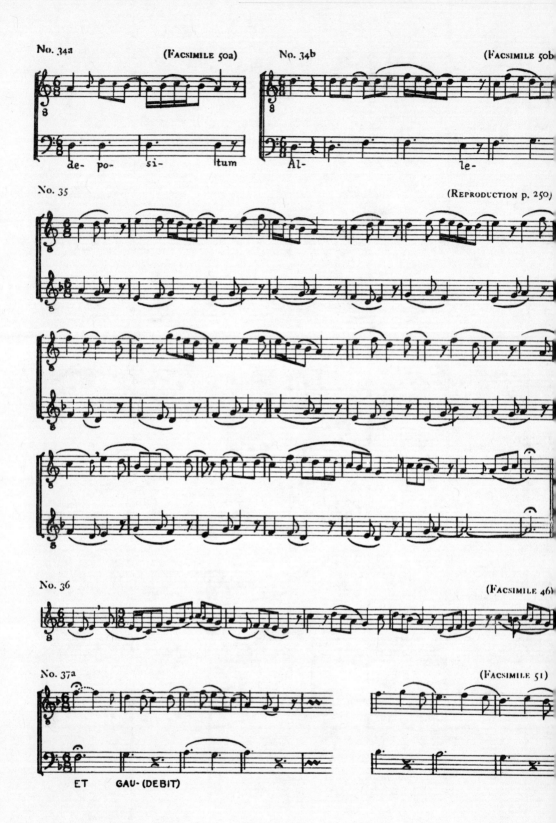

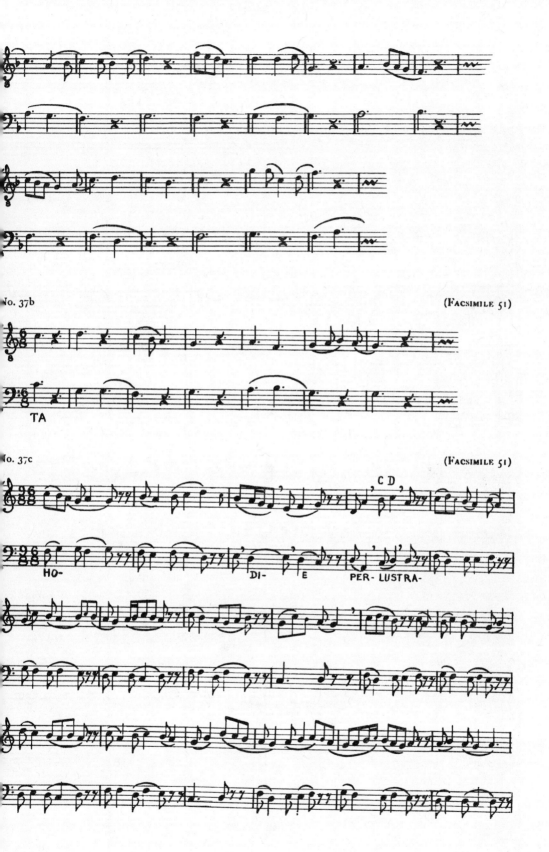

No. 37b   (FACSIMILE 51)

TA

No. 37c   (FACSIMILE 51)

C D

HO-

DI- E   PER- LUSTRA-

No. 38 (FACSIMILE 53)

MU- LI- E-

brace 2

brace 3

No. 39 (FACSIMILE 55)

Ms:E

hinc igi tur ho-mi- ni. hec con-ti- o tam pi- o do-mi- no.

lix gau-di- o ha-bi- ta-cu- lum jus-tissi- me

te- cum be- ne-di- cta tu in mu-li-

No. 43   (Facsimile 59)

por la joi- e dont a-mant sont sous-te- nu. Je vau-droi-e que mes-di-

li re-gars de ses veirs ieuz m'o- cist. He-las mes cuers trop ma

ET SUPER

sant fui-ssent sourt et a- vugle et mu. Ma-da- me les crient tant

prist quant si haute a- mour en-prist. Et ne por-quant sain je miex

No. 44   (Facsimile 63

Hu-ic ut placu-it tres ma- gi mistica vir-tu- te tri-pli-ci por-ta- bant

Hu-

(a) —

-ra po-ten- tia

No. 45   (Facsimile 65)

Au-cun ont trouvé chant par u- sa-ge mès a moi en doune o choi- son   amours qui resbaudist mon coura-ge si que mes

Lonc   tans me   sui te- nu de   chan-   ter

No. 46   (Facsimile 67)

(etc.)

(etc.)

In-   no- va fert a-   ni-mus mu-ta- tas   di-ce- re for-

mas

Ne pen- sez pas da- me, que je re- croi- e.
Car nul- le- ment fai- re ne le por- voi- e.

I.

A- quil' al te- ra

Cre- a- tu-

U- cel di di-

II.

La

La

La

Per-

piu non vo dir quan-to qud di mi piac-

piu non vo dir quán-to qúel di mi piac-

No. 52   (Facsimile 78)

Se   pron-   to   non   sa-   ra   l'uom

a   ben   fa-   re

No. 53   (Facsimile 79)

Nes-   sun pon-ga spe-   ran-   ça. Nel-la suo gio- vi-

ne-   ça.   Che   se'l   à in   se   va-ghe-   ça.

No. 54   (Facsimile 80)

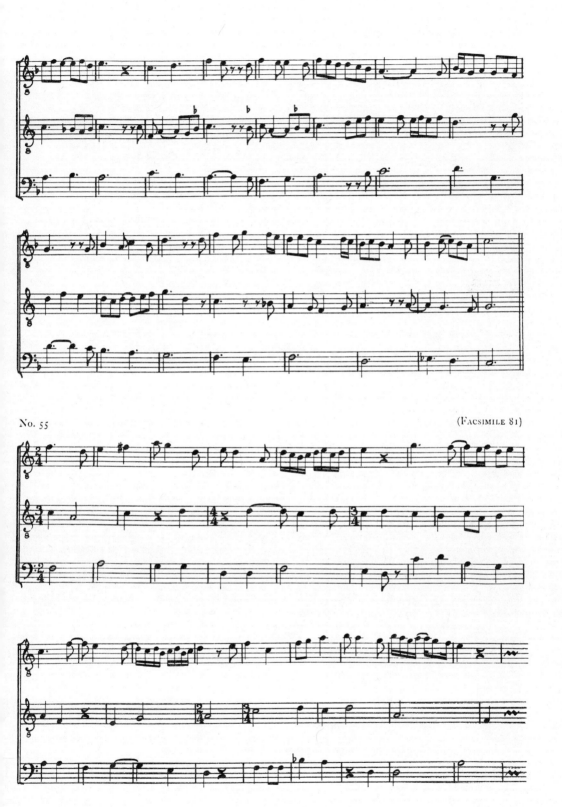

No. 55   (FACSIMILE 81)

ardans desir

The equations added in parentheses indicate the relationship between the note values of the soprano and those of the tenor.

Bel- le bon-ne sa- ge plai- sante et

T.

Ct.

gen- te A ce iour cy que l'an se

re- nou- vel- le, Vous fait le don

(Page 431 *Sumite karissimi*)